TECHNIQUES FOR
DIRECT ACCESS

Other books by the author:

Introduction to Computers

Documentation Standards, 1st ed., with Max Gray

Decision Tables

TECHNIQUES FOR DIRECT ACCESS

HARDWARE SYSTEMS PROGRAMMING

KEITH R. LONDON

FIRST EDITION

AUERBACH Publishers Inc.
PHILADELPHIA, 1973

Library of Congress Catalog Card Number: 72-89103
International Standard Book Number: 0-87769-1-149-5

First Printing

Printed in the United States of America

Library of Congress Cataloging in Publication Data

London, Keith R
    Techniques for direct access.

    Bibliography: p.
    1. Electronic digital computers--Programming.
2. Computer storage devices.   I.   Title.
QA76.6.L632   001.6'42   72-89103
ISBN 0-87769-149-5

CONTENTS

PREFACE

There has been a massive growth in the use of direct access devices such as disks and drums since the early 1960s. This growth is not due simply to the use of disk systems in large computer installations. It is due, rather, to the many small-to-medium installations having small disk devices, such as exchangeable disk stores. According to recent surveys, something on the order of 50 percent of all third-generation computers in the United Kingdom have some form of direct access device storage. In the United States, this percentage must be considerably higher—say, 70 percent.

There are many reasons why so many installations have adopted direct access devices. But there is a feeling in some quarters that many direct access devices are not used to attain full benefit of the facilities afforded. It is said that in the very early days of computers, they were used like "souped-up" tabulators. The early magnetic tape computers were commonly used like punch-card computers. And, in many cases, disk-based computers were used like the magnetic tape machines that preceded them

Many data processing managers, systems analysts, and programmers graduated from punch cards to magnetic tape, and thence to direct access devices. Some of the old methods and ideas have been a long time dying. It is only in very recent times that a new generation of data processing technicians have emerged who went straight on to direct access devices without the enforced apprenticeship on other devices. This book has been written to fill the growing need for a general reference work that covers all aspects of using direct access devices. No general text can replace the specific hardware specification, or programming manual, issued by a computer manufacturer, but it can lay a broad base for a better understanding of such technical material. This book goes further in that it discusses the use of direct access devices and how various techniques may be applied. The effective use of direct access devices depends really on the selection of the right devices for the work to be done in an installation. It also depends on good system design and on the selection of the right software facilities. Thus, briefly stated, the objective of this book is to give the reader a good all-round appreciation of direct access devices, prior to his specific study of a particular device or software package.

A prerequisite for a good understanding of this book is a knowledge of computer essentials, including basic units of a computer, the stored program concept, functions of the peripheral units, and basic data processing techniques.

In other words, the reader may be anyone who has at least studied an introductory textbook or attended a general appreciation course.

The first section of this book describes the characteristics of hardware devices and basic software approaches. It is in no way intended to be a definitive catalog of specifications. With the rapid rate of change in hardware and software technology, it is impossible to give a complete and up-to-date description or appraisal of all devices. Therefore, a selection has had to be made from the total range of devices that are most "popular" (from the sales viewpoint) and those that have proved to be the most reliable (on performance). From time to time exotic devices appear which, although technically innovative, have their short day and rapidly fade away. These devices are occasionally mentioned for historical interest, but are not otherwise emphasized.

In a book aimed at an international market, costs have presented a problem. Where costs are discussed, figures are presented in U.K. pounds and U.S. dollars. The problem has been whether to use a straight foreign exchange conversion rate or a more meaningful conversion factor. Without becoming embroiled in complex economics, a combination of approaches has been taken to provide a guide. Many manufacturers have been most helpful in supplying current technical specifications, but they have been naturally reluctant to give hard-and-fast prices. Similarly, the effects of separate charging, "unbundling," have yet to make themselves felt.

This book has been the product of many years of work. It has been based partly on personal involvement in developing systems, partly on a detached study of devices available and how they have been used, partly by day-to-day contact with many users concerned with training courses, and notes taken at informal meetings. In addition to formal acknowledgments to the many organizations listed elsewhere, I would like to acknowledge the personal help given by Miss Susan Wooldridge as a technical reader and advisor, and to Mrs. Ellie Scott-Allen for her work on draft preparation.

If there has been any one point that has been taken as a guide in writing this book, it is this: As with all other computer units, direct access devices are simply tools. The effective application of these tools to a particular problem depends on the expertise and creativeness of the technicians. Given powerful tools, it is the objective of the computer technician to make the best use of them. This book attempts to give the first step in doing this.

ACKNOWLEDGMENTS

This book could not have been written without the assistance of many equipment manufacturers, suppliers, and other organizations. I would like to acknowledge the assistance of the following companies, who contributed background information on hardware and software:

BASF United Kingdom Limited
Burroughs Corporation
Control Data Corporation
Data Recording Instrument Company
Honeywell Incorporated
International Business Machines Corporation
International Computers Limited
MAC Panel Company
Memorex Precision Products Limited
National Cash Register Company
Potter Instrument Company
Radio Corporation of American
UNIVAC Division of Sperry Rand Corporation

The following acknowledgment has been reproduced from the 1965 edition, U.S. Department of Defense, at the request of the Conference on Data Systems Languages:

> COBOL, Edition 1965, is the product of the CODASYL COBOL Committee and the European Computer Manufacturers Association (ECMA) efforts. Initially, the formulation and content was developed by members of the CODASYL COBOL publications subcommittee.
>
> COBOL is an industry language and is not the property of any company or group of companies, or of any organization or group of organizations. No warranty, expressed or implied, is made by any contributor or by the COBOL committee as to the accuracy and functioning of the programming system and language. Moreover, no responsibility is assumed by any contributor, or by the committee, in connection therewith.
>
> Procedures have been established for the maintenance of COBOL. Inquiries concerning the procedures for proposing changes should be

directed to the Executive Committee of the Conference on Data Systems Languages.

The authors and copyrightholders of the copyrighted material used herein—FLOW-MATIC (trademark of Sperry Rand Corporation); Programming for the Univac(R) 1 and 11, Data Automation Systems, copyrighted 1958, 1959, by Sperry Rand Corporation; IBM Commercial Translator Form No. F 28-8013, copyrighted 1959 by IBM; FACT, DSI 27A5260-2960, copyrighted 1960 by Minneapolis-Honeywell—have specifically authorized the use of this material, in whole or in part, in the COBOL specifications. Such authorization extends to the reproduction and use of the COBOL specifications in programming manuals or similar publications.

PART ONE

HARDWARE

CHAPTER 1

THEORY OF DIRECT ACCESS STORAGE

INTRODUCTION

A multiplicity of computer terms has grown up, nourished by each manufacturer, software house, major user, and standards organization. Because of this it is useful to go right back to basics: the storage requirements of a modern digital computer. It is also useful to review these basic points for those readers who are new to data processing. For others, this approach provides useful background before considering technical detail. This chapter examines the theory behind direct access devices or, rather, how they differ from other peripheral units. It also reviews the fundamental characteristics of direct devices and summarizes how they meet current information processing needs.

The usefulness of modern third-generation, general-purpose computers may be attributed to three characteristics:

> The stored program
> The high speed of calculation and data manipulation
> Compact mass data storage, and fast data retrieval

The first characteristic, the stored program, is fundamental, and its merits are extolled in every elementary textbook on computers. The second, in the early days of computers, was the major asset in a computer. In this book we are primarily concerned with data storage and retrieval, which is the most important aspect in commercial data processing.

Computer Storage Requirements

There are many ways in which the storage or memory of a computer can be described. In many textbooks, the classic representation of a computer is as shown in Fig. 1-1. This is a device-oriented representation. Consider now a conceptualization of the storage elements in a computer, shown in Fig. 1-2. The storage is divided into three levels, which we may call primary, secondary, and tertiary.

The primary level of storage has been known by many names:

> Internal storage
> Main storage
> Working storage

Immediate access storage (IAS)
High-speed memory (HSM)
Memory
Core storage (or "core")

The first term will be used in this book. The function of the primary level of storage has to a large extent remained unchanged since the very early days of computers; namely, to store the program instructions as they are obeyed and the data as it is manipulated and calculated. It is thus the heart of the computer, through which all input and output data passes, in which the program (or part of a program) is held, and much referenced data is stored.

The secondary level is sometimes referred to as backing storage. It functions as a direct extension of the primary level. It is thus used mainly for programs and to a lesser extent for data storage. Backing storage would thus hold programs prior to overlay or call into internal storage, to be called for subroutines, libraries of major software which will play an active role in program execution (i.e., part of an operating system), and high-volume reference data. The latter includes tables and constants. As a second level of storage, it can also be visualized as the extension to core for working storage; that is, holding large volumes of data during a transitory operation, such as sorting. The actual devices used for secondary level storage may be the same (and often are) as those used for tertiary level storage.

From a purist's point of view, backing storage is the provision of a large

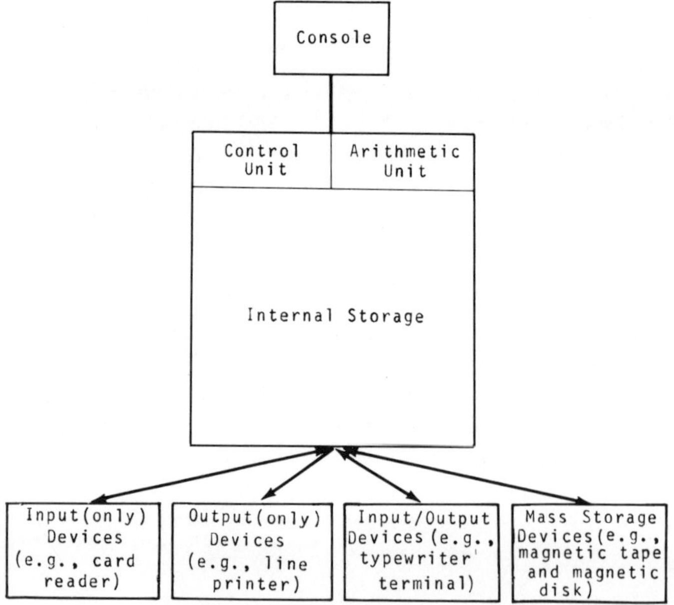

Figure 1-1. Units of a Computer

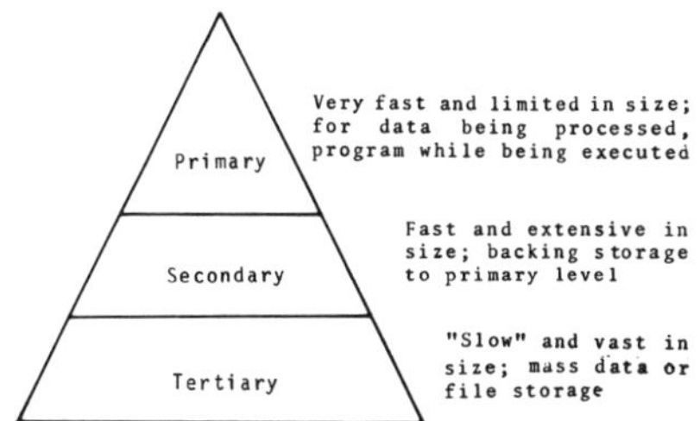

Figure 1-2. Storage Levels in a Computer

capacity storage unit, such as a magnetic drum, as an integral part of the operation of core. Such an approach was used in the ICL (then ICT) 1300 series computers in the early 1960s: a small core store, commonly not exceeding 2K, was supplemented by a much larger capacity magnetic drum which was an integral part of the central processor. The use of such large drum systems as backing storage (although not integrated into the central processor) has again become popular with the advent of terminal usage and time sharing. (An example of this is the use of FASTRAND drums, with a Univac 1108 computer, with time-sharing terminals.)

Tertiary-level storage is essentially "mass storage," used to hold either data or program. Later in this chapter we will see that there are other categories and classifications of tertiary storage according to usage.

This division of storage into three levels is conceptual. As stated earlier, devices used for second- or third-level storage requirements are often the same. But this division into levels gives an interesting picture in which to see the development of modern storage methods. The three levels have come about partly because of cost limitations and technical restrictions, and partly because of user (commercial) requirements. The former are the technological problems of hardware development; the latter are the requirements imposed by the type of data in industrial and commercial applications.

Development of Direct Access Devices

It has often been claimed that the ideal computer storage unit would be one in which *all* data was immediately accessible. That is, each item of data is directly addressable or locatable. And, the time that it takes to get any item of data would not be dependent upon *where* the data is stored. This means that the time to access data is constant for all items of data and it must, as an additional requirement, be *fast*. The obvious choice of device to meet all these requirements would be, in terms of current hardware, something similar to the storage devices used for primary-level storage; in other words, a ferrite core storage device (or its equivalent, thin film storage) or integrated circuit/monolithic devices. It would be a store that used a matrix system of addressing; e.g., a series of ferrite cores at the intersections of signal wires. Such devices enable, in effect, data to be accessed at the provision of an address. The address may be interpreted on the matrix coordinate system to reference a bit, a binary coded decimal, a byte, a character, or a word.

The use of such a device for mass data storage is outside the current state of technology for several reasons. First, there is the cost factor. There has been a general downward trend in the cost of internal stores. It is very difficult to make a straight comparison of costs over a long period of time because most machines are not offered for sale long enough. Similarly, speed and reliability have increased, but for a matching increase in cost. Even at today's costs (and in the immediate future), the use of some form of core storage or integrated circuits for secondary or tertiary mass data storage would be prohibitively expensive. (A medium-size store of eight million characters would cost on the order of £5 million ($10½ million), this is based on a linear increase in the price/size ratio in commercial available internal stores.)

A number of technical problems are also encountered with the construction of such a store. These include the technical viability of constructing such a store without many expensive components to obviate signal distortion, noise, and signal delays. If the same matrix arrangement were used as in current stores to access a character, bit, or word, the very nature of the cumbersome addressing system would present problems. Also, modern core storage techniques present problems in the temporary nature of the storage media. When power is removed or data is stored for a "long" time, magnetic seepage takes place and data is lost. Many alternatives to core stores also present similar problems.

Ultimately, however, a mass matrix storage device will be constructed and marketed commercially when the economic and technical problems have been solved. The use of such a massive primary store is out of the reach of the average computer user for the time being, and may be considered as an unobtainable ideal for the immediate future.

From the earliest times in hardware development, therefore, there has been the necessity of finding adequate methods for a lower level of storage. With the exception of the days of "high-powered number-crunchers," the quest has been for mass storage with the highest speed, the greatest ease of handling, and reliability at the lowest cost.

It is not unnatural that in the late 1940s and early 1950s, punched cards were used as the major form of input. Previous experience in using punched cards with conventional tabulators and calculators provided a ready-made technology for computers. The same was true of paper tape, originally developed for telecommunications purposes and readily adaptable for use with computers. Punched cards and paper tape provide a useful means of data collection and raw input, and are the basic method for men-to-machine communication. Equally important during the formative years of computer development, they served as a file storage medium. The distinction between a medium acting as a raw input carrier and as a means of file storage is important. Raw input, otherwise known as source input, is considered transitional. It serves as a man-to-machine information carrier that is usually a one-time function. A medium acting as a data "reservoir" acts as a true data store; that is, it holds data for repetitive use. This distinction can be demonstrated by a simple example:

Time sheets punched in cards = one time input = raw input.
Master company payroll punched in cards = repetitive references = file storage medium.

The whole field of input media and methods has broadened dramatically since the early days of computer usage. Although punched cards and paper tape are still industry favorites, many other means are available and in use: direct input via a terminal or via document reading, and data conversion by keyboard-to-magnetic tape or even to magnetic disk. However, to trace the development of direct access devices, we must look at file storage.

Serial Processing with Magnetic Tape

Cards provide for serial access. That is, one card record may be read at a time. A pack or deck of punched cards is read in the sequence in which the cards are stacked in the card reader. Even though cards are an inexpensive (though slow) media for raw input, they are rarely used in all but the smallest computer configuration as a means of file or mass data storage.

In the early 1950s a new means of file storage came into prominence: magnetic tape. This provided a faster means of reading the stored data; it was also more compact and easier to handle. But access to the records was still serial, the records being stored on the tape one after the other. It was also necessary to copy a record on which the data was changed, because updating in situ was not practical.

At this point we briefly examine the impact on systems technology of having only serial access storage devices available. Where only serial access is available, i.e., access to data record by record, systems tend to be *batch processed.* The time to access any one record is dependent on *where* the required record is located in the file. At this time a formal definition may be given: *Access time* is the time taken to locate and make available a specific record. Take the example shown in Fig. 1-3. This shows the time to access a selected record in a file of 292,000 records; the time could be 20.3 ms, if the record is in the first block, or a maximum of 9.9 min if the record is in the last block. (These times ignore housekeeping functions and are based on "active" data read times only, i.e., excluding label checking and tape switching.) To read or update any one record in this file will thus take up to about 10 min, depending on where the desired record is located within the file. Times like this preclude to a large extent single record processing. However, if sizable batches of records can be built up, then processing will become viable. If every record, or almost every record, in the file is to be processed, single record access time ceases to be important.

Serial processing using magnetic tape also had one other major limitation or

DEVICE

Reading speed, 96.6 kch/s
Packing density, 800 ch/in
Interblock gap, .75 in
Tape length, 3600 ft

FILE

292,000 records
10 records in a block
100 characters in a record,
    i.e., 1000 character blocks
       29.2 million characters in file
File occupies two reels (approx.)
2 X transports (units) available on-line

If a single record is required, access time may be
    20.3 ms
      (if record is in *first* block)
    9.9 min
      (if record is in *last* block)

Figure 1-3. Magnetic Tape Access Times

restriction. This was that a file had to be copied each time data in existing records was to be changed. The typical magnetic tape device does not permit updating in situ; i.e., it is not possible to read a record, change it, and write it back on top of the original record on the same tape. The traditional approach was thus a combined file update and copy as shown in Fig. 1-4.

To summarize the characteristics of serial file processing, using magnetic tape (or punched cards and paper tape):

Location of a specific record is by search, up to the entire length of the file.

The file had to be copied if data was to be changed, meaning that an entire pass of the file was commonly required to rewrite the file.

To make serial processing a practical method, batches of input transactions

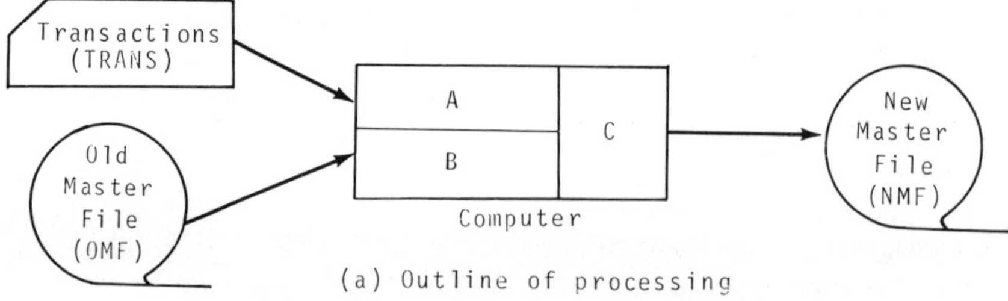

Figure 1-4. Traditional Magnetic Tape Update and Copy

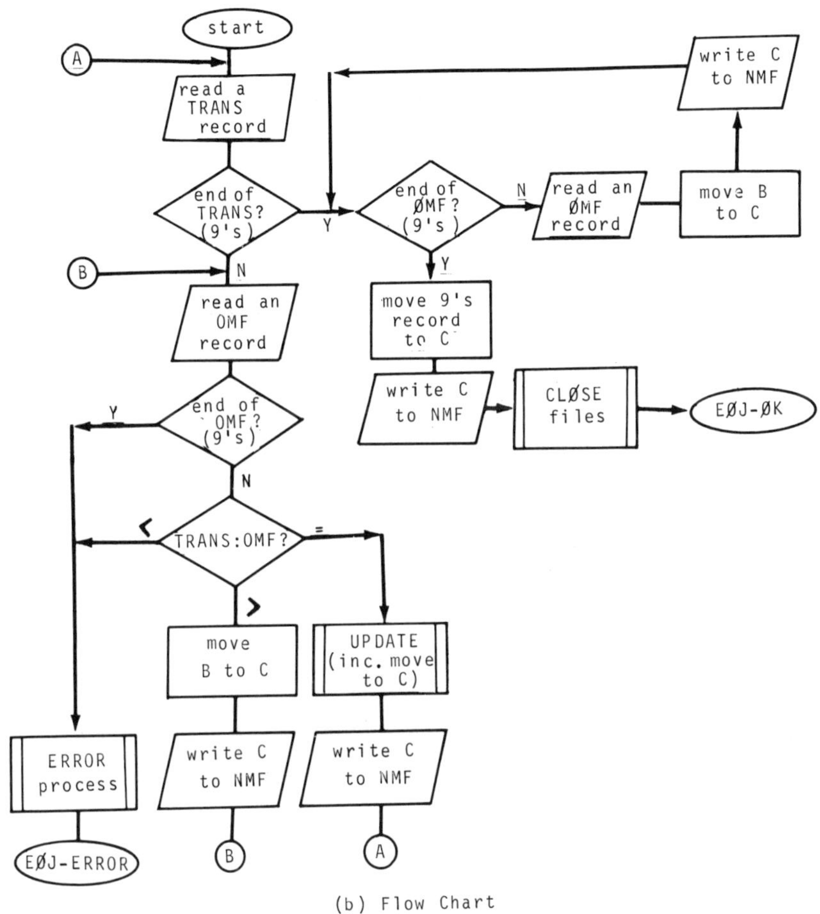

(b) Flow Chart

Notes: This flowchart has been presented to show
basic processing logic, and is therefore considerably simplified in that

1. Only one transaction applies to a master record; this has been checked by a previous program.
2. The logic allows only for alterations. Unmatched transactions are serious processing errors that cause an error halt so that the run has to be abandoned.
3. The last record in a file is a record consisting of all 9's.
4. Only single-tape reel files are allowed; the logic for OMF and NMF continuation reels is ignored.
5. Input/output operations are shown as a parallelogram; processing subroutines are shown as a box with two lines on the shorter sides.
6. The unpacking of records from blocks is ignored.

Figure 1-4. Continued.

must be accumulated, thus giving a higher file *hit rate.*[1] In many commercial systems, batches of input are formed by the very nature of the data itself; as in a weekly payroll, monthly billing, daily production control scheduling, etc.

Historically, additional serial processing techniques were developed to minimize the time spent in copying the entire file during an update pass. For example, large files with a low hit rate may be processed by using an exception technique as shown in Fig. 1-5. At a chosen point in the processing cycle, the "exception" tapes produced in method 1 in Fig. 1-5 are merged to produce a new consolidated master. In method 2, used for very low hit-rate cases, one exception tape is produced, but again consolidation takes place every so often in the processing cycle. However, the basic method of updating by file copy has one major advantage: *security.* No item of data is intentionally overwritten and master data can be preserved by generation cycling. This will be discussed later.

It is also obvious that file sequences are important, i.e., to have input in the same sequence as the master file to which it is to be applied. Where input is to be applied to a number of different files with different record sequences, intermediate sorts and expansions are required, as shown in the example in Fig. 1-6. In some installations using magnetic tape serial processing, up to 60 percent of computer time is used on sorting.

It was obvious that any attempt to introduce more sophisticated hardware and processing techniques would not make serial processing viable for some systems requirements. Thus, in the middle 1950s, development started to produce a commercially usable mass storage device to serve the functions of secondary and tertiary storage. Data was to be held in addressable units which would eliminate the need for a serial search. Whereas on magnetic tape, data was not addressable, on these new devices the data would be made available at the provision of an address. This would offer the whole scope of nonserial processing. These storage units are thus referred to by the general term *direct access storage devices.*

Early attempts produced a range of exotic and not always practical solutions— rather like the weird and wonderful forerunners of the modern aeroplane! Initial work was centered around the use of magnetic drums and magnetic loops, with most of the development of any import being done in the United States. Subsequent work was centered around the use of rotating disks, and thence to flexible magnetic-coated strips or cards. To place this development work in a historical context, the first disk-based device may be attributed to the U.S. Bureau of Standards in 1952. The first commercially available disk device was RAMAC marketed in 1956 by International Business Machines, followed closely by the Remington Rand RANDEX in late 1956. Now there is a plethora of devices available, ranging from 1 million to 200 million characters in capacity,

---

[1] At this time, the hit rate (or *activity rate* as it is also known) may be considered as a measurement of the number of records in a file which are to be altered during any one updating pass of that file.

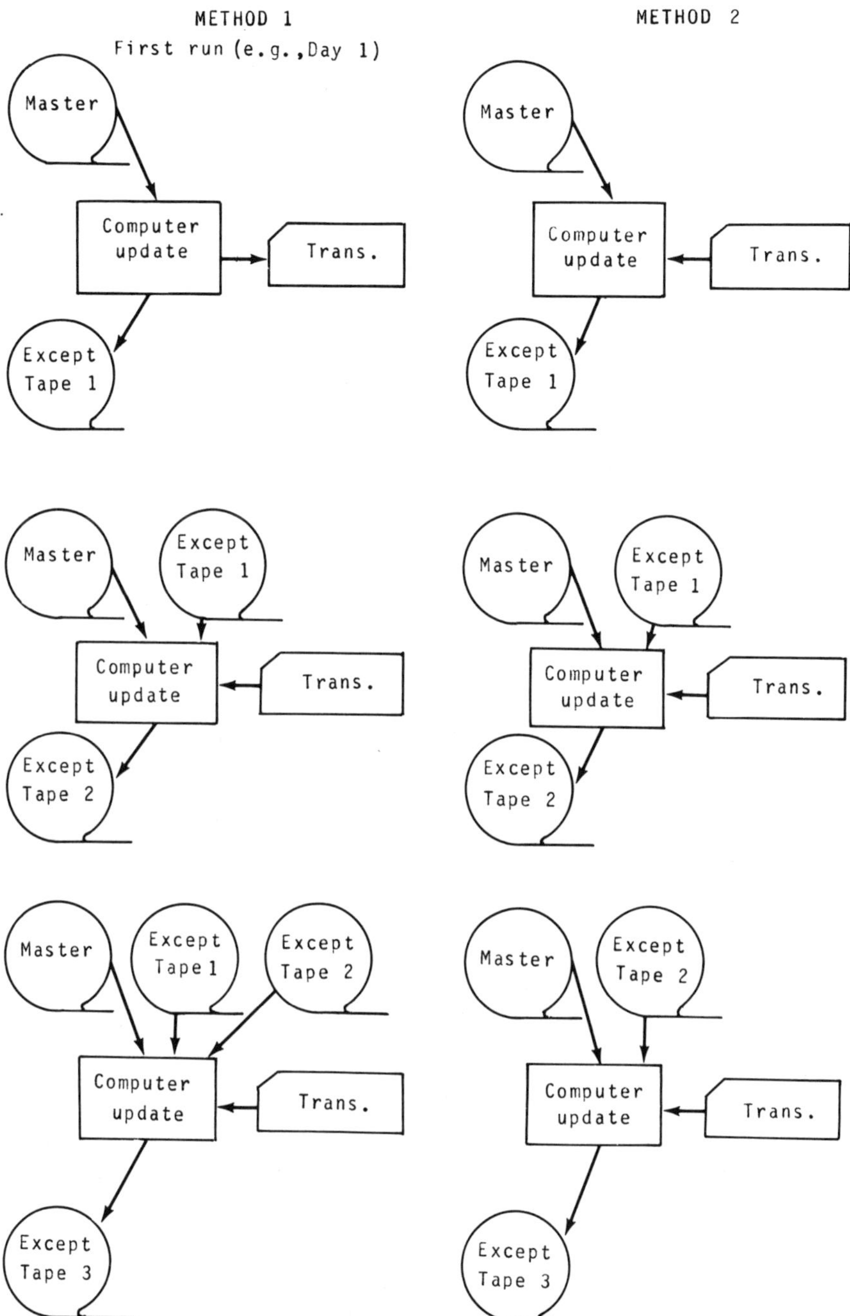

Figure 1-5. Exception Magnetic Tape Methods

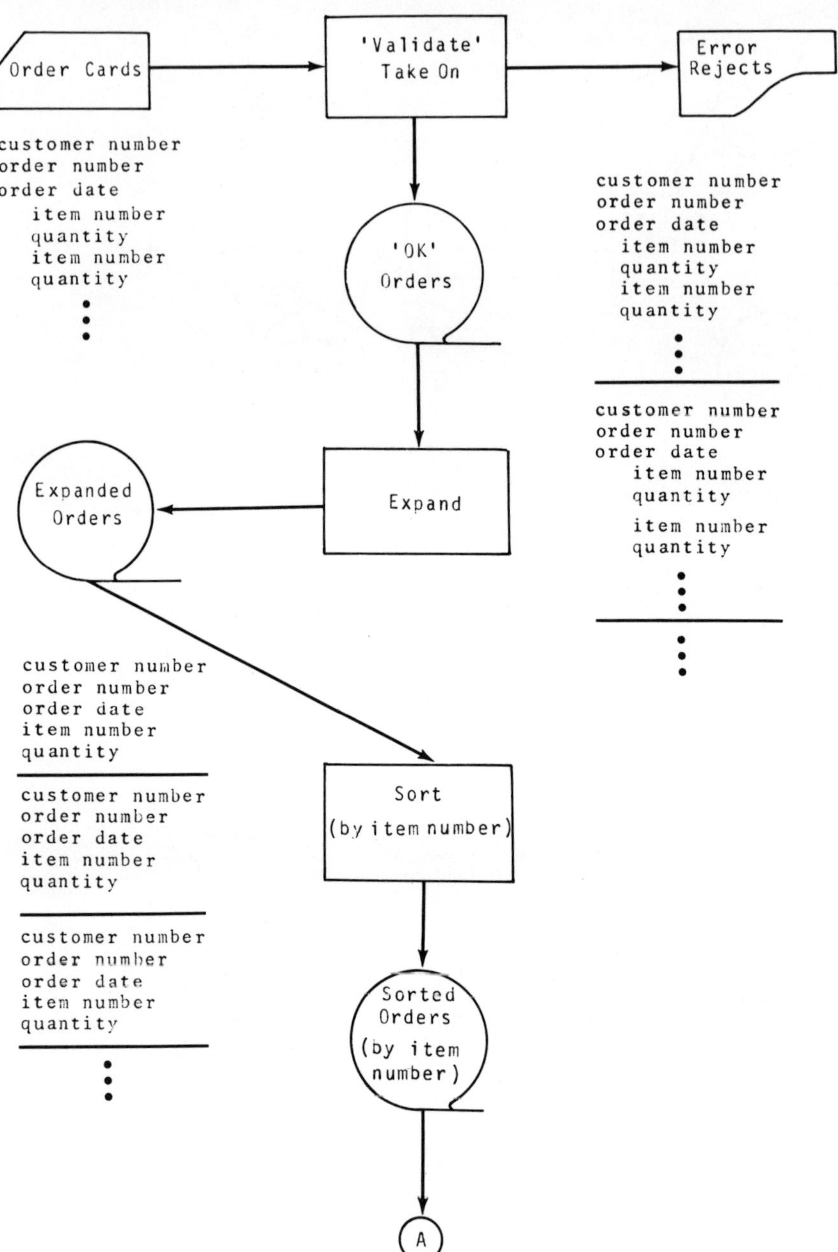

Figure 1-6. Example Tape-Based System

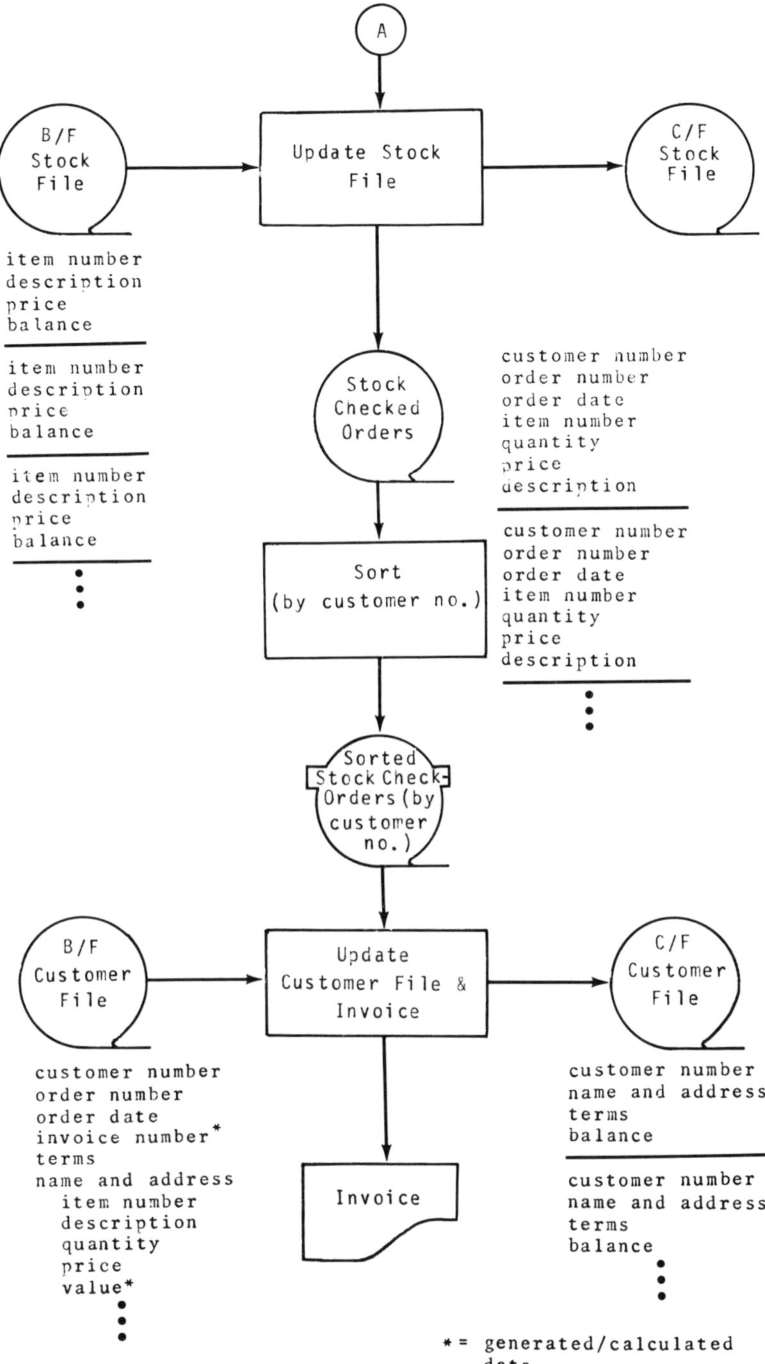

Figure 1-6. Continued.

0.3 sec and 20 ms in speed of access, and £5000 to £¼ million in purchase price.

The ingenuity of mechanical and electronic design has produced a large crop of device types. But the most important types of magnetic device (those covered in this book) fall into the following categories:

Drums
Disks, fixed
Disks, exchangeable
Strip/cards

These devices are discussed in detail in Chapter 2. All these devices, however, have certain common characteristics: a basic method of operation.

BASIC COMPONENTS OF DIRECT ACCESS DEVICES

The basic components of a direct access device are as follows:

A recording surface
Read/write heads
Transport mechanism
Control electronics

A device operates on the principle of moving the recording surface, by means of the transport mechanism, past the read/write heads (see Fig. 1-7). Data is recorded on the surface and is read back as required by the read/write heads. Data is transmitted between the device and the central processor as with any other peripheral unit. The device usually has its own control electronics (buffers, etc.) for internal operation. The functioning of the components is described below.

Recording Surface and Read/Write Heads

The recording surface may be of two different types: magnetic oxide coated or nickel-cobalt plated. In both types the recording surface comprises a non-magnetizable metallic substrate such as aluminum, a magnesium alloy, or brass. The surface is ground to optically flat tolerances by a diamond polishing technique. The substrate is then coated with a magnetic oxide coating or a nickel-cobalt plated layer.[2]

Magnetic oxide coating was a natural progression from magnetic tape technology. The recording surface is coated with ferromagnetic particles, fixed to the metal substrate by means of a suitable binder, usually a compound of organic resins. The magnetic constituent of the coating is fine particles of oxide: gamma

---

[2]The substrate for disk devices is on the order of 0.05 to 0.25 inch thick. Glass has been suggested as the ideal substrate! No device has (yet) been announced with a glass substrate.

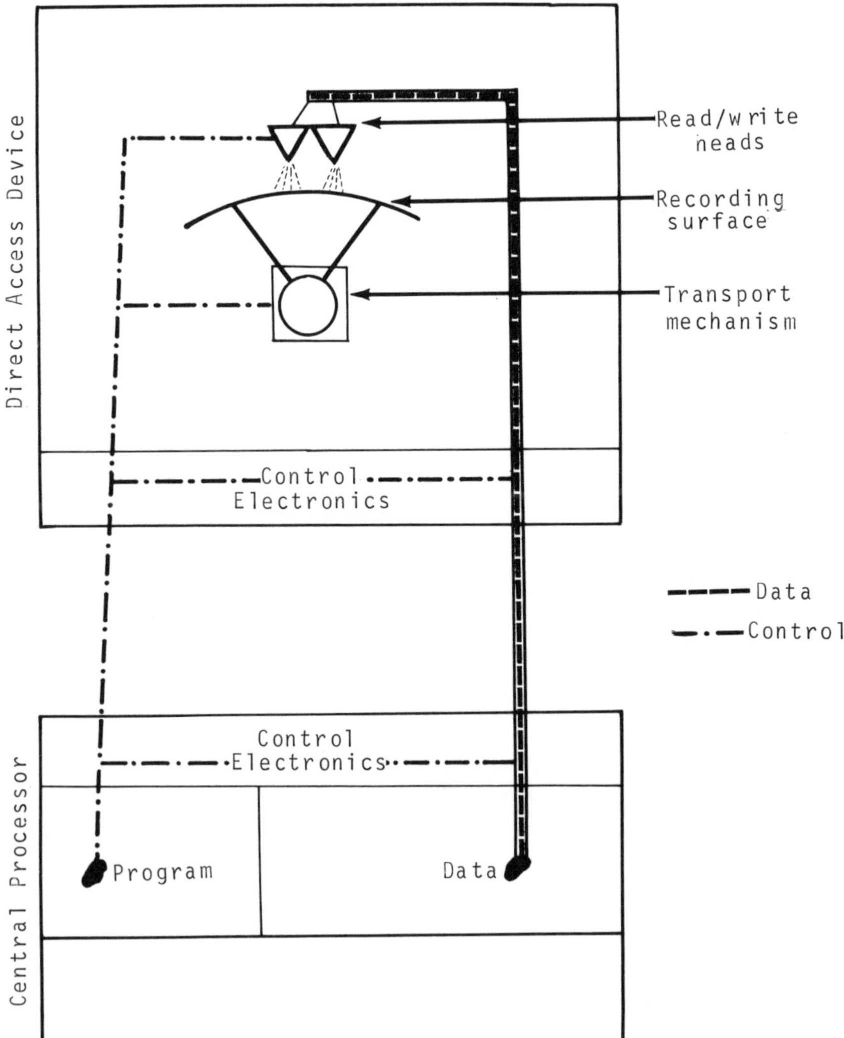

Figure 1-7. Basic Operation of a Direct Access Storage Unit

ferric oxide, Fe_2O_3. Particle dispersal, i.e., the integration and the alignment of the particles within the binder is an intricate process in manufacture. The particles must be distributed uniformally in the binder. At this stage in the manufacture, the coating has a thin consistency. After the coating has been placed on the base substrate, it is baked until it assumes a firm solidified form. The dimensions of each particle are such that there is generally a 7:1 ratio in length to thickness; in some cases the particles are aligned in the direction of rotation of the surface. An example of particle size is 0.1 micron thick and

0.7 micron long.[3] The thickness of the coating is on the order of 100 to 250 μin. (depending on the recording density as described below).

The percentage of oxide in the coating (known as the pigment loading) will determine the magnetic recording efficiency and characteristics of the surface. For example, ignoring all other factors, high-output devices will have a higher pigment loading than, say, regular devices. On average, the pigment loading will be in the region of 60 percent of the total composition of the coating. During manufacture all craters and protuberances will be removed so that the surface coating is optically flat. The oxide particles must be completely within the binder so that no particles protrude. Because ferric oxide is a highly abrasive substance (it is used as jewelers' rouge), contact with the working surfaces of the equipment, especially the recording heads on some devices, will cause considerable wear of the parts. (They will also interfere with the operation of floating heads, as described later in this chapter.)

The hardened surface is ground to a flat finish and is varnished to increase durability. The substrate and its coating are tested for mechanical suitability. The recording characteristics are then rigorously tested under controlled conditions for electrical properties.

The alternative recording surface in common usage is nickel-cobalt plating. In this case, a very thin layer of a nickel-cobalt alloy is deposited on the substrate by a plating process. The coating is much thinner than a magnetic oxide layer, about 15 to 30 μin. The plated layer is covered with a protective coating. This overlay (usually rhodium) provides a wear-resistant surface that also protects the sensitive coating from corrosive substances in the atmosphere. Nickel-cobalt recording surfaces are growing in popularity. This is attributable to a number of claimed advantages. The most important are as follows:

Finer surface finishes are possible.

The surface has better wearing characteristics for planned or accidental recording-head contact.

The surface provides a high-density recording medium, with a greater potential for higher densities than magnetic coated surfaces.

The recording heads are positioned opposite the recording surface. In some devices, recording is "in-contact"; this means that the heads rest directly on the recording surface. Or, the recording may be "out-of-contact" with the read/ write heads just above the recording surface. In-contact reading is usually found with nickel-cobalt surfaces. Either nickel-cobalt plated surfaces or magnetic oxide coated surfaces may be used with the out-of-contact recording method. The majority of modern direct access devices use the out-of-contact recording method. Moreover, the commonest method of suspending the heads over the sur-

---

[3] A micron is equal to one millionth of a meter. Hence, 0.1 micron (μ) is 0.0000001 meter, or approximately 0.000004 inch, i.e., 4 microinches (μin.)

face for out-of-contact recording is by means of a "floating head" technique (also known as the "flying head" technique). The heads are mounted on a delicately balanced arm. A hydraulic system presses the heads *down* toward the recording surface, which rotates at high speed. A thin film of air is generated between the surface and the heads by the rotating surface, thus pushing the head *back* from the surface. A constant gap (about 50 to 200 μin.) is thus maintained between the heads and the surface. The flying height of the heads is controlled by the intensity of the air stream, the aerodynamic design of the heads, and the "loading pressure" pushing the heads toward the surface. The head is held away from the surface by the air stream. The air stream is formed by the controlled (filtered) air intake acting upon the spinning surface. The read/write heads are fixed to retractable arms. Only when the surface reaches the appropriate rotational speed are the heads pushed out to float over the surface.

A detailed example of the floating head process is described here in terms of the Series 3371 exchangeable disk store manufactured by Data Recording Instruments Company, Ltd., England. This device has 6 disks, some 14 inches in diameter, which rotate at 2400 revolutions per minute. Only when the disk reaches approximately 70 percent of its nominal speed are the heads extended to float over the surface. During operation (reading/writing), the heads fly about 120 μin. from the surface. The head is aerodynamically designed with the lower surface cylindrical on a 16-foot radius. The density of recording (as explained later) is 765 to 1105 bits per inch.

In all floating head devices, safeguards are incorporated in an attempt to prevent a "crash"; i.e., the head's coming down on the recording surface while it is rotating. (In one month just prior to the time of writing, the author experienced two crashes in unrelated installations. In one, a stationary trolley was accidentally banged against a disk unit. In the other, there was a mainline power cut, which caused a major crash when the disk slowed and the "emergency retract" of the heads did not operate.) The popularity of the floating-head approach is attributed to several advantages:

1. The requirement for fine mechanical tolerances becomes less critical. In some devices the heads are mounted on a movable arm that traverses a specific area of the recording surface. Because the head positioning is not fixed, it is necessary to allow a wider variation in tolerances.
2. Since the heads are "pneumatically balanced" in relation to the recording surface, slight variations in rotation are compensated by head movement.
3. A further result from (2) is that, to a limited extent, the floating heads will make allowances for surface faults. However, in some respects, floating heads are still susceptible to gross surface eccentricities and foreign matter on the surface. Irrespective of the detrimental impact on recording quality, such surface faults may

> disrupt the air flow and cause the heads to be thrown out of alignment or even to crash on the sensitive recording surface.

The fourth advantage will be discussed in detail in Chapter 2. Essentially it is based upon advantage 1 above. That is, a floating head system permits the read/write heads to be positioned relatively easily over the surface. Thus, head movement is permitted across the recording surface. Rather than having one read/write head per unit area of surface for storing information, one head may be positioned, as required, over *many* such recording areas.

Read/Write Method

It is not necessary, of course, to understand the detailed method of operation in terms of electronics and magnetic theory in order to use direct access devices. This section may be considered one of "background and interest" that describes basic magnetic recording principles. The following explanation is in rather simplified terms for general readership. Thus, although the explanation is technically sound, its accuracy and completeness could be enhanced by the addition of many more technical qualifications and provisions. To do this, however, would detract from the basic aim of the book.

The recording of coded data on the device (or, in jargon, the *writing* of data *to* the device) is effected by means of a recording head positioned opposite the surface coating. The transport mechanism moves the circular surface past the recording head at high speed and data is transmitted to the head and recorded on the surface as a number of pulses. The fundamental concept of the magnetic recording process is explained briefly below.

Consider the diagram of a typical recording head structure, shown in Fig. 1-8 (a). This type of head is commonly referred to as a *ring* head, and its overall construction is shown in Fig. 1-8(b). Essentially, the core is laminated and is constructed in two parts merely for convenience of manufacture. The surface is transported past the front gap. An input signal current is applied to the core windings (i.e., the read/write coils). The input signal produces the phenomenon of "flux fringing" in the vicinity of the head gap; see Fig. 1-9. The flux fringing produced at the gap is capable of penetrating the recording medium (i.e., the sensitive coating on the substrate) and thereby magnetizing it.

Let us now consider the effects of this flux on the coating as the surface is placed within, and transported through, the field of the flux fringing. Each of the individual particles of the coating may be considered as a "domain" capable of receiving and retaining a "charge." Each particle has an associated magnetic field at all times, but in an unrecorded surface the individual domain fields are in random order of direction; see Fig. 1-10(a). As a result, the net magnetic charge of a number of domains is effectively zero. When the surface is within the area of flux fringing at the head gap, the penetration of the flux in the coating affects each individual domain within range so that a magnetic field is created,

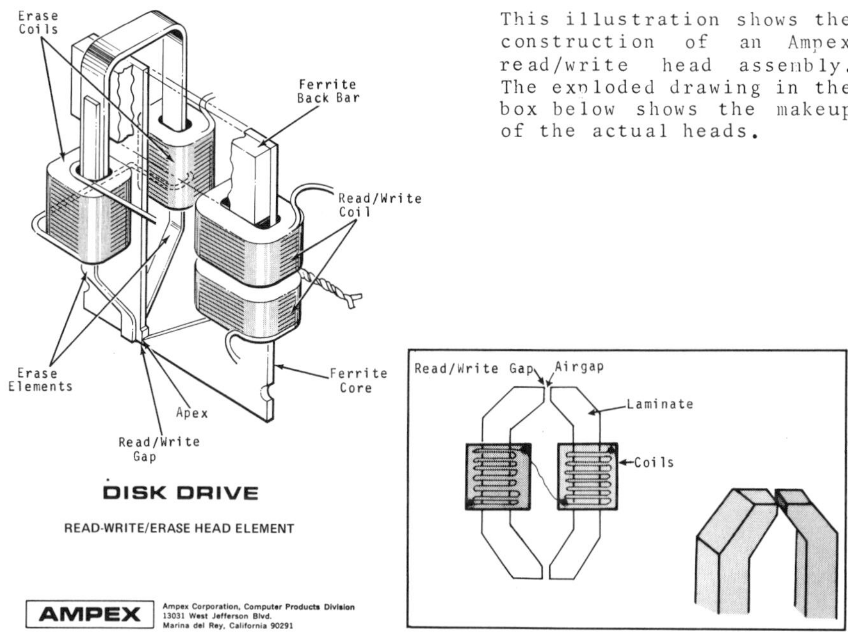

This illustration shows the construction of an Ampex read/write head assembly. The exploded drawing in the box below shows the makeup of the actual heads.

The photograph below shows the heads mounted on an arm. An upper arm and a lower arm are shown. This arrangement would be used on a disk device with the upper head positioned over the upper disk surface and the lower arm opposite the lower disk surface. The diagrams used to show the head arrangements in the explanatory text have been very much simplified, as can be seen by comparison with the actual head assembly shown above.

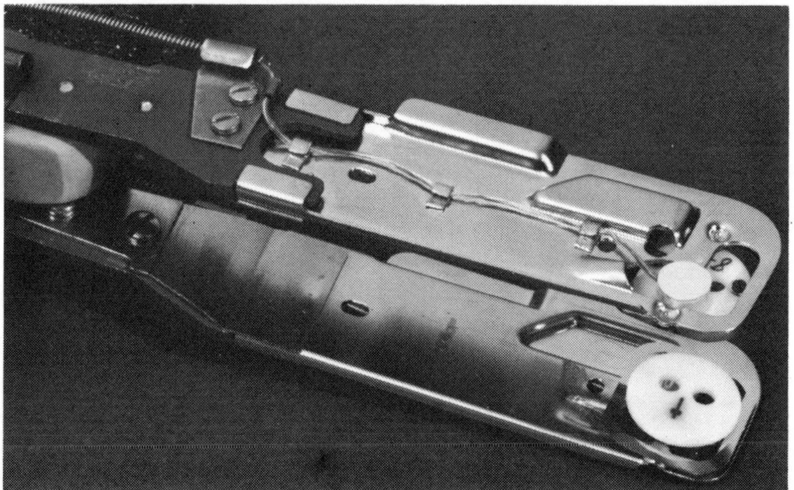

Figure 1-8. A Recording Head. Courtesy of Ampex Corporation, Computer Products Division.

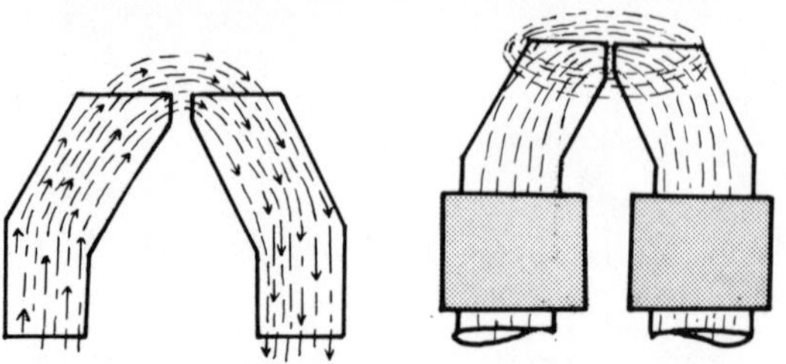

Figure 1-9. Flux Fringing

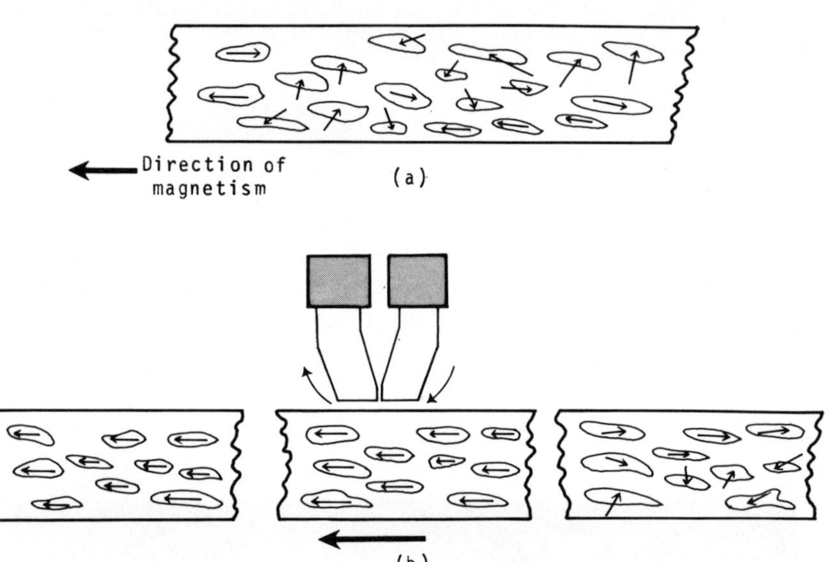

Figure 1-10. Recording Field Patterns

and the individual domains assume the pattern (or the direction of the lines of force) of the penetrating flux; see Fig. 1-10(b). Simply, then, the flux fringing induces a magnetic field in the coating such that the domain fields within range assume the same direction.

The net charge of the domains influenced by the head has now changed from its initial unrecorded state; it is no longer effectively zero but has been increased so that it is proportional to the intensity of the magnetic field induced by the head gap. When the magnetized area leaves the head, it retains its magnetic charge. Now, the magnetic charge retained depends on the electromagnetic properties of the coating and the magnetic intensity in the region of the gap, which is proportional to the current applied at the read/write coil.

The reading process is essentially the direct opposite of the recording process. Suppose a surface has been magnetized as shown in Fig. 1-11(a) and backspaced so that it is returned to its original position, Fig. 1-11(b); this surface is now to be read. As the surface passes the read head, the magnetic field "above" the surface induces a current in the read head. The passage of the coating past the head, from "unmagnetized" to "magnetized" areas thus produces an output signal from the head. This signal current is amplified and interpreted as data. It is important to realize that the signal generated in the head-core winding is *not* proportional to the magnitude of the flux but *to the rate of change* of the flux.

We have now reviewed the fundamental principle of writing and reading in a direct access device. The explanation given above has been greatly simplified, but can be made clearer by a brief examination of *digital* recording techniques.

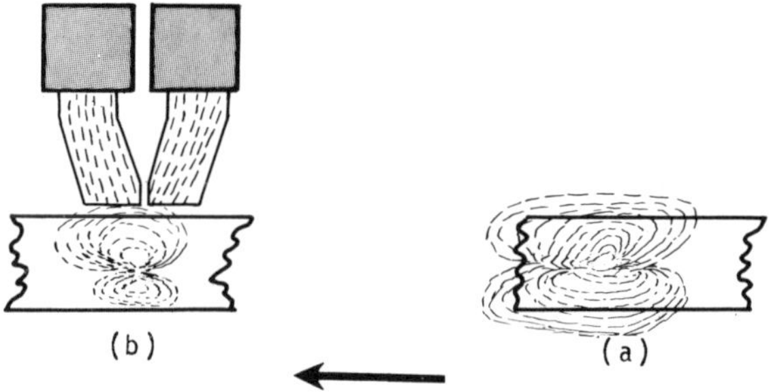

Figure 1-11. Magnetic Reading

FUNDAMENTALS OF DIGITAL RECORDING

The basic requirement of all computer magnetic device recording methods is that it must be possible to magnetize a surface from *two* signals of different values such that, on reproduction, two corresponding signals may be produced.

In the preceding explanation, writing and reading were considered to be operations that alternately energized and de-energized (i.e., "current" and "no current") the recording/reading head. Consider now the effect of reversing the current in the head; see Fig. 1-12. The reversal of current in the head will cause the fields in the coating to be aligned in opposite directions. Thus, according to the signal received at the head, magnetization of the surface may cause one of three effects:

Neutral (no current)
Saturation in one direction (+)
Saturation in the opposite direction (−)

Data may therefore be recorded on the surface and read from the surface by means of a three-level signal. This is shown diagrammatically in Fig. 1-12 and is the *Return-to-Zero* method (abbreviated RZ); i.e., a part of the surface is in its neutral condition before and after each energizing of the head. Note

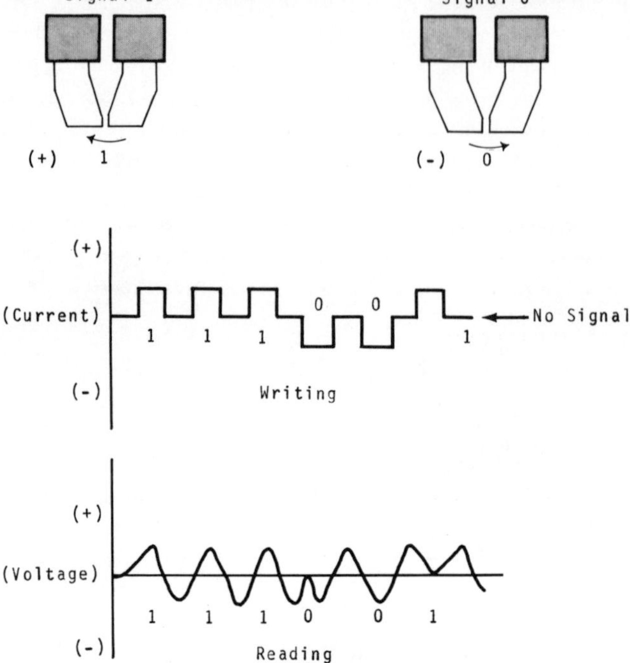

Figure 1-12. Basic Digital Recording (RZ)

that this system of recording meets the requirements outlined earlier, namely, that data in the form of pulse and no-pulse may be recorded on and later read from the surface, the two states being represented by saturation of the coating in opposite polarities (or direction).[4] In Fig. 1-12 the input pulses are represented by SIGNAL 1, SIGNAL 0, and NO SIGNAL.

An alternative method of digital recording is the *Non-Return-to-Zero-Change-on-One* method (abbreviated NRZ1). This method, and a modification of it mentioned below, are now used in most computer recording systems. It is similar to the RZ method in that "pulse" and "no pulse" input signals may be recorded on the surface by saturation in opposite directions. But, as its name implies, the surface is not recorded in a neutral state. The method is shown diagrammatically in Fig. 1-13. Note that whereas in the RZ method each signal type produces a flux reversal, the NRZ1 method requires that a flux reversal be produced only when a SIGNAL 1 (+) is input.

The third method of digital recording is *phase-modulation*, or *phase encoding*

---

[4] Saturation as used here may be considered to mean that the condition of the coating is such that an increase in the magnetizing force does not cause an increase in the magnetic intensity exhibited by the coating.

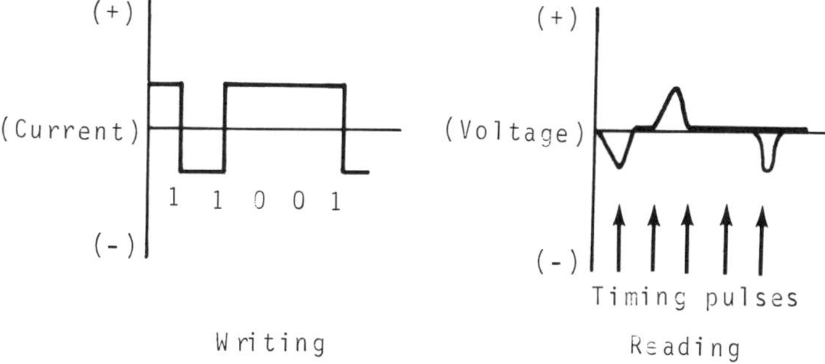

Figure 1-13. Basic Digital Recording (NRZ1)

(PE). This is essentially a modification of the NRZ method (with the square wave form smoothed by special circuitry). Most devices use the NRZ or PE method of recording. These techniques are used with both in-contact and out-of-contact recording devices. Generally, higher packing densities are achieved with the PE technique.

For those curious technically minded readers who would like to pursue the mechanics of digital recording, see Walker, 1967, in References.

We have seen how data, represented by two state signals, may be represented on the recording media. No attempt has so far been made, however, to relate the two state signals to any coherent coding system for digitalized data.

The data discussed in previous paragraphs dealing with magnetic recording may be considered to be information represented by the use of *characters*. A character is defined simply as the lowest meaningful element of information. It consists of the following:

Numeric	0 to 9
Alphabetic	A to Z
Special symbols	+ - . , ( ) @ £ $ / ? = * & ' %, etc.

We may assume that for normal commercial processing a character set of about 64 characters is required:

10 numerics
26 alphabetics
30 special symbols

The special symbols include certain control codes. The alphanumeric data to be recorded is held in the internal store of the computer's central processor. To write data, it must be possible to establish a unique code for each character. Further, the basic requirement of this code must be, as we have seen, that it is capable of representation by two state signals, i.e., signals of two different values such as "pulse" and "no-pulse." A code often employed for magnetic recording is the *binary coded character system.*[5] The basic code is shown in Fig. 1-14; at the present time, the column labeled "P" may be ignored.

The code is constructed on the following principle. There are seven bits per character, a bit being represented by 0 or 1. The seven bits may be considered as comprising two *zone* bits and four *numeric* bits. Since the maximum bit value is 2^5, the maximum number capable of being recorded is

$$2^5 + 2^4 + 2^3 + 2^2 + 2^1 + 2^0$$
$$32 + 16 + 8 + 4 + 2 + 1 = 63$$

Thus, 64 "numbers" (0 to 63) can be represented.

The four numeric bits are shown as having a value corresponding to $2^0, 2^1, 2^2$, and 2^3. Thus, decimal value may be represented as follows:

$$
\begin{array}{c c c c c}
 & 2^3 & 2^2 & 2^1 & 2^0 \\
0 = & 0 & 0 & 0 & 0 \\
1 = & 0 & 0 & 0 & 1 \\
5 = & 0 & 1 & 0 & 1 \\
9 = & 1 & 0 & 0 & 1 \\
 & & \cdot & & \\
 & & \cdot & & \\
 & & \cdot & & \\
\end{array}
$$

By using these four bit positions it is therefore possible to represent numeric value 0 to 9 (and, in fact, 10 to 15 as 1010 to 1111). However, it must also be possible to represent the alphabetic and special symbols. The code must therefore be extended by means of the zone bits. These two bits, when considered independently of the other bits in the code, may name the values

$$
\begin{array}{c c c}
00 & = & 0 \\
01 & = & 1 \\
10 & = & 2 \\
11 & = & 3 \\
\end{array}
$$

Thus, by combining the use of the zone and numeric components, $4 \times 16 = 64$ codes can be established. The relationship between the "value" of the zone component and the "value" of the numeric component may be seen by reference to Fig. 1-14. For example, the numeric 9 is represented by zone "0" and numeric "9" (i.e., 00 1001), the alphabetic character A is represented by zone "2" and numeric "1" (i.e., 10 0001), and so on. Bit 2^6, P, is the *parity bit.* This is a

---

[5] Since the binary system is basic to computers, it is assumed that the reader is acquainted with its purpose and use. Adequate descriptions of the binary system are given in most introductory books on computers.

Char	P	Z	Z	8	4	2	1	Char	P	Z	Z	8	4	2	1	Char	P	Z	Z	8	4	2	1	Char	P	Z	Z	8	4	2	1
0	1	0	0	0	0	0	0	(space)	0	0	1	0	0	0	0	@	0	1	0	0	0	0	0	P	1	1	1	0	0	0	0
1	0	0	0	0	0	0	1	! (exclamation)	1	0	1	0	0	0	1	A	1	1	0	0	0	0	1	Q	0	1	1	0	0	0	1
2	0	0	0	0	0	1	0	" (quotes)	1	0	1	0	0	1	0	B	1	1	0	0	0	1	0	R	0	1	1	0	0	1	0
3	1	0	0	0	0	1	1	# (number)	0	0	1	0	0	1	1	C	0	1	0	0	0	1	1	S	1	1	1	0	0	1	1
4	0	0	0	0	1	0	0	£ (pound)	1	0	1	0	1	0	0	D	1	1	0	0	1	0	0	T	0	1	1	0	1	0	0
5	1	0	0	0	1	0	1	% (percentage)	0	0	1	0	1	0	1	E	0	1	0	0	1	0	1	U	1	1	1	0	1	0	1
6	1	0	0	0	1	1	0	& (ampersand)	0	0	1	0	1	1	0	F	0	1	0	0	1	1	0	V	1	1	1	0	1	1	0
7	0	0	0	0	1	1	1	' (apostrophe)	1	0	1	0	1	1	1	G	1	1	0	0	1	1	1	W	0	1	1	0	1	1	1
8	0	0	0	1	0	0	0	((l.parenthesis)	1	0	1	1	0	0	0	H	1	1	0	1	0	0	0	X	0	1	1	1	0	0	0
9	1	0	0	1	0	0	1	) (r.parenthesis)	0	0	1	1	0	0	1	I	0	1	0	1	0	0	1	Y	1	1	1	1	0	0	1
: (colon)	1	0	0	1	0	1	0	* (asterisk)	0	0	1	1	0	1	0	J	0	1	0	1	0	1	0	Z	1	1	1	1	0	1	0
; (semicolon)	0	0	0	1	0	1	1	+ (plus)	1	0	1	1	0	1	1	K	1	1	0	1	0	1	1	[(l.bracket)	0	1	1	1	0	1	1
< (less than)	1	0	0	1	1	0	0	, (comma)	0	0	1	1	1	0	0	L	0	1	0	1	1	0	0	$ (dollar)	1	1	1	1	1	0	0
= (equals)	0	0	0	1	1	0	1	- (hyphen/minus)	1	0	1	1	1	0	1	M	1	1	0	1	1	0	1	] (r.bracket)	0	1	1	1	1	0	1
>(greater than)	0	0	0	1	1	1	0	. (stop)	1	0	1	1	1	1	0	N	1	1	0	1	1	1	0								
? (question)	1	0	0	1	1	1	1	/ (solidus)	0	0	1	1	1	1	1	O	0	1	0	1	1	1	1								
		No zones used								Zone 1 used								Zone 2 used								Zones 1 & 2 used						

Figure 1-14. Example of Character Coding System

special-purpose bit that is appended to the basic six data bits and is not considered in the basic interpretation of the code. Its use in checking is explained as follows: Once the complete code of 64 characters is established, a parity checking system is devised such that either

1. the number of "1" bits in any one character code is to be *even*; or
2. the number of "1" bits in any one character code is to be *odd.*

The two systems are known as *even* and *odd* parity checking, respectively. Suppose the seven-bit character code is to be checked for even parity; then, in any bit configuration representing one character, the number of "1" bits must be even. Character 7 has bit pattern 00 0111, which has three "1" bits. To make the number of "1" bits even, a parity bit is appended to the character 7: 1 00 0111. If the code has an even number of bits as in, say, character 5 (00 0101) no parity need be appended (0 00 0101). Similarly, in an odd parity checking system (as in Fig. 1-14), a parity bit is appended if the number of data bits is even. If the sum of the "1" bits in the seven-bit code is even, then the character is misrepresented.

In practice, a seven-bit code (such as ASCII) or an eight-bit code (such as EBCDIC) are used in modern computers. The codes are a straight extension of the six-bit code principle.

Units of Storage

The three methods of storing data in modern third-generation computers are named *character, word,* and *byte*. A character representation requires the use of six or seven data bits (plus a parity bit), as shown earlier in this chapter. A word machine has a fixed-length group of bits. For example, the ICL 1900 series computer is a word machine, with a word length of 24 bits; the UNIVAC 1108 has a word length of 36 bits. A word can hold a numeric value in serial binary form; for example:

ICL 1900—24 bit word—can hold a value from 0 to 8,338,607.

UNIVAC 1108—36 bit word—can hold a value from 0 to 34,359,738,367.

Alternatively, a word may be used to hold a number of characters in six-bit character form. Thus, an ICL 1900 series word can hold up to four 6-bit characters and a UNIVAC 1108 word can hold up to six 6-bit characters.

Byte representation of data uses eight data bits (and a parity bit). Examples of byte machines are the IBM 360 and 370 series, and the ICL System 4. One eight-bit byte can be used to hold

one coded character.

a value in serial binary, i.e., 0 to 65,535.

two digits in packed form; i.e., two digits in packed decimal form, with 4 bits each—no zone bits used.

(Four bytes may be used together to form a 32-bit word.) This book will refer to devices that use either the byte, the word, or the character method of representing data.

SUMMARY

In this chapter we have seen how direct access devices have grown in importance in data processing. They form a compromise between the high-speed addressable (but expensive) core storage and the cheap but low access time serial storage afforded by magnetic tape. We have also examined the restrictions imposed by serial access-only devices. The principles of recording and the characteristics of modern direct access devices have been summarized and the basic units of a direct access device have been described, together with the methods of coding and recording data. In Chapter 2, a more detailed survey of devices is given and a sample range of devices is described.

DEVICE TYPES AND BASIC TERMINOLOGY

TYPES OF MODERN DIRECT ACCESS DEVICES

As stated in Chapter 1, a number of components are common to all direct access devices. These are the transport unit, magnetic recording surface(s), read/write heads, and control electronics. The actual form of the recording surface and the relationship between the read/write heads and the surface determine the category of device. Devices fall into the following four categories:

Magnetic drums
Magnetic disks, fixed
Magnetic disks, exchangeable
Magnetic cards/strips

The characteristics of these devices are explained briefly below. Each of the device types is explained in greater detail in Chapter 3.

Magnetic Drums

The basic head/surface relationship in a magnetic drum is shown in Fig. 2-1 (a). Note that the recording medium is a cylinder fixed within the unit. The cylinder is coated with magnetizable material and rotates at high speed. Opposite the surface are a number of read/write heads. The area transcribed by a head on the circumference of the cylinder is called a *track*, or a *channel*. Data is transmitted from the central processor, via the control electronics, to a selected read/write head, where it is then recorded on a drum track. Some devices have a "one-per-track" arrangement in which there are a number of heads fixed opposite the drum surface. Alternatively, the heads may be movable. A common arrangement is to have a group of read/write heads mounted on a bar so that they can traverse the length of the drum. For example, a drum may have a length split into 200 circumferential tracks, with a group of ten read/write heads opposite the surface. In this case, the head system may be moved to any one of 20 positions, accessing ten tracks in any one position.

Fixed Magnetic Disks

The head/surface relationship is shown in Fig. 2-1(b). Note that the recording media is a large disk coated with magnetizable material. Opposite the sides of

28

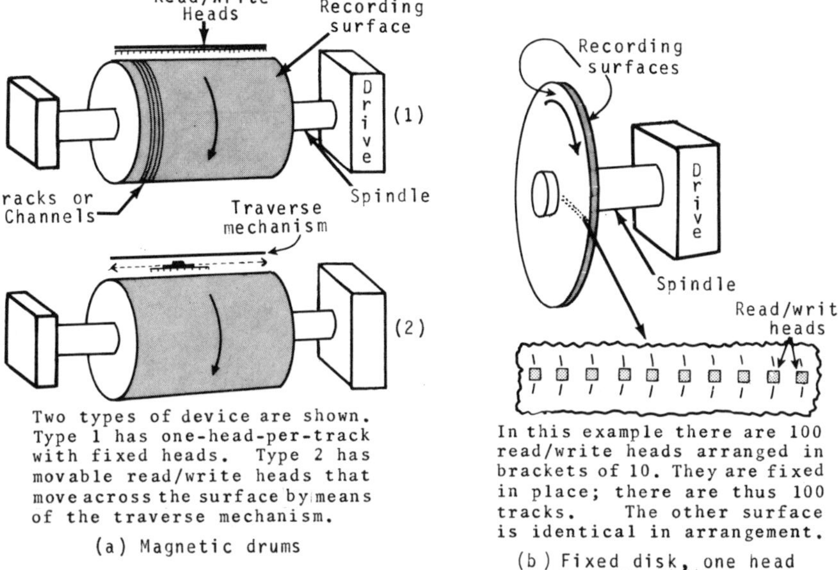

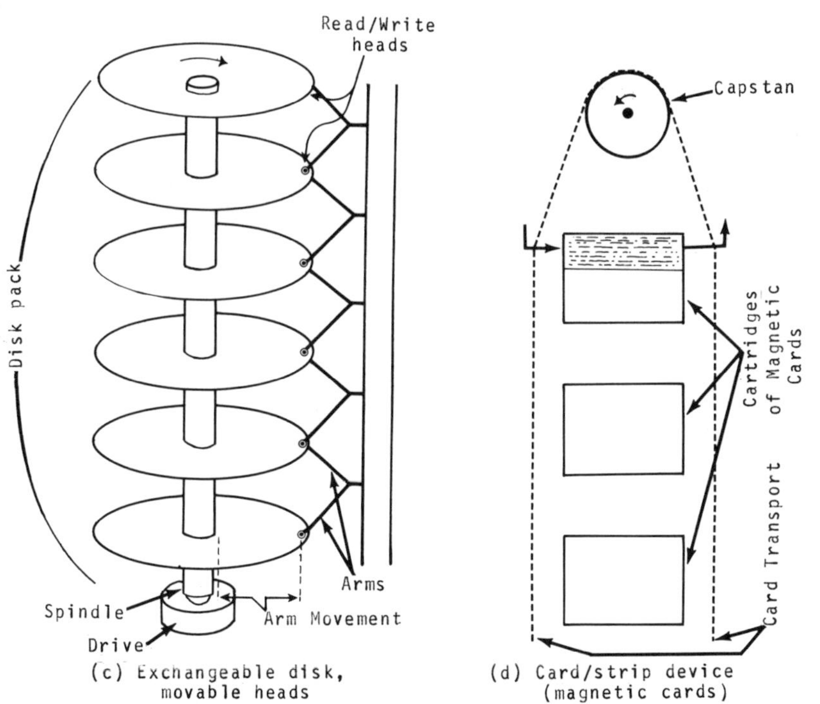

Figure 2-1. Direct Access Devices: Principles of Operation

the disk (as opposed to the circumference on a drum) are a number of read/write heads. The heads may be arranged on a "one-per-track" basis, or they may be grouped on a movable arm. Fig. 2-1(b) shows a one-head-per-track system. The disk is fixed within the device. However, there may be more than one disk per unit; in this case there will usually be a stack of disks fixed to a central spindle. Each disk surface will have its own array of read/write heads.

Exchangeable Magnetic Disks

The basic head/surface relationship is shown in Fig. 2-1(c). Note that the mode of operation is similar to the fixed-disk devices described above, except that

> the disks are considerably smaller.
>
> they are arranged in removable stacks, forming a portable cartridge or pack.
>
> there is a limited number of read/write heads on a movable arm.
>
> each disk surface has its own read/write head arm.

In most devices, the arms are linked together and move in unison. Thus, when one arm is moved to position the head over the first recording area (i.e., track 0), all the heads will be positioned over this track on each disk surface.

Magnetic Card/Strip Devices

The basic head/surface relationship is shown in Fig. 2-1(d). Note that the recording medium is not continuous as in the case of the devices described previously. The recording surface is broken up into a number of cards or strips. The cards/strips are of thin, pliable plastic coated with magnetizable material. They are stored in exchangeable magazines that can be loaded on to the device as required. The cards/strips can be extracted from their holders by the machine, transported to a capstan, and positioned opposite the read/write heads. The card/strip is wrapped around the capstan, where it is then used as if it were a magnetic drum. The heads may be arranged on a one-head-per-track basis, or they may be movable on an arm.

BASIC TERMINOLOGY

Despite the variety of possible physical arrangements in the head/surface relationship as described above, there is a common terminology for describing the performance of all devices. These terms may be classed in two groups: *timing terms* and *storage terms*. Both terms are described below prior to reviewing a number of direct access devices in detail.

Timing Terms

Any reading or writing operation on a direct access device may be considered as consisting of a number of actions. The first group of actions locate the appropriate area of the recording surface to be used in the operation, and a second set of actions actually perform the reading/writing operation. The actions are

1. *Location:*

   Unit selection
   Seeking
   Head switching
   Rotational delay

2. *Reading/writing:*

   Reading/writing
   Checking

Location

Unit Selection.   This is the selection or addressing of a specific device when more than one device unit is available on line at a time. It therefore requires switching within the control electronics. The unit to be used in any operation is addressed in a direct access instruction (either implicitly or via a parameter field). Because the operation consists of electronic switching, the time taken may be considered as negligible and of little or no significance.

Seeking.   Once a device has been addressed (unit selection), some form of mechanical movement may be necessary to access data on a particular part of the recording surface. The type of mechanical movement, if any, will depend on the device type. In devices that are organized on a one-head-per-track basis, no mechanical movement (or *seek*) will be required because each of the tracks is serviced by its own read/write head. Mechanical arm positioning *is* required on those devices that have movable heads. An instruction can be given which will cause the arm to move over the recording surface and to lock so that the heads are positioned over a specific track. In many devices, the heads move in unison, and thus an instruction such as "select track 50" will move all the heads to track 50 on all the recording surfaces (e.g., disk sides). Once the heads are positioned over a track, no further mechanical movement is necessary until data is required from another track.

Because a seek (track selection) involves mechanical movement, it is a relatively slow process. Moreover, the time taken to position the read/write heads over a desired track will depend on the distance the arm has to travel before the selected track is reached. To move the heads from track 1 to track 100 will obviously take much longer than a move from track 1 to track 2.

In a card or strip device, seeking is the selection of the appropriate card/strip from a holder, its transport to the capstan, and its wrapping around the capstan to form the read/write drum. Further seek time will be involved in positioning the read/write heads over the desired track(s) on the wrap-around drum. (In practice, many devices have provision for the positioning of the read/write heads while the card/strip is being transported to the capstan; it is not unusual for the whole of the head-positioning time to be overlapped by mechanical card/strip movement time.)

Head Switching.   Once the heads are positioned over a required track, it may be necessary to activate or select a particular head. In a device using a one-head-per-track system, track selection is by means of electrical head switching rather than by mechanical movement. As described previously, some devices have multiple movable arms, with one or more heads per arm. In this case, head switching is required to select the head that is positioned over the recording surface where the required data is to be read/written. In the example shown in Fig. 2-1(c), there are six recording surfaces. After the heads have been moved to the required track (say, track 11), the head opposite the appropriate recording surface must be activated. (Remember that the arms—and therefore the heads—move in unison.) If the data is located on track 11, disk surface 3, then the head over surface 3 must be activated. The head-selection process is an electronic switching operation and is thus a negligible time element.

Rotational Delay.   As described previously, all direct access devices have a recording surface that is rotated beneath or opposite a series of read/write heads. All devices thus have a built-in time delay that is caused by surface rotation. The example shown in Fig. 2-2 illustrates *rotational delay*, or *latency*, as it is also known. The data marked A in the diagram is to be read. Assume that the head has just been positioned over the appropriate track holding the data. The disk is spinning at high speed in the direction indicated by the arrow in the diagram. In Fig. 2-2(a), at the instant that the head is positioned, the data A is on the other side of the disk. Half a revolution must thus take place before the data is available at the head. The best case would be as shown in Fig. 2-2(b), where the data A is just approaching the head as it is positioned over the track. The worst case is shown in Fig. 2-2(c), where the data has just passed the head and almost a complete revolution must take place until it is available to be read.

Rotational delay or latency may therefore be defined as the time delay between the head's being positioned for a read/write operation and the appropriate area of the track's being available at the head for that operation. In practice, a device is often described as using "average latency"; that is, case (a) in Fig. 2-2. The time taken for rotational delay is thus a function of rotational speed and disk size. It is always more than electronic operations (unit selection or head switching), but is less than the mechanical movement of seeking.

Reading/Writing, Checking

So far it has been shown that a read/write operation may be preceded by a number of operations through several levels of addressing. The object is to lo-

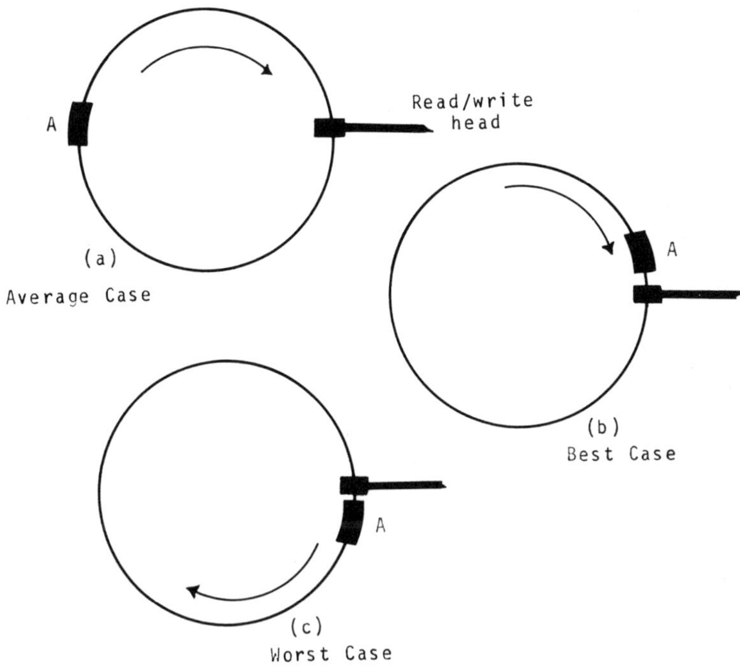

Figure 2-2. Rotational Delay

cate a specific area of the recording surface(s) which contains the data to be read or is to receive the data to be written. Each element in locating the recording surface area takes time:

(Unit selection, negligible)
Seek, considerable
(Head switching, negligible)
Rotational delay, small to considerable

The duration of the read/write operation will depend on the length of the data involved. The *transfer rate*—that is, the speed at which data is read or written once accessed—will depend upon the rotational speed and the packing density. Example transfer rates will be given in Chapter 3.

Many devices employ a check cycle after data has been written. Data is written on one revolution of the recording surface; on the next revolution, the data just written is read back to ensure that it has registered properly. This effectively doubles the nominal write time because two revolutions are necessary for each piece of data written.

The actual reading and writing process takes place as with any other peripheral device. Data to be written is assembled in contiguous storage locations. A single write instruction is given (with the core address of the data to be written and the destination location on the device), and the data is transferred to the device and recorded in the desired area. Similarly, a read instruction must refer to a specific area on the device which holds the data to be read and to an area in core which is to receive the data.

With this understanding of the operational characteristics of direct access devices, we may now look to the levels of storage.

Storage Terms

In the preceding discussion, a number of storage levels were implied. For example, a multidisk stack device with movable arms has three levels:

> Unit
> Track (seek plus head switching to give surface)
> Data (position of data on track)

For a magnetic card device, the levels are as follows:

> Unit
> Card (seek; card movement)
> Track (head positioning and switching)
> Data (position of data on track)

To show the basic principles of storage, let us first consider a fixed-disk device with a single disk, both sides of the disk being used as recording surfaces; see Fig. 2-3. A one-head-per-track system is employed. In this example, the sides of the disk are identified by 00 and 01, respectively, and there are 100 tracks per disk side. Each track thus has a unique address. The first track has address 000

side	track
0	00

to the last with address 199

side	track
1	99

Note that in this device each track is divided into a number of fixed-length *sectors.* A timing data point is used so that each of the ten sectors can be identified by the hardware and can thus be uniquely addressed, say sector 0 to sector 9. The device thus consists of a storage arrangement of

> 2 sides
> 1 side = 100 tracks
> total tracks = 200
> 1 track = 10 sectors
> total sectors = 2,000

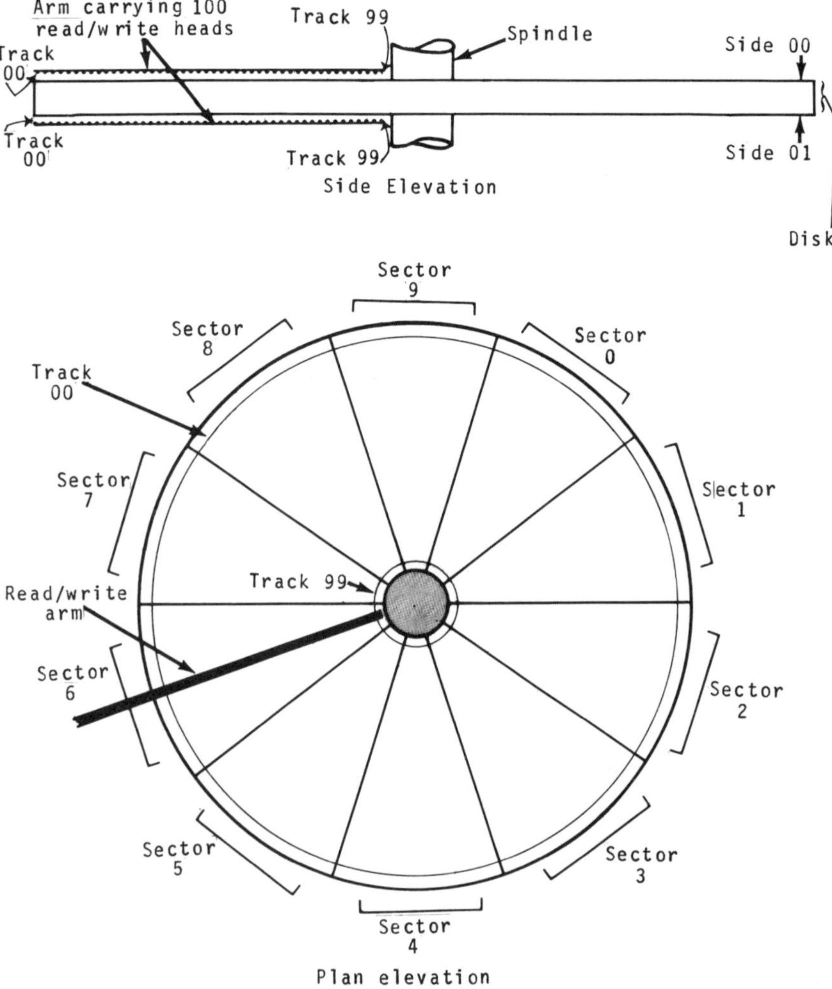

Figure 2-3. A Simple Track/Sector System—Fixed Head

In this example, each of the sectors is an area of a track holding 250 characters of data. Thus, this device has a total capacity of 500,000 characters, split into 2000 uniquely addressable units.

The curious reader may be puzzling over how it is possible to have 250 characters in a sector on track 00 where a sector is long, while at the same time have 250 characters in a sector on track 99, which is shorter. There have been several solutions to this problem. One is the use of variable packing densities. This technique is used on disks with a relatively small diameter and only a small difference in the length of the outside track and the inside track. In this solution the data is packed more tightly together on the inside tracks than on the outside tracks. By the use of this variable packing density, each sector consists of the same number of characters, and there is the same transfer rate for all data.

Alternatively, some devices have a fixed packing density but a variable number of sectors per track. The number of sectors per track will be determined by the position of a track relative to the outside of the disk. For example, on a 600 track system, the sectors can be arranged as follows:

> 25 sectors per track on the outside 300 tracks
> 20 sectors per track on the middle 200 tracks
> 10 sectors per track on the inner 100 tracks

This approach is generally adopted on large disks. Various other techniques have been used, such as "interleaving" data between tracks.

Now consider a movable head device as shown in Fig. 2-4. Again, a sector approach is used for addressing within a track. The capacity of the device is as follows:

> 10 surfaces (sides)
> 1 surface = 100 tracks
> 1 track = 10 sectors
> 1 sector = 250 characters

The device thus has a capacity in total of $(10 \times 100 \times 10 \times 250)$ 2.5 million characters in 10,000 addressable units. An example addressing system would be

$$xyyz$$

where x = surface (0 to 9)
         yy = track (00 to 99)
          z = sector (0 to 9)

In practice, it is very rare nowadays that a single instruction would be used with this composite address. Probably, two types of instructions would be used. The first would be an order to go to the appropriate track/surface, i.e., a SEEK instruction. Another instruction could then be given, referencing a sector, to initiate a read or write operation. Note that in these examples, a sector is a fixed length space, within a track, capable of holding a fixed number of characters. Some manufacturers call the equivalent of this a "block." The term *block* used in this context is totally different from a block of data on magnetic tape. A block on tape is variable in length according to the programmer's specification. A block or sector on a direct access disk device is a fixed-length hardware unit of storage.

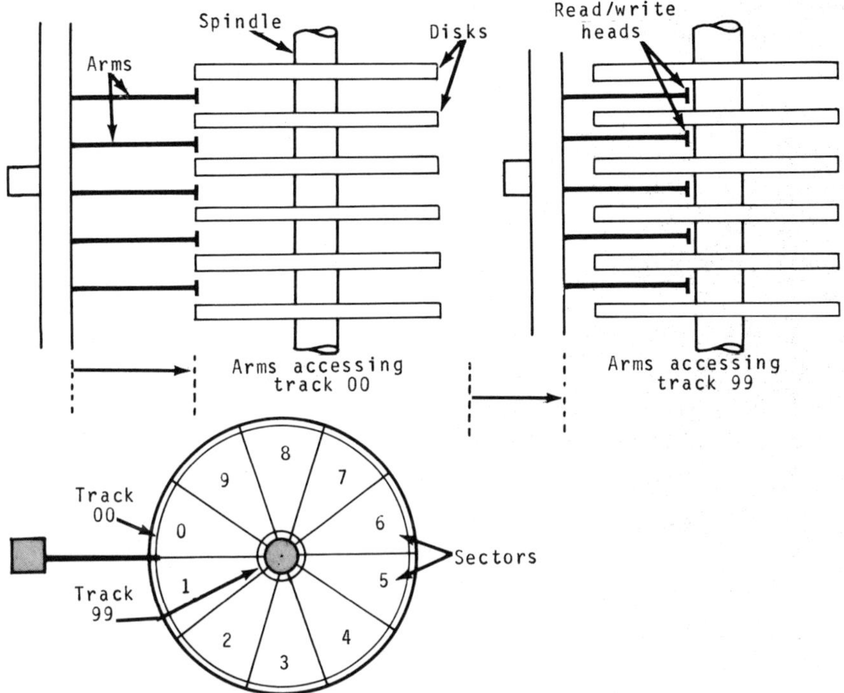

Figure 2-4. A Simple Track/Sector System—Movable Head

Cylinder/Bucket Concept

Thus far, units of storage on a direct access device have been described in hardware terms of tracks and sectors or blocks. This may be represented in a diagram by means of a simple two-dimensional storage map, as shown in Fig. 2-5, which shows a disk device divided into a number of uniquely addressable "cells" formed by surface/track/sector. The storage map shown in this illustration is a storage map of the device presented in Fig. 2-3. In many cases, it is easier for a disk user to think in different storage terms. All modern direct access devices are programmed via pre-prepared software. The relationship of user to device is thus

For example, some devices may be thought of in terms of blocks only. Each block is given a unique hardware address (say 0000 to 9999), with the software

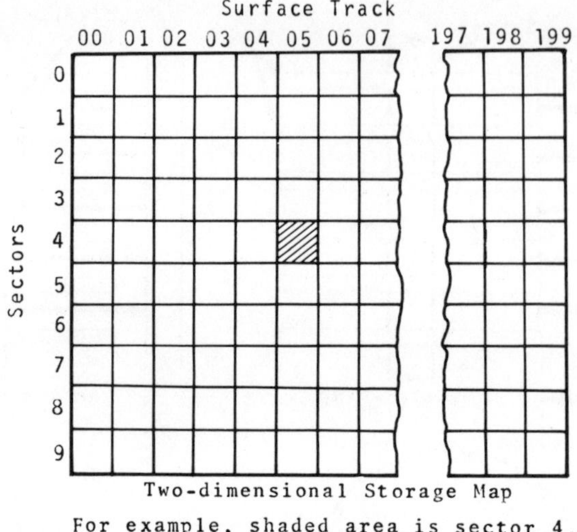

Figure 2-5. Two-Dimensional Storage Map. (For example, shaded area is sector 4, on track 5, on surface 0.)

assigning the physical hardware address to the logical address. Thus,

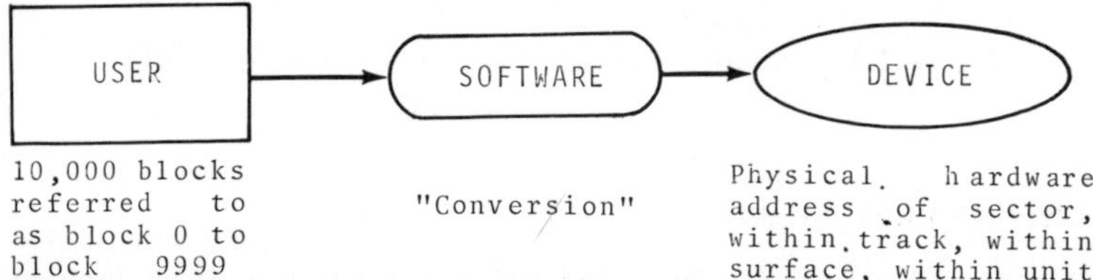

One of the most important concepts of direct access storage is the *cylinder* concept. To understand the reasoning behind the cylinder, and to understand its usefulness, it is necessary to briefly review three points.

1. The greater the number of read/write heads covering a surface, the higher the access speed because less seek time is involved. However, the greater the number of read/write heads, *the more expensive* the device.

2. Seek time is the longest time element in device access. Subject to engineering limitations, and the reduction of the number of read/write heads for economy, the greater the surface area under a head without head movement, the better; that is, fewer seeks will be required to cover the whole of the recording surface.

3. In a multiple surface device such as an exchangeable disk device with a stack of disks, all the head-carrying arms may be arranged to move in unison.

The concept of a *seek area* is to maximize the amount of data that can be accessed without mechanical movement, while at the same time keeping hardware costs to a minimum. A cylinder is one concept of a seek area; i.e., the recording area covered by one positioning of the heads. Given the device shown in Fig. 2-4, one cylinder equals ten tracks. That is, if the heads are positioned on track 1, they are positioned opposite track 1 on all surfaces because the arms move in unison. In this example there are 100 tracks; there are thus 100 cylinders, each cylinder with a capacity of 25,000 characters:

1 cylinder	= 10 tracks (one track per surface, with 10 surfaces)
1 track	= 10 sectors
1 sector	= 250 characters
10 X 10 X 250	= 25,000 characters

It is thus possible to access 25,000 characters worth of information without active seek time. If all the sectors are numbered 00 to 99 within a cylinder (i.e., there are 10 sectors X 10 tracks in one cylinder), a file map for the device would be as shown in Fig. 2-6. In Fig. 2-7 this is shown in hardware terms.

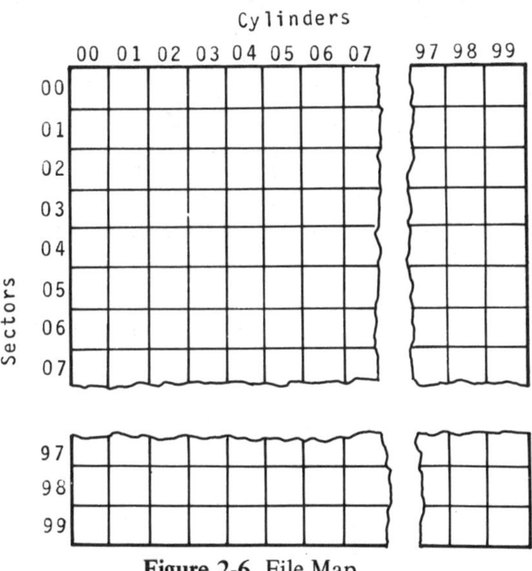

Figure 2-6. File Map

As an extension to this example, consider a device that has a similar design except that it has two read/write heads per arm. This means that two tracks per disk surface will be accessed for each arm position. Let us suppose that the two heads on one arm are positioned 50 tracks apart and that we call the innermost head A and the outer head B. When track 0 is under head A, track 50 is under head B; similarly, when track 49 is under head A, track 99 is under head B.

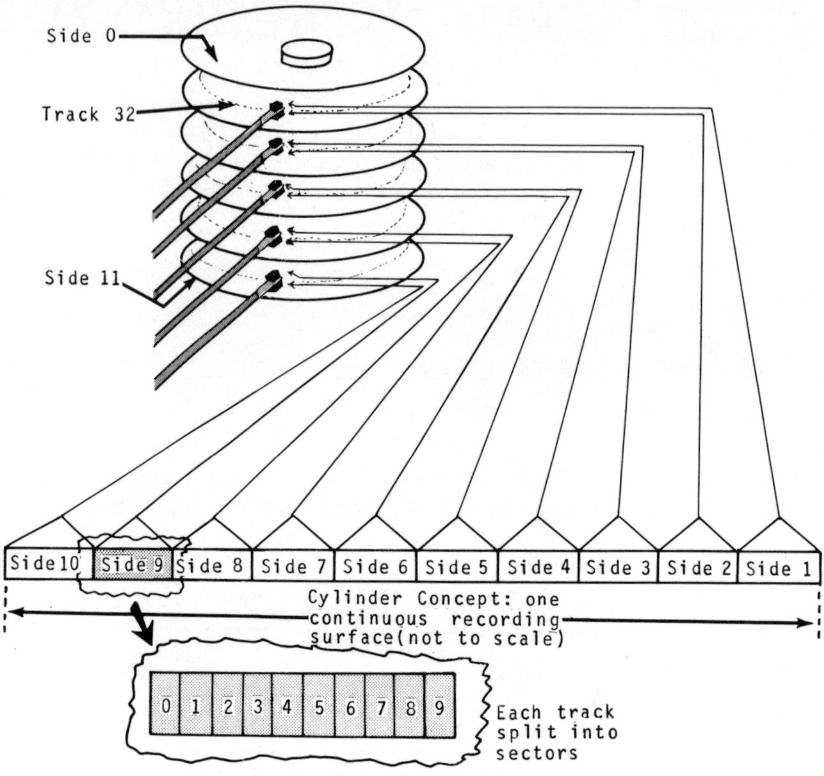

Figure 2-7. A Cylinder in Hardware Terms

The cylinder size is in effect doubled and the number of cylinders halved. The device is now organized as follows:

        1 cylinder = 20 tracks (10 surfaces × two heads per surface)
        1 track   = 10 sectors
        1 sector   = 250 characters
        1 cylinder = 20 tracks × 10 sectors × 250 characters
                   = 50,000 characters

and 100 tracks divided between 2 heads = 50 cylinders.

Again assuming that the sectors are numbered sequentially within a cylinder, a file map for the device would be as shown in Fig. 2-8. The cylinder concept therefore is a way of using the tracks in such a way that they are considered to be a continuous surface that may be accessed without mechanical movement (seek). The *bucket* concept is used in handling information within a *track*, i.e., at the sector/block level.

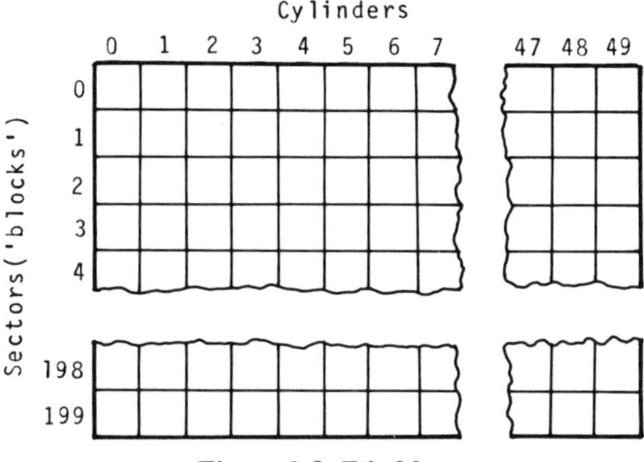

Figure 2-8. File Map

The bucket concept[1] is used by some computer manufacturers in place of the hardware sector approach. If a cylinder is defined as that area of storage available at each seek, a bucket is that area of storage used in one read or write operation. Rather than using the hardware sector address as shown in Fig. 2-6, the file map was introduced, in which it was stated "assume that the sectors within a cylinder are numbered sequentially 00 to 99." In practice, the user thinks in sequentially numbered buckets, which are converted by software to the hardware sector or block addresses:

However, a bucket may consist of more than one block; the number of blocks in one bucket depends upon the device and the software.

Using a bucket approach on the first example illustrated by Fig. 2-6, a file map of the device, assuming a two-block bucket, is shown in Fig. 2-9. The number of blocks making up one bucket is determined by the manufacturer and the device. For example, one manufacturer permits a bucket size of 1, 2, 4, or 8 blocks.

The bucket approach is a software concept (as is the cylinder), and the appli-

---

[1]In this chapter, a bucket has been defined as a unit of storage that is based on hardware blocks or sectors. A bucket may be defined in another way: "the smallest unit of addressing." (Thus, if addressing is on a variable format track device, a bucket may be defined as a data area on a track, or as a block of records, or as a fixed-length unblocked logical record.) The term *bucket* may therefore be defined *independent of hardware.* The use of "bucket" in this general sense is of great importance when random file organization techniques are used, as described in Chapter 8.

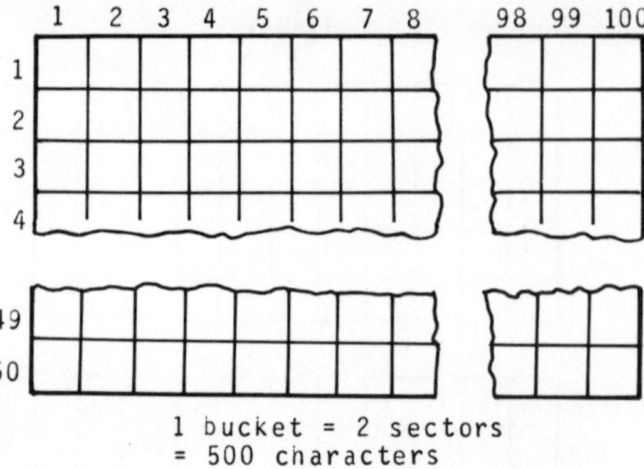

Figure 2-9. Two-Block Bucket

cation of the approach depends more upon the software than on the manufacturer. Thus far we have considered the storage of data in hardware terms
rather than as data handling such as that in storing files. To illustrate the logical
handling of data in cylinders/buckets, the following example is given.[2] It is
stressed that the actual software approach used depends upon the manufacturer
or the software house.

Example

The Device

1. An exchangeable disk store that has a stack (cartridge) of six
   disks.

2. The upper and lower disk surfaces are not used; thus there are ten
   recording surfaces available for use. There is one head per surface
   on a movable arm. All arms move in unison.

3. Each disk surface consists of 100 bands (tracks). Each band is
   divided into eight fixed-length hardware blocks. Each block consists of 512 characters.

4. The device thus has a capacity as follows:

   1 cartridge = 6 disks
   1 cartridge = 10 recording surfaces
   1 surface   = 100 bands
   1 band   = 8 blocks
   1 block   = 512 characters

   Device has a total capacity in characters of 4,096,000 (10 surfaces $\times$ 100 bands $\times$ 8 blocks $\times$ 512 characters).

---

[2] This example is loosely based on an ICL device and the basic EXECUTIVE software.
The device is an ICL 2801 exchangeable disk store. In no way should this example be taken
as a definitive description of the device or the operation of the software. In ICL terminology, track = band, and sector = block.

The Software

1. The cylinder/bucket concept is used. Because there is one read/write head per surface, a cylinder consists of ten bands.

2. The capacity of a cylinder is 4096 characters.

   1 cylinder = 10 bands
   10 bands   = 80 blocks (8 blocks per band)
   80 blocks = 4096 characters (512 characters per block)

3. The size of the bucket is selected by the user. The bucket size selected may be

   1 X block = 512 characters
   2 X blocks = 1024 characters
   4 X blocks = 2048 characters
   8 X blocks = 4096 characters

4. The total recording surface represented by the stack of disks is divided into *file* or *data areas.* The bucket size within a data area is constant. Data is read or written one bucket at a time.

5. Data areas are defined by the user. A data area is defined by the following information:

   (a) *start block number*; each block has a unique address; blocks are numbered from 0 to 79 within each cylinder

   (b) *end block number*

   (c) *start cylinder number*; each cylinder has a unique address; cylinders are numbered 0 to 99

   (d) *end cylinder number*

6. The number of blocks allocated to a file must be a multiple of 8.

7. Within a file area, bucket numbers are assigned by the software. A bucket number will be in the range 1 to *n*, where 1 is the number of the first bucket in the data area, and *n* is the last bucket number in the data area.

An example device containing three assigned data areas is shown in Fig. 2-10. In this example, the total available disk storage on a disk pack has been divided into three data areas: 1, 2, and 3, each with its logical bucket numbers as in Table 2-1.

Each of the three areas could be used to hold a logical unit of information; for example, each of the areas may be used to hold a file. Any item of data could thus be accessed from a data area by giving the logical bucket number; this would be interpreted by the software to give a seek and a bucket starting block address.

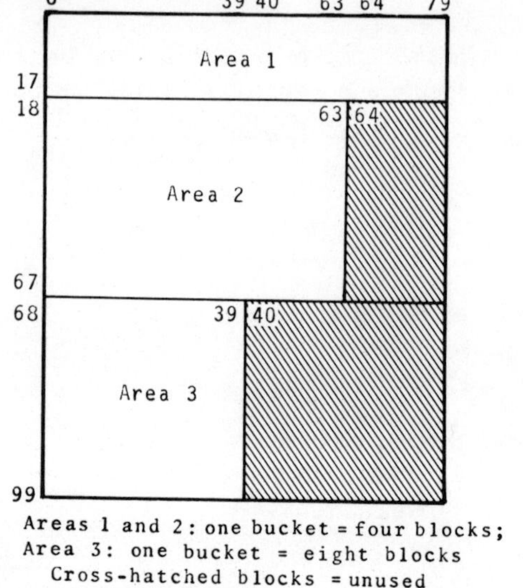

Areas 1 and 2: one bucket = four blocks;
Area 3: one bucket = eight blocks
Cross-hatched blocks = unused
unallocated space

Figure 2-10. Cylinder/Bucket Data Areas (after ICL)

Table 2-1. Logical Bucket Numbers

AREA 1

	Cylinder 0	Cylinder 1	...	Cylinder 17
	1	21		241
	2	22		242
	.	.		.
	.	.		.
	.	.		.
	20	40		360

AREA 2

	Cylinder 18	Cylinder 19	...	Cylinder 67
	1	17		785
	2	18		786
	.	.		.
	.	.		.
	.	.		.
	16	32		800

AREA 3

	Cylinder 68	Cylinder 69	...	Cylinder 99
	1	6		156
	2	7		157
	3	8		158
	4	9		159
	5	10		160

Variations of the cylinder/bucket approach have been used by several manufacturers, including RCA. Some manufacturers have adopted the cylinder level of file structure, but have left the addressing within a cylinder to a surface and block/sector address system. An alternative method of using a recording surface is the *cylinder/record* approach described below.

Cylinder/Record Approach

In the approach described above, the lowest level of conceptual storage is the bucket. The bucket size, selected by the user, is essentially determined by the physical characteristics of the device; that is, the fixed-length hardware blocks are grouped together in logical bucket units, and these units are numbered or addressed sequentially as required. Data, such as file records, are packed into a bucket. For example, five 100-character records can be stored in a 512 character block/bucket as follows:

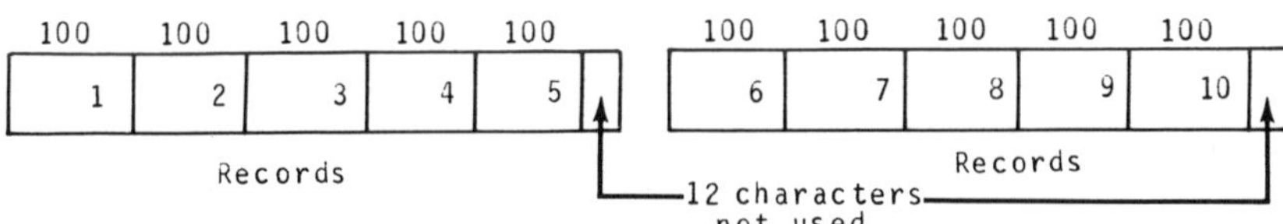

Or, two 550-character records can be stored in a 1024 character bucket:

Note that in both examples, unused space has been left in buckets. This follows the basic convention used in all software, that records must never be split across bucket boundaries. The bucket approach is thus one of fixed-length addressable storage units. An alternative approach is to make the lowest level of addressing a variable-length record. The greatest exponent of this technique is International Business Machines (IBM). The cylinder concept described previously is retained. The minimum or lowest hardware level of addressing is the *track*, i.e., arm position (cylinder) and within that, the head (disk surface). The track is not broken down into hardware blocks or sectors. Data is recorded on a track as a continuous series of characters. A device will have an index or data point that defines the start of a track. Information is recorded on the track as a series of special reference or "marker" records (nondata), followed by data records. For example, IBM requires the use of a number of different types of reference records:

Track address	Count areas
Track descriptor record	Data areas

Gaps are left between reference records and data records. The retrieval of information is thus totally different from the hardware block/sector approach. The latter approach is based on dividing up a track into small hardware addressable units. The retrieval of information is by access according to the hardware address. In the case of a record level of addressing, data is retrieved by accessing the reference records, which describe the contents of a track. The format of information stored on a disk track is now completely variable. Access is by means of special hardware and software features. Using IBM as an example, the position and use of the reference records is shown in Fig. 2-11.

In the scheme shown in Fig. 2-11, there are two ways in which data can be recorded: count-data format and count-key-data format.

The count area consists of an 11-byte field that contains the following format:

Flag
> One byte: special information about the status of a track; e.g., whether it is operative or defective.

Identifier
> Five bytes: This holds the cylinder and the head number (in a 4-byte field), and a record number. The record number is a 1-byte field holding a number in the range of 1 to 255. Records are thus numbered 1 to 255.

Key-Length
> One byte: a field that specifies the length of the record key (i.e., the user data that identifies a particular record such as a man number or product code). If a key is not present, this field is set to zero.

Data Length
> Two bytes: This specifies the length of a data area. In binary notation, it can hold a value of 0 to 65,535; a data area on a track can thus consist of up to (theoretically) 65,535 bytes.

Cyclic Check
> Two bytes: used for error detection.

In the count-data format, the majority of a track consists of count area (as described above) followed by data area, count area followed by data area, count area followed by data area, and so on through a track. Records formatted in this manner are said to be formatted *without keys.*

The count-key-data format is illustrated in Fig. 2-11(b). The key area may be from 1 to 255 bytes long. This key area can hold a logical key. A logical key is an information field that identifies data held in a record. For example:

> Customer record contains details of a customer, identified by a key, which is a *customer account number.*

> Payroll record holds all the pay information about an employee, identified by a key, which is a *man number.*

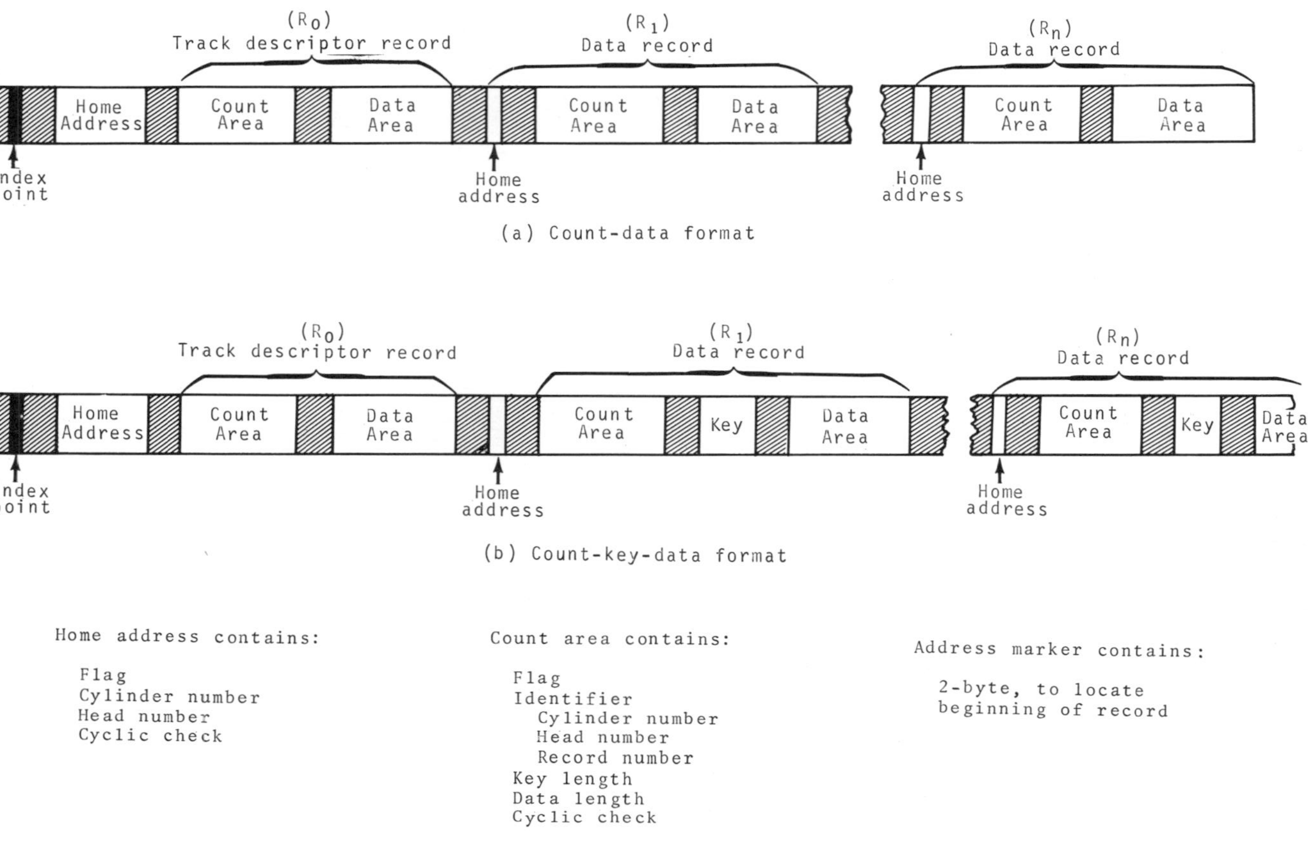

(R0)
Track descriptor record
(R1)
Data record
(Rn)
Data record
Home Address
Count Area
Data Area
Count Area
Data Area
Count Area
Data Area
Index point
Home address
Home address
(a) Count-data format

(R0)
Track descriptor record
(R1)
Data record
(Rn)
Data record
Home Address
Count Area
Data Area
Count Area
Key
Data Area
Count Area
Key
Data Area
Index point
Home address
Home address
(b) Count-key-data format

Home address contains:
Flag
Cylinder number
Head number
Cyclic check

Count area contains:
Flag
Identifier
Cylinder number
Head number
Record number
Key length
Data length
Cyclic check

Address marker contains:
2-byte, to locate
beginning of record

Product file with each record contains all information about a product, identified by a key, which is a *product code.*

The main difference between the two formats is thus the absence of a key area in the count-data format (i.e., key length in count area equals zero), or presence of the key area (i.e., key length in count area equals 1 to 255). Access to data is by means of the count area, which contains the addressing information, and by the key area, if present. This variable addressing facility permits considerable flexibility in how data records are arranged on a track. They may be arranged in any one of five ways:

Fixed, unblocked
Fixed, blocked
Variable, unblocked
Variable, blocked
Undefined

These are illustrated in Fig. 2-12. Note that the variable unblocked records require the use of two additional fields of reference information: *block length* and *record length.* This is necessary because both may vary from block to block and from record to record.

Why block records? The answer is twofold: space utilization and timing. The latter will be discussed in later chapters. Using the cylinder/record approach, the capacity of a track in terms of the number of data characters stored, will depend on the amount of space taken up by reference records (such as count and key areas). Each block will have *one* count area and a key area. If a block contains five data records, there are thus only one count area and one key area that cover five records. This is in contrast to a fixed, unblocked format for five records, which will require the use of five count areas and five key areas (i.e., one count area and one key area per record).

The number of records per track depends on the track format, i.e., count-data versus count-key-data format; an example of capacities is shown in Table 2-2. This shows the track capacity (in number of records) for fixed-block records, formatted with and without keys. Note that

1. The device on which Table 2-2 is based is an IBM 2311 exchangeable disk storage device.

2. Hardware track length is 3625 characters; this is reduced to 3605 characters because 20 bytes are used for track reference records (i.e., the Home Address and the Track Descriptor Record).

3. The count-data format and the count-key-data record formats are used in the example.

The commands available on the IBM 360 to access and process data stored on direct access devices are summarized in Table 2-2(b). These are shown to illustrate the way in which data stored in the cylinder/record manner can be processed, using the reference fields.

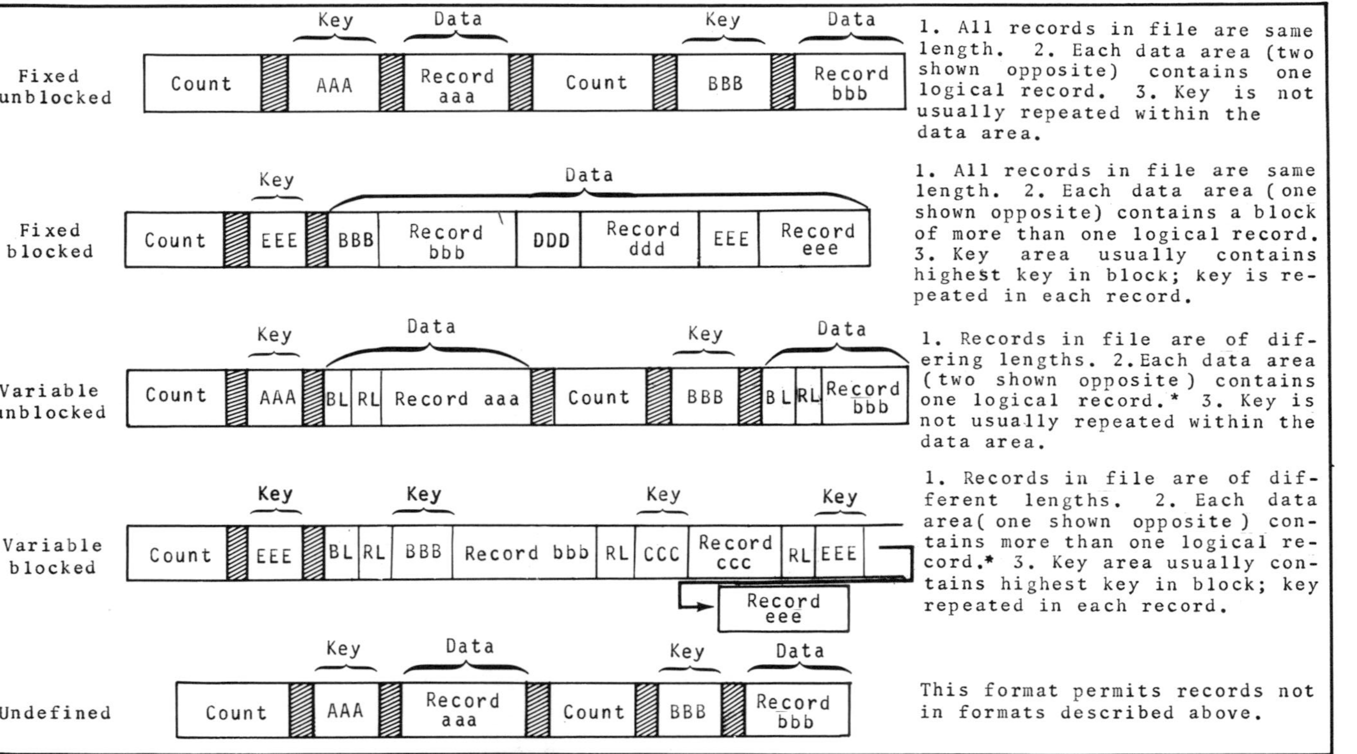

Fixed unblocked. 1. All records in file are same length. 2. Each data area (two shown opposite) contains one logical record. 3. Key is not usually repeated within the data area.

Fixed blocked. 1. All records in file are same length. 2. Each data area (one shown opposite) contains a block of more than one logical record. 3. Key area usually contains highest key in block; key is repeated in each record.

Variable unblocked. 1. Records in file are of differing lengths. 2. Each data area (two shown opposite) contains one logical record.* 3. Key is not usually repeated within the data area.

Variable blocked. 1. Records in file are of different lengths. 2. Each data area (one shown opposite) contains more than one logical record.* 3. Key area usually contains highest key in block; key repeated in each record.

Undefined. This format permits records not in formats described above.

* Note: For variable-length working, two additional fields have to be used: BL and RL (after IBM). BL specifies block length in bytes. RL specifies, for each record, the record length in bytes.

Table 2-2. Track Capacities

Data Record (including key) = 100 bytes; key = 10 bytes		
Format	*Block Size (records)*	*Number of Logical Records, Track Capacity*
Count-data	(1)	23
Fixed-unblocked (with key)		18
Fixed-blocked (with key)	2	24
	4	28
	10	32

(a)

	Location		*Reading/Writing*
SEEK	–to cylinder and read/write head –to read/write head	READ	–home address –track descriptor record –count –count, key and data –data –key and data
SEARCH	–home address equal –identifier equal –identifier high –identifier high or equal –key equal –key high –key high or equal –key and data equal –key and data high –key and data high or equal	WRITE	–home address –track descriptor record –count, key and data –data –key and data

(b)

It is important to realize the difference between *physical* and *logical* record access. Data stored in the count data format is accessed by the contents of the count area, which contains only *addressing* information. We may consider this as access by physical record. On the other hand, data stored in the count-key-data format can be accessed by logical record because a data key related to the logical *content* of the data record is included.

For simplicity, the cylinder/record method of storage and access has been described here, using IBM as an example. However, it is used in one form or another by many computer manufacturers, such as Honeywell (200 series) and ICL (System 4).

SUMMARY

In this chapter the basic operation of devices has been reviewed. It has been shown that direct access devices fall into four basic classifications:

Magnetic drums
Fixed magnetic disks
Exchangeable magnetic disks
Magnetic cards/strips

The type of device is defined by the shape of the recording surface. The first two types of device have a fixed on-line storage capacity, since the recording media is permanently held in the device. The last two types of device have removable recording media, providing unlimited off-line storage in the same manner as magnetic tape.

The devices may be further classified into fixed-head devices and movable head devices. To access data on the latter type, mechanical movement may be necessary to position the read/write heads over the required area of the recording surface. This is called *seeking*, and represents a major timing element in the accessing of data. Fixed-head devices do not require this mechanical seek time because the whole of the recording surface is covered by the heads. (Unit selection and head switching are electronic operations and the time required is negligible.) All devices have a circular recording surface and are thus subject to rotational delay. This is the time required for data on the spinning surface to become available at the read/write heads. This is also known as *latency*. Average latency is equal to one half-revolution of the surface, and is the mean between the best case and worst case (data just coming up to the heads and data just passing the heads, respectively).

The third element in timing is the actual read/write operation itself, which must be distinguished from the access time. The read/write time is the time to transfer the data to (or from) the central processor. Many devices employ a read-after-write check. The transfer rate depends on the rotational speed and the packing density of the recorded data.

Basic addressing is by track (band) and sector (block), although this may be in a number of levels:

Unit
Disk surface
Track on that surface
Sector on that track

A track is thus the surface under a read/write head; sectors are the segmentation of a track.

The two conceptual approaches to the storage were then introduced. The first was the cylinder/bucket concept in which a cylinder is that area on a device that is accessible without mechanical (seek) movement.

a bucket is the logical unit of storage (one or more blocks) within a cylinder.

Data is stored in buckets, and buckets are grouped into data areas. The bucket is based on the hardware division of a track into addressable units, i.e., sectors or blocks.

An alternative method of segmentation was described—the cylinder/record concept. The cylinder is the same as that described above. However, data is stored continuously on the track, which has no physical subdivisions such as sectors. Fixed-hardware addressing is replaced by a system in which reference records are recorded on a track. Access may be by physical or logical record. In this method of storage, reference or control areas (such as the IBM Home Address, Track Descriptor Records, Count Areas, and Control Areas, etc.) are used to locate data on the device.

From the hardware point of view, the two different storage methods mean that capacities can be measured either at the track level or to a block/sector level.

CHAPTER 3

MODERN DIRECT ACCESS DEVICES

It is not intended to provide a definitive catalog of hardware specifications in this chapter. Rather, it provides the reader with a practical appreciation of capacities, times, and costs to supplement the theoretical discussion given in previous chapters. In this chapter, a survey of common devices is made. These devices are freely available for operation with commercially available general-purpose digital computers. There are, of course, exceptional devices which are different from the representative selection given here.[1] The objective of this chapter, therefore, is to give a survey of current devices by presenting the key data about a representative selection.

TERMS USED

Before considering devices in detail, it is necessary to qualify the interpretation of a few terms defined in Chapter 2.

Seek Time. Wherever possible, three seek times are given: minimum, average, and maximum. Because seek time is mechanical movement, it is dependent upon distance covered. For example, if seek time is the time required for the mechanical movement of a head-carrying arm in a disk device, the time required for a particular seek will depend on the distance that the arm has to move; i.e., the number of tracks that have to be traversed. This is illustrated in Fig. 3-1; for the two devices represented in this figure, the seek times in milliseconds are given in the accompanying table.

	IBM 2311	*ICL 2802*
Minimum (one track)	25	30
Average	75	85
Maximum (all tracks)	135	145

Rotational Delay/Latency. Average latency is shown to indicate rotational delay; i.e., the time for one-half surface rotation. By and large, unit selection times have been ignored, as have head-switching delays.

---

[1] Manufacturers have been exceedingly helpful in providing technical data. At the time of going to print, however, some information was not available from official sources. With the rapid rate of development, all technical data is, of course, subject to change. Mention of a device does not mean that the device is still in production.

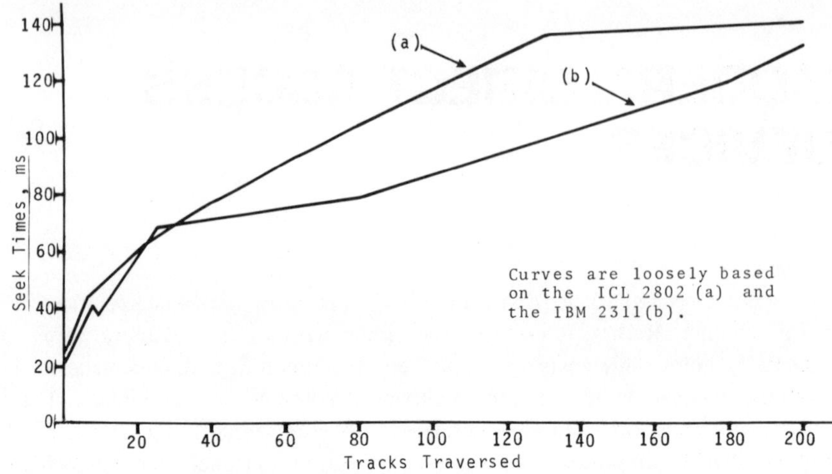

Figure 3-1. Variable Seek Times. (Curves are loosely based on the ICL 2802 and the IBM 2311, respectively.)

Units of Storage.   Wherever possible, the basic unit of storage has been taken as a *character*. This may be either a basic six-bit character, or six data bits plus a parity bit. Some devices are word or byte devices. As described in Chapter 1 ("Units of Storage"), a word consists of a fixed number of bits, which can be used to hold a number of characters in six-bit form. For example, a 36-bit word can be used to hold a number in serial binary representation, or six 6-bit characters. For comparison purposes, transfer rates will be quoted in characters per second (rather than words per second). A byte consists of a "word" of eight bits in length (or eight bits plus a parity bit). A byte can thus hold

> a character.
> two decimal digits (of four bits each).
> an eight-bit word, holding a value in serial binary form.

Generally, however, byte and character transfer rates may be compared without undue distortion. Packing densities will normally be quoted in bpi, bits per inch.[2] Capacities will be quoted in thousands or millions of characters. It will be remembered that a recording surface may be fixed hardware-block form, or it may be organized as a continuous stream of data on a track. In the latter case, the actual data storage capacity will be variable, as described in Chapter 1 in the subsection "Cylinder/Record Approach."

---

[2]Unfortunately, the terms *track* and *band* have come to have two different meanings. One interpretation is that a band is the lowest level of addressing. A band, however, consists of a number of bit tracks. Packing densities are quoted per track as defined as part of a band. However, in this chapter the terms *track* and *block* will be used as defined in the preceding chapter.

Terms of Storage.   The basic hardware terms used are *track* and *block*, as defined in the preceding chapter. Any alternative terms used by a specific manufacturer for a device will be given in brackets, if appropriate.

Read/Write Times.   Because devices use a variety of basic units of transfer (such as blocks, sectors, fixed-length buckets or variable-length records), the guide for read/write time will be the *transfer rate*, in thousands of characters or bytes per second (kch/s and kb/s, respectively).

Control Units.   To give the reader an appreciation of the on-line storage capacity of a type of device, an indication is given of the number of devices that can be linked to the central processor via a control unit. A number of control units may be attached to the central processor, but this will depend on the size and the power of the central processor.

Alternative Storage.   Most devices have alternative areas of storage. These are tracks that are not normally used, but are held in reserve. Should a defect or "bad spot" develop on an operational track, one of the reserve alternate tracks can be switched in, thus maintaining the full storage capacity of the device.

Costs.   Costs per character stored are given in the text as *indications*. Obviously, prices and pricing structures are variable among countries and among manufacturers, and are liable to change at relatively short notice. Usually, the purchase or rental of direct access equipment involves two different units of equipment: the transport(s) and the control unit(s). More than one transport may usually be linked to a control unit. Thus, the cost per character, in effect, decreases as more devices or transports are linked to one control. For example:

> Device X has a capacity of 100,000 characters and has a purchase price of $10,000.

> Device X has to be used with a control unit type Y, which sells at $5,000.

> Up to five type X devices can be linked to one type Y control unit.

The cost per character can thus be calculated as follows:

100,000 characters	1 × type X transport	$10,000
	1 × type Y control unit	5,000
		$15,000

Cost per character = 15¢.

200,000 characters	2 × type X transports	$20,000
	1 × type Y control unit	5,000
		$25,000

Cost per character = 12.5¢.

500,000 characters	5 × type X transports	$50,000
	1 × type Y control unit	5,000
		$55,000

Cost per character = 11¢.

Figure 3-2. Magnetic Drum Store. These photographs show the Univac FH432
the head assembly and lifting shaft are illustrated on the right. The actual drum
sitioning of the read/write heads. The drum rotates at 7,100 rpm ± 30 rpm.
ation, these heads fly at less than 0.0005″ from the drum surface. There are 54
at 889 bits per inch—tracks per inch, axially = 60.6. Courtesy of UNIVAC

(In the increasingly competitive field of selling computers, manufacturers are
increasing the performance and decreasing the cost by making better use of control units, i.e., offering a wider scope of transports that can be attached to one
control unit. Hence, this explains IBM's rationalization of their exchangeable
disk stores, which replace some units with a new range of disk devices that are, in
essence, making more effective use of the control units available.)

The indication of cost-per-character stored includes the control unit price
and the transport unit price[3] and is a *representative* value.

---

[3]The number of control units *does* affect the amount of overlap and simultaneity
among a number of different transports. This consideration will be a determining factor in
the way in which the transports are linked to the central processor via the control units.

Type 9102 Drum. The drum frame with base plats is shown on the left, and
cylinder measuring 10.5" X 9.0" is mounted in a casing with gaps for the po-
Positioned at the gaps in the casing are groups of read/write heads. When in oper-
read/write heads in a group, with up to nine groups per drum. Data is recorded
Division, Sperry Rand.

Device Descriptions and Comparisons

A range of devices is described under the headings of

Magnetic drums
Fixed magnetic disks
Exchangeable magnetic disks
Magnetic card/strip devices

Comments are made on the mode of operation of the devices, and one example
device is shown in detail. A summary is given at the end of the chapter, with a
survey of usage. It is stressed, however, that there are many criteria for comparing types of devices and for comparing the different products of manufacturers within a device type category. This is a survey of a general nature.

Table 3-1. Magnetic Drum Statistics

Manufacturer: Computer: Model Number:	UNIVAC 1108[a] FH 432	IBM 360[b] 2301	IBM 360[b] 2303	ICL 1900 SERIES[c] 1964	UNIVAC 1108[a] FASTRAND II
Drums per unit	1	1	1	1	2
Tracks per drum	128[d]	200[e]	800[f]	512[g]	6,144[h]
Blocks per track	2,048	Variable format	Variable format	1,024	64
Characters per block	6[i]	Variable format	Variable format	4[i]	168
Characters per track	12,288	20,483	4,892	4,048	10,752
Characters per unit	1,572,864	4,096,600	3,190,000	2,072,576	132,120,756
Transfer rate (kch/s or kb/s)	1,440	1,200	312.5	100	153.75
Head arrangement (fixed or movable)	Fixed	Fixed	Fixed	Fixed	Movable
Heads per drum	128	200	800	512	32 × 192 positions
Drum diameter (inches)	10.5	10.7		18.5	32.8
Drum speed (rpm)	7,100	3,490	3,428	1,500	870
Packing density (bpi)	627	1,250	1,105		1,000
Average latency (ms)	4.25	8.6	8.75	20.5	35
Seek, minimum (ms)	0	0	0	0	30
average (ms)	0	0	0	0	58
maximum (ms)	0	0	0	0	86

Average access time (ms)	4.25	8.6	8.75	20.5	93
Cylinder capacity (ch/byte)	Total capacity	Total capacity	Total capacity	Total capacity	688,128[j]
Number of units on line	9	32[k]	4[l]	4	8
Maximum on-line capacity (million)	14.155	130.99	12.76	8.39	1,057
Approx. cost per character stored,					
cent	8	5	4		0.2
new pence	3.2	2	1.4		0.08

[a] Quoted in characters. However, storage is in 36-bit words. Each word holds six 6-bit characters.

[b] Quoted in bytes.

[c] Quoted in characters. However, storage is in 24-bit words. Each word holds four 6-bit characters.

[d] There are 144 tracks, but 16 are reserved for hardware usage (timing, etc.) and spares.

[e] There are 220 tracks, but 20 are reserved (for spares, etc.). There is one additional track for timing, etc.

[f] There are 880 tracks, 80 being held in reserve as spares.

[g] Spare tracks are available.

[h] There are 6534 tracks per drum, but 390 are reserved for hardware usage (timing, etc.) and spares. Since there are two drums, the tracks available in one unit are 12,288.

[i] Addressing is therefore to a word level; 1 block = 1 word.

[j] There are 32 heads per drum, times two drums = 64 heads in unit. The two groups of 32 heads move in unison.

[k] That is, 4 drum units per control (2820) and up to 8 controls, number of channels and type of channel permitting.

[l] Assumes 2 devices per control (2841) with two controls on line.

Figure 3-3A. Fixed Disk Store. The photograph on the left shows the head/ far side of the disk. The heads are arranged in 12 groups, each group consists of (third row from the top, second in from the right) are for timing purposes. There separation is 40 to 45 mils. On the right is a general photograph of a Burroughs carrying casting and the disk surface, with mechanical and electronic compo-

MAGNETIC DRUM STORES

A magnetic drum unit consists of a cylindrical recording surface with a magnetic coating. Recording takes place on the circumference of the cylinder. The drum is permanently fixed within the unit. An example of a magnetic drum is shown in Fig. 3-2, and statistics of the various types are given in Table 3-1. Even with this limited sample of devices, there is a wide variance in unit capacities: 1½ million characters to 132 million characters, with transfer rates of 135 kch/s to 1440 kch/s. On-line capacity varies still more: from 8 million to 1057 million. (A Control Data Corporation device, the 863, has a maximum transfer rate of 2000 kch/s.) Some drum devices have very interesting characteristics. In terms of storage layout, the level of addressing can be to a very low level—for example, to a word on the ICL and UNIVAC devices. On the other hand, IBM permits variable record storage and addressing around a track, together with the cylinder concept.

surface relationship on a B9372, taken by double exposure—the heads are on the 13 read/write heads (cores). This can be seen in the plate. The bank of six heads is thus provision for 12 X 13 tracks = 156, giving six spare tracks; adjacent core disk device with the covers removed, showing the relationship between the head-nents. Courtesy of Burroughs Corporation.

The devices fall into two basic categories: head-per-track devices and movable head devices. Most of the devices listed in Table 3-1 use the head-per-track system. It can be seen that these devices have very fast access times—as low as 4.25 ms on the UNIVAC FH 432. These times are composed mainly of rotational delay, with no seek time. To obtain very fast access times, therefore, the rotational delay can be cut by speeding up the rotation and by keeping the diameter of the drum to a minimum.

With the wide range of device characteristics shown in Table 3-1, it is very difficult to generalize about drum devices. Generally, however, it is possible to divide drum units into two classes: those devices that provide limited on-line storage and very fast access times, and those devices that provide massive on-line storage and very much longer access times. An example of the latter are devices such as the UNIVAC FASTRAND II drums, which provide up to 132 million characters of on-line storage with a medium transfer rate of some 167 kch/s. This device has a fairly lengthy average access time, 93 ms. (This is calculated from an average seek time of the movable heads of 58 ms plus average latency of 35 ms.) Contrast this with another UNIVAC product, the FH 432.

This provides low-to-medium on-line storage capacity of up to 14 million characters, with a very high transfer rate on the order of 1440 kch/s. The device has a very short access time; the fixed-head, one-per-track system permits an average access time of 4.3 ms. It will be rare, in fact, to find just one drum transport attached to a modern computer. With the use of one or more control units, it is possible to have mass storage facilities available to the central processor. High-capacity devices thus have the penalty of longish access times, but the advantage of a "cheap" cost, less than a cent per character stored. Very fast access times (and low capacity) increase the cost to some 4 to 8 cents per character stored.

Generally, magnetic drums are used as true backing storage; i.e., as an extension of core storage (program/data/working space) rather than structured file storage. Certainly, for scientific usage, the ability to address down to a very low level, e.g., to a word level, is extremely useful. Drums have been given a new lease on life with the advent of time-sharing/terminal computer usage. In these cases, very fast access storage is required for such functions as repeatedly calling and loading many different programs. Similarly, for data storage, magnetic drums may be used for "dumping" data temporarily after input and before output.

FIXED-DISK STORAGE

Fixed-disk storage falls into two classes: fixed-head systems (Fig. 3-3) (one head per track) and movable head systems. The majority of devices in use these days are of the movable head type. The principle of fixed-disk stores is a stack of one or more large disks. The disks, mounted on a vertical or horizontal spindle (depending on make), are permanently fixed in the transport unit. Data is recorded on concentric tracks on the disk surface(s).

A sample of devices is summarized in Table 3-2. As with magnetic drums, the wide range of values shown in the table makes it difficult to generalize about device characteristics. It is obvious, however, that fixed-head devices have very much faster access times than have devices of the moving-head variety. Transfer rates of 150 to 300 kch/s are possible. This is about the norm for direct access devices these days. A notable exception is the IBM 2305, which has a transfer rate of 3000 kb/s. (The Control Data 6638 system gives a maximum of 1680 kch/s.) However, fixed-disk devices offer massive on-line capacity per device; for example, up to 600 million characters per device. Via control units, a number of such devices may be attached to the central processor.

The actual disk size is on the order of 25 to 39 inches (with the exception of the IBM 2305), as opposed to about 14 inches on exchangeable disk stores described later. This means that for movable-head devices, the seek time (arm movement) is quite high because the distances to be traversed are quite long; this gives seek times on the order of 100 ms. A number of heads may be attached to one arm, and a number of movable arms may be arranged to service *one* disk surface. On the other hand, fixed-disk stores permit the use of one-head-per track working, which is not possible on exchangeable disk stores (because of

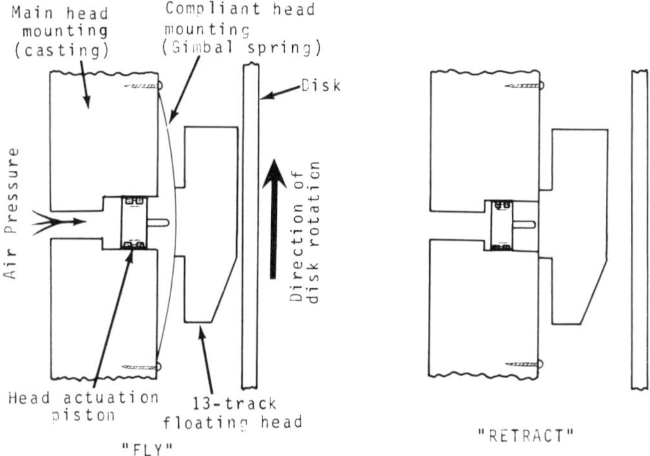

This schematic shows the operation of the floating head arrangement. The head is attached to an actuation piston, which is pushed toward the disk surface by air pressure from behind (22 psi ± 2) . In this case the heads are flown some 95 microinches from the disk surface. Note that the head is bonded to a compliant spring (a Gimbal spring), which is attached to the main casting. Removal of the air pressure thus causes the head to retract. When the head is in the "fly" position, it is repelled from the disk surface by the laminar rush of air caused by the disk rotation(1745 rpm) acting against the beveled leading edge of the head assembly.

Figure 3-3B. Schematic of Burroughs B9370 Floating Head

variable tolerances). This gives very fast access rates of 20 to 25 ms for rotational delay, and very fast transfer rates. But the fixed-head devices are very much more expensive than their moving-head counterparts. (About 5 cents per character stored as against 1 or 2 cents per character stored.)

Fixed-disk stores are usually to be found in very large installations with terminal or real-time working, where very large files have to be held on line. This type of device has dropped in popularity since the advent of the exchangeable disk store.

EXCHANGEABLE DISK STORES

There are two components in an exchangeable disk store: EDS, otherwise known as an RDS (replaceable disk store). First, there is the drive or transport unit; onto this drive is mounted a *disk pack* or *cartridge.* Some devices have a number of spindles and can thus hold a number of disk packs. A typical example is shown in Fig. 3-4.

The disk pack consists of a central spindle supporting a number of disks. When the disk pack is in storage, the stack of disks is encased in a plastic housing, a base and a cover. The base is unscrewed when the disks are to be mounted

Table 3-2. FDS Statistics

Manufacturer:	BURROUGHS[a]	BURROUGHS[a]	IBM[a]	ICL[b]	HONEYWELL[c]
Computer:	B2500/B3500	B2500/B3500	360	1900 SERIES	200 SERIES
Model Number:	B9372[d]	B9370-2	2305	2805[e]	262[f]
Number of Disks per Unit:	4	1	6	26[g]	72[h]
Surfaces used per unit	8	2	12	50	128
Tracks per surface	150[i]	100[i]	32[j]	256[i]	256[i]
Blocks per track	96	100	Variable	6 to 15[k]	Variable
Characters per block	100	100	Variable	512	Variable
Characters per track	9,600	10,000	14,136	3,072 to 7,680	9,381
Characters per unit	10,000,000	2,000,000	5,428,224	419,430,000	300,000,000
Transfer rate (kch/s or kb/s)	232.0	298.75	3,000	151.0	196.6
Head arrangement (fixed/movable)	Fixed	Fixed	Fixed	Movable	Movable
Read/write heads per surface	150	100	768[l]	6	4
Disk diameter (inches)	26.5	26.5	14	39	26
Rotational speed (rpm)	1,500	1,745	6,000	1,200	1,167
Packing density (bpi)					1,192
Average latency (ms)	20	17	2.5	25	26
Seek, minimum (ms)	0	0	0	15	15
average (ms)	0	0	0	92.5	78
maximum	0	0	0	205	120

Average access time (ms)	20	17	2.5	117.5	104
Cylinder size (ch/byte)	Total capacity	Total capacity	Total capacity	638,400	1,179,648
Units on line	100	2[m]	4[n]		4
Maximum on-line capacity (million)	1,000	4	21.71		1,200
Approx. cost per character stored,					
cent	0.5	2.0	3.0		0.1
new pence	0.2	0.8	1.2		0.04

[a]Quoted in bytes.

[b]Quoted in characters. However, storage is in 24-bit words. Each word holds four 6-bit characters.

[c]Quoted in characters.

[d]The basic unit is a module of four disks; figures given here are for one module.

[e]Three versions are available, consisting of 7, 14, or 26 disks. The 26-disk version is described here.

[f]Another version is the 261; this has half the capacity of the 262.

[g]One disk is reserved, leaving 25 disks for use.

[h]The total of 72 disks is divided into two 36-disk stacks.

[i]Spare tracks are available.

[j]An additional 48 spare tracks are provided and held in reserve.

[k]Because of the disk size, the surfaces are divided into zones. Each zone is serviced by two read/write heads, and each zone has different packing densities and transfer rates.

[l]There are two heads per track. These heads are 180 degrees apart. Because a track is effectively split into two halves by the two heads, the time for one revolution is 10 ms, but the *maximum* latency is only some 5 ms.

[m]Based on two units per control. Number of controls depends on the number of channels available.

[n]Assumes 1 × 2835 control with 2 × 2305 units on that control; linkage is by a 2880 block multiplexor channel.

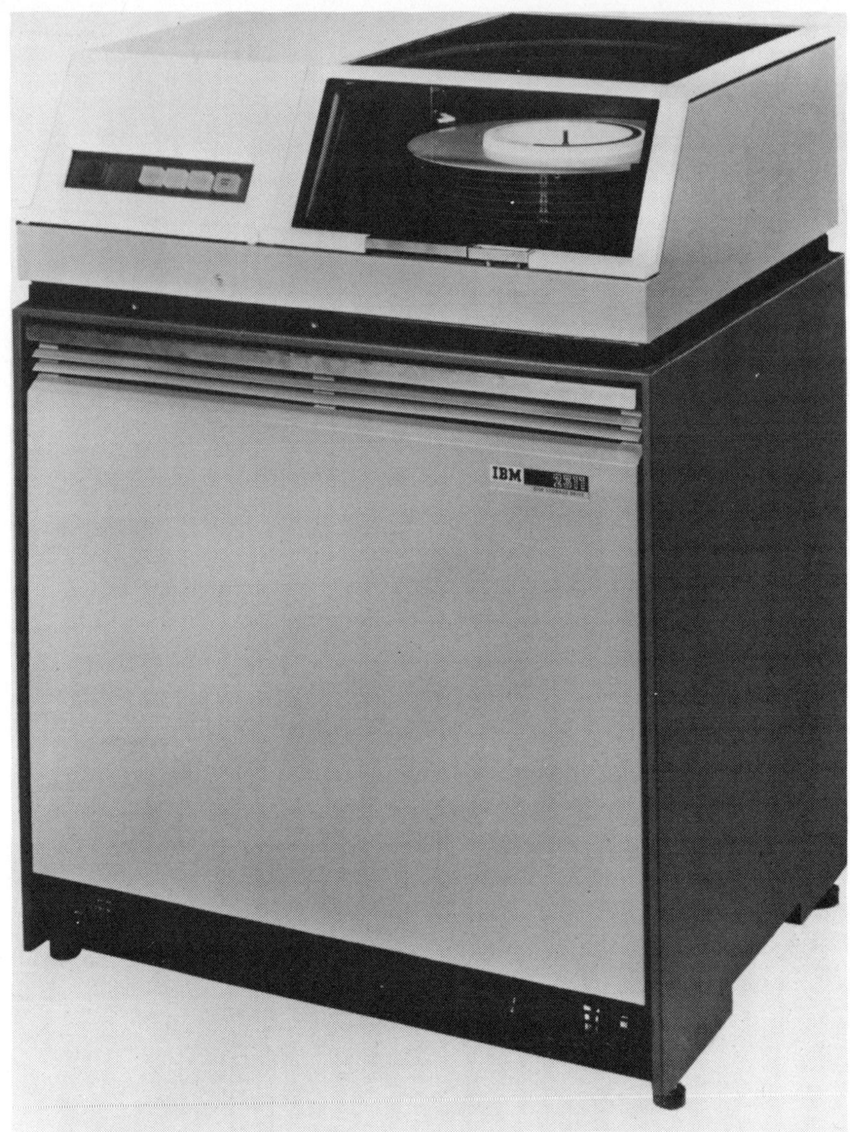

Figure 3-4. IBM Exchangeable Disk Store Device. On the left is an IBM 2311 disk drive with pack loaded. On the right is a close-up of the head/disk surface relationship on the IBM 2311. Courtesy of IBM Corporation.

on a transport, and the disk pack is lowered onto the spindle on the drive. The disk is locked down in position and the top cover is removed, after which the disks are available for use.

Figure 3-4 (Continued)

A representative selection of devices are summarized in Table 3-3. Note that Table 3-3 shows both single-spindle (drive) units and multispindle units.

Common characteristics of exchangeable disk stores are discussed below.

Transport
   1. The number of heads on a movable arm is limited to not more than five read/write heads per arm. (Rarely is there more than one read/write head per arm.)
   2. Heads retract when the device is inoperable, e.g., when a disk pack is being loaded. When the device is to be used for read/ writing the heads are moved out over the disk surface(s).
   3. All devices work on the floating head principle, using the out-of-contact recording technique. (See full description in Chapter 1, "Recording Surfaces and Read-Write Heads.")
   4. There is a wide range of packing densities and transfer rates, depending on manufacturer and model; for example, 250 to 3333 bpi, 13.3 to 420 kch/s. However, a transfer rate in the range of 150 to 350 kch/s is usual.
   5. The number of tracks per disk surface is generally 100 to 200.

Table 3-3. EDS Statistics

Manufacturer: Computer: Model Number:	CDC[a] 3100/3300 853[d]	IBM[b] 360 2311	ICL[c] 1900 SERIES 2802	HONEYWELL[a] 200 SERIES 259A	IBM[b] 360 2314	IBM[b] 360 3330[e]
Spindles in unit	1	1	1	1	8[f]	2
Disks in pack	6	6	6	6	11	11
Disk diameter (inches)	14	14	14	14	14	14
Disk surfaces used in pack	10	10	10	10	20	19
Tracks per surface	100	200[g]	200[g]	200[g]	200	404[h]
Blocks per track	16	Variable	8	Variable	Variable	Variable
Characters per block	256	Variable	512	Variable	Variable	Variable
Characters per track	4,096	3,650	4,096	4,602	7,294	13,030
Characters in unit	4,096,000	7,250,000	8,192,000	9,200,000	233,408,000	200,000,000
Transfer rate (kch/s or kb/s)	288.33	156	208	147.5	312	806
Arrangement of heads (fixed/movable)	Movable	Movable	Movable	Movable	Movable	Movable
Heads per disk surface	1	1	1	1	1	1
Disk speed (rpm)	2,400	2,400	2,400	1,700	2,400	3,600
Packing density (bpi)	1,105	1,100		1,100	1,100	4,040

Average latency (ms)	12.5	12.5	12.5	17.5	12.5	8.35
Seek time, minimum (ms)	30	25	30	30	25	10
average (ms)	85	75	85	79.6	60	30
maximum (ms)	145	135	145	150	130	55
Average access time (ms)	97.5	87.5	97.5	97.1	72.5	38.35
Cylinder capacity (ch/byte)	40,960	36,250	40,960	46,020	145,880	237,570
Units on line	8[i]	8[j]	8	8	1	4
Maximum on-line capacity (million)	32.788	58	65.536	73.6	233.4	800
Approx. cost per character stored						
cents	0.5	0.8		0.6	0.1	0.01
new pence	0.2	0.32		0.24	0.04	0.04

[a] Quoted in characters.

[b] Quoted in bytes.

[c] Quoted in characters. However, basic unit of storage is a 24-bit word. Each word can hold four 6-bit characters.

[d] Identical in capacity to the ICL 2801.

[e] The 3330 is a 2-spindle module; 2, 4, 6, or 8 modules may be put on line. Figures quoted are for basic 2-spindle module.

[f] There are actually 9 spindles. but one is held in reserve.

[g] Three tracks are held in reserve as spares; there are thus actually 203 tracks per surface.

[h] There are 7 reserve tracks on each surface.

[i] That is, 8 × 853 on line via a 3234 control.

[j] That is, 8 × 2311 on a 2841 control.

Disk Pack

1. The number of disks in one disk pack depends on the manufacturer and the model, but can be 1, 2, 6, 10, or 11. In most cases, the top and bottom disk surfaces in the stack are not used for recording.
2. The diameter is about 12 to 14 inches. Suppliers appear to be about evenly divided between the use of nickel-cobalt plating and and ferric oxide coating.
3. Disk packs are portable and easy to handle. As an example, the disk packs for the device shown in Fig. 3-4 consist of six disks (14 inches in diameter by 0.05 inch thick). The pack weighs about 10 pounds and can be changed in about a minute.

With this brief description of common technical characteristics, it is possible to summarize the major points of usage.

The EDS devices have proved to be the most popular of all direct access devices on the market. They provide reasonably high transfer rates, 150 to 312 kch/s, and medium access times. Taking the "average" access time as average seek time plus average latency, the range of single-spindle units shown in Table 3-3 is on the order of 80 to 110 ms. These devices have two other major factors in their favor. The first is that there is unlimited off-line storage (in the same manner as reels of magnetic tape), although the on-line capacity is limited (say, 10 million characters per spindle). Additionally, the user may have relatively large volumes of data on line (if required) by putting a number of transports on line via the appropriate control units. Thus, four disk drives could permit about 35 million characters of on-line storage. This modular approach to providing on-line storage has enabled many small- to medium-sized computer users to make use of direct access facilities at a relatively low cost. (The cluster approach to disk drives is gradually replacing the fixed-disk movable arm devices.)

MAGNETIC CARD/STRIP DEVICES

Magnetic card/strip devices are feats of electromechanical engineering. The primary objective of these devices is to provide massive on-line storage at medium access and transfer rates. Three devices are worthy of mention:

NCR CRAM† (Card Random Access Memory), National Cash Register

IBM DATACELL, International Business Machines

ICL-MCF* (Magnetic Card File), International Computers, Ltd.

Mass Storage Unit,* Radio Corporation of America†

> *Notes:* *Available on a number of computers; originally the RCA 3488 device. Sold in the U.K. by ICL (with the 1900 series) and in the U.S. by RCA (with Spectra 70 series).
> †Marketed in four versions with the 315 computer (CRAM 353); now offered with the Century (CRAM 653).

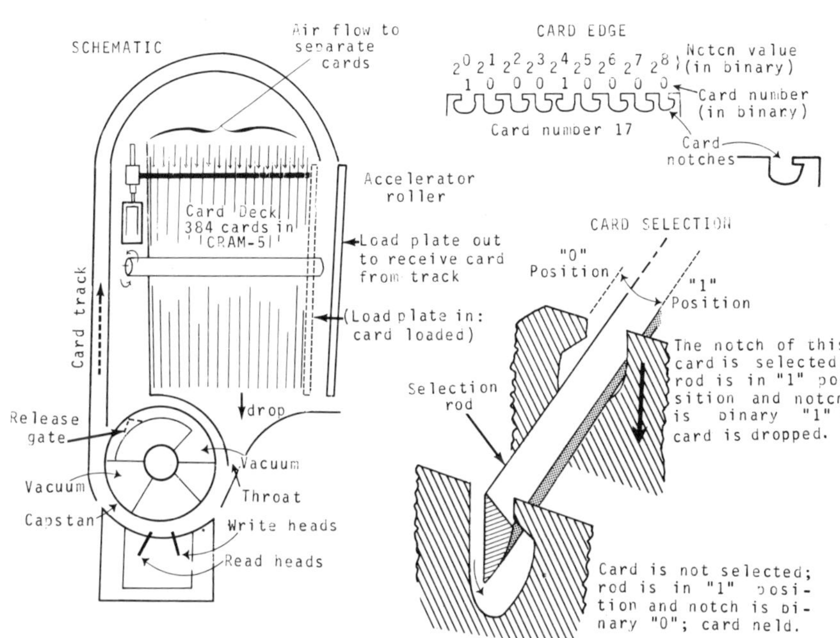

Figure 3-5. Card/Strip Devices

The operation of these devices is shown in Fig. 3-5. Key statistics are summarized in Table 3-4. Each of these three devices is described below.

NCR CRAM

The CRAM device first made an appearance as second-generation computer equipment in May 1961. The principle of operation is shown in Fig. 3-5(a). The basic unit of storage is a magnetic card measuring 3½ X 14 inches. The card is made of 5-mil Mylar coated with 200 μin. of oxide. Each card has a pattern of notches along one edge, which uniquely identifies that card. A deck of these cards is stored in a canister or cartridge. Early CRAM units had 256 cards; this was later increased to 384. Canisters are quite portable and are exchangeable; it takes about a minute to change a cartridge. When a deck of cards is in position on the device, any card can be selected by means of a rod mechanism operating on the edge notches. A selected card is "dropped" onto a transport mechanism, which moves it to a capstan. Card travel is accelerated to 380 inches per second as it approaches the capstan. It is wrapped around the 7 inch diameter capstan frame by vacuum suction.

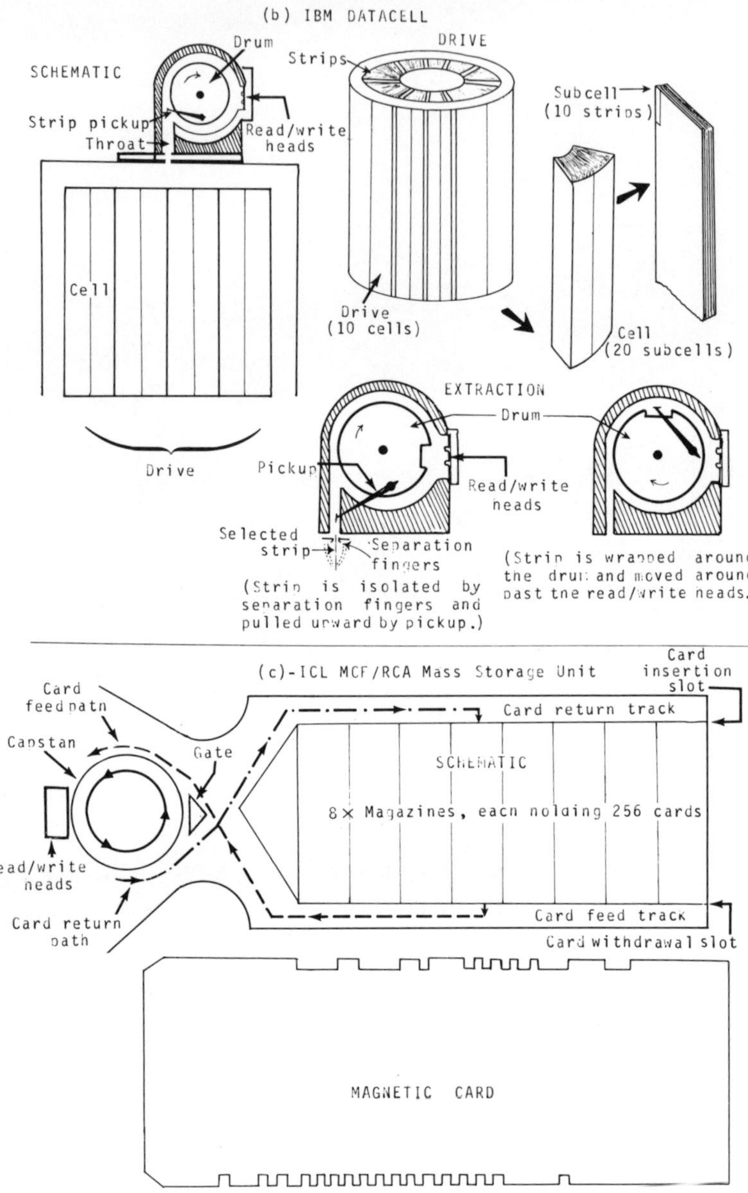

Figure 3-5 (Continued)

    The card can then be used in much the same manner as a magnetic drum. The card rotates opposite read/write heads. Data is read from or written to tracks on the card. When the read/write operation is completed, the card is released from the capstan and transported back to the end of the deck. (The

Table 3-4. Card/Strip Statistics

Device	Basic Media Unit	Tracks per Media Unit	Characters/ Bytes per Track	Characters per Media Unit	Units per Group	Characters Bytes per Unit (million)	Groups per Device	Characters/ Bytes per Device	Average Access Time (million)	Maximum Transfer Rate (k/s)
NCR, CRAM (5) (characters)	Magnetic cards	144	1,500	216,000	284/deck	82.9	1 deck	82.9	145	50.7
ICL-MCF (characters)	Magnetic cards	64	2,592	165,888	256/ magazine	42.5	8 magazines	340	515	80
RCA, mass storage unit (bytes)	Magnetic cards	128	2,048	262,144	256/ magazine	67.1	8 magazines	536.8	515	70
IBM, DATACELL (bytes)	Magnetic strips	100	2,000	200,000	200/cell (in 10 subcells)	40	10 cells	400	575	55

sequence of the cards within the deck is immaterial because the rod-selection mechanism identifies a card by its notch pattern, not by its position within a deck.) In CRAM-5 units, a block of 36 read/write heads are positioned opposite the capstan. These heads can be moved to any one of four positions, thus giving 144 data tracks on a card.

To a certain extent, deck-to-capstan movement, read/write head movement and capstan-to-deck movement can be overlapped. Basic operating data is listed in Table 3-5.

Card life on CRAM-5 is claimed to be in excess of 300,000 capstan revolutions.

Table 3-5. CRAM Operating Data

	CRAM-1	CRAM-2	CRAM-5
Capacity			
Cards per deck	256	128	384
Tracks per card	7	56	144
Characters per track	3,100	1,120	1,500
Characters per card	21,700	62,720	216,000
Characters per unit (mil)	5.6	16	82.9
Reading			
Number of read/write heads	7 (fixed)	55 (fixed)	36 ($\times$ 4 positions)
Packing density (bpi)	263	700	936
Transfer rate (kch/s maximum)	100	38	50.7
Access			
Deck-to-capstan access-drop card (average in ms)	235	235	125
Average latency (ms)	24	24	24
Maximum access time (ms)	333	333	200

IBM DATACELL

The DATACELL is the type 2321 for use with IBM 360. The principle of operation is shown in Fig. 3-5(b). The basic unit of storage is an iron-oxide strip, measuring about 2¼ $\times$ 13 $\times$ 0.005 inches, with coding tabs for identification. Ten of these strips are grouped together to form a "subcell," 20 subcells making one cell. The data cell thus holds 200 strips; it is portable and exchangeable. Each data-cell drive can hold up to 10 cells, giving a total on-line storage capacity per drive of 2000 strips (10 cells $\times$ 20 subcells $\times$ 10 strips). The data cells are mounted on the device in a circular holder. To access any required strip, the holder is rotated until the desired subcell is positioned under a capstan. By means of a simple hole-tab system, the appropriate strip in that subcell can be selected. It is isolated by means of separating fingers, extracted by a pickup, and lifted up to the capstan. Cell positioning and strip withdrawal takes from 175 to 400 ms. The strip is wrapped around the capstan to form a temporary drum that rotates at 1200 rpm. Positioned opposite the capstan is an array of 20 read/write heads, movable to five positions. Data is written to or read from the strip by means of these read/write heads. The head arrangement thus gives 20 heads X 5 positions = 100 tracks per strip. When the read/write operation has been completed, the strip is returned to its original subcell. This is done by separating adjacent strips and reversing the direction of rotation of the capstan, forcing the strip back into its original position. Basic operating data is listed in Table 3-6.

The cylinder concept is used, with variable record storage along a track. (The number of bytes per track is thus an estimate based on one record per track.) Because there are five positions of 20 read/write heads, each strip consists of five cylinders, each of 20 tracks. This gives 10,000 cylinders in a full array (on a drive), each cylinder holding 40,000 bytes.

Table 3-6. DATACELL Operating Data

Capacity	
Strips per subcell	10
Subcells per cell	20
Strips per cell	200
Cells per array (drive)	10
Strips per array (drive)	2000
Tracks per strip	100
Bytes per track	2000
Bytes per array (drive)	400 million
Reading	
Transfer rate (maximum, bch/s)	55
Number of read/write heads	20 (X 5 positions)
Packing density (bpi)	1750
Access	
Average latency (in ms)	25
Minimum strip access time (in ms)	175
Maximum access time (in ms)	600

ICL-MCF and RCA Mass Storage Unit

The ICL Magnetic Card File (MCF) has been in existence for many years, having been used in the early 1960s with second-generation computer equipment. The principle of operation is shown in Fig. 3-5(c). The basic unit of storage is a magnetic card measuring 16 X 4½ X 0.0075 inches. The cards are notched top and bottom and are stored in portable (exchangeable) magazines. Up to 256 cards can be stored in a magazine. Depending on the model, up to eight magazines can be attached to one retrieval unit (drive). A card may be selected from any magazine and transported via a pinch roller system to a capstan.

Card selection takes 303 ms; card feed to the capstan takes from 136 to 235 ms. The card is wrapped around a capstan where read/write operations can be carried out (1000 capstan revolutions per minute). These are performed by a group of eight read/write heads.

Magazine-to-capstan, head positioning, and capstan-to-magazine movement may be overlapped. Data is recorded along bands (tracks) on a card, using the cylinder/bucket approach; each track is divided into a number of hardware blocks. The basic operating data is listed in Table 3-7.

Table 3-7. ICL-MCF and RCA Mass Storage Unit

	ICL-MCF*	RCA 70/568-11
Capacity		
Number of magazines per unit	8	8
Cards per magazine	256	256
Tracks per card	64	128
Characters per track	2,592	2,048 (bytes)
Characters per card	165,888	262,144 (bytes)
Characters per magazine	42,500,000	67,108,864 (bytes)
Characters per unit	340,000,000	536,870,912 (bytes)
Reading		
Transfer rate	80 kch/s	70 kb/s
Eight read/write heads†		
Access		
Latency (ms)	30	30
Maximum card select (from eighth magazine, ms)	538	530
Minimum card select (from first magazine, ms)	439	439

*One track is split into four 648 character blocks.

†Heads movable to 16 positions; gives 16 cylinders of eight tracks each.

Summary

Key statistics for these devices are summarized in Table 3-4. They provide massive on-line storage with the facility of exchangeable cartridges or magazines; this provides unlimited off-line storage. The mass storage capability gives a very low cost per character stored, about 0.03 or 0.06 cent (about 0.012 to 0.024

of a new penny). Access times are classed as high to medium, compared with other devices. In practice, these devices have not proved popular. The market, in terms of potential users, must be limited. The general problem in some cases has been one of mechanical reliability; the devices have been viewed with some skepticism by people in the data processing field. Several users have reported considerable doubts about media life. Should the basic recording media rip or tear in a wreck, reconstruction and recovery is very difficult and messy. For these reasons, computer users have turned away from these devices in favor of the more reliable disk and drum units.

COMPARING DEVICE TYPES

Many criteria and yardsticks are used in comparing device types. Some criteria follow:

    Initial capital outlay
    Rental/amortized purchase
    Cost per character stored
    Average access time
    Number of update cycles (read/write back) per second
    Number of reference cycles (read only) per second

These comparisons can be made only in a given circumstance. A *general* comparison chart is shown in Fig. 3-6. This shows an approximate division in capacity and access times across a range of devices. Some general summary notes are given below.

Magnetic drums tend to be used as true backing storage in scientific/time-sharing configurations. Fixed disks tend to be used where a very fast response rate is required (fixed-head models) and where there is a medium to large amount of data. Card/strip units are losing ground to very fast exchangeable disk stores, notably the IBM 3330. These devices thus provide massive on-line storage with medium access times. Exchangeable disk stores may be considered the bread-and-butter direct access device, a multipurpose storage medium that is adequate for most commercial and industrial applications.

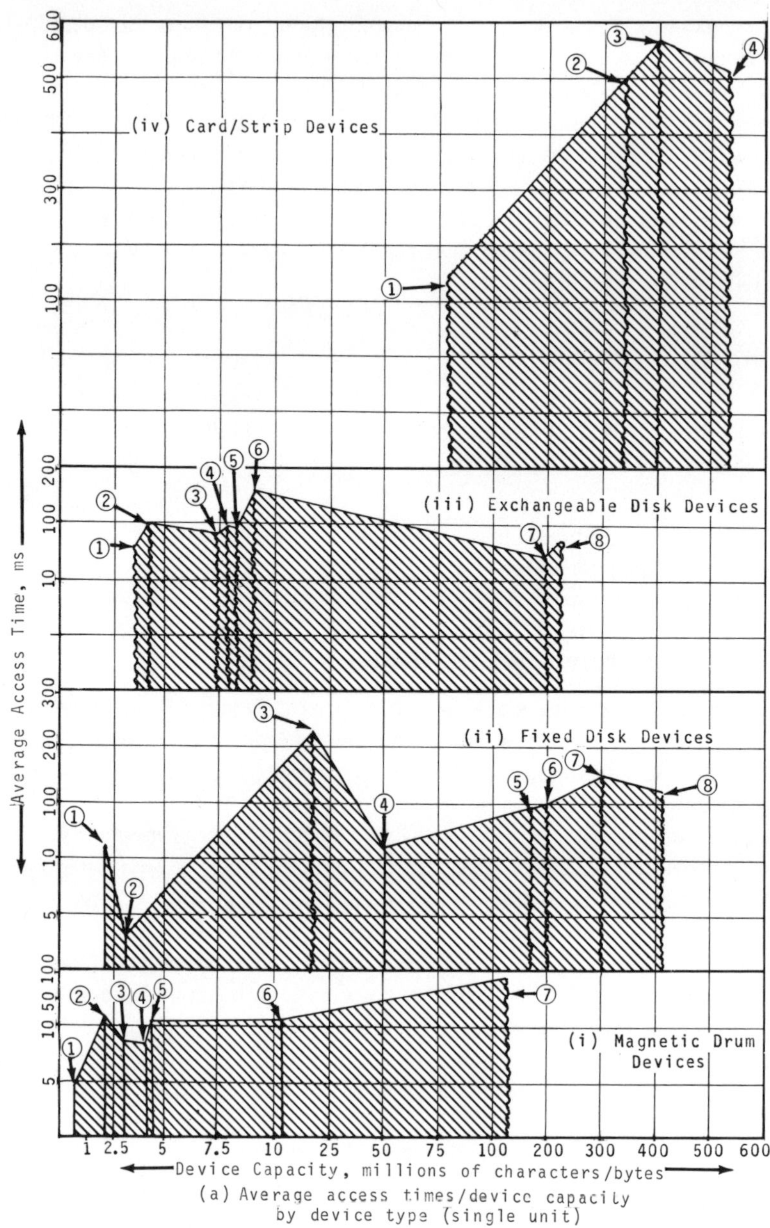

Figure 3-6. Comparison Charts

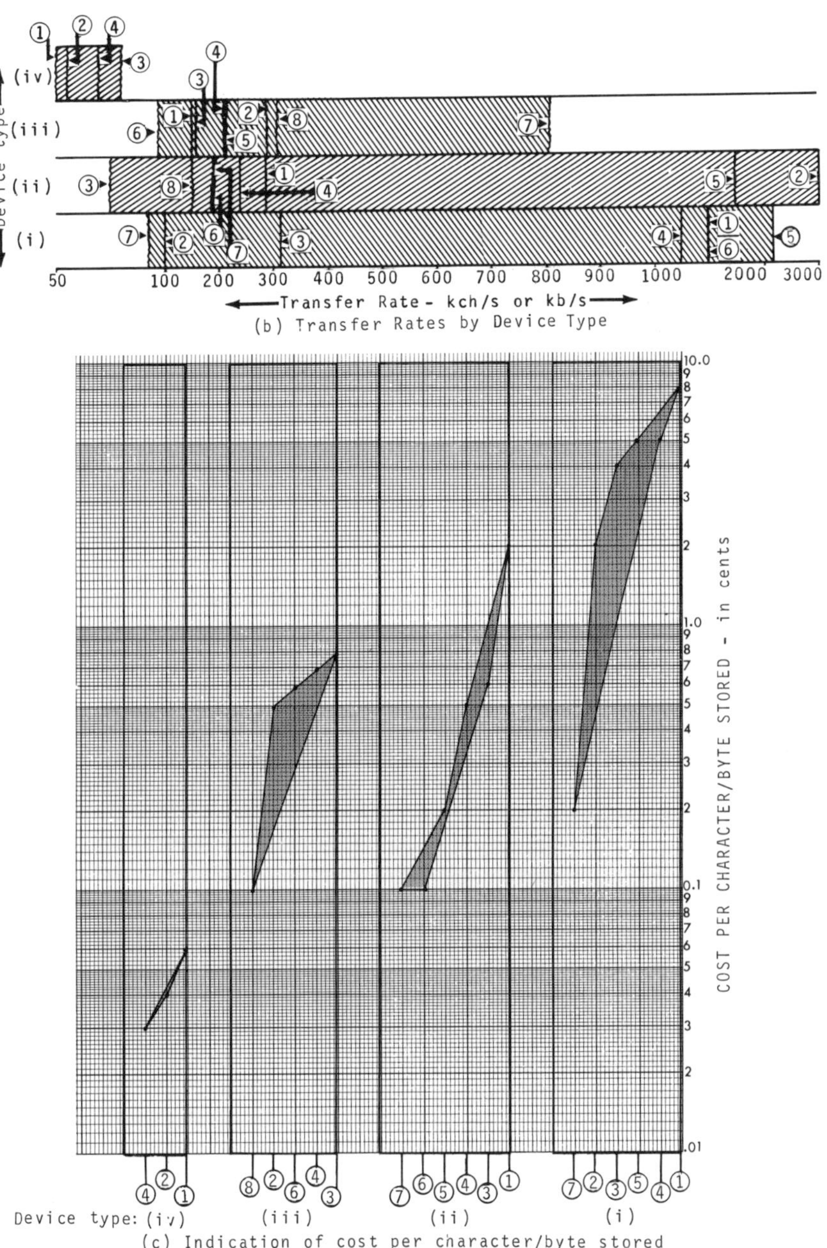

Figure 3-6 (Continued)

These charts indicate the range of capabilities
and costs by device type.

Actual devices (indicated in circles) are

	(i) Drums		(ii) Fixed Disks
①	Univac FH-432	①	Burroughs B9370-2
②	ICL 1964	②	IBM 2305
③	IBM 2303	③	GE DSU204
④	IBM 2301	④	Burroughs B9372
⑤	CDC 863	⑤	CDC 6638
⑥	Univac 1782	⑥	CDC 814
⑦	Univac FASTRAND II	⑦	Honeywell 262
		⑧	ICL 2805

(iii) Exchange Disks

① Honeywell 200/115	⑤ ICL 2802
② CDC 853	⑥ Honeywell 259A
③ IBM 2311	⑦ IBM 3330
④ GE DSU160	⑧ IBM 2314

(iv) Card/Strip

① NCR CRAM(5)
② ICL MCF
③ IBM DATACELL
④ RCA MASS STORAGE UNIT

The wavy lines indicate movable-head devices; straight lines,
fixed-head devices.

Figure 3-6 (Continued)

PART TWO

FILE ORGANIZATION AND PROCESSING

CHAPTER 4

THEORY OF FILE ORGANIZATION AND PROCESSING

Direct access devices provide the computer user with powerful storage tools. Devices such as magnetic drums and disks give backing storage facilities for programs, intermediate data (such as mathematical matrices), and sorting. The major facilities offered, however, are *in file data storage*. This chapter introduces the basic methods of organizing and processing files. Each method, its advantages and problems, will be reviewed in depth in later chapters.

BASIC PRINCIPLES

In previous chapters it was demonstrated that direct access devices provide addressable storage. Individual records, or groups of records, are stored in addressable "cells," the structure length and form of a cell being determined by the hardware characteristics of the device. The use of software enables the user to store and retrieve information by locating and accessing a selected addressable area (cell) within the device. Such an area, according to device and software, may be a cylinder, a track, a block, a sector, or a bucket, etc. An alternative to the serial-searching required when using magnetic tape is thus provided.

It is possible to view most direct access devices as having two-dimensional addresses, i.e., devices that work on two levels of storage such as

First Level	*Second Level*
track	sector (block)
cylinder	bucket
cylinder	track
cylinder	record

and so on, depending on the software approach taken. An example of this two-dimensional representation of storage is shown in the file map in Fig. 4-1. This shows part of a direct access storage device that consists of 5 cylinders with 10 tracks per cylinder; the track size in this example is fixed at 3600 characters per track. Let us now consider the alternative methods of storing a file in this area.

A file is defined as a collection of information about a specific "topic." Examples of information about employees to be paid, information about vehicles to be serviced, information about what customers have bought and how much

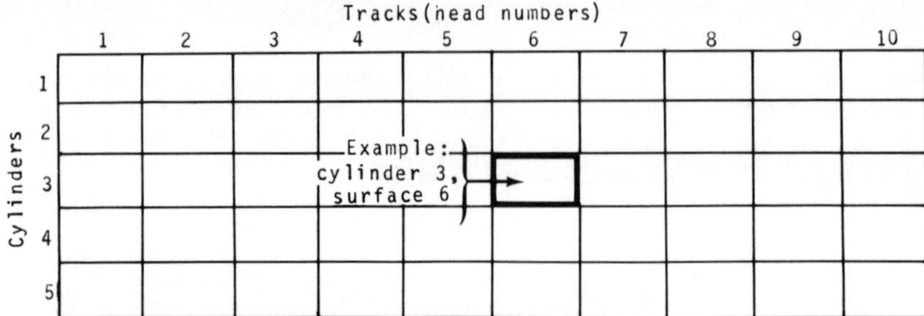

Figure 4-1. Two-Level Storage Map

they have paid, and so on. A file consists of a number of records, each record containing information about a specific item that makes up the detailed "topic." Taking the example files mentioned above, we have the following records:

Payroll File: one record for each employee, giving name and address, tax code, department code, basic rate, tax paid to date, gross pay to date, etc.

Vehicle File: one record per vehicle, giving registration number, type of vehicle, department to which vehicle is allocated, date last serviced, date of acquisition, costs incurred to date, etc.

Customer
Sales Ledger: one record for each customer, showing name and address, terms of business, current balance, etc.

Each record in a file is identified by a *key*; i.e., a unique reference number that identifies the particular item or event to which this record relates. In the case of the three files mentioned above, each record in the file would be identified by a key such as

Payroll File: each record identified by a key, which is an *employee number.*

Vehicle File: each record identified by a key, which is a *vehicle number.*

Customer
Sales Ledger: each record identified by a key, which is a *customer account number.*

The file to be stored in the device shown in Fig. 4-1 is a parts file. There is one record for each part manufactured by the company. A part record contains all details of description, raw material, and machining operations required to manufacture the part. Each part record is identified by a key that is a *part code*; a part record is 800 characters long. An example list of part codes is given in Table 4-1; note that 100 part codes are shown and that each part code is four characters long. This is in fact an extraction from a real list of part codes used

Table 4-1. Commercial Keys*

0003	0282	032V	0801
0006	0283	0354	088A
0011	0284	0355	097A
0014	0285	0397	097J
0015	0286	0401	097S
001A	0287	0402	097T
002C	0288	0403	0980
002D	0289	0408	0981
002X	028A	040E	0982
0081	028B	040G	0983
0082	028C	040K	0984
0089	028D	040S	0985
008F	028E	040T	0986
008M	028L	0410	0987
0100	028N	060A	0988
0102	028∅	060B	0989
0109	0319	060F	098A
023J	0321	060H	098B
0264	0322	060M	098C
0267	0324	060N	098D
027A	0329	0731	098E
027X	032D	0736	098F
027Y	032F	078A	0990
027Z	032H	0792	099B
0281	032S	0794	099K

*These are the first 100 keys in an example file. The collating sequence (which agrees with the logical sequence) is numeric 0 to 9, followed by alphabetic A to Z.

by an electronic spares servicing company. The list of parts has been in use for some time, and because of deletions and additions to the range of parts, "gaps and clusters" have formed within the sequence of keys. That is, many keys in the total range 0000 to 099K are absent. Of those keys that are present, there are a number of clusters where adjacent keys are in use; 0980 to 098F, for example.

This file is to be stored in the area of a direct access device defined in Fig. 4-1 by the various standard methods of organizing data. Once the file is set up (i.e., all 100 part records stored), transactions are to be posted. (In this simplified example, the "transactions" are alterations to description, raw material, sequence of machining operations, and so on. Each of the transactions will be identified by the key, namely, the appropriate part code of the part record that is subject to the particular change.) Processing will be by overlay. This means that the appropriate record will be retrieved from the device and read into internal storage, where it will be changed and the altered record written back to the file, *overwriting the original record.*

Serial Processing

The simplest method of storing the file is to sort the records into sequence by key (i.e., part code) and to write the records to the device in that order. The

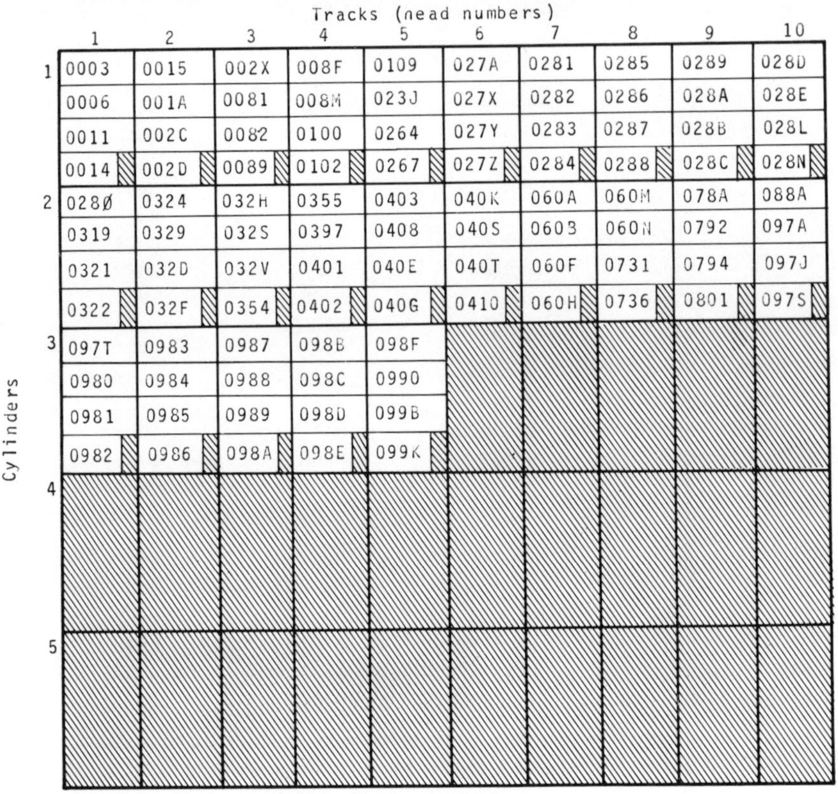

Figure 4-2 — Sequential File Storage. The grid is labelled "Tracks (head numbers)" across the top (columns 1–10) and "Cylinders" down the left side (rows 1–5). Cross-hatched squares indicate unused space.

Cylinder	1	2	3	4	5	6	7	8	9	10
1	0003	0015	002X	008F	0109	027A	0281	0285	0289	028D
	0006	001A	0081	008M	023J	027X	0282	0286	028A	028E
	0011	002C	0082	0100	0264	027Y	0283	0287	028B	028L
	0014	002D	0089	0102	0267	027Z	0284	0288	028C	028N
2	0280	0324	032H	0355	0403	040K	060A	060M	078A	088A
	0319	0329	032S	0397	0408	040S	0603	060N	0792	097A
	0321	032D	032V	0401	040E	040T	060F	0731	0794	097J
	0322	032F	0354	0402	040G	0410	060H	0736	0801	097S
3	097T	0983	0987	098B	098F					
	0980	0984	0988	098C	0990					
	0981	0985	0989	098D	099B					
	0982	0986	098A	098E	099K					
4										
5										

Cross-hatched squares indicate unused space.

Figure 4-2. Sequential File Storage

records would be stored four to a track, starting with the first four records going into the first track, the next four into the next track, and so on, until the first cylinder is full. The next four records would then be stored in the first track of the next cylinder, and so on, until all records are stored. (Note that the track size was fixed at 3600 characters and that each of the part records was 800 characters long.) Remembering that it is not feasible to store records by "splitting" them across track boundaries, they are stored four to a track (4 × 800 characters = 3200 characters) with 400 spare characters on each track. This is shown in Fig. 4-2.

A file stored in this manner can be updated by *serial processing*. This would mean taking each record in each track in turn and comparing its part code with that of an incoming transaction. As with magnetic tape, to make this method of processing viable, the transactions would have to be sorted into the same key sequence as the master file; i.e., part-code sequence. The procedure would thus be something like this:

1. Read the first track in the first cylinder.

2. Compare the transaction with each of the records in that track (in internal storage); when equality is found between the transaction part code and the master file part code, the master file record is changed to reflect the transaction. Read more transactions as required until all records in the track have had all transactions in the input applied to them.

3 When all master records in the track have been updated by the input transactions, write the four records back to the area of the device from whence they were originally read. This will overwrite the original records.

4. Read the next track. *Go back to step 2.*

5. If, after reading a track, no records in that track are to be updated, then read the next track in sequence. *Go back to step 2.*

Serial processing thus involves taking each of the file records in turn by *physical sequence*. In this example, the physical sequence was the same as the logical key sequence. In what circumstances could the physical sequence and the logical key sequence be different? One of the most common reasons in a direct access device is "overflow" caused by insertions. Consider inserting three records in the file shown in Fig. 4-2. The records are

	Location in file in which records must
Key	*be stored to preserve sequence:*
032B	cylinder 2, track surface 2
088B	cylinder 2, track surface 10
098G	cylinder 3, track surface 5

All these records could be inserted by doing a copy of the file. That is, writing the file onto, say, magnetic tape, merging the existing records with the new records, and then writing out the complete file back on to the direct access device. An easier way (short term) is to assimilate the records into the file by using a *tag* system. A tag (also known as a *pointer*) is a special reference field that is inserted into a track in place of the entire record. The tag gives the key of the new record and the address of where that new record is stored on the device. Alternatively, only the address of the new record may be induced in the tag, with the key being "implied" by the absence of the record from the track. The track into which the addition should be placed is the *home track*; the track into which the addition record is actually placed is called the *overflow track*. Thus, the tag is read as: "record so and so should be here but isn't; it will be found in cylinder/track such and such."

Serial processing would be ineffective on this file because the physical sequence of records no longer corresponds to the logical sequence by key. As we will see later, however, serial processing is very useful for basic file housekeeping, such as copying, where the logical key sequence is immaterial in processing.

Sequential Processing

Sequential processing is the accessing of records, one after the other, in ascending sequence by logical key. (Contrast with serial processing, in which records are accessed one after the other by ascending *physical* sequence.) Using the example given in the preceding section, it would mean that all records in the file are accessed one after the other (key sequence = physical sequence) but with the tags being followed. One method of processing would be as follows: When there is no transaction-to-master match in a track, a tag, if present, is inspected; if a match (tag key-to-transaction) is equal, the track containing the tagged record is accessed. The record is updated, and the sequence of record by record processing is followed until another tag needs to be followed.

To the user, therefore, records are "presented" one by one in logical key sequence, irrespective of whether they are actually located in this sequence in the device. If sequential processing is desired, most software has facilities to follow tags automatically when they are encountered. As far as the user is concerned, therefore, sequential processing using a direct access device is very much like sequential processing using magnetic tape. The major difference is that records can be updated in situ (by overlay).

Self-Indexing

Serial and sequential processing are searching methods of access. There are, of course, cases where sequential access is very useful. These are cases where each record in the file needs to be inspected. These situations include 100 percent hit-rate processing, as in a payroll where a pay notification of some form needs to be prepared for every employee on a file, or where a summary report is to be produced from data extracted and accumulated from every file record. There are many cases, however, where selected record retrieval is desirable. This generally applies when there is a low-hit rate, or where file sequences are not matched, or when a fast response is required. These cases will be looked at in more detail in Chapter 5. The point here is this: There are many cases when selected record retrieval (without searching) is either necessary or desirable. The problem of accessing selected records is simply this: Given a record key, how is it possible to find the "cell" address of the location that holds the record? At first sight, the most obvious solution to this problem is to make the record key equal to the physical address. For example:

Cylinder 0

Track/surface 0   Record key = 0
1   Record key = 1
2   Record key = 2

    3   Record key = 3
    4   Record key = 4
    5   Record key = 5
    6   Record key = 6

This is *direct addressing*, otherwise known as *self-indexing*. It is ideal for locating the data. Where a track can hold more than one record, the file is stored with more than one record on a track, a fixed number of records on each track. A simple arithmetic operation can be used to find the home track address; for example, divide the key by the number of records per track, quotient equals the track address:

Cylinder 0

Track/surface   0   Record keys 0, 1, 2
                 1   Record keys 3, 4, 5
                 2   Record keys 6, 7, 8
                 3   Record keys 9, 10, 11
                 4   Record keys 12, 13, 14

Example: key = 7; address = 7/3 = 2

The file is stored in ascending sequence by key. Either sequential processing (record by record) or selected record retrieval is possible.

Ideal as self-indexing may seem, it is rarely possible to use it with commercial file keys. It is rare indeed to find a commercial file without clusters and gaps, as described previously. Where there are gaps in the key sequence, poor store utilization occurs because space must be left for every record key (and associated record) that is not present. Another problem is in the key format itself. Even when most keys are present, problems are caused by alphabetic characters and long keys. Given, say, a four-digit address that represents a track address, and a six- or seven-digit key, there is the problem of condensing the key size to address range. These are the main reasons why self-indexing is so rarely used.

However, where the data processing specialist has control over the allocation and distribution of the keys, and where the number of records is relatively small and the record length is short, self-indexing can be used. Examples are small—relatively static—master reference files such as tax codes or, say, two to three hundred job codes assigned after the computer system is implemented. Self-indexing can also be used with scientific/technical applications, such as the creation and processing of matrices for cumulative or mathematical processes.

Indexed-Sequential Processing

Indexed-sequential processing is another attempt to locate the data for selective record retrieval. This approach, also known as *partial indexing*, is certainly more practical than self-indexing and has been more widely adopted. Let us start with the simplest approach: the creation of a total index. This index would have one entry for each record in the file:

record key: address

To locate the required record, the index is searched until a matching key entry is found. The address of that record is then extracted and used to access the desired record. In this case the only file searching required will be the searching of the track. (This will be necessary if the index references a track and if more than one record is stored per track.)

With such an index, the file need not be stored in logical key sequence. The only saving in time is that the search is made on short index-entry records rather than on the long records in the actual file area. This approach of a one-for-one entry index is very rarely used.

For a file of any size, however, such an index (otherwise known as a *directory*) would be large and cumbersome to access. A far more practical approach is to segment a total index into a number of levels. These levels are sometimes called *rough* and *fine* indexes. Let us take an everyday example of levels of index.

The Greater London telephone directory comprises four volumes: A–D, E–K, L–R, and S–Z. Let us assume that there is a total of 2 million listed subscribers, an average of 250,000 per volume. Each volume has *the equivalent* of "tab cards" dividing the total contents of a volume down into alphabetic sections: A, B, C, and so on. On each page there is a three-column list of subscribers, giving the surname followed by Christian name or initials in alphabetic sequence by subscriber's surname. On the top of each page, however, there are two subscribers' names, surnames. The first, on the left-hand side of a page, gives the first subscriber's name on that page; i.e., the first name on top of the first column. The second heading, on the right of the page, gives the name of the last subscriber on a page; i.e., the name at the bottom of the third column. To find any telephone number, therefore, involves a "split level" search:

Select volume (by volume reference A to D, E to K, etc.).

Select part of volume (by alphabetic "tabs").

Select page (by heading).

Select name (by search of page).

A similar approach may be used to index a file on a direct access device. Just as the telephone directory works because it is in alphabetic order, so a file-indexing method will work only if the file is stored in ascending key sequence.

The principle of indexing a file is to create a number of levels of index, each index having entries that show "highest record on *storage level*." The storage level may be a unit, a cylinder, or a track. Location of a record is by a progressive search of each level of index. An example index is shown in Fig. 4-3. This index is based on a large file, stored on three disk drives (on line at the same

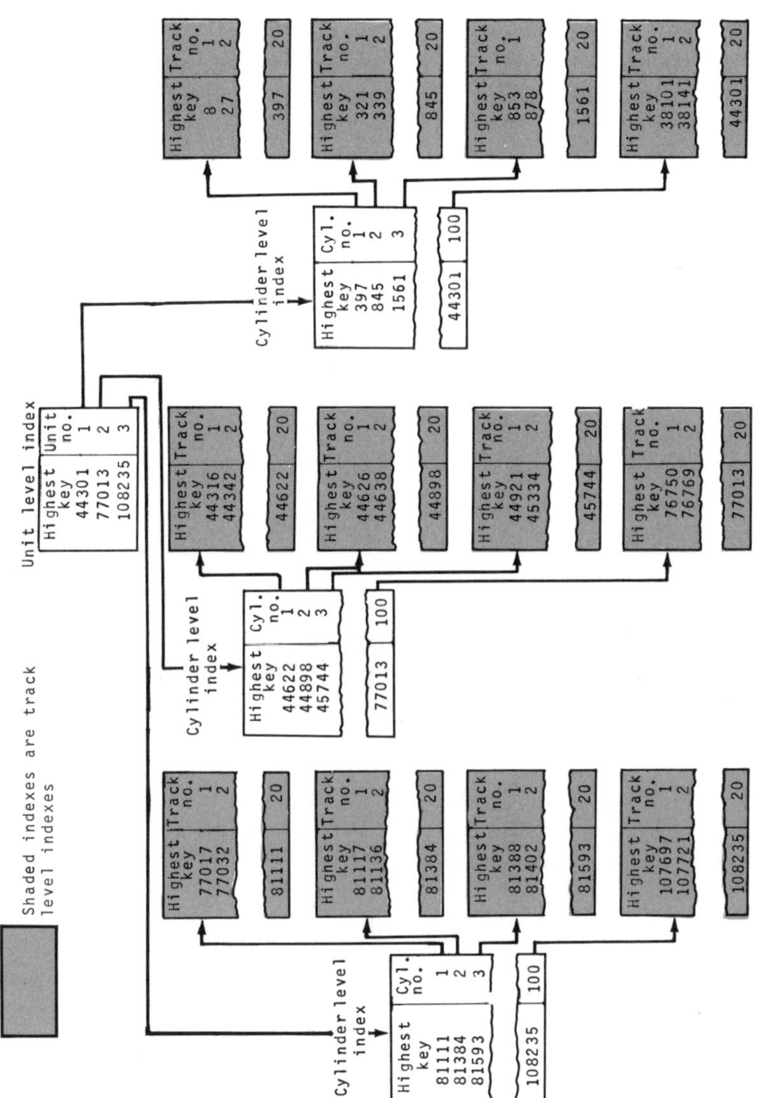

Figure 4-3. Split-Level Indexes

time), 100 cylinders per drive (unit), with 20 tracks per cylinder. The file is stored 10 records per track. The file thus consists of 3 X 100 X 20 = 6000 tracks, holding 60,000 records. Note that there is one index entry for each address; a three-level index approach is used:

Unit level	Three entries
Cylinder level	One index per unit, each index holding 100 entries, one per cylinder
Track surface level	One index per cylinder, each index holding 20 entries, one per track

To find any one record in a file, the following searches of the indexes are necessary:

1. Go to unit index; find unit number.

2. Go to cylinder index for that unit; find cylinder number.

3. Go to track index for that cylinder; find track number.

A cylinder level index, giving track numbers, is shown in Fig. 4-4. To search an index such as this one, it must be brought into internal storage; it may, however, be resident on some direct access device, each level being called into internal storage as required. Once in internal storage, the search takes place. A number of methods may be used and these will be discussed later in more detail in Chapter 7.

The simplest method is to use a straight serial search of the index. The key of the required record is matched with the first index entry. If the key is less than or equal to the index entry, the address is picked up and that track is accessed. If the key is greater than the entry, it is matched against the next entry until a "less than" or "equal to" condition is found.

Since the file is structured, overflow may take place if records are added. The indexes are built up as the file is created. Additional records are inserted in their home tracks, if space is available, or a tag reference to an overflow bucket is inserted. How will such insertions affect the validity of the indexes? Provided the "highest record key" is not exceeded in any track, the indexes need not be altered; see the example in Fig. 4-5. As with any structured file that is subject to additions and deletions, the index must be periodically reorganized from time to time to tidy it up. Indexes will be updated during this reorganization to represent the new status of the file.

Indexed-sequential processing thus provides for either selected record retrieval or sequential (record by record) access; the latter is possible because the file is stored in ascending sequence by key. Unlike self-indexing, the characteristics of the keys (the format, size, clusters and gaps, etc.) is of little significance. Because selective record retrieval without file searching is possible, the input (i.e., transactions or movements) may be either in sequence or in random order.

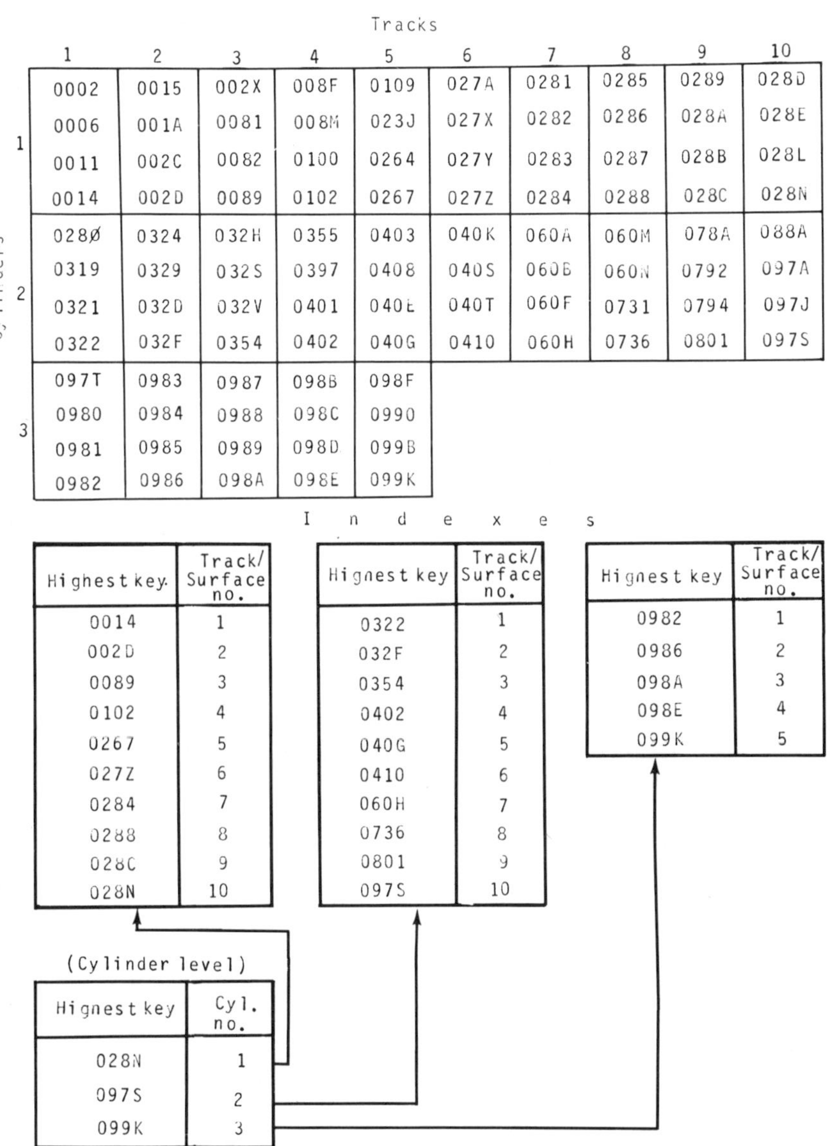

Figure 4-4. An Indexed-Sequential File

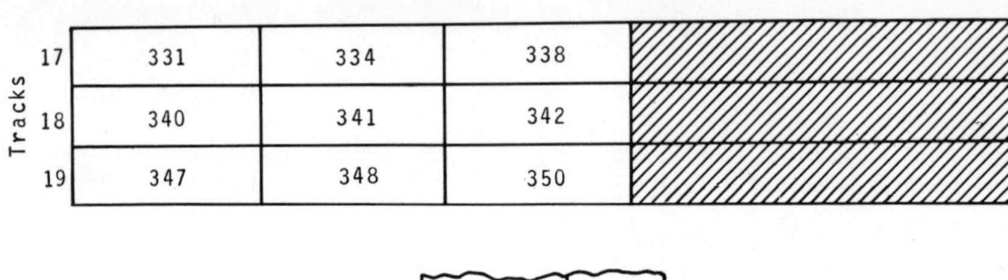

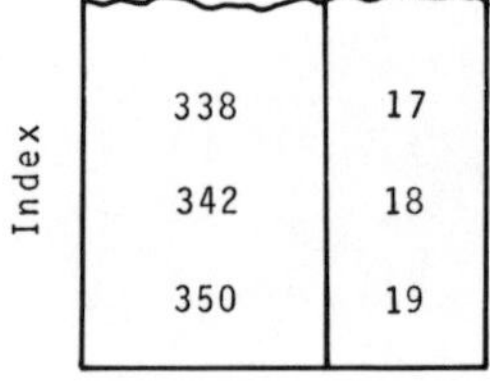

Two records are to be inserted:

339	349

Records inserted thus:

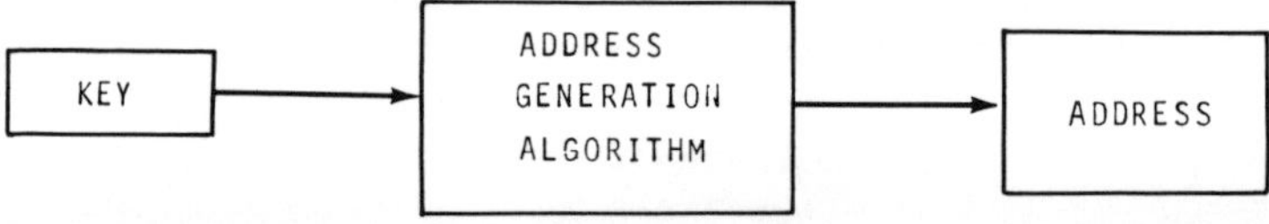

Index is unchanged.

Figure 4-5. Overflow in an Indexed-Sequential File

Address Generation

In all the methods described previously, files are stored on a direct access device in record key sequence. In essence, the file is sorted into ascending sequence by record key and then loaded. Indexing, either self or partial, is fitted into the pattern of the stored records. It is thus the position of a record in key sequence which dictates the location of the record in the device. The principle of address generation is radically different in that the keys are subjected to a computational process that produces the device storage address:

KEY	→	ADDRESS GENERATION ALGORITHM	→	ADDRESS

The interesting point here is that the device address is computed from the key, and in some cases there is a random distribution of records over the device.

Using this technique, selected data is retrievable without index searching. This method thus enables very fast record retrieval. It does, however, present a number of technical problems.

For example, if there are clusters or gaps in the file keys, this must not be transmitted to the device addresses. If gaps are present in the range of keys and this is carried into the device addresses, inefficient storage utilization will result. On the other hand, if a range of keys produces the same physical address, competition for space results. This, in turn, may result in an overflow problem in which records cannot be stored in their home track but have to be allocated to an overflow area. Although quick retrieval of information is possible, the random order of records in the device makes it very difficult to produce sequential reports.

SUMMARY

Each of the methods described here will be discussed in detail in subsequent chapters. The basic methods of accessing data on a direct access device are summarized below.

Serial

Access by taking all records in turn; records are accessed in *physical* sequence.

Access to selected records is by means of serial searching.

Sequential

Access by taking all records in turn; records are accessed in *key* sequence.

Access to selected records is by means of serial searching.

Indexed-Sequential

Access to selected records by means of indexes; input may be in key sequence or random.

Access to records may be sequential, as above, to produce sequential reports.

Random

Access by address generation, giving very fast retrieval of selected records; input may be in key sequence or random.

Records are stored randomly in the device and sequential reports are difficult (often impossible) to produce.

The basic methods of storing and accessing records are summarized as follows:

	Storage	
Access	*Sequential*	*Random*
Serial	Yes	Yes
Sequential	Yes	Difficult/impossible
Indexed-sequential	Yes	Yes
Random (retrieval with unsorted input)	Yes	Yes

Selected record retrieval is possible only when the keys are self-indexing, the file is indexed-sequential, or an address generation scheme is used.

CHAPTER 5

FUNDAMENTALS OF FILE DESIGN

In Chapter 4, the storage and retrieval of data on direct access devices was treated in a rather abstract and theoretical manner. That is, given a device with structured storage (with addressable locations), what ways are there of holding and using data on such devices? Given that we have these methods of handling data, this chapter provides an introduction to file design: the use of these devices in a practical environment. The fundamental job of the computer specialist, systems analyst, or systems designer is the interpretation of the user's processing requirements and the construction of a method of holding and manipulating data on the computer to give the appropriate output.

COMPUTER-BASED SYSTEMS

It is impossible in a short space to cover all aspects of computer-based systems and their development. In this chapter, therefore, only those factors that directly influence file design will be highlighted and discussed in depth. However, file design cannot be considered in complete isolation from all other activities in a system, and therefore other functions will be mentioned briefly.

A system in modern commerce and industry is a complex entity, a series of procedures that generate and manipulate information. It must therefore be viewed in wider terms than just pieces of paper, as a series of interrelated procedures that operate within an equally complex organization and which are performed by people with differing aptitudes and attitudes. Because of the wide range of business methods and requirements, it is difficult to generalize on the structure of commercial computer-based systems. However, it is possible to describe a computer-based system in terms of a number of basic steps. These are shown in Fig. 5-1.

Steps in Computer-Based Systems

As shown in Fig. 5-1, the steps fall into three general groups: the input subsystem, getting the information into the computer; the computer subsystem, processing the information on the computer; and the output subsystem, where the information is checked and distributed. Note that each input type and output document represents a "subsystem."

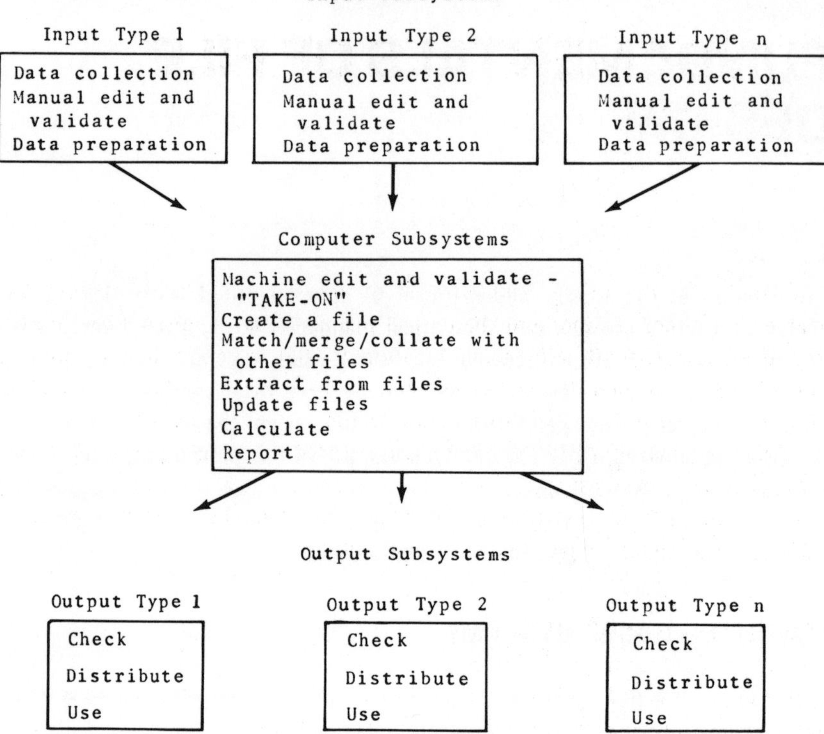

Figure 5-1. Steps in a Computer-Based System

Data Collection/Data Capture

All systems start with the collection of data, i.e., recording details of an event or an activity. In the majority of systems today, data collection is still a relatively unsophisticated activity; principally, it is the simple process of recording information by filling out a form. For example:

Event	*Data Collection*
Employee joins company.	"New employee form" completed by personnel department.
Customer changes name and/or address.	"Customer detail change form" completed by accounts.
Job completed on the shop floor	"Job completed docket" filled in by foreman (including good quantity produced/hours worked).

Customer places   "Order form" completed by salesman.
order.

    .   .

    .   .

    .   .

Some systems use a *turnaround* document, produced by a computer or head-office department, to which a limited amount of data is added by the user. Sometimes just the return of the form is "recording" that a particular event has taken place. The information produced by the computer is readable to both humans and the computer. Only the additional information entered by the user needs to be encoded for subsequent computer reading.

An example of a simple turnaround document is an interpreted punched card produced by the computer and issued to the men on the shop floor. When a job has been completed, the hours worked and the quantity produced are written on the card, and the card returned to the computer department. The added information is punched in the card and this, together with the prepunched information, forms the complete record of the event.

Again, further development of "form filling" includes the use of *terminals* on line to the computer for direct entry of data (typewriters, etc.). Data capture also includes the new field of completely automatic "data logging," where input media is produced automatically as events are taking place.

Manual Edit and Validate

After data has been collected, it is usually subjected to some form of human check. The check (validate) may be made to ensure that the data collected is authentic, complete, accurate, and legible. This process may include an editing function whereby data is added to or deleted from the collected data.

Data Conversion/Data Preparation

This is the encoding of the collected and checked data into a computer-readable form, via a keyboard operation such as punching cards or paper tape, or encoding magnetic tape. Data may already be in an input form such as magnetic ink encoded or optical character recognition encoded documents.

These three stages may be called the *input subsystem.* That is, they are concerned with getting the data into the computer. During all these stages, checks will be carried out to ensure the accuracy, completeness, and reasonableness of the data. Once the data is in a computer-readable form, it is input to the *computer subsystem.* This processes the data to produce the appropriate output, which passes into the *output subsystem.* The output subsystem is concerned with getting reports into a form for dispatch (bursting, collating, trimming, punching, folding, etc.), quality control, and the actual distribution procedures. In describing the techniques of using direct access devices, we are primarily concerned with the computer subsystem, which is discussed in more detail below.

Computer Subsystem

The computer subsystem is the computer-based processing that manipulates and calculates data from the input to the output subsystems. Data coming into the computer subsystem is subject to a *machine edit and validate*, which is generally coupled with a transcription from a slow-input medium (punched cards, paper tape, encoded documents, etc.) onto a fast file media, such as magnetic tape or disks. The checks at this stage may be

> range checks, checking that the data lies between certain preset limits.

> format checks, checking that the data consists of the appropriate array of spaces, numerics, and alphabetic characters.

> batch totals, checks of record counts, hash totals, financial totals, etc., formed in the input subsystem.

> check digits, checking that a key is correct by means of a simple arithmetic check.

> presence checks, checking that there are matching keys in a master file for input records.

Subsequent processing is concerned with matching/merging/collating information, and extracting and altering information on files. Calculation may take place at this stage, and reports may be produced and passed to the output subsystem.

The basis of the computer subsystem, therefore, is the processing of computer-based files. Input for example, after it has been checked, may be matched against one master file, the master file updated, and that master file matched against another file, which is itself input to another computer procedure. In this chapter we are primarily concerned with the fundamentals of file design, i.e., how direct access devices may be used to hold and manipulate the data once it is in the computer subsystem. For this, we need to take a brief look at the starting point for file design, which is concerned with the information that the designer needs to have available before detailed design work can take place.

INPUT TO FILE DESIGN

Considerable work will have taken place prior to the design stage. This work is summarized in Table 5-1. In short, the input to the design phase is the result of analysis. After it has been decided *what* is to be done (and the information available to do it), the task of the designer is to decide *how* it is to be done. We can break down the starting point of design into a number of steps:

> 1. What has to be done; that is, a statement of processes that have to be undertaken in the system.

2. The data available for use, and the format of output reports that are mandatory.

3. The problems in the existing system that have to be solved in the new system.

Thus we can simply state the objectives of system design succinctly as

> To do the tasks (1) using the data (2), in such a way that the problems (3) are solved, thus meeting the objectives and aims laid down—and agreed to—by the user.

If there is one requirement for good computer file design, it is this:

Know your data!

Given this problem specification, the designer can get to work. His first tasks will be the definition of the necessary raw input, computer stored files, and report output. The review of this basic classification into three parts is iterative. The designer is continuously trying to strike a balance between arriving at a system that is easy for the user to operate—a human-oriented input subsystem, and a computer subsystem that is effective and efficient on the machine. The first major step is to make a decision on the nature of the input and output data. The constraints made on the designer at this point will be, by and large, imposed by the user area: the quality, attitude, and time available of the people submitting the input, and the requirements and format of the output—again laid down by the user's system requirements.

The first step is to look at data against *usage*. For each element of data in the system, it is necessary to know and understand the following:

1. *Nature of the element:* what the data is and what it is used for in the system.

2. *Relation of the element:* how the data is related to the raw input and the report output.

3. *Characteristics of the element:* length of the element and its format; whether it is fixed length or variable length.

4. *Volumes and growth of the element:* incidence of the data, the existing volume of the element (the number of times that it occurs), and the expected growth rate over the life of the system.

All this must be known before detailed file design can begin. Let us now look at the considerations for organizing the data into computer-based files: the content of the files, the method of organization and access, and the device(s) to be used.

Review the data elements in terms of the *function* of each element. All elements of data will fall into one or more of the following classifications:

Managerial, used for decision making

Operational, used in day to day activities

Table 5-1. Summary of Systems Development

Phase	Task	Major Involvement	Objectives and Scope	Output Documentation
A. Project initiation	1. User request	User, senior management, senior data processing staff	User examines his own objectives and environment. Preferably, puts forward a formal statement of assistance required. Statement is reviewed by senior company management against corporate data processing plan. Setting basic terms of reference for future tasks.	*User request:* Formal statement of (a) objectives (b) boundaries and constraints (c) time scales (d) mandatory reports (e) user suggested system/solutions (f) relationship with other systems
	2. Feasibility study	User, senior systems staff	Senior technicians investigate and review user's environment and requirements. Senior technicians can include computer systems analysts, O & M people, work study, etc. Come up with range of alternative solutions to problems as stated in user request.	*Feasibility study report:* (a) objectives, etc., as entered in the user request above, possibly modified (b) basic description of current system (c) range of solutions that may include: do nothing, O & M solution, accounting M/C solution, computer solution (d) for each solution, development/operational costs, expected benefits (objectives met), time scales, etc.
	3. User review	User, senior systems staff	Review of feasibility study report, and selection of solution that appears to meet the problem as stated in the user request. Issue of formal terms of reference for subsequent development work.	*Systems definition:* Formal statement of terms of reference for detailed development work. User-selected solution is extracted from feasibility study report and modified if necessary.
B. Requirements definition	1. Fact-finding	User, systems analysts	Investigation of current system in detail, primarily by interviewing (with observation). Should be done in depth: review of job functions,	*Data organization:* Documentation of results of fact finding; includes (a) organization chart (b) functional chart

	2. Analysis	User, systems analysts	organization, procedures, information flow (including volumes), growth, data elements used, field lengths, etc. To examine the outputs of data organization and to identify the essential processes (functions), the problems in these processes which must be solved by the new design, and the essential data.	(c) document flowchart (d) document specifications (e) systems description (including description of key procedures) *Interim report* to user, showing the information opposite, so that the analyst/ designer has confirmation of the key information prior to design
	3. Design	User, systems analysts, lead programmers	Based on the outputs of analysis, the designer (systems analyst with programming support?) defines (a) the input subsystem: data collection, vetting, and data conversion (b) the computer subsystem: all file creating, file update, extraction and calculation and reporting programs (c) the output subsystem: procedures for distribution and use of reports	*The System specification:* (a) specification of system objectives and principles (b) full descriptions of user procedures (c) input and output formats (d) test plan (e) conversion and implementation plan and schedule (f) program specifications (for each program description of what must be done, inputs, outputs, files, etc.) (g) timings and operational schedules
C. Implementation	1. Programming	Programmers, systems analysts	Production of proved, documented programs as defined in the program specification.	*Program manual*

Table 5-1. (cont.)

Phase	Task	Major Involvement	Objectives and Scope	Output Documentation
C. Implementation (cont.)	2. Systems testing	User, systems analysts, programming	Final testing of user and computer procedures and programs, according to the test plan, to ensure the system is acceptable to the user.	Approved, actioned *test plan:* Test cases, results expected, results obtained, test procedures
	3. Conversion	User, systems analysts, operations	To achieve all necessary changeover tasks, prior to committing to the new system. For example: file conversion, final documentation check-out, training, acquisition of forms	Various *procedure manuals,* especially for training user staff. File conversion may itself represent a major systems project and a systems specification prepared accordingly.
	4. Changeover	User, systems analysts, programmers, operators	To effect the changeover from old to new systems; may be by parallel, pilot, gradual, or immediate conversion.	Most documentation has been produced at earlier stages; principally, final user documentation is prepared.
D. Post-implementation	1. Maintenance	User, systems analysts, programmers	Making changes in the operating method (manual procedures of computer programs) to remove a bug, incorporate changes in business methods or organization, provide additional or different information for the user, improve the efficiency of the system or to enable new hardware/software to be used	*Updated documentation:* All the documentation concerned is updated to record the change fully.
	2. Evaluation	User, systems analysts, programmers	A formal review study of the operational system after it has been in use for a certain time, to ensure that the system has met the objectives laid down in the user request and that the system is operating efficiently.	*Evaluation Report:* Repeats the user request feasibility study and compares the operational system to these. Comments on method of development (where, schedules adhered to, were they wrong), efficiency of the system and changes in user requirement.

Source: K. R. London, *Decision Tables* (Philadelphia: Auerbach Publishers Inc., 1972).

Recordkeeping, historical for regular usage

Transitory, passes through the system but does not form part of a permanent data set

Archival, a detail to be stored off-line after processing

Historical, a summary item kept on line for reporting purposes (example: last year's sales).

A check list for information about a data element may include

Name of data item

Source

Ultimate usage

Characteristics (format and length)

Availability

Time cycle (if relevant)

How updated and how often

Reports used in

Other items it affects or is affected by (for example, "total annual quantity produced" would be the sum of "monthly quantity produced")

Finally, data in a system can be reviewed by its basic type:

Control, used for validation/editing

Reporting, produced on printed report for use

Supporting, reference tables, etc.

Indicative/qualitative, descriptive or identifying information like names and addresses

Quantitative, numerical or status information

Computational, constants and formulas.

All these types of data classification will help the designer understand and catalog the information that will be handled in the system.

FILE DESIGN CONSIDERATIONS

A file is a collection of records, each record holding a group of data associated with one activity, event, or entity. Any computer-based system is defined as a series of computer-based procedures (programs) that process, directly or indirectly, files. At this point, let us look at the relationship among *process, program,* and *file.*

A process is a function that must be performed in a system. A system may have a number of processes. For example:

Credit control

Sales/invoicing recording

Cash receipt posting

Overdue account notification

Statement preparation

Sales statistics (by cost of goods by type of customer)

In a simple insurance system, the processes in the system may

Record the receipts of monthly premiums.

Identify those policies that have premiums 15 days or more overdue.

Issue notifications of agent premiums becoming due.

These processes define *what* has to be done. For each process, there may be a number of computer-based procedures, i.e., programs or runs. Any file will generally have at least three different types of procedures applied to it: file maintenance procedures, updating procedures, and reporting procedures. It is necessary to differentiate between *indicative* and *quantitative* data. Consider the sales accounting system in the first example above. The basic file in the system may be a computerized Sales Ledger File. This file will have to be maintained by adding new customer details, deleting "dead" customers, and altering details: address, credit limit, delivery address(es), terms of sale, etc. This type of information is indicative in that it defines or identifies and is constant. The other type of information is quantitative because it defines a particular financial or other quantity at a certain time. Quantitative data is changed on a regular cyclical basis. An example of quantitative information is the customer balance (how much he owes or the amount that he has in credit), which is updated on a regular basis according to purchases and receipts. In this example, there will be a series of file-maintenance programs to keep the indicative data up to date, and one set of programs to keep the quantitative data up to date. In practice, it may be possible to use the same programs to effect types of change.

In determining the structure of files, the designer must bear in mind *all* processes for which that file is to be used. The actual file design is an iterative process: As a file is developed, it is considered against each of the processes in which it is to be used. This may result in basic changes in the file structure (and even in the process) to satisfy one processing requirement, to reassess file utility for other processes, or to accommodate special functions.

It is possible to draw up a number of check lists of design considerations; these are summarized in Fig. 5-2. The design of each file and its use in each process must be judged against these criteria, discussed briefly below.

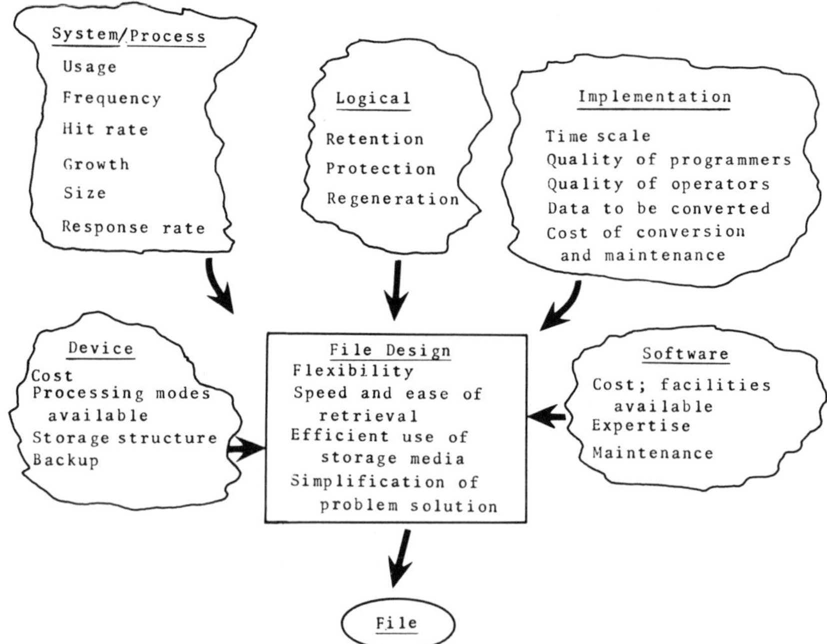

Figure 5-2. File Design Considerations

System/Process Considerations

The primary components of a file are usage, frequency, hit rate, growth, size, and response rate. Each is discussed below.

Usage. During design, the usage (or relevance) of each element of the file is considered against each process, i.e.: Is it necessary to have this element of data on the file for this process. It may be beneficial to create a number of files rather than one megolithic file. However, before any decision can be taken, all other functions must be considered. The segmentation of a large file into a number of smaller files may itself result in problems. For example, new data (a new policy, customer, product, etc.) may be too cumbersome to fit into a new system because a new record has to be "exploded" to a number of files rather than just one file.

Frequency. The number of times a file is to be passed influences the organization and method of access. For example, a file that is to be run a number of times each day will need to be designed with processing time very much in mind. A file that is processed twice in an operational shift must be designed for efficiency, whereas a file that is to be run once every six months is not subject to the same stringent criteria.

Hit Rate. This is the number of records in a file that have to be accessed in each process. For example, consider the hit rate and frequency of a customer Sales Ledger File used in the sales processes listed below. There is one record for each customer, with two quantitative fields: account balance (sales minus payments) and sales to date this year (sales only). Procedure is as follows:

1. *Credit Control.* Done daily on all orders. The total number of customers, i.e., number of records in the customer Sales Ledger is 10,000. An average of 3000 orders are to be credit-checked each day. Hence, on the basis of daily frequency,

$$\text{Hit rate} = \frac{3000 \times 100\%}{10,000} = 30\%$$

2. *Sales/invoicing.* Done daily, with values of all orders being posted to the customer file. At a daily frequency,

$$\text{Hit rate} = \frac{3000 \times 100\%}{10,000} = 30\%$$

3. *Cash receipts.* Done weekly. An average of 600 cash receipts are to be posted in a week. At weekly frequency,

$$\text{Hit rate} = \frac{600 \times 100\%}{10,000} = 6\%$$

4. *Overdue account reporting.* Done weekly. All records are inspected and those accounts that are more than a certain amount overdue are reported for attention. All records, therefore, need to be inspected on a weekly frequency basis.

$$\text{Hit rate} = \frac{10,000 \times 100\%}{10,000} = 100\%$$

5. *Statement preparation.* Monthly. Statement for all accounts produced each month.

$$\text{Hit rate} = \frac{10,000 \times 100\%}{10,000} = 100\%$$

6. *Sales statistics.* Monthly. Summary of all sales by type, etc. Frequency: monthly.

$$\text{Hit rate} = \frac{10,000 \times 100\%}{10,000} = 100\%$$

7. *Inquiries.* Special customer status inquiries are run once an hour against the file. There are about ten inquiries to be processed at each inquiry processing run. Frequency: hourly.

$$\text{Hit rate} = \frac{10 \times 100\%}{10,000} = 0.1\%$$

In this simple example we have seen how one file can have different frequencies and hit rates, depending on the process. In practice, some of the processes described above may be performed on the same processing run, i.e., doing the cash receipts and the overdue reporting at the same time on the same run.

The distribution of hits over the file must be considered also. In the preceding example it may be the case that sales are concentrated on a few customers, with the majority of customers buying very rarely in comparison to this active percentage. The designer must be aware of any special distribution of activity over the data as a whole.

Growth. It is useless to design a system that will cope with today's data, but will break down after volumes have grown, say, in the first year or six months. Company growth will be reflected in a growth in the quantity of information to be processed. Thus, a rise in sales activities can result in a greater number of customer records caused by an increase in number of customers, a greater number of input transactions (orders, etc.), and perhaps an extension in the *size* of records rather than just the *number* of records.

It is necessary to know not only the *rate* of growth but also the *pattern*: Are records deleted from the beginning, end, or "at random" over the file? Are records added at the beginning, end, or scattered through the file? And so on.

Size. The number of records in a file and the number of characters per record, giving the file size, will be an important factor. In the case of fixed-length working, where the content and size of a record is constant for all elements of data in a record and all records in a file, the calculation of file size is a relatively simple matter. Where variable-length working is used, three different factors will have to be taken into account:

> File size based on maximum field/record sizes (to determine maximum storage area required and maximum processing time)

> File size based on minimum field record sizes (to determine best case of storage area and processing time)

> Average or most common record sizes, with deviation for larger and smaller records, to give the typical storage and processing time.

Response Rate. This is the speed at which data in the file is to be updated, and the speed with which reports are to be produced from the time that they are requested. A real-time system in which stock is being dynamically allocated will be a very fast response rate. For example, an airline seat reservation system is a fast-response system, since there must be immediate access to updating of, and reporting from, seat/flight status. In a fast-response process control environment, data must be immediately available for inspection and calculation if a feedback signal is to be used to control an operation. On the other hand, many systems in commerce are batch processed on a regular cycle: monthly sales statistics, weekly payroll, daily invoicing, etc.

Putting the Factors Together

To summarize: The computer subsystem is primarily concerned with the processing of files. It will consist of a number of processes: *what* must be done. These processes will be performed by a number of computer-based procedures (*how* done), i.e., programs/runs. One file is usually used by a number of programs. The designer must really know the characteristics of the data in depth. File design is an iterative process whereby initial ideas are considered, some discarded, and some followed up by more detailed design. This detail design is followed by further assessment, modification of the original idea, or total abandonment of ideas, etc. The key considerations as regards the actual structuring of the file are shown in Fig. 5-2. Note that these factors will vary from file to file and program to program. An example of the application of these factors is shown in Fig. 5-3. Note that the information shown is independent of device and software, and that files are defined in terms of the content and usage only. When related to hardware available, it may be necessary to make changes. This is part of the iterative process of file design.

In addition to the file data characteristics shown in Fig. 5-3, there will be general logical considerations, as shown in Fig. 5-2. These apply to the overall processing requirements of the system. Essentially, they are related to the security of the data, the need for ensuring the integrity of the data and the provision for regeneration should a processing failure occur. They also include retention requirements such as how long the data is to be preserved and held available in the system.

Against these factors, there are the device and software characteristics summarized in Fig. 5-2, truly demonstrating the repetitive nature of the design process. All these factors must be considered if a file is to be developed which meets all the systems processing requirements. The general objectives of file design may be summarized as flexibility, speed and ease of retrieval, efficient use of storage media, and simplification of problem solution. These objectives are quite often conflicting. For example, a system that gives a lot of flexibility in processing will almost certainly lead to inefficient use of the storage media. Or, a fast-response system with the files structured accordingly will certainly not be simple in either concept or implementation. The relative importance of each objective will depend on the goals of the project and the characteristics of the systems.

There is thus a considerable amount of work to be done in sketching out the content and processing requirements of a file before detailed device characteristics can be considered. In subsequent chapters a number of different methods for storing and retrieving data are discussed. After each technique has been described, comments are made as to how the method can be applied against the file design objectives discussed above.

PROCESS		Establishment to Budget Reporting	Staff Change Notification
	Frequency:	Monthly	Daily
	Response Rate:	24 hours	6 hours
File	Characteristic[d]		
Personnel File			
Employee number	5NF	X[f]	X
Employee name	20A/NV		/[g]
Job code	4NF	X	/
Organizational unit	3NF		/
Level	1NF		/
Position title	22A/NV	X	/
Sex	1AF		
Date of birth	6NF		
Skill 1[a]	3NF 100%		/
2	3NF 82%		/
3	3NF 23%		/
4	3NF 11%		/
Actual salary	5NF		
Growth	15%		
Size	12,540 record		
Hit rate		100%	1.2%
Organization File			
Organizational unit	3NF	X	
OU it reports to	3NF	X	
OU name	20A/NV	X	
Job code[b]	4NF	X	
Position title[b]	22A/NV	X	
No. of OU's authorized [b]	$X \rightarrow 13$[e] 2NF	X	
Authorized salary[b]	5NF	X	
Number of employees	4NF	X	
Employee number 1[c]	5NF	X	
Employee number 2[c]	5NF	X	
	$X \rightarrow 73$[e]	X	
Employee number n[a]	5NF	X	
Salary budget	7NF		
Growth	1.5%		
Size	738 record		
Hit rate		100%	

(a) Percentage indicates the number of records containing skill.
(b) Repeated for each job code.
(c) Repeated for each employee.
(d) Characteristic = number of characters; = type: N = numeric, A/N = alphanumeric, A = alphabetic; = format: V = variable length, F = fixed length.
(e) $X \rightarrow$ = up to so many times.
(f) X = is used.
(g) / = may be used.

Figure 5-3. Process Characteristics

CHAPTER 6

SEQUENTIAL STORAGE AND SEQUENTIAL ACCESS

THE BASIC METHOD

Sequential storage and processing is the simplest method of using a direct access device for file processing. It is an area, however, where we hit a basic problem of terminology differences among various manufacturers and users. The major problem is in the use of two terms: *serial* processing and *sequential* processing. Serial processing has been previously defined as the extraction and processing of records, one after another, by physical sequence. This means that we start at the beginning of the file and work through to the end, taking the next record from the next higher location. Sequential processing on the other hand, starts at the beginning of the file, takes the record with the lowest key, and works through the file toward the end, taking as the next record the record with the next higher key. The difference, therefore, is that serial processing works in physical sequence of records and sequential processing works in logical sequence. In this chapter, sequential storage and access is taken to mean the latter, i.e., access by *logical sequence*.

The principle involved requires that the file be stored and sorted into ascending order by key. The file is then loaded onto the direct access device in this sequence. The file is subsequently processed by taking each record in turn and transferring it to the central processor, where it can be examined and processed. This continues until the file processing is complete (the last record wanted has been accessed) and/or the end of the file is reached.

FILE LAYOUT AND PROCESSING

The structure of the file will depend on the hardware characteristics and the software to be used. The various storage methods are summarized as follows:

1. *Bucket approach*: Records are located in fixed-length buckets that comprise in hardware terms a number of blocks or segments.

2. *Variable-track approach*: Records are stored according to the level of addressing that is to be used. For example, in IBM terms, the records may be formatted with or without keys. They may be blocked or unblocked.

A Bucket Approach

If a bucket approach is used, the records are loaded so many to a bucket. Each bucket is then accessed in sequence and the contents (one or more records) are unpacked and examined in core. If the records are to be updated, all that have to be changed are altered in core and the complete bucket of information is written back to the device. This means that the whole contents of the original bucket is overwritten. The processing is shown diagrammatically in Fig. 6-1.

Timing of a read-only file is very simple. Since every bucket on every cylinder is to be accessed, timing for a complete read of the file is

$$(C_n \times C_t) + (B_n \times B_t)$$

where:

C_n = number of cylinders occupied by the file

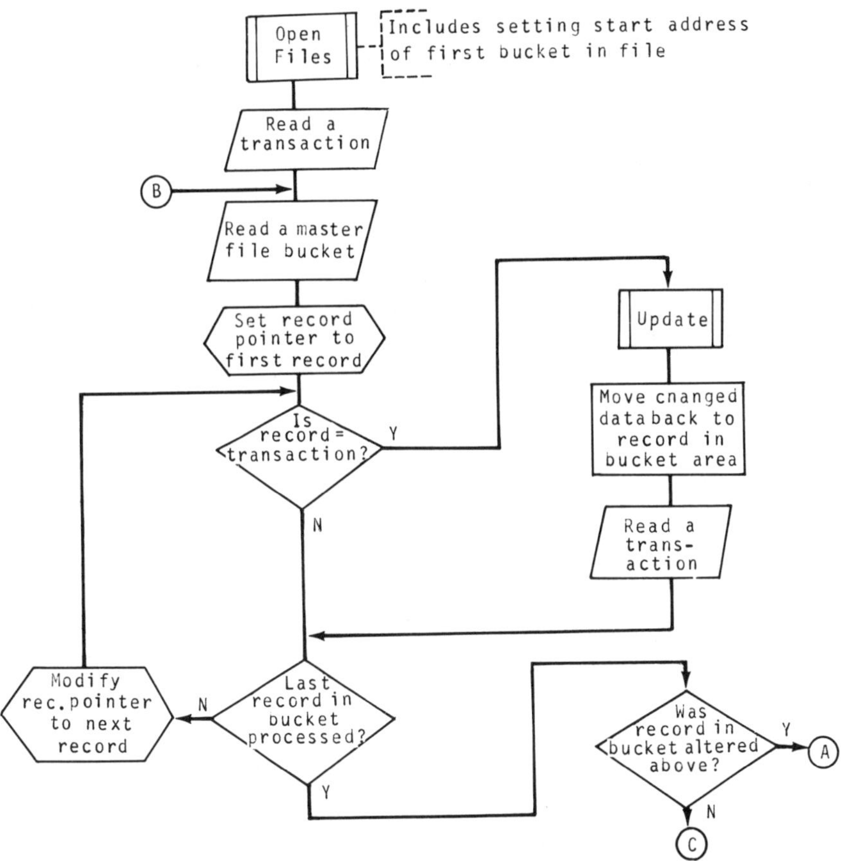

Figure 6-1. Sequential Processing

C_t = minimum seek time to change cylinders
B_n = number of buckets in the file
B_t = time to read a bucket

This simple timing formula applies to reading the whole of the file as, for example, in producing a sequential report. The seek time used in the calculation is the *minimum* seek time, the time to move from one cylinder to the next. In a fixed-head device, of course, this will be zero time. The bucket read time should include average latency. For example:

Read a file consisting of 80,000 records stored 10 to a bucket, with 80 buckets to a cylinder; the file thus covers 100 cylinders. The device being used has a minimum seek time of 30 ms with a bucket read time of 25 ms. Latency of 12.5 ms is assumed. Read time for the whole file is

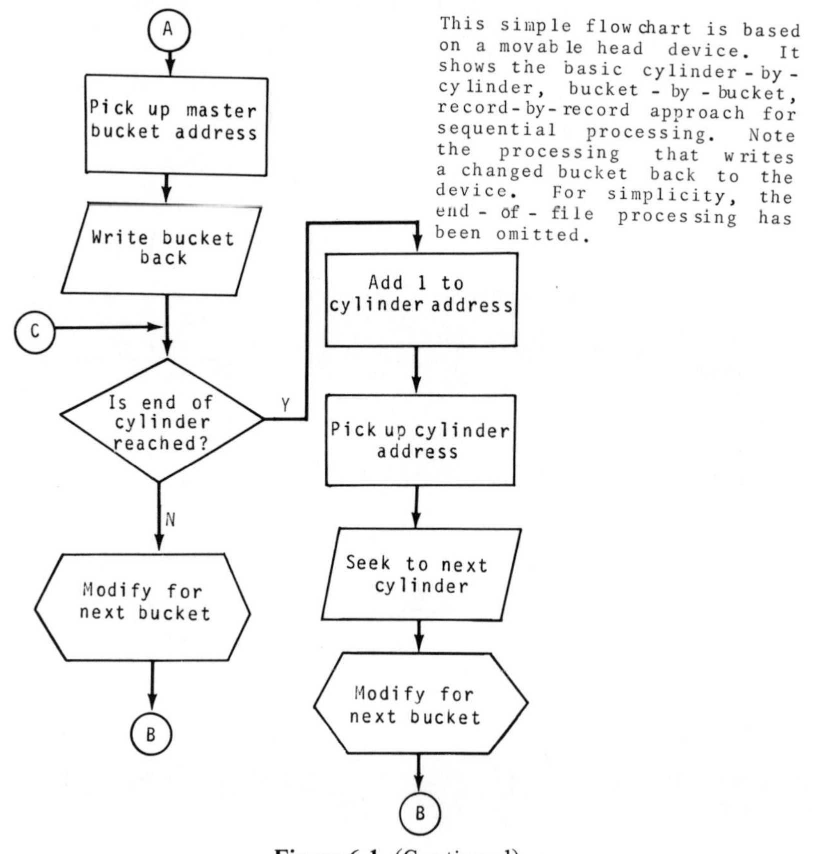

Figure 6-1. (Continued)

$$(100 \times 30) \text{ ms} + (8000 \times 37.5) \text{ ms}$$

which is 5 minutes, 3 seconds.

The next case is one in which records in the file are not only to be read but also to be updated. This leads us to a very interesting problem. If the records are stored one to a bucket and one input transaction will apply to one file record —i.e., each file record may have no more than one transaction applied to it in any one updating run—then we must add onto the basic formula an allowance for the write time. If we assume that the whole file is to be read and each of the transactions updates one of the file records, then the timing is

$$(C_n \times C_t) + (B_n \times B_t) + (T \times B_w)$$

where T is the number of transactions and B_w is the bucket write time.

The situation is complicated, of course, when multiple record buckets are considered, or where the processing is to cease when the last transaction is applied. The file described in the previous example is to be updated by 1000 transactions. These transactions have been sorted to the same sequence as the main file. For the purposes of this example, one transaction relates to a master file record, and one master file record gets only one transaction. The best case, in terms of processing time, will be when 1000 transactions hit the first 1000 records in the file. This means that the first 1000 records in the first 100 buckets are hit. These 100 buckets will be on the first two cylinders, and thus the timing is

$$
\begin{array}{ll}
(2 \times 30) & \text{for seeking} \\
(100 \times 37.5) & \text{for reading} \\
(100 \times 62.5) & \text{for writing}
\end{array}
$$

where a write takes 50 ms per bucket, plus 12.5 ms for latency. This gives about 10 seconds. The worst case, in terms of processing time, will be where there is no more than one transaction per bucket to be applied and the last bucket contains a transaction to be applied. This would result in a complete file read, which would take 5 minutes, 3 seconds, plus a write time of 1000×62.5 ms:

$$(1000 \times 62.5) \text{ ms} + 5 \text{ min } 3 \text{ sec} = 6 \text{ min } 5 \text{ secs}$$

One could decide on an average time by taking the mean of these two times. This might provide a very rough and ready estimate. It may be the case that examination of the application characteristics will show that there is a pattern in the hit rate: This could then be used as the basis of the timing.

Rule-of Thumb Approach

Another rule-of-thumb approach is to use very simple statistical techniques. These are described in detail in Appendix A. Essentially, they are based on a random distribution of hits over the file. "Random" in this sense means that the chance of any record being hit is the same as any other record being hit.

If there is a bias in that some records have a higher activity than others and will therefore be hit more often, this random distribution of hits will not apply. Assuming a random distribution of hits over the file, it is possible, given the number of buckets and the number of records per bucket, to estimate the number of buckets that will be a hit for a given number of transactions. Again, this will assume that a master file record does not have more than one transaction applied to it on any given run.

An example table of bucket hits is given in Appendix B (Table B-2). For any file it is possible to use these tables to get an indication of the number of buckets hit. It is stressed that these tables assume a random distribution and can be read as *"buckets hit in the long run."* Any bias in the transaction-to-master file record relationship will cause a corresponding bias in the pattern of hits over the file. Ignoring for the moment the hit rate on cylinders and considering only the hit rate on buckets, we can compute the read time for the example given in the preceding section as follows: Table B-2 shows that the assumption that 1000 buckets is hit is reasonable. In this case, the number of records per bucket is not a major determining factor. Thus, the timing is

> 5 minutes 3 seconds for a complete file read, plus 1000 × 62.5 for the write of the buckets that have a changed record. File time is thus 5 minutes 3 seconds + 1 minute 2 seconds = 6 minutes 5 seconds.

What this does not show explicitly, of course, is how many buckets must be read before the last transaction has been applied. This would influence the file timing for reading the buckets, and would affect the number of cylinder changes that must take place. The safest way of producing a conservative timing estimate is to assume a complete file read, using the statistical approach to give the number of altered buckets to be written back. Let us now change the volume of transactions in the example here to 10,000. The table in Appendix B shows that the expected number of buckets hit is about 6500. This figure could be used in the timing estimates.

What these tables do not show, of course, is *what* buckets are hit. It would be very wrong to assume in this last example that the 6500 buckets hit are the *first* 6500 buckets in the file; nor would it be correct, based on this reasoning, to assume that only 6500 buckets are to be read. In no way does the table indicate this. It merely shows that 6500 buckets of the total 8000 buckets will be hit on average in the long run.

Variable-Track Format

As described previously, records in the variable-track format, such as on an IBM device, can be blocked or unblocked. The processing is very similar to that described for the bucket approach described above. The records may be formatted with or without keys. In practice, however, a file that is to be processed only sequentially should not be formatted with keys; there is no advantage to be gained because the records are to be read one after another. A multiple-record block may be assumed to be like a multiple-record bucket for timing purposes. Since records can be blocked, the optimum blocking factor will be determined by the amount of core available to receive the input block and the characteristics of the track—the available-data area after deductions are made for the various reference fields.

OVERFLOW

The description of sequential processing thus far can be taken as referring to serial processing—if the records are in logical key sequence. Where we find the major distinction in serial versus sequential processing is in the treatment of overflow records. These are insertions to the file after the file has been created. The IBM definition of "sequential" processing is equivalent to serial processing, because additions to an IBM-sequential file have certain requirements: The entire file must be copied so that the new records can be inserted into their rightful positions to maintain the logical key sequence within the file. Deletions can be handled by leaving the record in its place on the file and identifying it by means of some form of delete marker. This is read during processing as "the record is physically here but should be considered as deleted." Periodically, the file is copied and reorganized, with new records being inserted and old records actually deleted. The latter is achieved by inspecting each record as the file is reloaded after it has been copied and by omitting any record with a delete marker.

Another method of handling record insertions in a sequential file is to use a **tagging** or chaining system. This was demonstrated in Chapter 4 in the section "Serial Processing." (Using IBM software, sequential processing in the sense of all records being accessed in key sequence (including overflow records) is handled by means of an indexed-sequential file, as described in Chapter 7.) The file is created with the current records loaded in key sequence. The file area is divided into three parts. The first is the *prime*, or *home*, area. It is into this area that the records are initially loaded. A number of buckets are left empty on each cylinder; these buckets will take the additional records that will be inserted during the life of the file. This is commonly known as the *cylinder overflow area*. The third part of the file area is an *independent overflow area*, located at the end of the main file. This is shown diagrammatically in Fig. 6-2.

The principle of operation is as follows: When the file is created, or reloaded during periodic reorganization, the records are loaded at maximum packing density. This means that each bucket receives as many records as it can take. Some spare space is usually left in a bucket to take tags, as described later.

As shown in Fig. 6-2, a number of buckets are reserved on each cylinder to take all the overflow records from the home buckets on that cylinder. When a cylinder overflow area becomes full, overflow records are transferred to the

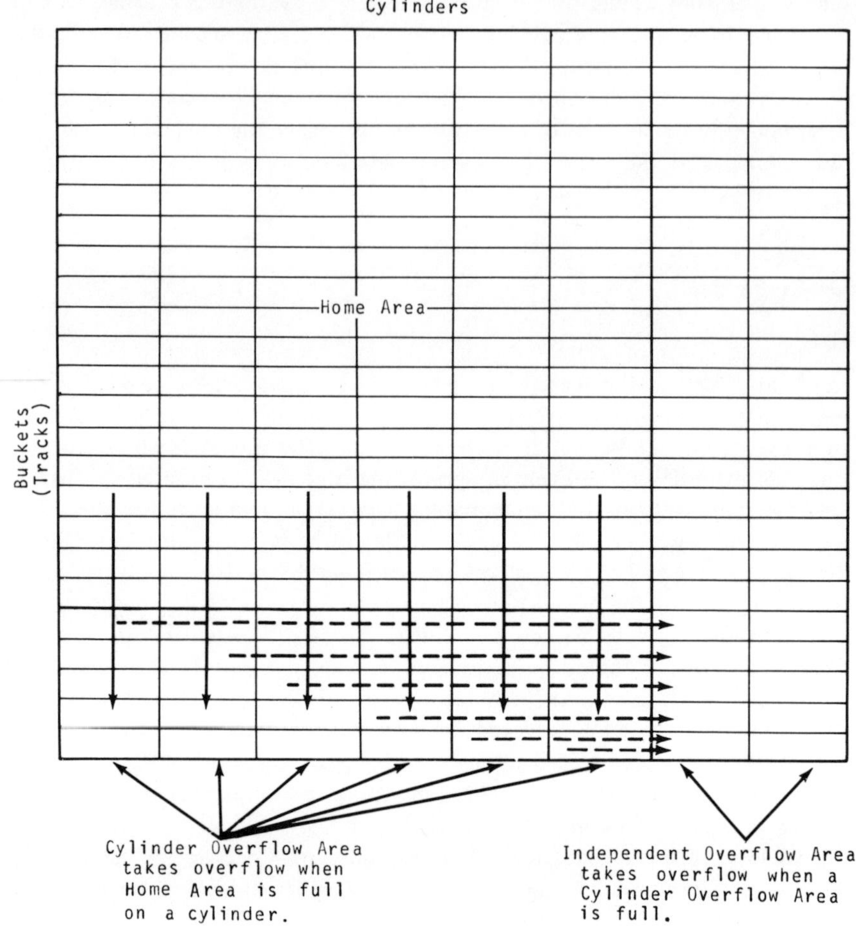

Figure 6-2. Overflow Areas in a Sequential File

independent overflow-area-reserved cylinders on the end of the file. An example of one cylinder of a file is shown in Fig. 6-3(a); this shows the state of the file area after the file has been loaded.

One system of dealing with insertions is to use a key/address tag. When a record is to be inserted but there is insufficient space in the home bucket and the record cannot be inserted in sequence, a tag inserted in the home bucket gives the key of the missing record. The cylinder overflow area is then searched for a space to take the record. If a space is found, the new record is inserted in that space and the address of the bucket put in the tag in the home bucket. Examples of this are shown in Fig. 6-3(b). If no space is found in the cylinder overflow area (i.e., it is full), then the record is placed in the independent overflow area at the end of the file. This is shown in Fig. 6-3(c); the address of the

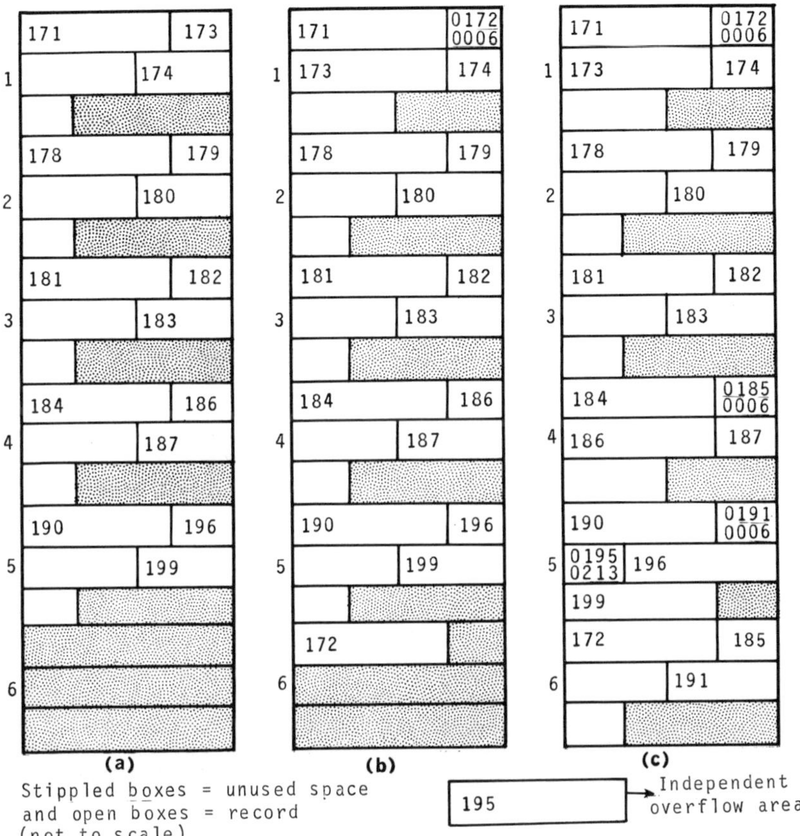

Stippled boxes = unused space
and open boxes = record
(not to scale)

One cylinder in a file is shown. For simplicity, the cylinder consists of five home buckets plus a one-bucket cylinder overflow area.
One bucket consists of 500 characters of storage. Records are fixed
length, 160 characters each. A tag consists of eight characters,
four for the key and four for the address.

(a): This shows the file immediately after it has been loaded.
     Each of the home buckets consists of three 160 -character
     records; this leaves 20 unused characters of storage in each
     bucket.

(b): One record (key 172) is inserted in the file. Its home
     bucket to retain the sequence is bucket 1. A tag is
     inserted in the appropriate position in this bucket, tagging
     it to the cylinder overflow area (bucket 6).

(c): This shows the file some time after loading. Note that three
     records have been inserted. The sequence of insertion has
     been: 172,185,191. Note the placing of tags for these records.
     An additional record (key 195) is to be inserted. There is
     therefore assigned to the independent overflow area (bucket
     213) at the end of the file area and tagged accordingly.

Figure 6-3. Example of Sequential Overflow

overflow record is put in the tag in the usual manner. If the independent over-flow area becomes full and a further overflow record is to be inserted, there is little option but to abandon processing and to produce an appropriate message on the console.

A number of refinements can be made to the basic processing:

> As a home bucket is searched for space in which a new record is inserted, existing records are inspected for delete codes. If a deleted record is found it is omitted and the new record inserted in its place.

> The first bucket in the overflow area can be reserved for control purposes. This bucket can be used to show the next available space for a new record. This will obviate the need for searching the area each time a new record is to be inserted. The area can also be used to flag an "overflow-area full" condition so that reference can be made directly to the independent overflow area.

Under this system, we have the problem of what do we do if a home bucket is full, a new record is to be inserted, and there is no space to insert the tag. One way in which this condition can be dealt with is to move a home record from the bucket and insert two tags in the space left. One tag will be for the new record and one tag will be for the moved home record. A very general overflow processing flowchart is shown in Fig. 6-4.

The preceding description shows only one way in which overflow can be dealt with. Most bucket systems use an approach like this, but there are many alternative methods of handling overflow. Another method is to omit the address field in the tag altogether; a small index can be incorporated at the beginning of the cylinder overflow area to give the location of all records in that area. In some applications where the overflow is very small indeed, it is possible to omit an index altogether and just search the overflow area until the desired record is found. Yet another alternative is to omit all forms of tags entirely. If a record is not in its correct position on the file, a search is made automatically of the overflow areas. If it is not located there, it is assumed that the record is not present in the file. This will obviously be a time-consuming process if there are many overflow records. Thus it is suitable only for systems with a very low insertion rate. It does, of course, reduce the space taken up in the file by tags; in a low-insertion file this space will probably be minimal.

Processing Overflow

The method used for dealing with overflow must be chosen after the insertion/deletion rate of the file has been examined, and will depend on the software available. The amount of space to be allocated to the overflow areas will depend on the pattern of insertions. In some systems, insertions may be made anywhere in the file; in others, insertions occur almost exclusively at the end of the file.

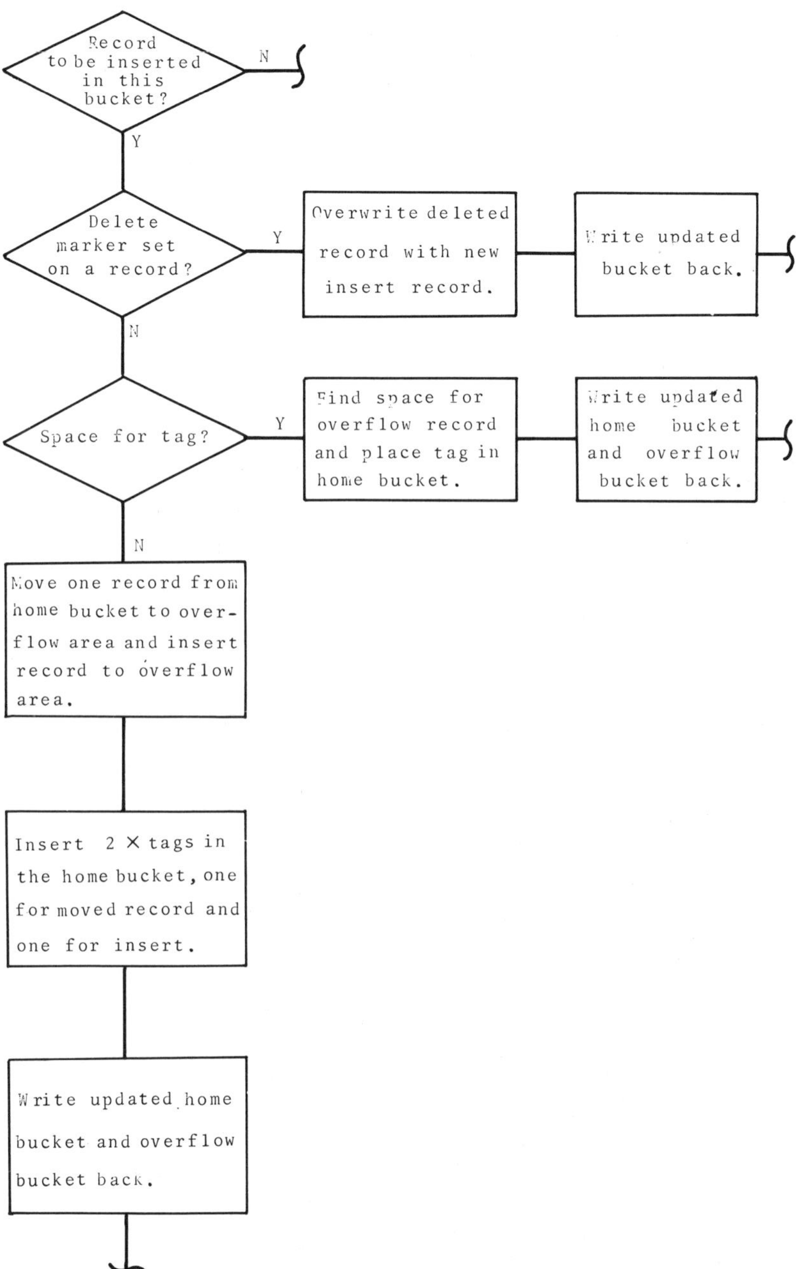

Figure 6-4 Tagged Overflow Procedure

In some files, deletions take place "at random," while in others they take place on the early records in the file. The pattern of insertions will thus influence the number of overflow cases generated from record insertions. If it is known that insertions will take place in certain parts of the file, it may be possible to have cylinder overflow areas larger than in other parts of the file. Variable-length records that "grow" in size with processing may also create an overflow case, as shown in the example in Fig. 6-5.

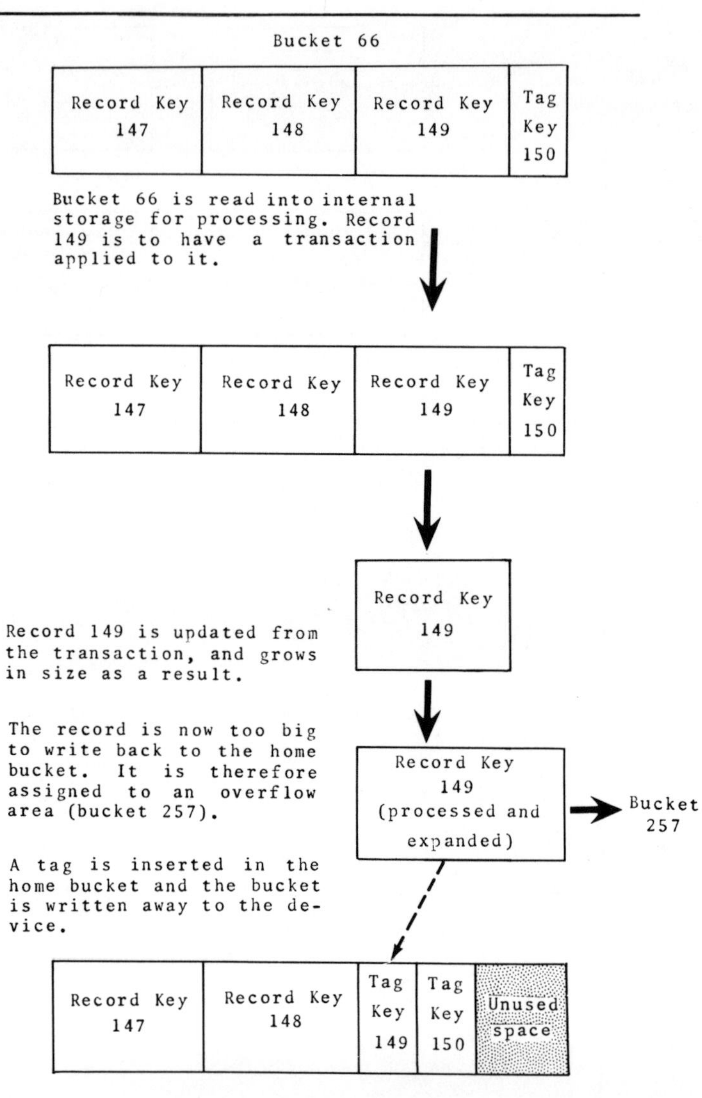

Figure 6-5. Record Growth Overflow

One possible method of handling the overflow problem in a very volatile file is to load the records at less than 100 percent during file creation or reorganization, which means that many new records can be accommodated in their home buckets without any overflow cases being generated. This can result in poor space utilization and longer processing times. Taking the example file timed earlier (see section "A Bucket Approach"), suppose the file was loaded with seven records per bucket and the file area enlarged accordingly. In the original example the file area was

> 10 records per bucket
> 80 buckets to a cylinder
> 8000 buckets
> 100 cylinders
> 80,000 records stored

By keeping the number of buckets to a cylinder constant, we now have a file area of

> 7 records to a bucket
> 80 buckets to a cylinder
> 11,430 buckets (rounded)
> 144 cylinders
> 80,000 records stored

The time for a straight sequential read of the whole file is now about 7 minutes 4 seconds as opposed to 5 minutes 3 seconds on the first organization. If we are considering a very large file, the difference in processing times will be considerable.

The use of a low record-packing density to allow for possible insertions should be carefully examined. Only in systems where there will be a large number of insertions over the whole file area should it be considered. If it is applied as a general principle, it may be using a sledgehammer to crack a nut! On the other hand, it is wise to leave room in each bucket for at least a tag of the appropriate form.

Monitoring Insertions and Overflows

It is vital to monitor the number of insertions made during processing and the number of overflow cases that result. For the early life of the file, this monitoring may be a computer report of the number of records in the cylinder overflow areas and the number of records in the independent overflow area. If the file is subject to a fair number of insertions and deletions, then it should be periodically reorganized. The time interval between reorganizations will be determined by the volatility and the decrease in processing time caused by the handling of overflow records. The worst case from the timing point of view is a large number of records in the independent overflow area. This will mean that each overflow record to be inserted results in a seek, followed by a read, to locate the appropriate bucket that holds the overflow record. Because the independent area is physically at the end of the home area, average seek time will have to be allowed. Similarly, the retrieval of a record from the cylinder overflow area will require an additional bucket read. The insertion of a new record in the cylinder overflow area will result in a read of the home bucket, followed by a read of the overflow bucket control area (if there is one), followed by a read of the overflow bucket and the insertion of the record into that bucket.

If only one input area has been allowed in internal storage, then the reading of the overflow area buckets will overwrite the home bucket contained in internal storage, as shown in Fig. 6-6. This can be very time consuming, and at least two areas should be allowed in internal storage, or the appropriate record moves should be made during processing. One example of internal storage allocation to various bucket areas is shown in Fig. 6-7. This diagram illustrates the principle of minimizing the number of re-reads caused by overwriting an area of core, as in Fig. 6-6.

It is again possible to use basic statistical techniques to attempt to predict over the long run the amount of overflow that will occur. These techniques assume the use of a random distribution of insertions over the entire file area. Table B-3 in Appendix B shows an estimate of the number of records that will probably overflow for a given number of insertions. If a file is loaded at 100 percent, then every additional record will result in an overflow condition. For a record-packing density of less than 100 percent, it will be possible for some insertion records to be stored in their home buckets. The following information is needed to make the estimate:

> Average space left in file for additional records: This is based on the number of records stored in the available buckets since the file was created or last reorganized. For example, if there are 10,000 records stored in 5000 buckets with a bucket capacity size of 4 records, then there is room for 10,000 more records. Thus, there is room for 2 more records per bucket.

> Number of records added since the last reorganization: This requirement assumes that a number of records will be added from the time at which the file was created or reorganized. The worst case, if overflow is going to occur, will be just prior to the next file reorganization. An estimate is to be made of the number of added records that will overflow.

Assume that 5000 records are to be added to the file described above. What percentage of these records will cause overflow conditions? Table B-3 shows that an expected 26.4 percent of these records will overflow. This will amount to some 1000 records. Again it is stressed that this is based on insertions, records that are not added onto the end of the file but are inserted "at random" all through the file area. Table B-3 does, however, illustrate the importance of periodic reorganization.

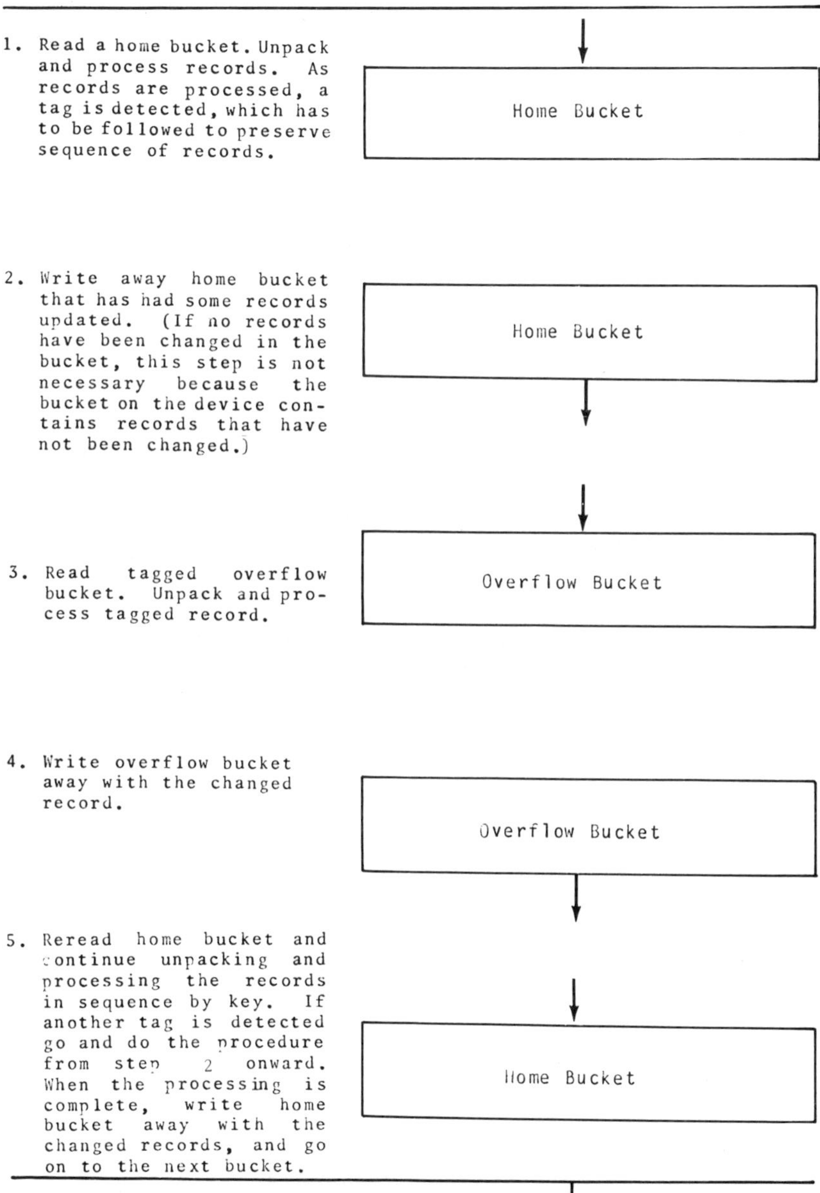

Figure 6-6. Input Areas and Overflow Handling Timing

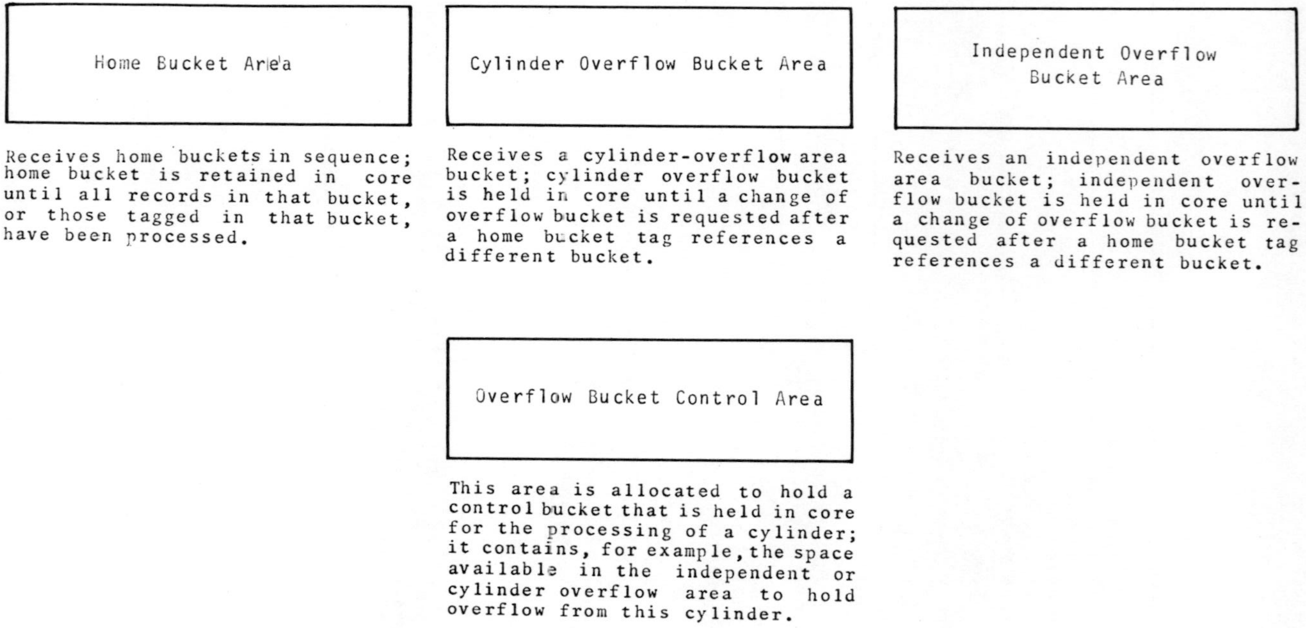

Home Bucket Area

Receives home buckets in sequence; home bucket is retained in core until all records in that bucket, or those tagged in that bucket, have been processed.

Cylinder Overflow Bucket Area

Receives a cylinder-overflow area bucket; cylinder overflow bucket is held in core until a change of overflow bucket is requested after a home bucket tag references a different bucket.

Independent Overflow Bucket Area

Receives an independent overflow area bucket; independent overflow bucket is held in core until a change of overflow bucket is requested after a home bucket tag references a different bucket.

Overflow Bucket Control Area

This area is allocated to hold a control bucket that is held in core for the processing of a cylinder; it contains, for example, the space available in the independent or cylinder overflow area to hold overflow from this cylinder.

Figure 6-7. Bucket Areas for Overflow Handling

SUMMARY

Sequential processing is the retrieval of records one after another in logical key sequence. Processing logic is essentially very simple for a file without overflow. There are many different ways in which overflow can be handled. For all methods, however, it is necessary to monitor the efficiency of processing as records are inserted and deleted. During systems design, estimates must be made of basic file space utilization and processing times without overflow, and similar estimates for worst overflow conditions. Procedures for periodic file reorganization must be built into the system at the design stage.

Sequential processing is generally used when a complete file analysis is required or when a sequential report is to be produced. It is also used in file updating runs where there is a very high hit rate of transactions. Selected record retrieval is impossible; desired records have to be located by searching. Random inquiry processing in a fast-response system must thus use another method of organization: indexed-sequential or address generation, as described in later chapters. These are the obvious cases when sequential processing is impractical. There are many borderline cases, however, when a choice between sequential and indexed-sequential processing is far less obvious. This will be discussed in Chapter 7, after the indexed-sequential method has been discussed in detail. To all intents and purposes, therefore, sequential processing on a direct access device may be considered very similar to the serial processing using magnetic tape —with the important difference that data on a direct access device can be updated by overlay.

INDEXED-SEQUENTIAL STORAGE—SELECTIVE SEQUENTIAL ACCESS AND RANDOM ACCESS

THE BASIC METHOD

Indexed-sequential storage is a method of structuring a file for selective record retrieval. This is access to a desired record without serial or sequential searching through the file records. As demonstrated earlier, this facility for going directly to a selected record is vital in many systems for a number of reasons, of which three are

1. *Low hit rate:* Some systems, through their very nature, require only a small portion of file records to be accessed. In these cases, sequential searching to find a small number of selected records may be inefficient.

2. *Unmatched sequence of input:* This is where the sequence of the input is not the same as the sequence of the file. To avoid sorting, a method whereby records can be retrieved in a "nonsequential" manner is very useful.

3. *Fast response:* File searching is too time consuming in fast-response systems such as inquiry processing or real-time systems. Selective record retrieval is vital in these types of systems.

Indexed-sequential processing has proved to be the most popular method of directly retrieving records from a file. In this chapter we consider all aspects of creating and processing indexed-sequential files. First, the general method of operation will be considered. Next, index formats and search processing methods will be discussed. Finally, the alternative methods of processing a file will be considered.

The principle of indexed-sequential storage was introduced in Chapter 4 in the section "Indexed-Sequential Processing." Simply, a file is loaded onto a device with the records in logical key order; this procedure is the same as for serial or sequential files. As the file is loaded, indexes are created. The indexes show how the file is arranged on the device. Each index shows which records are stored on a part of the device. For example,

"highest record on a device unit"
"highest record on a cylinder"
"highest records on a bucket/track/block/etc."

These indexes can be used to locate and retrieve a desired record. Once a record has been located, it can be called into internal storage, updated, and written back, i.e., updated by overlay. Figures 4-3 and 4-4 show files with various levels of index.

The format of the index, the number of index levels, and the method of index retrieval and searching will depend on the device, the software, and the systems characteristics. To illustrate the basic principle, consider the following example:

A file is stored on an exchangeable disk-storage device. The file occupies all 100 cylinders of the device. The device is addressed by giving the cylinder number and the number of the track (head) on that cylinder. Each cylinder consists of ten tracks, and each of the tracks is used to store five logical records. The first track holds an index of the highest record stored in each of the 100 cylinders. There are thus 100 entries in this index, one for each cylinder. The first record on each track of the remaining cylinders is a track-level index. This has one entry for each track and shows the highest numbered record on a track. (In the case of the first cylinder, the track-level index is held as the first record on the *second* track.) This is shown diagrammatically in the form of a file map in Fig. 7-1. The processing logic for this file is shown in simplified form in Fig. 7-2. Record processing is by reference to the various levels of index. The general procedure shown in the flowchart may be described in narrative as follows:

1. At the start of the file processing run, the cylinder-level index is read into internal storage. It is held there during the whole of the run.

2. As a file record is required, the record key is matched against the cylinder-level index in core. The matching process determines which cylinder holds the record.

3. The appropriate track-level index determined in step 2 is read into internal storage.

4. The key is matched against the track-level index. The track address that holds the record is picked up from the index and that track is read. The track is inspected, record by record, until the desired record is located and processing can begin on that record.

5. After a record has been updated, the track with the change receives the updated record.

This example shows the basic processing logic, and as we shall see later, there are certain refinements that can be added to speed up the processing. As pointed out earlier, the format of the index will depend on the software approach used—

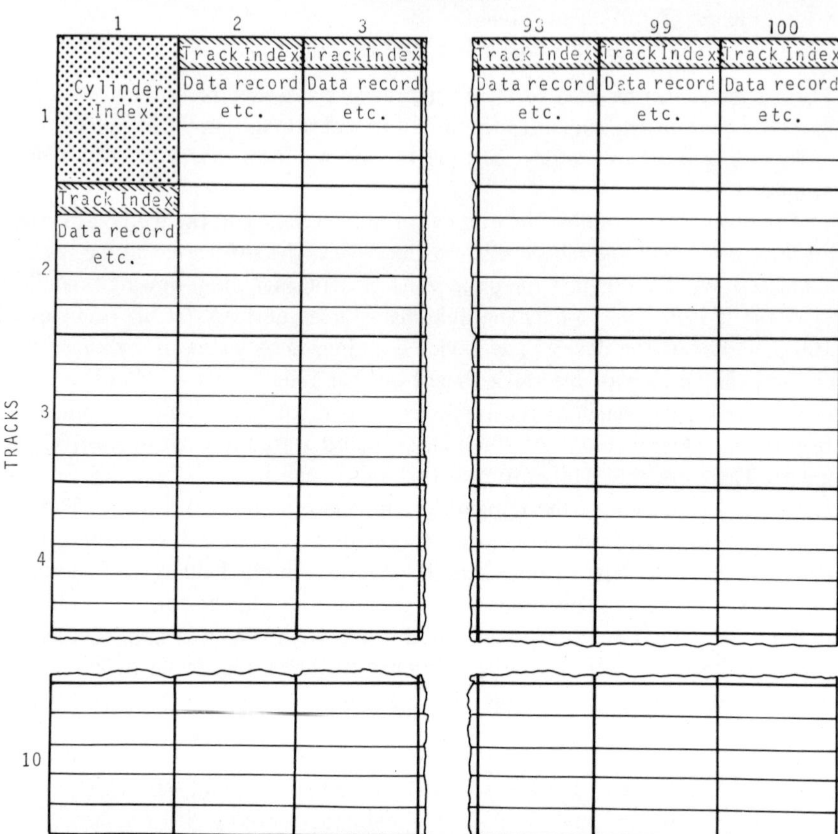

Figure 7-1. Cylinder/Track Indexes—File Map

this is primarily a difference in how overflow records are handled. The number of levels of index and the storage levels that are indexed will also depend on the type of device.

Levels of Index

The number and level of indexes are dependent on the size of the file and the type of device. The highest level of index, if present, is a type of master index. If a file covers a number of hardware units, such as a number of exchangeable disk drives, the highest level of index may well be a unit index. This will show the highest record on each device unit. As a small index, it is usually held in core during the whole of the file processing run. It can be held anywhere on one of the file units or on another device or type of device entirely.

In a movable head drum/disk device, the next level will probably be a cylinder-level index showing the highest record key on each cylinder. In a large file, it may not be feasible to hold the entire index in core for the whole of the

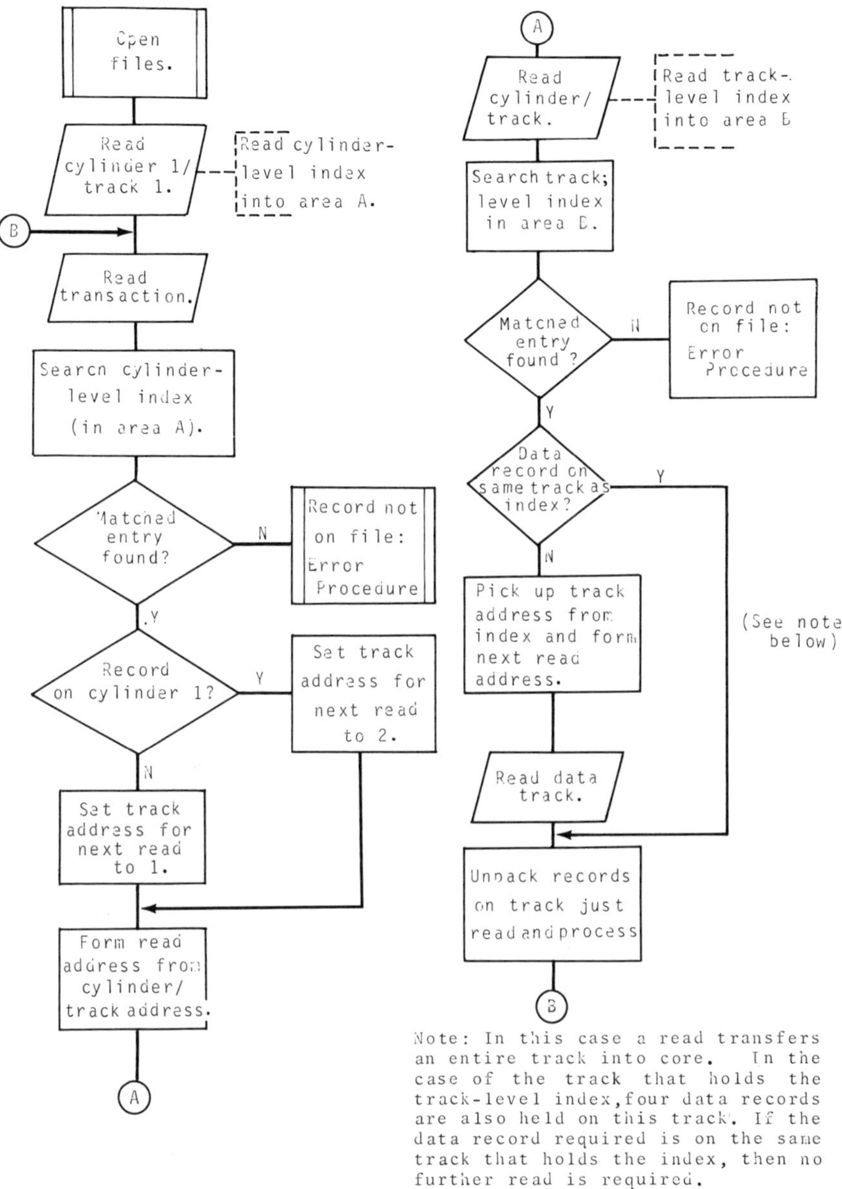

Figure 7-2. Cylinder/Track Indexes—Processing

processing run. In this case the index will be segmented and a higher level of index will be used so that the appropriate part of the index can be called for a given record. Again, the cylinder-level index may be stored anywhere on a file or on another device or type of device. In a magnetic card/strip device, this level of index would be to a card or strip level, to the highest record key on a card or strip. If the device has no hardware level of storage for a rough index, then some artificial segmentation may be necessary to produce an index that is manageable in core. An example of this is a large fixed-head drum or disk that has one head per track. In effect, the whole device forms one cylinder. A track-level index would probably be the highest level of index on a unit.

For a movable head device, the lowest level of index will be to either a bucket or track level. To keep access time to a minimum, this level of index is usually held on the cylinder to which it is related, as in the example shown in Fig. 7-1. Similarly, in a magnetic card/strip device, the track/bucket level index is usually held on the card or strip to which it refers. One seek will therefore access the required cylinder that holds both the data record required and the level of index which shows where that record is held on the cylinder.

In the case of a variable-format track device, there will be one entry per track, showing the highest logical key on a track. If the data records on a track are blocked, then the records are formatted with keys. This means that the key area holds the highest key in the following block. Each of the logical records in a block will also contain its key. Similarly, if a bucket approach is used, there will be one bucket-level index on a cylinder, one entry per bucket showing the highest record key in each of the buckets.

The exact location of the indexes—where they are stored in the file area or the device used to hold them—will depend on the software approach used.

INDEX FORMATS

The format of an index depends primarily on the method of device addressing, i.e., bucket versus variable-format track. For this reason, the two methods will be discussed separately.

Bucket Level Indexes

The layout of the file area for an indexed-sequential file using the bucket approach will be the same as for a sequential file, as described previously. That is, the file is created by loading records in ascending logical key sequence into the home or prime area. Later additions that cannot be fitted into the home area will be treated as overflow records. These overflow records will be tagged from their home buckets in the required sequence, and the records will be assigned to the cylinder overflow area or the independent overflow area at the end of the file (see Chapter 6). During the loading of the file records, the various levels of index will be created and these indexes will be written to the appropriate locations on the device. Records are subsequently retrieved by reference to the indexes. However, because the file has been created with the records in logical key sequence, straight sequential processing without reference to the indexes may be performed if required.

Subsequent additions to (or deletions from) the file will be treated in the same manner as for a sequential file. These additions and deletions will not affect the structure and accuracy of the indexes. Because the highest record on a storage area is used as the index entry, additions are inserted in such a manner that this highest key entry is not affected. For example, record 205 is to be inserted in the file. In this case, the new record is inserted in bucket 332, but

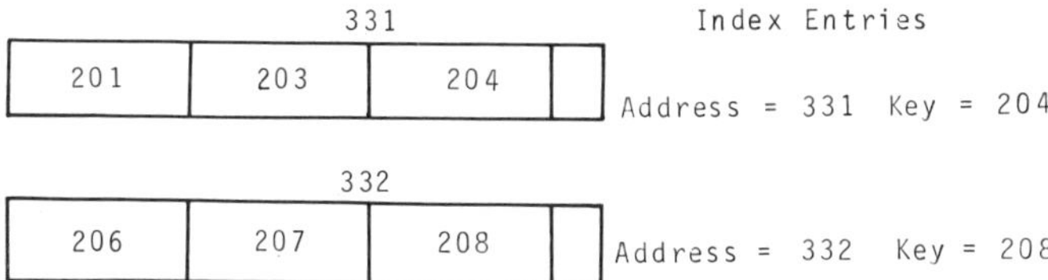

there is no space in this bucket. A tag is therefore inserted in bucket 332 referencing the new record, which is assigned to an overflow area as shown below.

The index is thus not affected by the insertion. A similar approach is used if the insertion comes at the end of a cylinder, to preserve the accuracy of the cylinder-level index.

An example of a bucket-level index is shown in Fig. 7-3. This index is an interesting modification of the basic "address-highest key" format entry. Here the bucket contains a header record that gives certain control information about this particular index: number of entries, address of index, size of key, and so on. Each of the entries consists of highest key in bucket. As the index is searched, a count is kept of the number of entries inspected before a match is found. The method used to search the index is a serial search, starting at the beginning of the index and working "down" the index until a "less than" or "equal to" condition is found. This count is added to the address of the first index bucket to give the bucket address. In a large file, the index may occupy more than one bucket, in which case the addition of the count is adjusted accordingly. The use of this relative addressing by means of a count thus obviates the need for an address field to be present in each index entry.

Variable-Format Track Indexes

The format of a variable-format track index is radically different from the bucket approach as described above because an overflow tagging system on the home tracks is not used. In effect, *overflow tags are inserted in the index rather than on the home tracks.* A file is initially loaded in the normal manner, records being stored in ascending logical key sequence in the home area. The records may be blocked or unblocked, but they must be formatted with keys. A cylinder overflow area and an independent overflow area may be assigned in the normal manner for a sequential file. For each track, however, there are *two entries*. One entry is the highest key on track, the normal entry in an index. The second entry for a track is an overflow tag entry. An example of a file immediately after loading (with no overflow) is shown in Fig. 7-4. Note that the cylinder-level index holds the home address of the track-level index, which is stored on the first

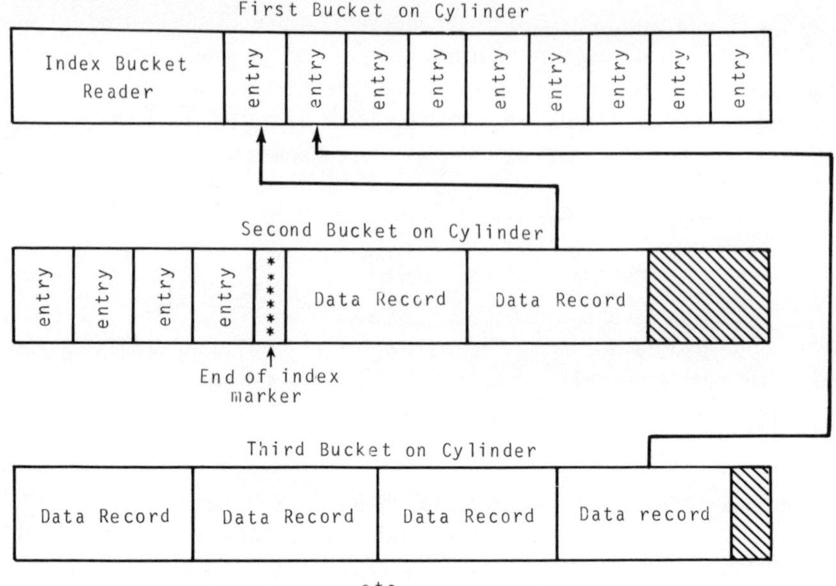

Figure 7-3. Example Bucket-Level Index

track of a cylinder. Each entry in the cylinder-level index has an address field that holds a home address, which is a cylinder number in the range 00 to 99 as the first two digits and a head number as the next two digits. The head number in this case is always 00, thus referring to the first track of a cylinder. Note that the last entry in the index is a "dummy" representing unallocated or unfilled cylinders in the file area.

The track index contains two entries for each track in a cylinder and is stored on the first track of a cylinder. Note the use of a dummy to mark the end of the index. Data records follow immediately after the end of the index. One of the entries for each track is the "highest key on track" in the normal manner. The other entry is an overflow entry. In the example shown in Fig. 7-4, this is set to a special value, since there will be no overflow immediately after the file is loaded. (In this case, the "no overflow" condition is denoted by an address entry of 255.) If subsequent overflow occurs on a track, then the overflow record is inserted in, say, the cylinder overflow area, and the address of the track that receives the overflow record is inserted in the index. Where more than one overflow record occurs on a track, a simple tagging system is used in the overflow area. Let us see how this works with some example record inserts.

A cylinder overflow area is allocated, which is track 31. Consider the case of an insertion record, key 0988. This record has a home track of 0001. The new record is inserted in its correct position on track 1, i.e., between records 0987 and 0990 and all the records are moved up accordingly. The last record, key 1120, is in effect "squeezed off" the end of the track. This bumped record is assigned to the cylinder overflow area, track 0031. The highest record key on track 0001 has thus now become 1119:

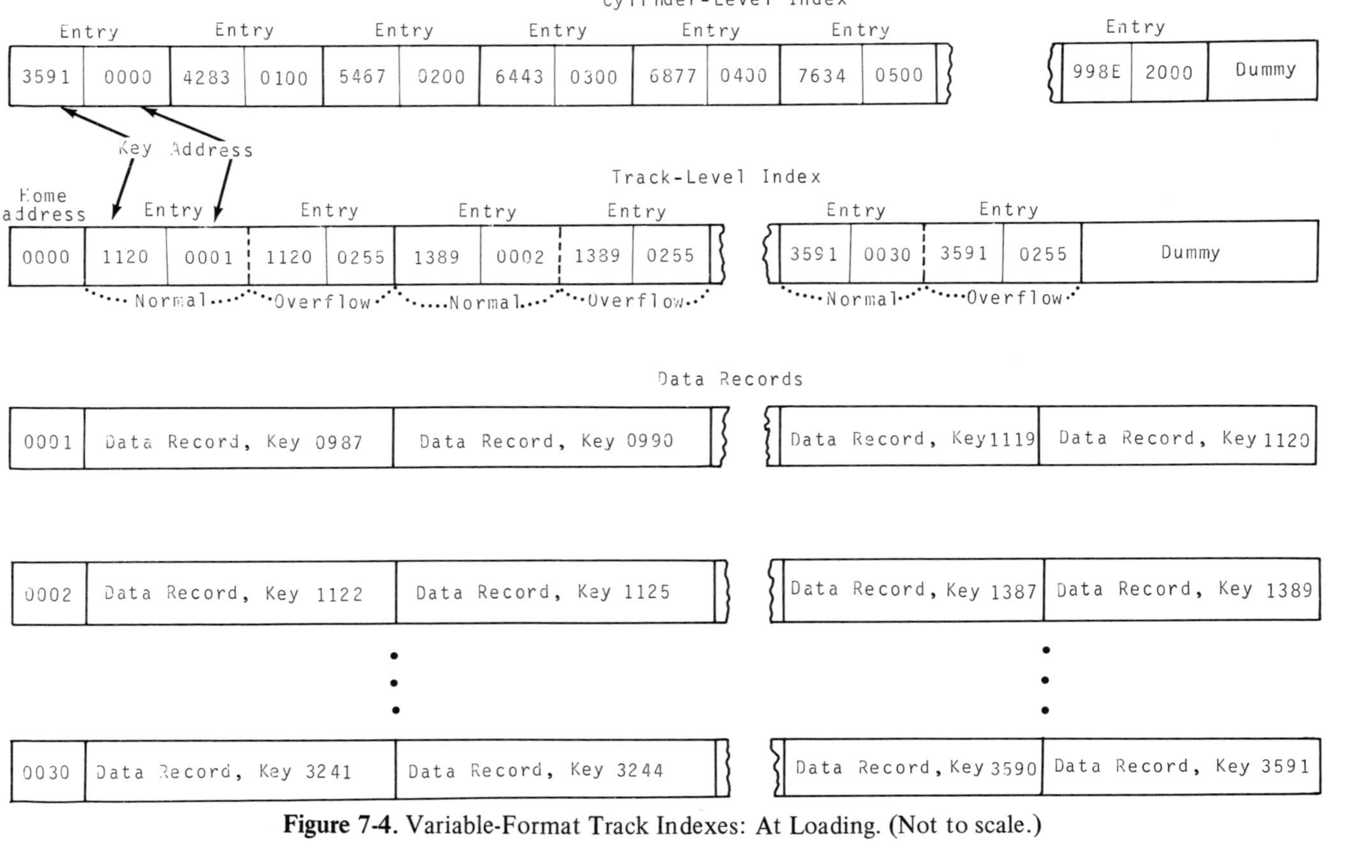

Figure 7-4. Variable-Format Track Indexes: At Loading. (Not to scale.)

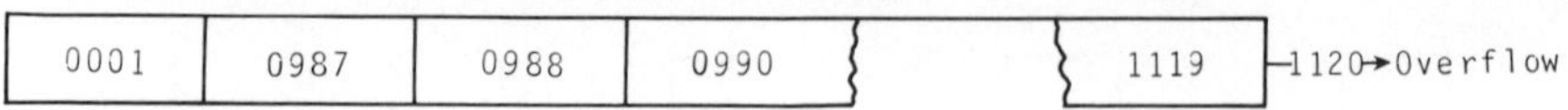

The normal index entry for track 1 is

The overflow record, 1120, is assigned to the cylinder overflow area, track 0031, and is placed there thus:

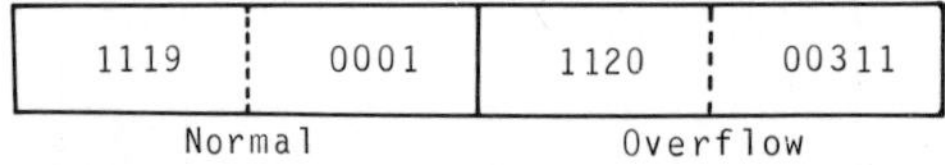

The preceding graphic shows the home address (0031) followed by a count field (00311) followed by a key field (1120). The count, it will be remembered, contains the cylinder number 00, the head number 31, followed by the record number. In this case the record number is 1 because the record is the first on the track. There then follows a special marker field, a *link field.* This is set to a value of 0255, which is an end-of-chain indicator, signifying that there are as yet no other overflow records in this area from track 1. This is followed by the data record, key 1120. The overflow entry for track 1 is set to a reference for this record in the overflow area. The complete track index entry for track 1 is thus:

This is the procedure for the first overflow condition on a track. Let us consider another addition: record 1121. To preserve the sequence of entries, this record is inserted on track 2, thereby not disturbing the highest record entry for track 01. The procedure is the same as before because 1121 is the first overflow insertion to track 0002.

1. Insert 1121 on track 0002 and move up subsequent records:

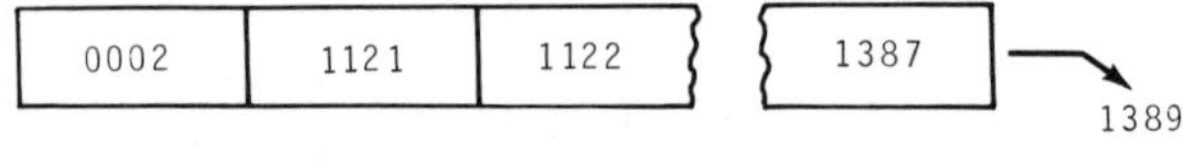

Normal index entry:

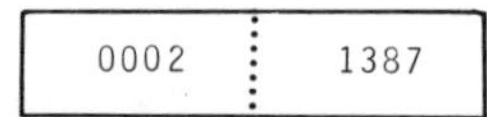

2. Move bumped entry to cylinder overflow area, track 0031, writing the record in the first available place:

Home Address	Count	Key	Link		Count	Key	Link	
0031	00311	1120	0255	Data Record 1120	00312	1389	0255	Data

Record Key 1389

	Index							
0000	1119	0001	1120	00311	1387	0002	1389	00312
	Normal		Overflow		Normal		Overflow	

Subsequent additions are handled by a slightly modified procedure. The address in the overflow entry must always refer to the lowest key in an overflow chain. The link address is used to enable overflow records for a particular track to be extracted, up to the last record in the chain. The last record in the chain will be the record with the highest key and will have a link of 0255 (end of chain). Let us consider some examples. Fig. 7-5 shows one track of a file with a one-track cylinder overflow area. The first two entries in the index are also shown.

1. Record 025 to be inserted. In this case the new record is greater than the last record on the prime track (023) but is less than the highest overflow record for that track (027). The new record is assigned to the overflow track (track 20), and is chained to the highest record. The overflow index entry is altered to show the address of the inserted record. This is shown in Fig. 7-6(b).

2. Record 008 is to be inserted (Fig. 7-6(c)). This record is placed on the prime track and the records moved up. The bumped record, 023, is moved to the overflow track and tagged in the chain. The key for the normal entry is altered to reflect the new highest record on the track. The address field of the overflow entry is changed to the address of the new overflow record. This is shown in Fig. 7-6(c).

Note that the links in the overflow chain are always set to show the sequence of records. For example, suppose an overflow track (track 25) holds two records overflowing from track 6: These are record keys 058 and 060. The index entry for track 6 is

Normal		Overflow	
057	0006	060	00252

The overflow track (25) is

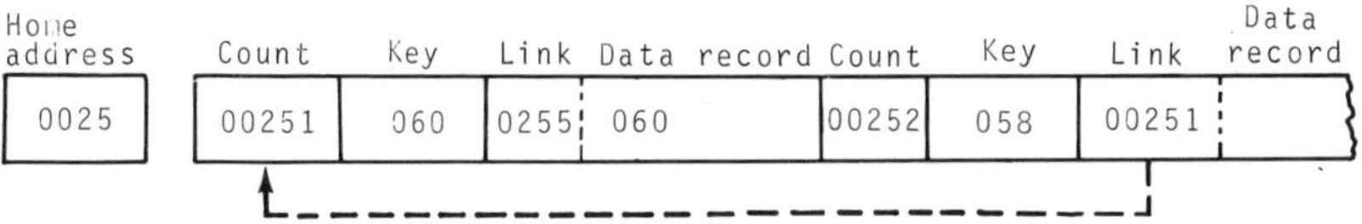

Home address	Count	Key	Link	Data record	Count	Key	Link	Data record
0025	00251	060	0255	060	00252	058	00251	

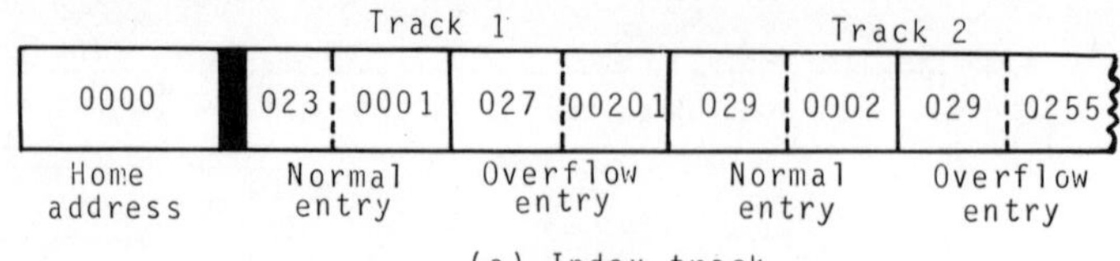

(a) Index track

This shows the first entries on the index track. There are two entries for each data track. The entries for track 1 show that overflow has occurred. The normal entry shows that the highest record on the prime track (1) is key 23. The address in the overflow entry shows the location of the lowest record key in the cylinder overflow area for track 1. Because there is only one overflow record for track 1, the address is the location of that record. The overflow address entry for the second track is set to 0255 (an end-of-chain marker), which indicates that there is no overflow for this track.

(b) First data track

The data records are recorded one after another on the track. When the file was originally loaded, the lowest record key on the track (i. e., the first record) was key 010. A subsequent addition took place, record key 009; this record was placed on the track and all other records moved up. Record key 027 was "bumped" from the end of the track and placed in the cylinder overflow area (track 20) and the index was updated accordingly.

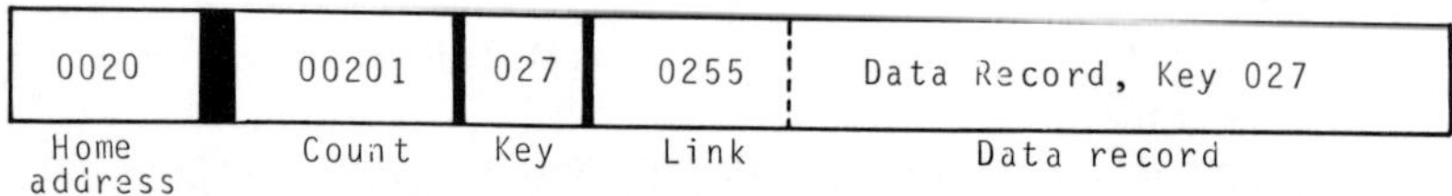

(c) Overflow track

One record is shown above (record key 027), the overflow record from the first data track. Note that the count shows that it is the first record on track 20. The link field is set to 0255 to indicate that it is the last overflow record in the chain.

Figure 7-5. Variable-Format Track Indexes: With Overflow

Record 059 is to be added. This can be done by placing the new record on track 26 and altering the links in the chain with the index entry unchanged; then the overflow track (26) is

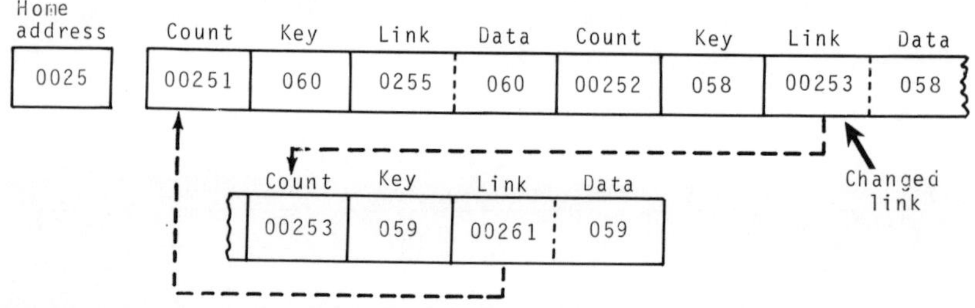

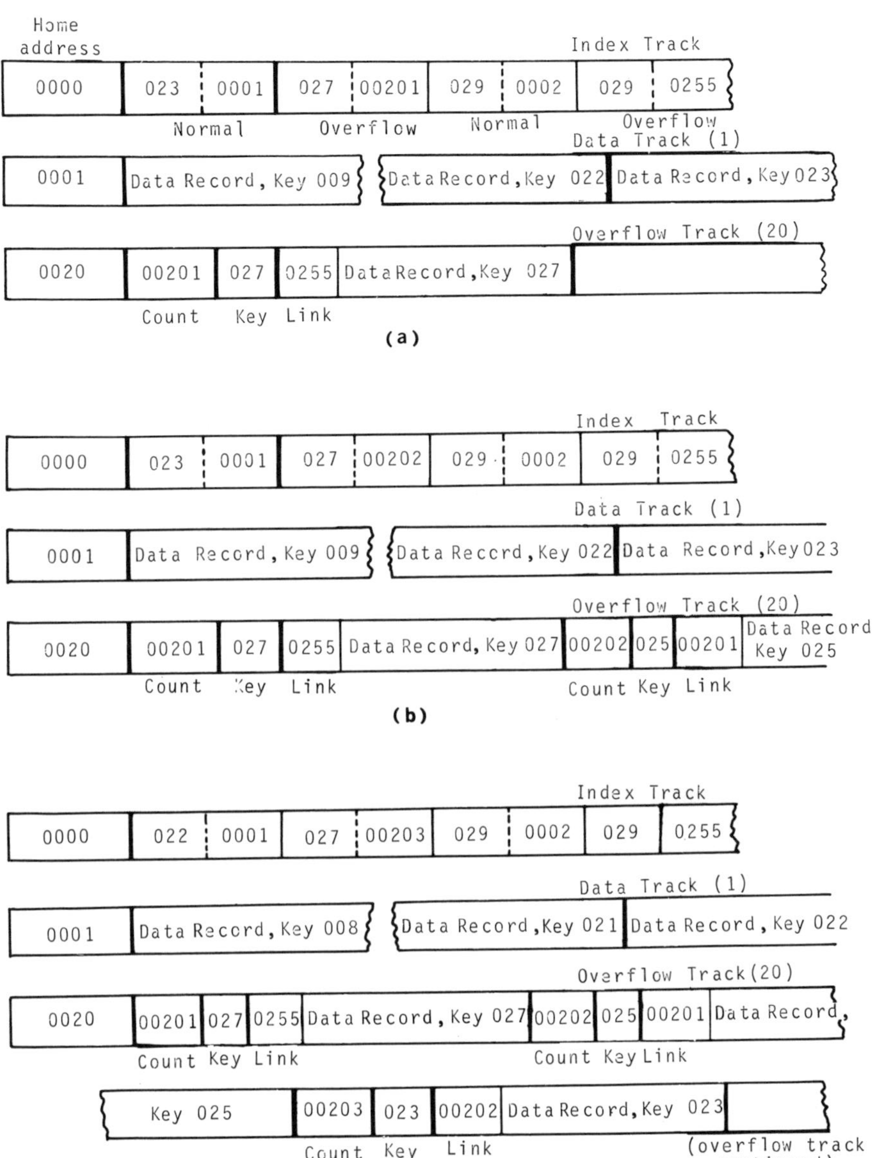

Part(a) of this figure shows the file as described in Fig.7-5; i.e.,there has been one addition. The addition was of record 009, which was put on the prime track 0001, and record 027 was bumped to the overflow track. Part(b) shows the addition of record key 025, and part(c) shows the subsequent addition of record key 008. The procedure is described in the text.

Figure 7-6. Examples of Subsequent Additions to Figure 7-5. (Not to scale.)

The principle of overflow handling by tagging in the index is thus quite simple. The normal entry records the highest key on the prime track. The overflow entry for a track shows the highest overflow record key for the track and the address of the lowest overflow record for the track. In essence, therefore, the logic of the two entries is similar. Both keys in an index entry are the highest: one for the prime track and one for the overflow chain. Both addresses in an index entry are the address of the lowest record in a location: one for the prime track (which is in effect the lowest record) and one for the lowest record in an overflow chain. By reference to these index entries, records can be retrieved in logical key sequence or, alternatively, can be retrieved directly by reference to the indexes. Because of the logic of storing additions, all records on the overflow track will be "greater than" the highest key on the prime track. This means that they will be greater than the prime index key entry. The additions will be "less than" or "equal to" the overflow key index entry. The actual logic will be considered when processing methods are described later in this chapter.

SEARCH TECHNIQUES

The procedure of matching an input key against the index entries to find the location of a specific record is called *searching*. The input key is known as the search key. There are two basic methods of searching an index, although there are many variations of these two methods. The two methods are serial searching and binary searching.

Serial Searching

The simplest way of searching an index is the serial method. The logic is shown in Fig. 7-7. This is based on a bucket approach. Similar logic is used for a variable-format track index. The search key is matched with the first index entry. If the search key is greater or less than the entry key, the address of the bucket is picked up and this is used to form the read instruction. If, on the other hand, the search key is greater than the entry key, the search key is matched against the next entry in the index. The process is repeated until a comparison gives a satisfactory match or the end of the table is reached. All indexes have some form of end-of-index marker. There are two approaches. One method is to use a maximum value as an index key entry. This means the search key will be invariably less than the last entry. The address field shows a bucket number. This means that all added records, if greater than the last proper key entry in the index, will be stored in or tagged from this bucket. If a search is made of this bucket and the record is not found, then the record is not on file. This procedure is used to avoid updating the index for each additional highest key in file. The alternative (and more common) approach is to use an end-of-index marker; this is the approach used in Fig. 7-7.

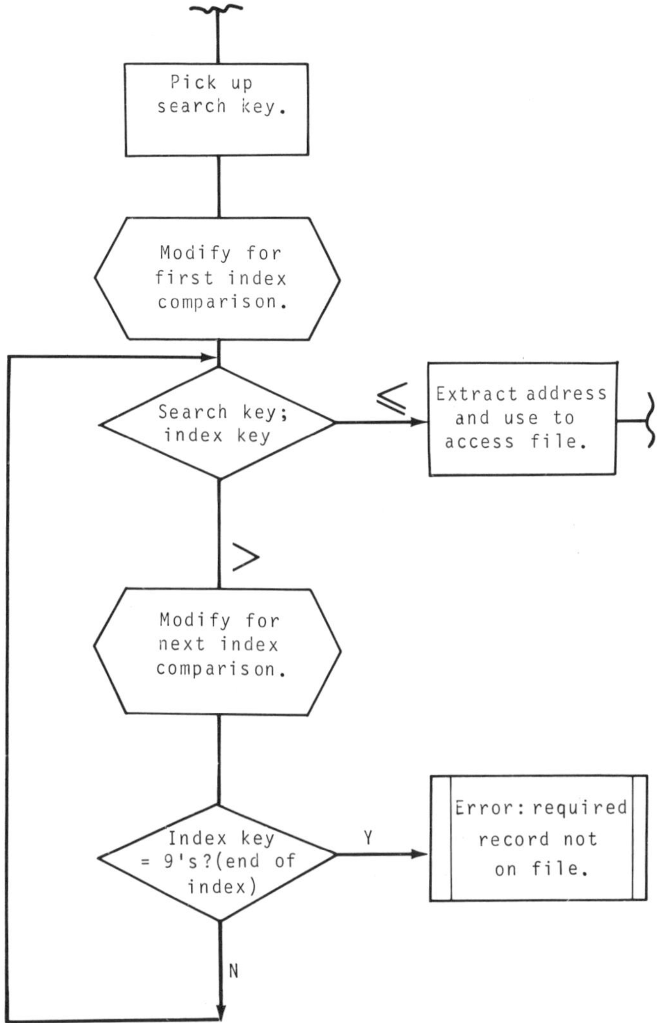

Figure 7-7. Serial Search Logic

The number of comparisons made before a selected record is found is determined by the position of the matched entry relative to the start of the table. It could be on the first entry that a match is found, or it could be on the last. The average is thus half the entries that must be compared before a match is found. In a large index used for, say, random inquiries in a fast-response system or multiple references in a batch system, the search time may become excessive when using this method. In this respect, the binary search technique is useful in cutting down index search times.

Binary Search

The logic of the binary search has far more variations than the simpler serial search. The procedure is an iterative "halving" of table size until a match is found. A simplified procedure is shown in Fig. 7-8. The first comparison is made with the midpoint entry in the index. This may be the entry required. If it is not the required entry, the next comparison determines which half of the table contains the desired record. The next match is to the midpoint of that half of the table. In this case, with an eight-entry table, the match is to find out which *quarter* of the table contains the entry, and then which *eighth* of the table contains the entry. Note that each matching operation may require *two* actual comparisons to find the required entry.

If there is an "equal to" condition, a match is found. If the result of the first comparison is "search key less than index," a comparison is made to the lower adjacent entry. If the result is now "search key greater than index entry," the preceding entry contains the required record. An example of this procedure follows:

Index key, comparison 1	*Search key*
029	
038 37	
045	

Search key is less than index entry.

Index key, comparison 2		*Search key*
0001	029 · · · · · . .	
0002	038	 37
0003	045	

The search key is greater than index entry. Therefore go back to previous entry and pick up address 0002.

Detailed processing logic for a binary search is shown in Fig. 7-9. The logic applies to an index of the form shown in Fig. 7-10. The technique uses a "counter-relative addressing" system, which may be new to nonprogrammers. A few words of explanation are thus in order before reviewing the processing logic.

Each of the index entries in Fig. 7-10 is 10 characters long. The last character in the first key in the index is called INDEX. If we refer to INDEX + 10, we thus refer to the last character of the next key entry. For example,

key	address
000461	0001

INDEX

key	address
000461	0001
000512	0002

INDEX + 10

That is,

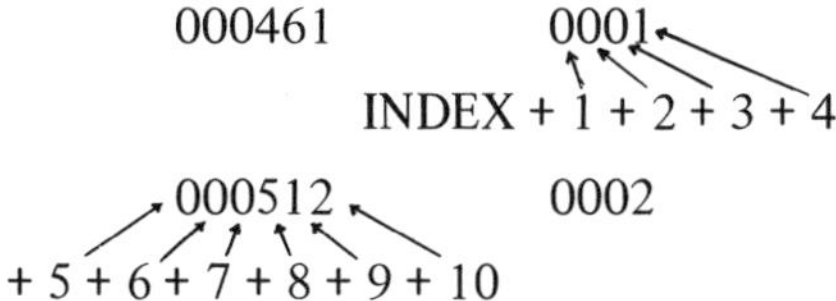

The relative addresses of the keys are shown in the left-hand column in Fig. 7-10. In the processing logic, we refer to an entry by means of INDEX + C, where C is the value set earlier in the program. Thus, if we set C equal to 70, and then refer to INDEX + C, we reference INDEX + 70, which is the midpoint of the table. There are two dummy records (one at the start of the table set to the lowest value of 000000 and one at the end of the table set to 999999). These have a special code, which is an error value. This is inspected after the address has been picked from the index. If it is an error, the appropriate procedure is taken. The following general notes clarify the operation of the logic. The italic paragraph letters are cross-references to the circled letters given in Fig. 7-9. It is stressed that the version of the logic discussed here has been chosen for ease of explanation, although it will work in practice. Many refinements may be made, which will decrease both amount of storage used and execution time.

Explanation of Operation (refer to Fig. 7-9)

(a)   This is an initializing step. The value C is set to 70; since the first time (b) is tested, reference will be made to INDEX + C = INDEX + 70, the midpoint of the index. K is a special count that is used to go up or go down the index. This is used on steps (k) and (h).

(c)   This step is performed when the first test (b) produces a "less than" condition. It modifies INDEX so that the next lower key is tested at step (d). For example,

(1) Search key 1991.

(2) First test (b) compares.

Search key: INDEX + C, where C = 70; then 1991: 1992.

This "less than" causes

(3) Subtract 10 from C. This makes C = 60.

(4) Second test (d) compares (now):

Search key = INDEX + C, where C = 60; then 1991: 1771.

(5) In this case, result is "greater than," and thus step (e) is performed.

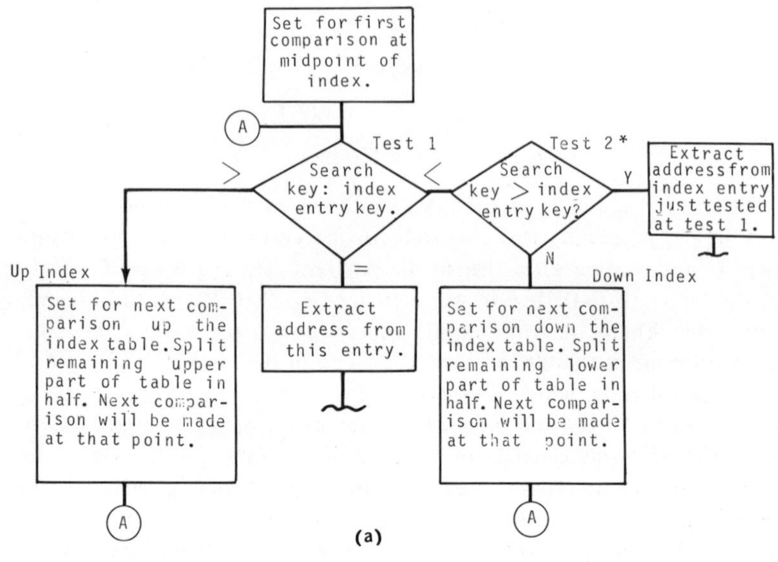

(a)

EXAMPLE 1:
Search key is 17
(home track = 007).

Key	Address	
(Dummy) 00	XXX	
02	001	
04	002	
09	003	
11	004	←(i)
14	005	
16	006	←(ii)
20	007	←(iii)
(Dummy) 99	XXX	

The first test is made at the midpoint of the index (indicated opposite by (i)). The result of the comparison at test 1 gives search key > index key. The next comparison is thus made at (ii), which is the midpoint of the remainder of the upper part of the index. This test again produces a condition where the search key is greater than the index key. The next comparison is thus made at point (iii), which is the midpoint of the remainder of the upper part of the index; i.e., the last entry. The result of this comparison is that the search key is less than the index key. A comparison (test 2) is thus made with the preceding entry. This gives a "greater than" condition; the address is thus extracted from the entry previously tested at test 1. (Test 2 is shown opposite by means of the dotted line.)

EXAMPLE 2: Search key is 03 (home track = 002).

Key	Address	
(Dummy) 00	XXX	
02	001	←⋯
04	002	←(ii)
09	003	
11	004	←(i)
14	005	
16	006	
20	007	
(Dummy) 99	XXX	

The first test is made at the midpoint of the index (indicated opposite by (i)). The result of the comparison at test 1 gives search key < index key. Test 2 is then carried out on the preceding index entry; the result of this test is that the index is halved downward. The next test 1 is at point (ii). This produces a search key less than index key condition so that test 2 is made at the preceding entry (indicated by the dotted line). This test results in a "greater than" comparison and the address is extracted from the entry (ii).

(b)

* The logic shown in part (a) has been very much simplified and **must** be read in conjunction with the examples shown in part (b). This test is "search key > adjacent previous index entry."

In part (b) examples are shown of a binary search made on a simple 7-entry index (with high and low dummies at either end). The logic used here should be followed through on part (a).

Figure 7-8. Binary Search: Simplified Logic

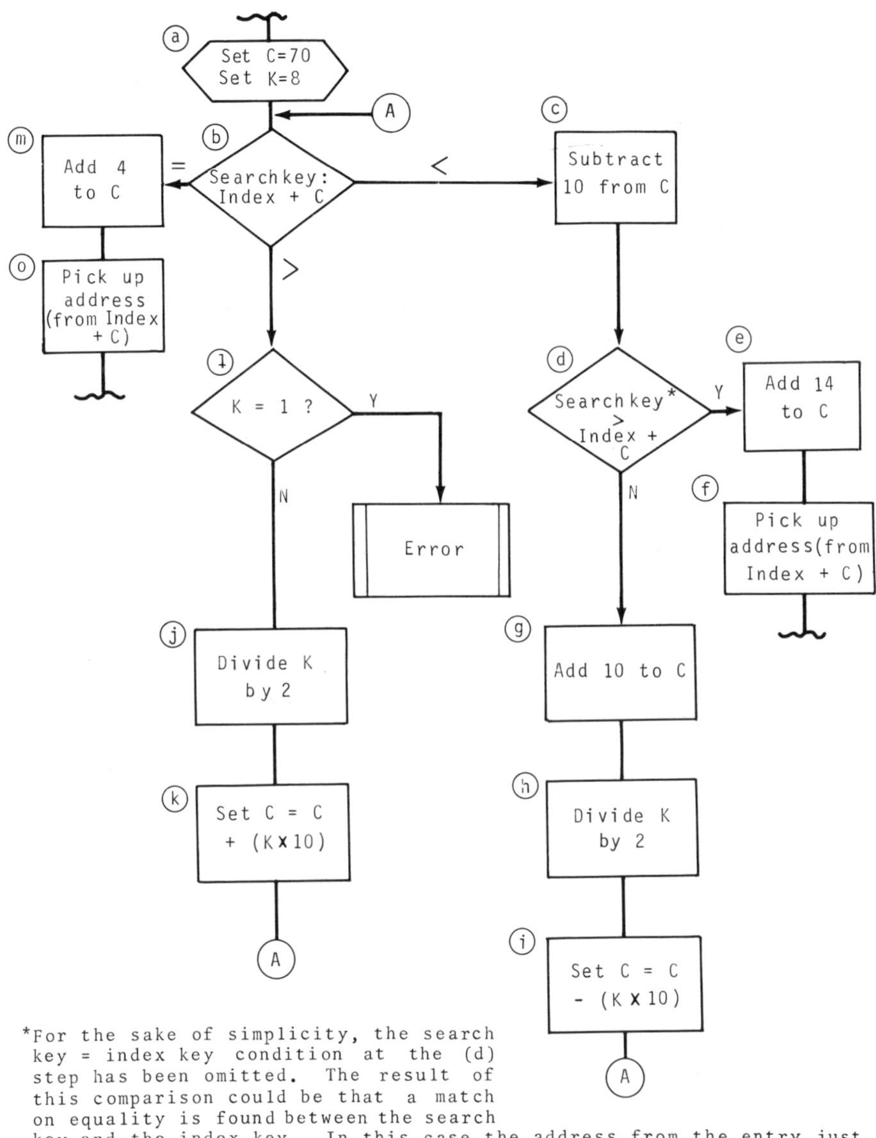

*For the sake of simplicity, the search key = index key condition at the (d) step has been omitted. The result of this comparison could be that a match on equality is found between the search key and the index key. In this case the address from the entry just tested would be extracted. To complete the logic, therefore, an additional test is required at this point if the "no" branch is taken. If equality was found, then steps (m) and (o) should be taken.

Figure 7-9. Binary Search: Processing Logic

```
            Key    |Address
          Field    |Field
          000000 XXXX  ◄──── "Low dummy"
Index     000461 0001
  +10     000512 0002
  +20     000844 0003
  +30     000998 0004
  +40     001321 0005
  +50     001542 0006
  +60     001771 0007
  +70     001992 0008
  +80     002273 0009
  +90     002488 0010
 +100     002751 0011
 +110     003009 0012
 +120     003111 0013
 +130     003771 0014
 +140     004210 0015
 +150     004371 0016
          999999 XXXX ◄──── "High dummy"
```

This is an example index used with the binary search technique shown in Fig. 7-9. The "low dummy" will have a relative address of INDEX— 10. The "high dummy" will have a relative address of INDEX + 160.

Figure 7-10. Binary Search: Index

(*e*)   This sets C so that INDEX + C references the address field of the matched entry. Continuing the example given above,

> (6) Result of comparison (*d*) means that desired record 1991 is on previous tested entry. C was previously modified to 60 (on step 3). Adding 14 to C gives 74; INDEX + 74 refers to the appropriate address field (0008).

> (7) Now INDEX + C is used to extract the address field on step (*f*).

(*g*)   This step is done if the tested entry (INDEX + C on step (*d*)) does not indicate that a match has been found. The addition of 10 to C resets C to its value when test (*b*) was performed.

(*h*), (*i*)   This simple procedure enables a step to be made *down* the index. K was originally set to 8 on step (*a*). Assume that the search key is 000461. The values of C and K will be as follows:

	C	K	
First test at (*b*)	70	8	INDEX + 70
First (*h*)	70	4	$(\frac{8}{2})$
First (*i*)	30	4	70 – (4 × 10)
Second test at (*b*)	30	4	INDEX + 30
Second (*h*)	30	2	$(\frac{4}{2})$
Second (*i*)	10	2	30 – (2 × 10)

		C	*K*	
Third test at (*b*)		10	2	INDEX + 10
Third (*h*)		10	1	($\frac{2}{2}$)
Third (*i*)		0	1	10 − (1 × 10)
Fourth test at (*b*)				INDEX + 0: Test gives equality.

(*j*), (*k*) These two steps operate in much the same manner as (*h*) and (*i*), but they modify *C* so that we go *up* the index. For example, assume that the search key is 004210. The values of *C* and *K* will be as follows:

	C	*K*	
First test at (*b*)	70	8	INDEX + 70
First (*j*)	70	4	($\frac{8}{2}$)
First (*k*)	110	4	70 + (4 × 10)
Second test at (*b*)	110	4	INDEX + 110
Second (*j*)	110	2	($\frac{4}{2}$)
Second (*k*)	130	2	110 + (2 × 10)
Third test at (*b*)	130	2	INDEX + 130
Third (*j*)	130	1	($\frac{2}{2}$)
Third (*k*)	140	1	130 + (1 × 10)
Fourth test at (*b*)	140	1	INDEX + 140: Test gives equality.

(*l*) This test prevents going over the top of the table. Suppose the search key was 004215. This is not on the file, since 4210 is shown as the highest key. A test is made at (*b*); *C* = 140, *K* = 1. The result at (*b*) is "greater than" (004215: 004210). The test at (*l*), with *K* = 1, gives an error condition.

(*m*) This is a modification of *C* to enable the address field to be accessed in much the same manner as step (*c*).

To prove the logic to find a record, say, search key 00310, the reader is invited to "walk through" the logic, noting the values of *C* and *K*. Note the importance of the first dummy record, key 000000. This record contains the lowest possible value key. If record 000011 is being sought, a comparison will be made of search key against INDEX + 0. This will result in a "less than" condition. The steps (*c*) and (*d*) will be performed. This produces (at step (*d*)), a comparison of search key against INDEX − 10, which is the dummy

000000. This will result in a "greater than" condition, which causes the address field at INDEX + 4 to be extracted.

The use of binary searching has distinct advantages over ordinary serial searching. It will be remembered that the maximum search in serial searching is the total number of entries compared; the average is half the number of entries compared. By use of the binary search technique, however, the maximum length of search will be $\log_2 N$, where N is the number of entries in the index. Theoretically, therefore, the maximum length of search in a 16-entry index, as in Fig. 7-10, is 4 (i.e., $2^4 = 16$). Similarly,

$$32 \text{ entries} = \text{maximum search of 5 entries}$$

$$64 \text{ entries} = \text{maximum search of 6 entries}$$

$$\cdot \qquad \cdot$$

$$\cdot \qquad \cdot$$

$$\cdot \qquad \cdot$$

$$2048 \text{ entries} = \text{maximum search of 11 entries, etc.}$$

The number of comparisons given here is, in fact, the number of tests made at step (b) of the flowchart shown in Fig. 7-9. (That is, the number of "lower record entry" comparisons made at step (d) has been ignored.) The *average* number of comparisons for a binary search is marginally lower than the maximum. For example,

$$32 \text{ entries} = \text{average search of 4.22 entries}$$

$$64 \text{ entries} = \text{average search of 5.12 entries}$$

$$\cdot \qquad \cdot$$

$$\cdot \qquad$$

$$\cdot$$

$$2048 \text{ entries} = \text{average search of 10.01 entries}$$

For a 2048-entry index, serial and binary search comparisons may be contrasted thus:

Serial search		*Binary search*	
Minimum	1	Minimum	1
Average	1024	Average	10.01
Maximum	2048	Maximum	11

In practice, it is necessary to insert dummies to build up the number of index entries to a power of 2 (± 1, depending on the search logic being used). The binary search technique is thus eminently suitable for searching large indexes for random inquiry processing in fast-response systems. As will be shown later, serial searching has advantages in systems where the input search keys are in the same sequence as the main file.

Activity Index Loading

Index loading is a special modification of the serial search technique. It is based on building an index that has, as the first entries, the most sought after records. One method of operation adds an additional field to each index entry. This is the *activity count*. In the following example, the activity count is two digits long:

<pre>
lowest key   highest key   address
  004290   004321   0001 00
                                           activity count
</pre>

Each time a search key is matched against the entry and the address is extracted, one is added to the activity count. Periodically, the index is read off the device and sorted by key within activity count. This places the most requested records at the beginning of the index. The file is still stored sequentially by logical key, but the index is now no longer in this key sequence. This, however, does not matter as long as there is only one key stored in the index entry. (There must thus be one index entry per key for the whole or part of the entire file.) This technique is suitable for files in fast-response inquiry systems where the difference in activity for records is pronounced. The disadvantage is, of course, in the increased internal storage required for larger index entries.

PROCESSING METHODS

There are three main ways in which an indexed-sequential file can be processed. These are shown in Table 7-1. The timing of the various approaches is discussed below. A comparison is made at the end of this chapter, together with a summary of the advantages and disadvantages of each method.

Sequential Processing

This is the same as that discussed in Chapter 6. Because the file is stored in logical key sequence, it is possible to read the records, record by record, in key sequence. If the bucket approach is used, tags will be followed as they are en-

Table 7-1. Summary of Indexed-Sequential Processing Methods

Indexes	Input Sorted to Same Sequence as Main File	Input Unsorted
Need not be used*	*Sequential*	Difficult/impossible
Used for selected record retrieval	*Selective-sequential*	*Random*

*Indexes are not required for sequential processing on a file structured by using a bucket approach with overflow tags in buckets. Indexes *will* be required if a variable-format track index is used, since the tags are, in effect, contained in the overflow entries in the index.

countered. If the file uses a variable-format track index, the overflow tags are picked up from the index or the link fields in the records in overflow area(s).

The principle of sequential processing of such a file is as follows: The highest level of index is read once at the beginning of processing to locate the start of the file area. The general procedure is shown in Fig. 7-11. The overflow entry, if not the end of the chain (0255), is used to pick up the first overflow record for that track. The addressed record will be "greater than" the last prime record from the home track and the lowest record in the chain.

The link addresses in the overflow record chain are as follows: When the end of the chain is reached, the first record on the next track is read and so on. The records are thus presented to the user in logical key sequence. The timing will be similar to that discussed in Chapter 6 ("A Bucket Approach") except that

> One seek is required for each prime track.
>
> Two seeks are required for each record in the independent overflow area (one to get the record, and one to return to the prime track).
>
> One read is made for each record or block of records.
>
> One write is made for each updated record (if updating is being performed).
>
> One read is made for each pair of entries in the track indexes.

If the records are unblocked, then every hit record will result in a write. If records are blocked, then the rule-of-thumb procedure given in Chapter 6, "A Bucket Approach," can be used to estimate the number of blocks hit.

If the overflow for a file occurs to the extent that records are placed in the independent overflow area, processing time may be increased considerably. The extent of overflow must therefore be carefully monitored so that the file can be periodically reorganized to minimize overflow processing time.

Selective-Sequential Processing and Random Processing

This processing is the direct retrieval of selected records, *with the input records in the same sequence as the main file.* Contrast this with random processing, which is the direct retrieval of selected records *with the input records in random (unsorted) key order.*

As will be demonstrated, there are inherent timing advantages in the selective-sequential mode of processing. Because the input is in the same sequence as the main file, the retrieval updating program is working progressively *forward* through the file. This minimizes the number of index reads and the number of track or block reads. For example, suppose that there are three input records

$$01714$$
$$01723$$
$$01725$$

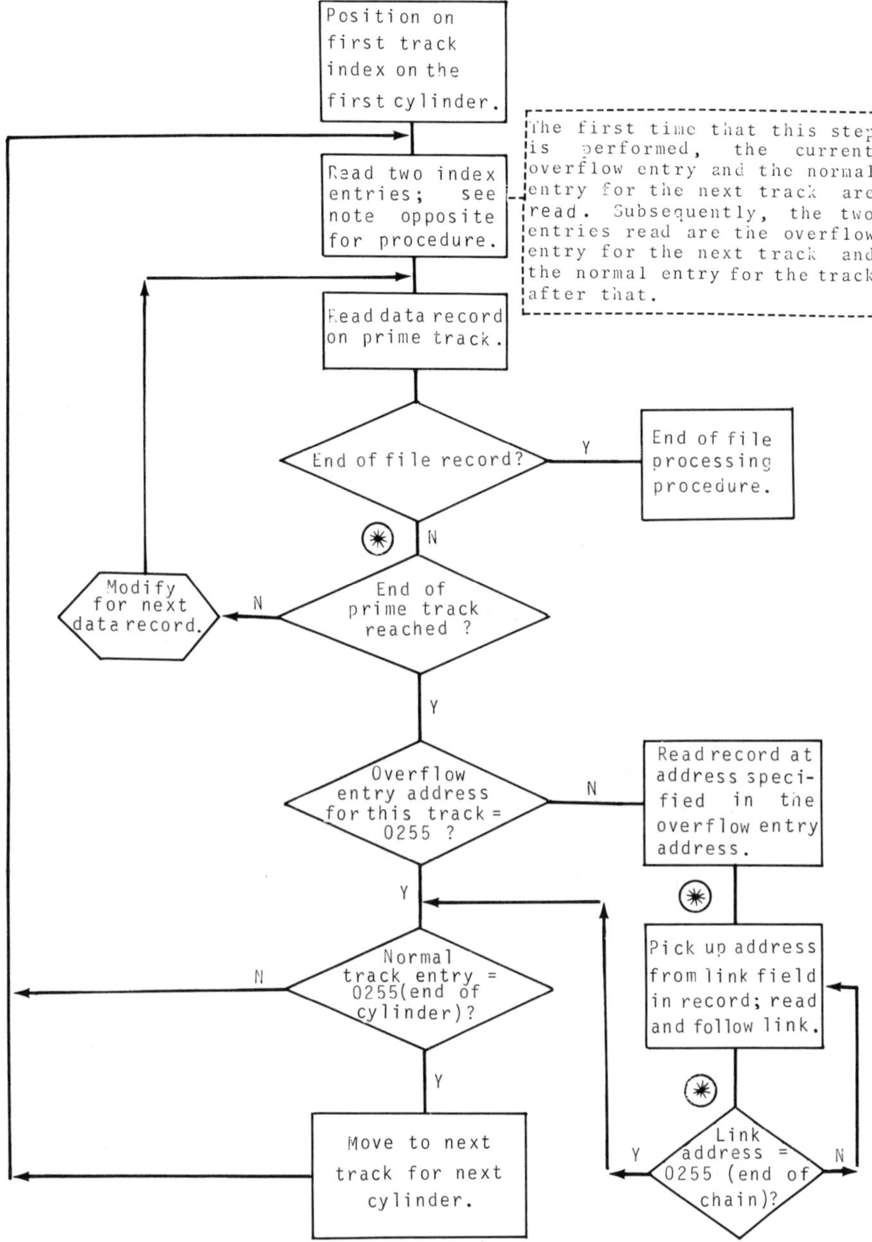

Note: The circled asterisk indicates that at this point in the process, the record is subjected to some user processing (not shown in this flowchart).

Figure 7-11. Sequential Processing of a Variable-Format Track File (with Indexes)

and masters for all these records are held in the same block. Only one index read will be required to locate the block that holds record 0 1 7 1 4, and only one read is needed to bring that block into core. All three input records can then be processed without any further reads.

For random processing, on the other hand, each record will have to be treated independently of any other record. There *may* be the case that two records are in sequence, but this cannot be relied upon for timing purposes. Each input record may therefore result in at least one index read, followed by a data read, followed by a data write.

Selective-Sequential Timing

The characteristics upon which processing depends fall into two groups. The first group is the actual hardware timing details of the device. The second set of details is the storage characteristics of the file.

The *device timing*, which must be known, is as follows:

1. *Minimum seek time:* This will be used for changing from cylinder to cylinder. Because the input is in the file key sequence, the heads (on, say, an exchangeable disk store), will be moving progressively through the device. The only exception to this will be access to the independent overflow area to retrieve records (if any). For this, average seek time will need to be used.

2. *Read time:* This depends upon whether a bucket or variable-format track device is being used. The read time should include average latency.

3. *Write time:* Same condition as for read time. Many devices permit a write/verify mode. This causes a read of the data just written; the read-after-write is used to check that the data has been properly recorded.

The *file structure information* must include the following:

1. *Number of input records:* The number of input records (transactions) is crucial in determining process time. If processing takes place in batches, it is advisable to do *two* file timings. One timing is based on the maximum number of transactions ("worst case") and one based on the average, i.e., "most common" number of transactions.

2. *Number of cylinders hit:* This is the number of times a seek is made to a new cylinder. The factors determining the number of cylinders hit are as follows:

    Number of transactions

    Number of cylinders

Number of records per cylinder

Distribution of input over cylinders (i.e., any bias in the pattern of input transactions)

3. *Number of data areas hit:* This is the number of tracks, buckets, or blocks that have input records to be applied to them. Again, this is a function of

number of transactions,

number of data areas (buckets, tracks, blocks, etc),

number of records per data area, and

distribution of input over data areas (i.e., any bias in the pattern of input transactions).

In addition to these factors, the incidence of overflow will be important. This will be discussed later.

With the exception of very large files, or where internal storage is severely restricted, the cylinder-level index will generally be stored in core for the whole of the processing run. Where the index is segmented, one index read will have to be assumed for each segment. This will be (in most cases) negligible. The major part of the timing will be based on reading tracks or buckets.

For each cylinder that has at least one record to be applied, there will be one read of the track/bucket level index. For each track/bucket/block that has at least one record to be applied, there will be a read and a write or write/verify. The timing formula is

$$\text{Total time} = \text{data time} + \text{index time}$$

in which

$$\text{Data time} = (C_h \times S_m) + [B_h \times (B_r + B_w)]$$

where: C_h = cylinders hit
S_m = minimum seek time
B_h = track/buckets hit
B_r = track/bucket read time
B_w = track/bucket write time

Note in this formula that tracks and buckets have been used; however, it applies equally to blocks, etc.

Index time will depend upon the number of levels of index used. Assuming the use of a bucket/track level index,

$$\text{Index time} = C_h \times B_r$$

where: C_h = cylinders hit
B_r = track/bucket read time

The most difficult factor to estimate is the number of hits, on cylinders or buckets/tracks. If there is a "bias" of hits due to the characteristics of the data itself, and it is possible to determine what this bias is, it may be used in estimating the hits. An alternative approach is to assume a random distribution of input transactions over the file and to use a statistical approach. It is assumed that each record in the file stands an equal chance of being hit as any other record. In turn, this means that each cylinder/bucket/track in the file stands an equal chance of containing a record that matches an input transaction. Figures and tables in Appendix B may be used to *estimate* the number of storage areas hit. A comprehensive timing example is shown in Fig. 7-12(a).

In practice, the use of minimum seek time in a large file (i.e., many cylinders) with few transactions will give an incorrect result. It is better in this case to use an estimated time nearer average seek time.

One point must also be made here on the type of index search procedure used. For selective-sequential processing, a serial search technique is generally the best approach because of the "progressively forward" nature of the input. Some systems use a freeze technique. Because the next search key to be applied to the index will always be up the index, a pointer is used to record the last index entry tested. Further searches take place from the entry indicated by the pointer, rather than from the start of the index.

Random Processing: Timing

For random processing, each input transaction is independent of the preceding or following key. Only when the number of input transactions is high, relative to the number of main file cylinders/tracks, can it be assumed that more than one contiguous input relates to one file location. For example, if ten transactions are to be applied to a two-cylinder file, it is reasonable to assume that a number of adjacent transactions apply to one cylinder. If, on the other hand, ten transactions are to be applied to a 100-cylinder file, the chances of two or more adjacent transactions being applied to the same cylinder are far more remote. By and large, therefore, it is relatively safe to assume that each input transaction will result in a seek, an index read, a data read, and a data write.

A rule-of-thumb approach is to assume that the number of seeks is equal to

$$1 + \left[T\left(1 - \frac{1}{C}\right) \right]$$

where T is the number of transactions and C is the number of cylinders occupied by the file. It can be seen that T must be very large compared with C before the rule of "one input = one seek" is altered.

The basic timing formula is thus

$$(C_h \times S_t) + [T \times (B_{dr} + B_{dw})] + T \times B_{ir}$$

where: C_h = cylinders hit (as described above)

S_t = seek time (see below)

T = number of transactions

B_{dr} = data track/bucket read time

B_{dw} = data track/bucket write time

B_{ir} = index track/bucket read time

```
Device: cylinder/bucket method used | File: cylinder-level index
        exchangeable disk store     |       bucket-level indexes
        seek time: minimum: 30 ms   |       60,000 records
                   average: 85 ms   |       10 records to a bucket
                   maximum:145 ms   |       60 buckets to a cylinder
        bucket read time: 25 ms     |       100 cylinders for file
        bucket write time: 50 ms    |       6000 buckets for data
        (inc. verification)         |       100 buckets for track-
        latency: 12.5 ms            |       level indexes
```

```
Input: 10,000 transactions to be posted to the file, sorted to
       the same sequence as the main file. Assume random
       distribution of input. Also assume that no main file
       overflow records are involved.
```

```
Timing: Index time = cylinders hit × bucket read time
Formula:Data time =(cylinders hit × minimum seek time)
        + (buckets hit × (bucket read time + bucket write time))
```

```
Hits:  10,000 transactions over 100 cylinders = 100 cylinders hit
       10,000 transactions over 6000 buckets  = 4500 buckets hit
```

Actual file timing

```
Index time = 100×37.5 ms = 4 s
Data time =(100× 30 ms) = 3 s
          + 4500  × (37.5 + 62.5) = 7 min 30 s
          Total time = 7 min 40 s
```

```
Additional Processing Time(not shown) Will Be Required For
    Reading 10,000 Record Input Transaction File.
```

(a) Selective-sequential processing example

```
Device: as in part (a).     |     File: as in part (a).
```

```
Input: 5000 input transactions, unsorted.
```

Hits: Number of seeks $= 1 + T\left(1 - \dfrac{1}{C}\right) = 1 + 5000\left(1 - \dfrac{1}{100}\right)$

$\qquad\qquad\qquad\qquad = 4951$

Number of data buckets read/written = 5000

Actual file timing:

```
Seeks time = number of seeks × average seek time
           = 4951× 85 ms = 7 min
Index time = 4951 × 37.5 ms = 3 min 6 s
Data time  = 5000×100.0 ms = 8 min 20 s

    Total time = 18 min 26 s
```

Additional processing time same as in part (a).

(b) Random processing example

Figure 7-12. Indexed-Sequential Processing Timing

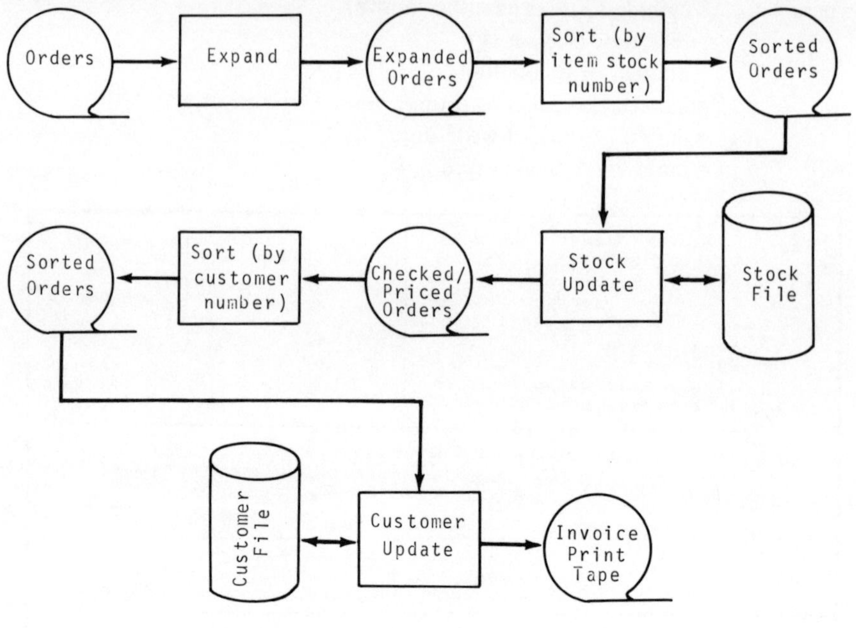

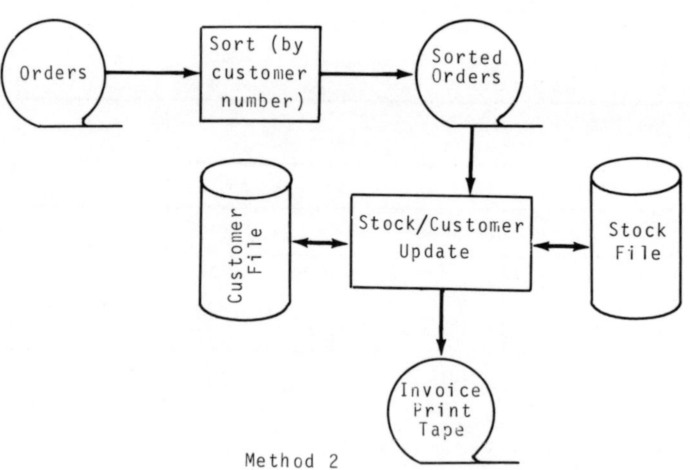

(c) Comparison of selective-sequential processing, with sorting, and random processing without sorting

Figure 7-12. (Continued)

The seek time used—minimum, average, maximum—will depend upon the number of cylinders in the file. If the file occupies only a few cylinders, then the seek time used is lower than that for a file with a large number of cylinders. A comprehensive timing example is shown in Fig. 7-12(b), and is diagrammed in Fig. 7-12(c).

OVERFLOW HANDLING

The additional timing for overflow record retrieval will be similar to that discussed for a sequentially processed file as discussed in the section "Processing Overflow," Chapter 6. Some summary notes of special cases in an indexed-sequential file are discussed below.

Bucket Approach

One additional bucket read/write is required for each record retrieved from the cylinder overflow area. If the record is in the independent overflow area, then there will be one additional seek. If selective-sequential processing is being used, then the provision for a number of bucket input areas is very useful. For example, three bucket areas could be used: one for the prime bucket, one for the current bucket index, and one for the current overflow bucket. Timing advantages when using this three-bucket system during random processing will be minimal.

Variable-Format Track Approach

There will be *at least* one additional read for a record in the cylinder overflow area. Because of the link-address system, the record required could be at the start of the chain (best case) or at the end of the chain (worst case). An average should therefore be used, based on the most common length of chain.

The amount of overflow and the importance of monitoring with a view to periodic reorganization is the same as that described for a sequential file (see "Monitoring Insertions and Overflows," in Chapter 6).

SYSTEMS CONSIDERATIONS

The indexed-sequential method of processing is the most versatile method of structuring direct access files. It permits sequential, selective-sequential, or random file processing. What are the problems in using such a file? The first and most obvious is the storage overhead for storing the indexes and the time required for creating and maintaining the indexes. To a certain extent, a bucket approach with overflow chaining is more efficient than the variable-format track approach because the latter may require a modification to the index for an insertion record and the maintenance of the link fields.

Most prewritten software will include programs/instructions that permit index creation on file loading and automatic index searching for retrieval. To a large extent, therefore, the systems development time for indexed-sequential versus straight sequential is not that excessive. Certainly, program testing and systems testing take longer for an indexed-sequential file. This time penalty occurs because indexes and dummy indexes for file test data take longer to prepare for a structured than for a straight sequential file. Timing will play a large part in the decision of sequential versus indexed-sequential versus random. In some cases, the decision as to which approach is to be used is dictated by the characteristics of the system. For example, sequential processing is used when a sequential report has to be prepared with a very high hit rate of the file records. Similarly, random processing is essential for individual or small batches of inquiries.

Interesting problems arise when there is a systems processing choice between sequential and selective-sequential, or between selective-sequential and random. Let us consider some timing comparisons of different processing methods. As demonstrated earlier, the hit rate of "number of file records" hit is *less* important than number of device storage areas hit, e.g., number of cylinders hit, number of tracks hit, number of buckets hit, etc. The smaller the device storage space occupied by the file, the higher the hit rate. As an example, consider a bucket device with a file stored

> 8 records to a bucket
> 64 buckets to a cylinder
> 100 cylinders in file

This gives 512 records per cylinder, or 51,200 records in file. This file structure is the first attempt by the designer in the iterative process of file design. There are 60 transactions to be applied on one run. This, by the use of statistical techniques, gives an estimate of about 46 cylinders hit, 60 buckets hit.

The designer considers the rate of insertions; the file is very volatile, with many insertions at random over the file. He therefore decides to consider loading the records at less than eight to a bucket. He decides to use a loading factor of 50 percent, i.e., to put only half the number of records in a bucket. This enlarges the storage area occupied by the file; in this case, the number of buckets per cylinder is to be kept fixed at 64 and the number of cylinders doubled. This gives

> 4 records per bucket
> 64 buckets per cylinder
> 200 cylinders in file

With 60 transactions, the estimated hit rates are 55 cylinders and 60 buckets. Conversely, from the starting point of eight records per bucket, the designer may inspect the content of the file record and decide that some data in the record is redundant. By judiciously "pruning," the record size is reduced so that at a loading factor of 100 percent, the file is stored

16 records per bucket
64 buckets per cylinder
50 cylinders in file

With 60 transactions, the estimated hit rates are 38 cylinders and 60 buckets.

Small figures have been used here to demonstrate the impact of file size on hit rate. If the values given above are uniformly multiplied tenfold, say, there will be a radical difference in seek time.

The principle of minimizing processing time is to maximize the loading factor and reduce the space occupied by the file. Against this, however, are two vital considerations. Maximizing the loading factor may cause overflow for every record insertion other than those records inserted at the end of the file. Reducing record sizes to a minimum can cut processing time, but it may cause processing problems in the system as a whole. For example, file record X is part of a very large file. Examination of the record X shows its content to be

$$A \quad B \quad C \quad D$$

Items A are used in process 1.
Items B are used in processes 1 and 2.
Items C are used in processes 2 and 3.
Items D are used in process 4.

Items D are longest. The creation of a number of files rather than one large file will certainly reduce individual process times. However, the insertion of a new record X will need an "explosion" of one input to a number of files. The size of the file—by loading factor and record size—is thus crucial to file timing.

Random processing can occur on a batch of data that is in a different sequence to that of a main file to which the records are to be applied. Two example approaches (Methods 1 and 2) are shown in Fig. 7-12(c). Input orders are to be matched against two files:

Stock file: to reduce stock, and price items

Customer file: to pick up name and address and to post customer balances

The first task must be the stock file access. The approach shown in Fig. 7-12(c), Method 1, is similar to the tape-based system shown in Fig. 1-6. The accepted input is expanded and sorted to stock item number. It is then matched, selective-sequentially, against the stock file. The file is then re-sorted to customer account and the orders are matched against the customer file selective-sequentially.

The alternative approach in Fig. 7-12(c), Method 2, is radically different. For user purposes, the output is required in customer account number sequence and therefore the input is sorted into that sequence. The stock file is accessed with the item codes in random order. The customer file is accessed on the same run. This file is updated selective-sequentially.

Let us now stipulate sizes of the files and time the principle runs for comparison. The comparison is between the two methods of Fig. 7-12(c);

Method 1	*Method 2*
Expansion and sort by item number (tape)	Sort by customer number (tape)
Sequential stock update	Random stock update
Sort by customer number (tape)	Selective-sequential customer update
Selective-sequential customer update	

File Sizes

The file sizes are as follows: The input order record ranges in size from 200 characters to 600 characters; an average of 420 will be used for timing purposes. There are an average of 200 orders per day, with an average of 50 items per order. The two files are

1. *Stock file:*
   150,000 records
      3 records per bucket
      100 buckets per cylinder
      500 cylinders in file (50,000 buckets in file)

   File indexed with cylinder and bucket level indexes (by item number)

2. *Customer file:*
   15,000 records
      1 record per bucket
      50 buckets per cylinder
      300 cylinders in file (15,000 buckets in file)

   File indexed with cylinder and bucket-level indexes (by customer number)

Operational Device Runs

Seek time:	minimum	= 30 ms
	average	= 85 ms
	maximum	= 145 ms

Read bucket	= 25 ms
Write/verify bucket	= 50 ms
Average latency	= 12.5 ms

Method 1.   From Fig. 7-12(c), the timings are as follows:
   Expansion and sort: 6 min

Selective-sequential stock file update:

200 orders × 50 items = 10,000 items/day against 500 cylinders

Cylinders hit = 500 (from Appendix B)
   10,000 items against 50,000 buckets
Buckets hit = 9000 (from Appendix B)

Timing (rounded):

500 seeks = (500 × 30 ms for minimum seek)	= 15 s
500 index bucket reads = (500 × 37.5 ms for read + latency)	= 20 s
9000 data bucket reads = (9000 × 37.5 ms for read + latency)	= 5 min, 40 s
9000 data bucket write/verifies = (9000 × 62.5 ms for write + latency)	= 9 min, 20 s
Total time	= 15½ min

Sort = 2 min
Selective-sequential customer file update:
   200 orders per day against 300 cylinders
Cylinders hit = 195 (from Appendix B)
   200 orders against 15,000 buckets
Buckets hit = 200 (from Appendix B)

Timing (rounded):

195 seeks = (195 × 30 ms for minimum seek)	= 6 s
195 index bucket reads = (195 × 37.5 ms for read + latency)	= 7 s
200 data bucket reads = (200 × 37.5 ms for read + latency)	= 7.5 s
200 data bucket write/verifies = (200 × 62.5 ms for write + latency)	= 12.5 s
Total time	= 33 s

The total of these times is 24 minutes.

To keep the problem simple, a number of additional times have been ignored. These include the reading of the transaction order file, the printing of invoices, etc. One of the major timing elements omitted is *the operator setup times for each run.* The time derived above will, however, serve for a comparison with the processing in Fig. 7-12(c) for Method 2.

Method 2.   From Fig. 7-12(c),
   Sort = 2 min
Random stock update:

200 orders × 50 items = 10,000 items

$$\text{Number of hits} = 1\left[T\left(1 - \frac{1}{C}\right)\right] \quad \text{or}$$

$$1 + 10,000\left(1 - \frac{1}{500}\right) = 9981 \text{ seeks}$$

Timing = 9981 $\times$ 80 ms for average seek = 13 min, 15 s

$$
\begin{aligned}
9981 \text{ index bucket reads} \quad &= 6 \text{ min, } 10 \text{ s}\\
10,000 \text{ data bucket reads} &= 6 \text{ min, } 15 \text{ s}\\
10,000 \text{ data write/verifies} &= 10 \text{ min, } 25 \text{ s}\\
\textit{Total time} \quad\quad\quad &= 36 \text{ min}
\end{aligned}
$$

Selective-sequential customer file update (same for Method 1)
= 33 s

The total time for this method is thus 34½ minutes. A detailed comparison of times follows:

Method 1		*Method 2*	
Expansion and sort	= 6 min	Sort	= 2 min
Stock update	= 15½ min	Stock update	= 36 min
Sort	= 2 min		
Customer update	= ½ min	Customer update	= ½ min
Total	= 24 min		= 38½ min

When the additional transaction and print times are considered, we could well have a break-even situation on timing. The additions of the operator setup times would probably mean that Method 2 is a fair solution.

In this type of situation, the reduction of sort times to resequence input may well be offset by the increased random processing time.

CHAPTER 8

RANDOM STORAGE AND RANDOM ACCESS

THE BASIC METHOD

In Chapters 6 and 7, sequential methods of storage have been considered. In these methods the records are stored in a device in ascending sequence by record key. It was demonstrated that records can be accessed either sequentially (i.e., one record at a time, one record after another in key sequence) or selectively by means of indexes. In this chapter, we discuss a radically different method of storage and retrieval, namely, storing data that is *not* in sequence by key, and the accessing of records by a calculation process rather than by the use of indexes. In the United Kingdom this method of storing and accessing records is commonly called *address generation* or *indirect addressing*; in the United States it is known as *randomizing* or *key transformation*.

Address generation is the computation of a direct access storage device address from a record key:

The location of a record is determined by the address generation algorithm. Contrast this to sequential storage, in which the location of a record is simply determined by the position of the key in relation to the preceding and succeeding keys. In address generation, the "sequence" of the records in the device is determined by the algorithm, not by the sequence of the file keys. Because the address generation algorithm is used to assign a record to a location in a device, the same computational procedure may be used to locate and retrieve a selected record after it has been stored. To demonstrate how address generation works, let us review a similar (but very much simpler) approach: self-indexing, or direct addressing.

It will be remembered that in self-indexing the key is used to form the device address of where the record is stored. It was pointed out that self-indexing can become a viable proposition where

> one record is stored in each device storage location.

> the range of the keys is similar to the range of addresses (i.e., a four-digit key is used to give a four-digit storage location address).

> the keys in the file are consecutive, without the clusters and gaps formed by the characteristics of the keys themselves or by the addition or deletion of keys.

The last point is the most important with regard to the characteristics of keys found in practice. It is rare indeed that a file consists of a numerically sequenced set of keys with no gaps in sequence. As a file ages, keys are often deleted, and this in itself results in gaps in the sequence. Similarly, keys are often added to the end of a file. If one can imagine the creation of a new file in which numbers (keys) are issued in a purely chronological sequence, at the inception of the file it may consist of ten keys:

$$
\begin{array}{c}
0 \\
1 \\
2 \\
3 \\
4 \\
5 \\
6 \\
7 \\
8 \\
9
\end{array}
$$

A year later, the file may have doubled in size to give 20 keys, which may have been straight additions to the initial sequence, i.e.,

$$
\begin{array}{cc}
0 & 10 \\
1 & 11 \\
2 & 12 \\
3 & 13 \\
4 & 14 \\
5 & 15 \\
6 & 16 \\
7 & 17 \\
8 & 18 \\
9 & 19
\end{array}
$$

Equally likely in many commercial systems, the file may double in size, but as records are added, other records may be deleted. The following range of keys shows that the file will have doubled in size to give 20 keys, but the range will now be 0 to 32, as opposed to 0 to 19:

0	20
2	21
3	24
5	26
9	27
10	28
11	29
15	30
16	31
17	32

In short, record movements have been

Records retained		Records deleted		Records added and since deleted	Records added and retained	
0	11	1	13	22	20	29
2	15	4	14	23	21	30
3	16	6	18	25	24	31
5	17	7	19		26	32
9		8			27	
10		12			28	

If one record is stored per storage location, then at the end of year 1 we will have 32 locations employed to store 20 records. The storage area used is thus

$$\frac{20}{32} \times 100\% = 62.5\% \text{ efficiency}$$

The area of the file will continue to expand at a linear rate as the number of keys used expands. This will be acceptable in some cases where the file is small and the rate of change in keys is low; an example of this is the use of 300 expense account codes. It is not feasible to re-allocate the file storage locations by packing the file records closer together. If this were done, then the storage address would no longer be equivalent to the key.

There is also the problem of gaps and clusters at the inception of file processing. Consider a produce code of six digits:

nnn   xx   c

where *nnn* is a type of product, *xx* is a size code, and *c* is a color code. Thus, 312 12 4 is a dress shoe (code 312), size 12, and the color is yellow (code 4). There cannot possibly be a contiguous sequence of file keys because of the very nature of the key itself. But it may be possible to re-allocate code numbers to coincide with the characteristics of the device itself. For example, the code

312 12 4 may be changed to 546 (i.e., record number 546 in the file). User acceptance and cost of overall recoding will rarely permit this to be done except in the case of a small number of special type codes.

The last set of problems are associated with the characteristics of the storage device addresses. The most obvious case of imbalance is where the length of the keys themselves are longer than the device storage address; for example, where the file keys are seven digits long and the device address is six digits long. Or, there may be the requirement to store more than one record in a device location (track or bucket). In the former case, the reduction of the key from seven to six digits may result in a doubling-up process that exceeds the storage capacity of the device. If the dropping of the units digit of the key is chosen to make the key fit the storage address, then duplication of addresses for a range of keys must occur; for example:

$$
\begin{array}{c}
1234561 \\
1234562 \\
1234563 \\
1234564 \\
1234565 \\
1234566 \\
1234567 \\
1234568 \\
1234569
\end{array}
$$

will all go to storage location 123456. Also, the storage address may be outside the range of addresses on the device. A simple arithmetic operation may be performed in an attempt to reduce the size of the key and to assign the desired number of records to a track or bucket. However, one is relying on a contiguous sequence of keys to give an even distribution of records over the file.

Address generation may be considered as an extension of self-indexing where the generation of the address from a key attempts to provide an even distribution of records over the storage space available. This will be discussed in more detail below. Why look to address generation when indexed-sequential provides a means of selected record retrieval? Why use address generation (producing a random sequence of records in the file) that prevents the production of sequential reports at ease? Part of the answer lies in the timing problems of indexed-sequential processing. It was shown in Chapter 7 that if the sequence of input is random, or the batch is equal to one record (i.e., single-record inquiries), then one or more access of an index will be required before the wanted data is located in the device and can be accessed. Assuming that a rough index is held in core and a fine index is held on the device, then it will take at least two accesses before the data can be retrieved. Also, indexes in a large file will occupy both core (rough index) and possibly considerable space on the device (fine indexes).

For a large file, the index storage overhead, in terms of both core and device space allocated, may be considerable; then index search may take some time. Address generation is thus mainly considered where a very fast response rate is required in an inquiry system where the file is large. The characteristics of address generation may be summarized as follows:

1. Records are assigned to device storage locations by means of a calculation procedure (algorithm) that produces an address from a record key.

2. Records are stored in the device in a "sequence" dictated by the algorithm, which is not the sequence of keys within the file.

3. The same algorithm may be used to retrieve the records after they have been stored. This obviates the need for index searching.

4. Because the file is not stored in key sequence, sequential processing and reports are very difficult to obtain.

5. Address generation is usually used for random interrogation of large files in systems that require a very fast response.

6. The function of the address generation algorithm is to produce a series of addresses from a series of keys,

   giving: an address within the address range allocated to the file on the device.

   a uniform distribution of records over the allocated file area (i.e., the right number of records per bucket or track).

   efficient file storage utilization (i.e., minimizing unused storage space).

   given: a range of keys that contains clusters and gaps.

   a set of keys that may be longer than the address.

THE TRANSFORMATION PROCESS

W. P. Heising (1963) in his excellent paper "Note on Random Addressing Techniques," gave a very fine and succinct description of the key-to-address transformation process ". . . a method of mapping a sparse set of keys into a dense set of addresses." Before considering the actual methods whereby keys may be transformed into device addresses, let us look in a little more detail into the characteristics of file storage. The relationship between keys and addresses is summarized in Fig. 8-1. A file stored on a device by means of address generation has two major constraints: under-utilization of storage space and synonyms.

A *synonym* is the same device address produced by more than one key. If the number of synonyms produced exceeds the track/bucket capacity, then synonym overflow will occur. This will require the use of tags, and the access time for any record in the file will increase because the tags will have to be followed

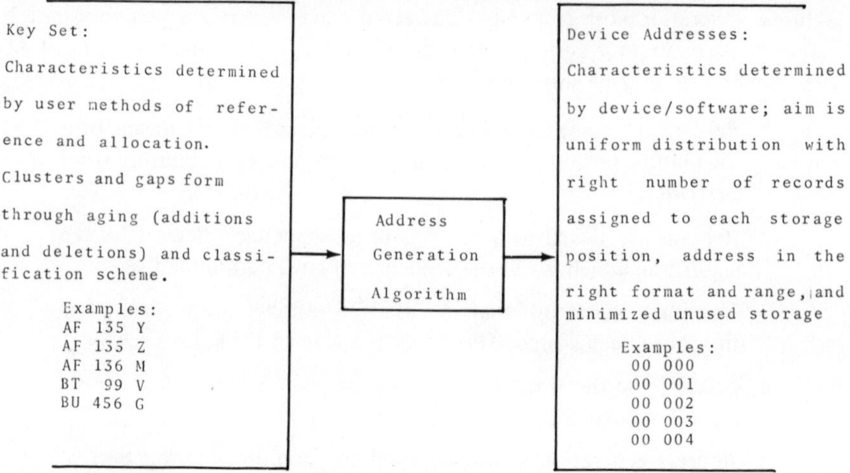

Figure 8-1. Address Generation—Key to Address Transformation

to locate and extract the appropriate record from the overflow area. On the other hand, some buckets/tracks may contain no records, or some may be used far below the bucket/track capacity, such as only one small record held on a location that could hold five records. The greater the area of storage occupied by a file, the greater the access time (as demonstrated earlier).

If a file could be packed into one cylinder, then only one seek would be necessary. If the file is enlarged to cover a number of cylinders (a smaller number of records being held on a cylinder), the processing time for random inquiries will be increased. It has often been stated that the best method of address generation is one in which the key transformation process produces a random distribution of keys over the available addresses. This, as we shall see below, is a debatable assertion. What is certain is this: There is no known method that can be universally applied to all key systems to give a good distribution over the storage area available. And, certainly, it is impossible to transform *random* keys to device addresses without getting some synonym overflow or inefficient use of storage space.

A Pattern of Keys

Let us consider and discuss three possible distributions in a range of keys constituting a file—i.e., the number of key values that are present in the range and the pattern in which the keys are present or absent. They may be

completely uniform.
irregular clusters and gaps.
completely random.

The first case is the best as far as address generation is concerned. All keys in a range are present and the keys have a uniform step between them. Thus,

$$0000$$
$$0001$$
$$0002$$
$$0003$$
$$0004$$

.

.

.

$$5648$$

would be a set of completely uniform keys: 5649 keys in the file, files and keys in ascending order by increments of 1. Similarly, the keys shown below are uniform in that they are separated by increments of 20

$$0000$$
$$0020$$
$$0040$$
$$0060$$
$$0080$$
$$0090$$

.

.

.

Again, a set of file keys can be said to be uniform if they are arranged in regular gaps. An example of this would be a five-digit key that has the first two digits taking a value of 00 to 57 in steps of 1, and the next three digits having values of 000 to 120 in steps of 6. Examples of the codes would be 00 000, 00 006, 11 120, etc. The file would thus consist of $58 \times 21 = 1218$ keys. Given that the range and uniformity are known, then the address generation algorithm would be used to map the records against the device accordingly.

The second case is one in which nonuniform grouping occurs as irregular clusters and gaps. An example would be where each digit (or alpha character) in a key has a special significance.

$$ptttssc$$

where: p = product type (alpha)
          ttt = code number for specific product (numeric)
          ss = size code (numeric)
          c = color code (alpha)

Given that the starting code is C14304R and the "highest" code is (at present) T32701Y, the distribution of keys may be completely nonuniform. Product type K, for example, might consist only of 17 different types of product, while

L might consist of 450 different types of product. Given that the products are continually changing, the lack of uniformity presents a problem to the address generation algorithm. Nevertheless, there will be some uniformity on which to capitalize.

In the last case, the keys are completely random, a very rare occurrence indeed. (In fact the author and his colleagues have never come across such a case!) Each number used as a key is assigned on an arbitrary basis and each key is completely independent of any other key. In effect, this would be equivalent to assigning keys with a random number generator! This case, it is claimed, represents the worst case as regards the use of an address generation algorithm, since the distribution of the keys over the file can never be better than random.

Experience shows that the majority of commercial keys fall into the second class: keys in nonuniform clusters and gaps. In this case, the only way in which an address generation algorithm can be developed is by a "trial and error" method, which will be described later in this chapter.

Despite the fact that random distribution of keys is rarely found, it is useful to consider this as a starting point because statistical methods can be employed to demonstrate the importance of various factors in using an address generation technique.

A Pattern of Addresses

Before considering an example random distribution, it is necessary to look at the type of address that must be generated and to slightly redefine the term "bucket." The address to be generated could be a logical bucket number. In this case, a file area will be defined in which all buckets are numbered sequentially through the area. Each bucket will have a fixed length, consisting of one or more hardware blocks.

Where a variable-track format is used, a number of options are open. The first is to address at track level. Alternatively, the generated address may be to the "record" level or to "block" level. On an IBM 360 device, for example, the difference can be viewed as follows:

> *Addressing to track level:* Commands used are SEEK, SEARCH KEY EQUAL, READ DATA.

> *Addressing to record level:* Commands used are SEEK, SEARCH IDENTIFIER EQUAL and READ DATA.

A track or block level of addressing is considered synonymous with a multiple-record bucket.

For ease of reference, the term *bucket* will be used in this chapter to refer to the lowest level of addressing within the file. Thus, a bucket can be

> one or more blocks (in a bucket device).
> a record.

one or more logical blocks in a variable-format track device.
a track in a variable-format device.

A Random Distribution

Let us assume that we have a group of keys and an address generation algorithm that will produce a truly random distribution of records over the available storage space. (For simplicity of explanation a "bucket" device will be used.) We must be very careful in our understanding of the term "random distribution." It means that each bucket is equally likely to be hit. It *does not* mean that each of the buckets will be equally occupied. It means that all buckets stand an equal chance of receiving any record that has to be assigned. This means that some duplications in numbers are likely, and in fact inevitable.

The starting point in considering this problem is the number of records to be stored, the available storage space (number of buckets), and the number of records to be assigned to a bucket. Example values are

$$\text{Number of records} = 6$$
$$\text{Number of buckets} = 10$$
$$\text{Bucket capacity} = 1 \text{ record}$$

Six records are to be assigned at random into ten buckets, and each bucket can hold only one record. The first record can be assigned without any trouble. The second, however, has only nine out of ten chances of being assigned to an unused bucket. Another way of looking at this is that there is one chance in ten that it will be assigned to a bucket that has already been filled (by the first record). The third record has eight chances in ten of being located to an unfilled bucket. Again this can be viewed as two chances in ten that the record will be allocated to a bucket that has been filled by the first two records. Thus, continuing this sequence, we will have the following ratios:

Record	*Chances of assigning record to "empty" bucket*	*Chances of assigning record to "full" bucket*
4th	7/10	3/10
5th	6/10	4/10
6th	5/10	5/10

This can be summarized as follows:

Record	*Chances of assigning record to empty bucket*
1st	10/10
2d	9/10
3d	8/10
4th	7/10
5th	6/10
6th	5/10

By applying simple rules of probability theory, we can calculate the chance of all six records being allocated to empty buckets as

$$\frac{10}{10} \times \frac{9}{10} \times \frac{8}{10} \times \frac{7}{10} \times \frac{6}{10} \times \frac{5}{10} \times 100\% : 15\%$$

Conversely, 85 percent of the time there will be at least one record overflowing as a result of competition for space, i.e., synonym generation. By the use of statistical techniques we can try to predict the number of records assigned (randomly) to a number of buckets on the basis of how many buckets will have

No records assigned.
One record assigned.
Two records assigned.
Three records assigned. . . .[1]

Figure 8-2(a), (b), and (c) shows three file distributions. In each case the file consists of 1000 records; the space allocated to the file varies in each distribution. Figure 8-2(b) shows, therefore, that

68 buckets have no records assigned.
135 buckets have one record assigned.
135 buckets have two records assigned.
90 buckets have three records assigned.
45 buckets have four records assigned.
18 buckets have five records assigned.
6 buckets have six records assigned.
2 buckets have seven records assigned.
1 bucket has eight records assigned.
no buckets have more than eight records assigned.

(Note that numbers in Fig. 8-2 have been rounded-off considerably to produce whole numbers.)

If there were not a random distribution of records over the available storage space, then the calculations shown above would not hold true. How is the lack of "randomness" caused? Quite simply, by the bias in the keys—either a uniform structure in the keys or because of irregular clusters and gaps. The former can be capitalized upon to give a better (i.e., more uniform) distribution, and the latter will have to be smoothed by the use of the appropriate address generation algorithm. The choice of the appropriate algorithm will be made by a study of the characteristics of the keys and by simulation (trial and error) of various address generation procedures. Given that it is inevitable that some synonym overflow will occur, how should it be dealt with in the file?

---

[1] The statistical proof for the preparation of the charts and tables is given in Appendix A. The basic assumption is that a Poisson distribution applies. This proof is for the mathematically minded; the systems analyst or programmer without the appropriate background is asked to accept the results as shown.

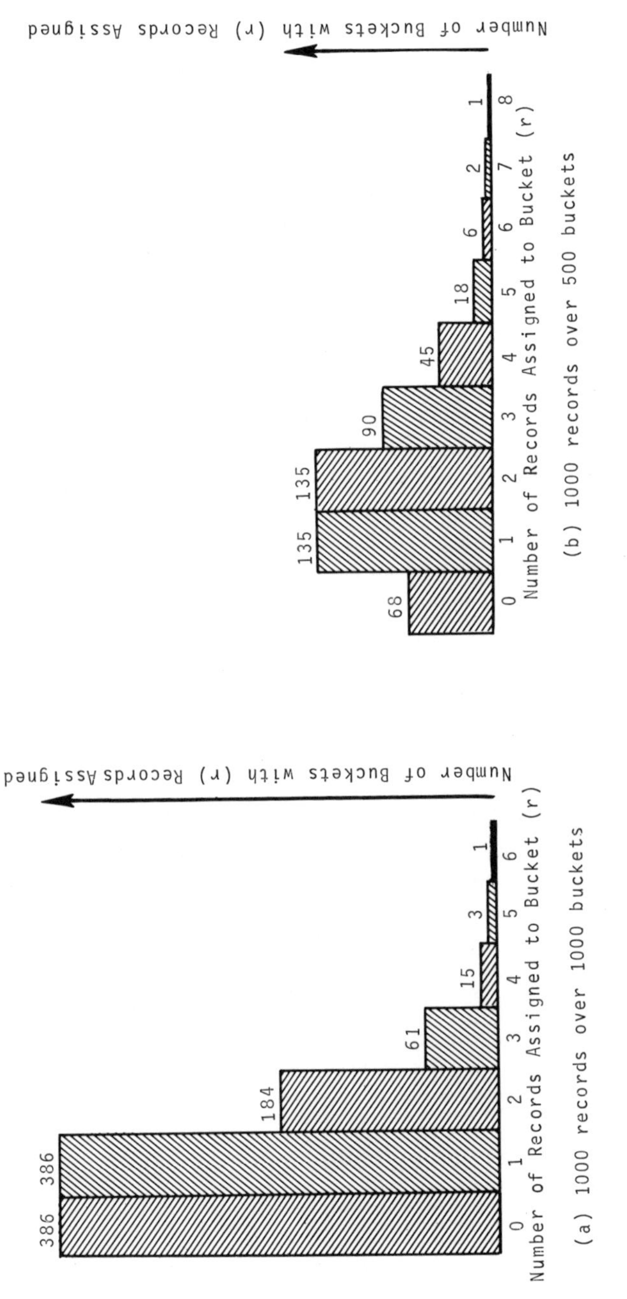

Figure 8-2. Storage Utilization in a Random Distribution

Synonym Overflow

There are two ways to deal with synonym overflow. The first is to allocate an area of storage space for it. This is much the same procedure used in indexed-sequential files, as described previously. An area of storage is allocated, say, at the end of each cylinder into which all overflow records are loaded. Tags are inserted in the home buckets to reference the location in the overflow area that holds the absent record. Note, however, that should this area become full, the overflow records will need to be located in another cylinder, and this will considerably increase the processing time. On the other hand, the provision of an overflow area with the file home bucket area puts further constraints on the range of addresses available to the address generation algorithm. In practice, the allocation of an area at the end of a cylinder to hold overflow records is rarely possible because of software constraints. Commonly, the only viable method is to assign a separate area of the device: This results in the use of time-consuming seeks to locate and access overflow records.

The alternative method is to assign any unused space in the home buckets to hold overflow records without using a separate overflow area. This requires a search of the file area to locate unused storage or requires the use of an index of available space. Various methods of dealing with overflow will be discussed later in this chapter.

TRANSFORMATION METHODS

Usually, the transformation method is in two parts. The first is used to transform the key into a format that can be easily processed by the arithmetic hardware of the computer. If a straight decimal numeric key is available, then transformation is simple. At most it will involve conversion of a decimal-character format to a binary number in a fixed-word-length machine (such as on a UNIVAC 1108 or ICL 1900 series computer). If the key includes alphabetic characters, then these will have to be transformed to some numeric value so that arithmetic can be performed. There are a number of ways to do this. Since most computers use a six-bit (or an eight-bit) character code, the easiest is to split the total six-bit representation into an octal representation of two three-bit values. For example:

letter E 6-bit character code equals 010101

octal representation: 010   101

                      2   5

This may be used to generate two decimal-digit codes for the one original alphabetic character

000010   and   000101

in a character machine, or

00100101

in a packed decimal on a byte machine, or some other appropriate form in serial binary representation in a fixed-word-length machine. In the latter case it may also be necessary to compress the value so that it fits into a word for arithmetic processing. An example of key reduction is shown in Fig. 8-3. The second phase of the transformation process is the reduction of the key number to a range suitable for use as an address within the storage device being used. Let us now consider some ways of processing keys to produce addresses.

```
(a) Byte working
    1. Basic key in six-bit character form is

            0   0   0   0   0
            0   0   0   0   0
            1   1   1   0   0
            0   1   0   0   0
            0   0   1   0   0
            0   0   1   0   1
            0   1   0   1   0
            1   1   0   1   0

            A   T   L   3   4
        That is, key ATL34 is held in five adjacent bytes.


    2. Split six-bit characters into two groups of three
                                              bits each.

            (1    (1    (1    0    0
          4{0   6{1   5{0    0    0
            (0    (0    (1    0    0

            (0    (0    (1    (0    (1
          1{0   3{1   4{0   3{1   4{0
            (1    (1    (0    (1    (0


    3. Put each of the three-bit groups formed from the alpha
       characters into separate bytes to for numeric key.

            0   0   0   0   0   0   0   0      0   0   0   0
            0   0   0   0   0   0   0   0      1   1   1   0
            0   0   0   0   0   0   0   0      0   1   0   1
            0   0   0   0   0   0   0   0      0   0   1   1
            0   0   0   0   0   0   0   0      0   0   0   0
            1   0   1   0   1   1   0   1      0   0   1   1
            0   0   1   1   0   0   1   0      0   1   0   0
            0   1   0   1   1   0   1   0      1   1   0   0

            4   1   6   3   5   4   3   4      packed decimal
```

```
(b) Word working:

    1. Key in character form stored in 24-bit words.
```

000000000000000000100001	110011101100000011000100

```
    2. Can be treated as a serial binary number in
       double-length working arithmetic operations.
```

Figure 8-3. Character-to-Numeric Conversion of Keys

Division

One of the simplest ways of computing an address from a key is to divide the numeric key (after the first step) and use the result as an address. Consider the simplest approach of division:

Number of available device addresses = A
Start address   = F
Any key   = K

Address for record key K is

(remainder formed by dividing K by A) + (F)

For example, a file is to be stored in 100 buckets. The start bucket address is number 24; the range of addresses is thus 24 to 124. Compute the address of key (K) 3652:

3652/100, remainder = 52;   52 + 24 = bucket 76

Since the remainder will never be greater than 99, but could be 0, the address range is F to F + A − 1. The lowest address would be a remainder of 0 from the K/A step plus 24; the highest would be a remainder of 99 plus 24, i.e., 123.

The use of division thus achieves the first requirement of the second step; namely, the key has been compressed to give a number within the required address range on the storage device. If one record is to be stored in each storage location, the number of addresses allocated should equal the number of records to be stored. Figure 8-4 shows the allocation of 21 records over 21 storage locations. Note that a consecutive *string* of key numbers produces a consecutive run of addresses. (The sequence of addresses are considered circular: i.e., the addresses run 1,2,3 . . . 20, 0, 1, 2 . . . , etc.) This demonstrates the statement made above, namely, that it is sometimes useful to maintain the uniformity in the keys during the transformation process—if this uniformity can be transferred to the storage addresses. If we inspect a sequence of keys, it is obvious that providing a "string" consists of less records than the divisor; all the remainders (i.e., addresses) will be different.

Now consider Table 8-1. This shows a series of keys to be distributed over 20 addresses (buckets). In Series A there is a set of 20 keys separated by a "gap" of 1. In Series B there are 20 keys with a key interval of 5. Series C, D, E, and F each shows a series of keys separated at intervals of 10, 15, 20, and 25, respectively. The distribution of these keys over the available buckets is shown in Fig. 8-5. It varies from a nice even distribution in Series A to a massive 20-record cluster in Series E. The same sets of keys are shown in Table 8-2, but this time the divisor (number of addresses) has been raised to 23.

Looking at the distribution of records shown in Fig. 8-6, it can be seen that the clusters of records experienced in the distribution in Fig. 8-5 have been smoothed out considerably. Why is this? One of the major factors is that the divisor used in Table 8-2, 23, is a *prime number.*

Key	Bucket Address
0377	20
0378	0
0379	1
0380	2
0381	3
0382	4
0383	5
0384	6
0385	7
0386	8
0387	9
0388	10
0389	11
0390	12
0391	13
0392	14
0393	15
0394	16
0395	17
0396	18
0397	19

Figure 8-4. Address Generation: Results of Division. [Keys assigned to buckets by division (by 21).]

In Series A, Table 8-2, the statement made earlier is further substantiated; namely, that a string of keys in ascending sequence, going up in steps of 1, will produce a unique series of keys if the string is less than A (i.e., the number of addresses . . . the divisor). The same thing happens if the interval between the keys and the divisor is "prime"; i.e., with the exception of 1, the key interval and the divisor have no factors in common, or very few. This can be shown by various mathematical proofs. In terms of the examples given earlier, note the relation between key interval and divisor as regards common factors ("1" is an exceptional case and is ignored). Take for example Table 8-1 with divisor (20), factors 2 X 2 X 5:

Series B: interval between keys = 5; therefore divisor and interval are related.

Series C: interval between keys = 10; therefore divisor and interval are related.

Series D: interval between keys = 15; therefore divisor and interval are related.

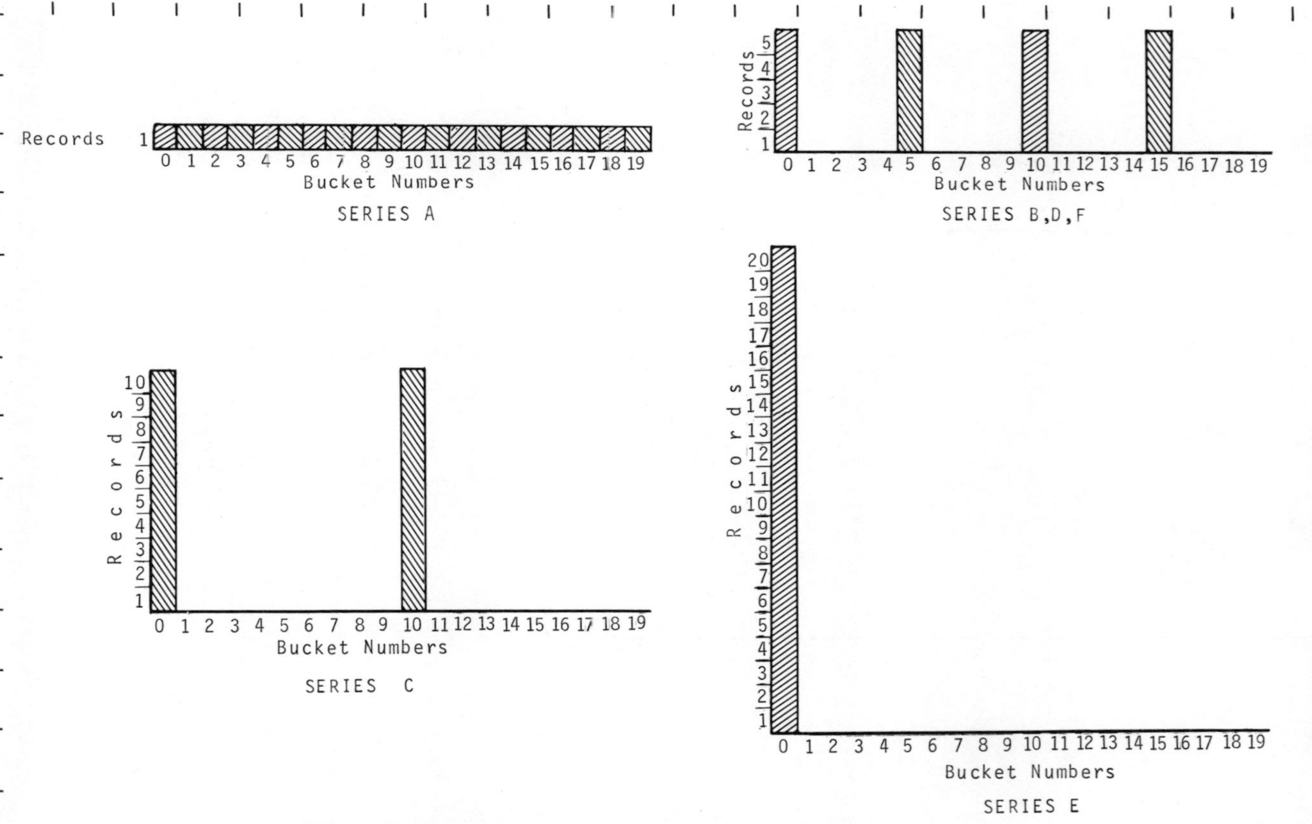

Figure 8-5. Distribution of Twenty Addresses for Key Series A-F

Table 8-1. Address Generation—Results of Division by 20

| *Series A,* | | *Series B,* | | *Series C,* | | *Series D,* | | *Series E,* | | *Series F,* | |
| *Increments of 1* | | *Increments of 5* | | *Increments of 10* | | *Increments of 15* | | *Increments of 20* | | *Increments of 25* | |
Key	*Address*	*Key*	*Address*	*Key*	*Address*	*Key*	*Address*	*Key*	*Address*	*Key*	*Address*
2000	0	2000	0	2000	0	2000	0	2000	0	2000	0
2001	1	2005	5	2010	10	2015	15	2020	0	2025	5
2002	2	2010	10	2020	0	2030	10	2040	0	2050	10
2003	3	2015	15	2030	10	2045	5	2060	0	2075	15
2004	4	2020	0	2040	0	2060	0	2080	0	2100	0
2005	5	2025	5	2050	10	2075	15	2100	0	2125	5
2006	6	2030	10	2060	0	2090	10	2120	0	2150	10
2007	7	2035	15	2070	10	2105	5	2140	0	2175	15
2008	8	2040	0	2080	0	2120	0	2160	0	2200	0
2009	9	2045	5	2090	10	2135	15	2180	0	2225	5
2010	10	2050	10	2100	0	2150	10	2200	0	2250	10
2011	11	2055	15	2110	10	2165	5	2220	0	2275	15
2012	12	2060	0	2120	0	2180	0	2240	0	2300	0
2013	13	2065	5	2130	10	2195	15	2260	0	2325	5
2014	14	2070	10	2140	0	2210	10	2280	0	2350	10
2015	15	2075	15	2150	10	2225	5	2300	0	2375	15
2016	16	2080	0	2160	0	2240	0	2320	0	2400	0
2017	17	2085	5	2170	10	2255	15	2340	0	2425	5
2018	18	2090	10	2180	0	2270	10	2360	0	2450	10
2019	19	2095	15	2190	10	2285	5	2380	0	2475	15

Table 8-2. Address Generation—Results of Division by 23

Series A, Increments of 1		Series B, Increments of 5		Series C, Increments of 10		Series D, Increments of 15		Series E, Increments of 20		Series F, Increments of 25	
Key	Address	Key	Address	Key	Address	Key	Address	Key	Address	Key	Address
2000	22	2000	22	2000	22	2000	22	2000	22	2000	22
2001	0	2005	4	2010	9	2015	14	2020	19	2025	1
2002	1	2010	9	2020	19	2030	6	2040	16	2050	3
2003	2	2015	14	2030	6	2045	21	2060	13	2075	5
2004	3	2020	19	2040	16	2060	13	2080	10	2100	7
2005	4	2025	1	2050	3	2075	5	2100	7	2125	9
2006	5	2030	6	2060	13	2090	20	2120	4	2150	11
2007	6	2035	11	2070	0	2105	12	2140	1	2175	13
2008	7	2040	16	2080	10	2120	4	2160	21	2200	15
2009	8	2045	21	2090	20	2135	19	2180	18	2225	17
2010	9	2050	3	2100	7	2150	11	2200	15	2250	19
2011	10	2055	8	2110	17	2165	3	2220	12	2275	21
2012	11	2060	13	2120	4	2180	18	2240	9	2300	0
2013	12	2065	18	2130	14	2195	10	2260	6	2325	2
2014	13	2070	0	2140	1	2210	2	2280	3	2350	4
2015	14	2075	5	2150	11	2225	17	2300	0	2375	6
2016	15	2080	10	2160	21	2240	9	2320	20	2400	8
2017	16	2085	15	2170	8	2255	1	2340	17	2425	10
2018	17	2090	20	2180	18	2270	16	2360	14	2450	12
2019	18	2095	2	2190	5	2285	8	2380	11	2475	14

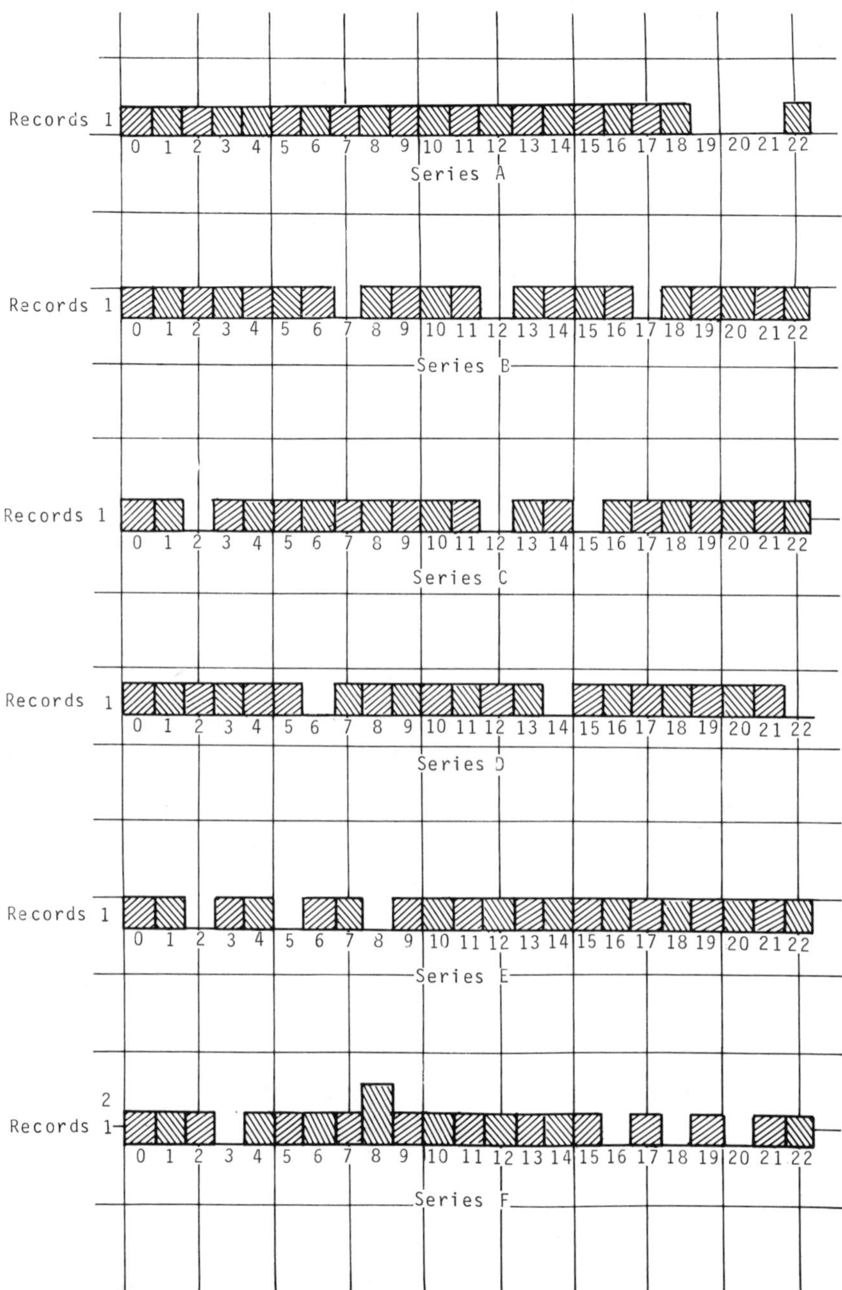

Figure 8-6. Distribution of Twenty-three Addresses for Key Series A-F

and so on. The use of a prime, which has only 1 times itself as a factor, thus reduces the incidence of common factors between the key interval and the divisor.

We have seen the use of a prime divisor in cases where there is a single string of keys. A string was defined as a group of keys separated by a constant interval. We must now consider the case of clusters and gaps within the keys. Each cluster can be considered as a string, and this may cause a duplication of addresses.

Taking a very simple example, consider the keys shown below:

2001	1	2203	3
2002	2	2204	4
2003	3	2408	8
2004	4	2409	9
2101	1	2410	10
2102	2	2411	11
2103	3	2509	9
2104	4	2510	10
2201	1	2511	11
2202	2	2512	12

Opposite each key is the address generated by the division of 20. Consider the first three clusters:

2001	2002	2003	2004
2101	2102	2103	2104
2201	2202	2203	2204

The starting key in each string is separated from the starting number of the previous string by a constant: 100. In the last two strings the starting address of the last string (2509) is separated by 101 from the previous string (2408). The same series of keys is shown below, but this time divisor 23 is used to produce the address:

2001	0	2203	18
2002	1	2204	19
2003	2	2408	16
2004	3	2409	17
2101	8	2410	18
2102	9	2411	19
2103	10	2509	2
2104	11	2510	3
2201	16	2511	4
2202	17	2512	5

We can apply the same sort of reasoning used in looking at the impact of using a prime as a divisor within a string. There was considerable duplication of addresses between the first three strings when using the divisor 20. This happened because the difference between the start keys in all three strings was 100, with many common factors to the divisor 20. When using the prime divisor 23, this relationship was broken, since 23 and 100 have no common factors. Note, however, that the use of 23 as a divisor has generated overlap between the second and fourth clusters. A prime is useful in preventing too much of the repetition of addresses. As Buchholz (1963) said in his paper: "If the starting points of two rows [*strings*] differ by a constant D, their starting addresses will not coincide as long as D has no factors common to the divisor A." Thus, there will be at most a partial overlap between the addresses obtained from two runs (strings) of keys. It is impossible to avoid overlap altogether, but the use of a prime will cut down the incidence of its occurrence. A prime divisor is a useful technique for transforming keys to addresses. The usual technique is to take the next lowest prime downward from the address limit (A). Thus, if a file is to be placed in 980 addresses, a suitable prime limit is 983, which could be used as the divisor. In the preceding discussion, we have been mainly concerned with storing records one per address. It has been pointed out, however, that most key sets will invariably generate synonyms. The facility to store one record per address is therefore useful, provided storage is not radically underutilized.

Unfortunately, prime division is not always suitable for all sets of keys. Also, certain primes are better than others for a particular range of keys.[2] On the whole, however, division by a prime will prevent a serious maldistribution in assigning records to addresses.

Truncation, Extraction, and Folding

We define *truncation* essentially as a type of division. The key is divided by a power of the radix in which the key number is expressed. Examples are division of a decimal number by a power of 10 or binary number by a power of 2. The low-order digits (or bits) are retained to give the home address. For example, truncating the key 178142165 by dividing by 100,000 gives a remainder of 42165, which is used as the device address. Address ranges produced through truncation are thus 0 to (R^n - 1). Of course division of this nature would not be performed by an actual arithmetic dividing operation. It is performed by shifting or by digit selection. This thus provides a useful alternative to ordinary division, which is commonly the most time-consuming of all arithmetic operations.

Truncation is suitable for key sets with a uniform distribution of keys, i.e., consecutive keys with few gaps. Where there is considerable clustering, trunca-

---

[2] An excellent note to this effect is given in Buchholz's paper (1963): "Prime divisors of the form $kR^n \pm 1$ should be avoided for keys that are in radix R, where k is a small integer. As may be seen from the binomial expansion of $(R^n \pm 1)^{-1}$, the remainder after division is essentially a superposition of successive n-digits groups of the dividend, and this superposition tendency is retained for small $k > 1$. Hence, for decimal keys in the range of 10^2 to 10^5, such primes as 101, 199; 401, 499, 601, 701, 1999, 2999, 3001, 4001, 4999, 7001, 8999, 9001, 19999, 59999, 70001, 79999, and 90001 had better be avoided."

A Note on Primes

For those readers to whom the technicalities and concept of primes have been lost in the distant days of the schoolroom, the following notes are given. It is certainly not the intention that this book be an introductory text in number theory; these notes are intended as refreshers to the nonmathematically minded.

A prime number is any number that cannot be expressed as the product of two numbers each smaller than itself. That is, a prime number cannot be divided evenly other than by itself and 1. Thus, 15 is not a prime because it can be expressed as 3×5. But 13 is a prime because it can be evenly divided only by 13 or 1. (Note that it can be said that 13 has factors 13×1, but this breaks the first definition: one of the factors, *13*, is not smaller than itself.) Tables of primes are published in volumes of mathematical tables. There is no shortcut that automatically identifies a particular number as being positively prime or nonprime. Any good mathematical textbook will describe primes in depth and will tell how to identify them. One of the best "nontechnical" write-ups I have come across is called "Prime Quality" by Isaac Asimov, in *The Left-Hand Side of the Electron*, Doubleday & Company, 1972.

---

tion can be grossly inefficient. It is, however, useful for reducing a very long key prior to division by a prime, etc.

The selection of the low-order digits in truncation is based on the fact that these digits are subject to the most change. For example, it is usual to find the units position changing from key to key. *Extraction* is simply the use of digits other than the low-order digits in the key to form the address. In effect, extraction is performed by a variation of truncation. For example, extraction of the middle five digits of a key is by radix division, followed by dropping the low-order digits of the remainder:

Key = 178142165
Divide by 10^7 (equivalent to a 7-position shift).

Remainder = 8142165
Drop the two low-order digits (65).

Address = 81421

Examination of the characteristics of the key set will reveal those digits that most often change, those that sometimes change, and those digits that change hardly at all. Since extraction is a modification of basic truncation, the characteristics of the keys will determine the effectiveness of the method.

Clusters and gaps in the key distribution will be carried through to the record distribution over the available storage space. By themselves, truncation and extraction are of little use *unless* there is a uniform key distribution. On the other hand, these techniques are very useful for compressing keys in conjunction with other techniques. Key reduction is a necessary process in those computers that constrain the length of the dividend by virtue of having fixed-length arithmetic registers. The key in these cases will have to be reduced in size, or an alternative method of division will have to be found. In any case, the time taken over a division operation on a long key, i.e., in a division by prime, may be excessive; although key reduction is not mandatory, it may certainly be advisable.

Folding is an alternative to truncation and as such can be considered a method of shortening and compressing keys. The key is divided into two or more parts and these parts are then added together. For example, the following eight-digit keys are compressed into four-digit numbers (note that the overflow-rightmost-digit is ignored):

Key	*Folding*	*Address*
46753984	4675 +3984 —— 8659	8659
46753985	4675 +3985 —— 8660	8660
67864096	6786 +4096 —— 0882	0882

As stated earlier, key reduction is often necessary in an address generation algorithm. Folding, as demonstrated above, is a superior method to truncation in some cases. Only part of the key is used in truncation; the other part of the key is, in effect, discarded. Any variability in the discarded part of the key is thus ignored in the formation of the address, and this may lead to production of many synonyms. Folding, on the other hand, retains the whole key in some form and thus retains all the variability.

It will be remembered that division by a prime retains a sequence in a string of keys, and this sequence is useful in the generation of addresses. If the sequence is in that part of the key discarded in truncation, then the division by a prime cannot capitalize on this sequence. Duplication will occur in the folded keys. If folding is carried out prior to prime division, the prime division will become inefficient if it is carried out on duplicated keys. Let us suppose that a series of six-digit keys are folded to produce a three-digit value; this three-digit value is to be used as the dividend in prime division. If duplicates are generated by the folding process, then duplicate remainders will be generated in the division stage, as shown in the table.

Keys	Folding	Prime Division (by 19)	Address
23234425	2323		
	+4425	6748	
		19	3
32143534	3214		
	+3534	6748	
		19	3
56361112	5636		
	+1112	6748	
		19	3

The extent to which folding will generate duplicates depends, of course, on the characteristics of the keys. In some classification schemes, duplicates may occur often; in others, duplications may be very rare indeed. Folding can be performed in several ways. The technique of *boundary-folding* (also known as *fold-boundary*) is to fold the key rather like folding a number written on a piece of paper:

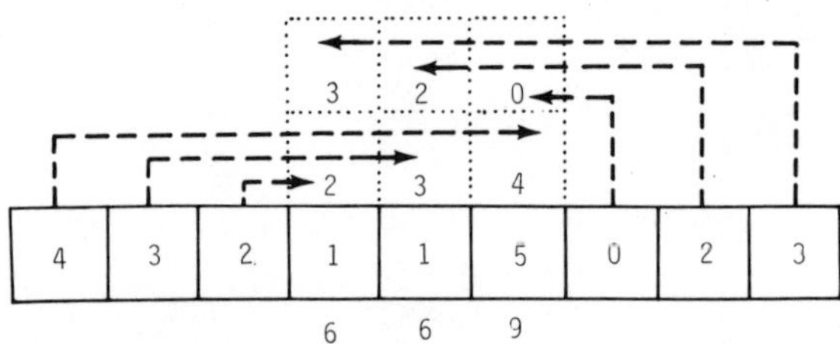

The technique used in the examples given above is sometimes called *shift-folding* (or *fold-shifting*). This consists essentially of adding high-order digit to high-order digit, and low-order digit to low-order digit:

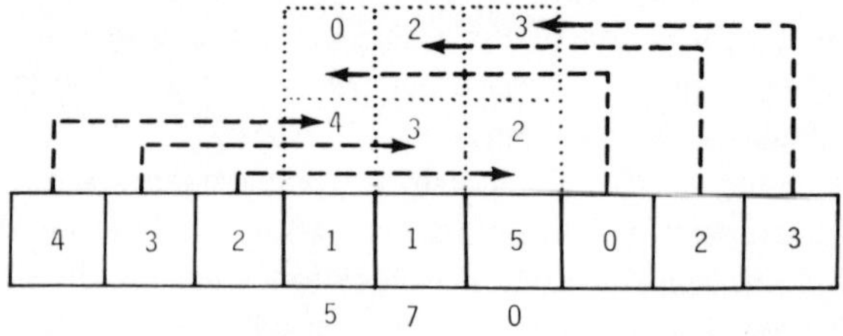

By the use of ingenious number juggling it is possible to use combinations of the preceding techniques to produce the required distribution of records over the available storage space. An example of this has been reported (Kaimann, 1968, part II). The basic problem to be solved was as follows: A number of student records were to be stored on a direct access device. Each student was identified by a nine-digit key and there were 48,950 keys used in the evaluation of the address generation scheme. In all, some ten different methods of key-to-address transformation were tried. The best result was obtained by the following method:

Trial Number 9:

> This trial selects five of the digits, extracting the two low-order digits of subfield 1 and three low-order digits from subfield 2:

> ID Number: 123456789
> Home Address: 34789

This method worked for this particular file. Of course it would be grossly wrong to assume that this method would be the best in every file! However, it demonstrates how variations of the basic extraction technique can be used with good results.

Randomizing: Radix Transformation

Thus far we have considered two major methods for generating addresses from keys. The first was division by a prime, which can produce good results; the second required truncation/extraction/folding, which by and large are methods of key compression. We now consider a different approach, that of trying to produce a random distribution of records over the available storage space. The most common method of randomization is by means of *radix transformation*, as described below. Before considering this method, however, it is useful to review one method of randomization that seems to have gained popularity but which theoretically has little or no substantiation. This is *key number squaring*. Part of the key is multiplied by itself and the resulting value is used as the address. In actual fact, the result produced is commonly so large that some form of truncation has to be performed before it can be used as an address. Many keys also produce a large number of zeros in the result and these may result in a maldistribution. An example of the squaring technique is

Key = 43216788

> extract middle four digits = 2167
> square extracted figure   = $2167^2 = 4,695,889$

The result would have to be truncated in some way, or further extraction performed, to reduce this large value to the required device address range. On the four occasions that the author has tried this approach, none of the results was encouraging; in one case, they caused a very bad maldistribution. Buchholz (1963) came up with a very interesting comment:

> Another randomising scheme that is sometimes suggested is to multiply the key by itself (presumably stemming from the erroneous analogy to the centre-squaring method of generating random numbers).

A Note on Radixes and Mathematical Notation

Before considering radix transformation, the following notes may be useful to the nonmathematically minded, by way of a refresher in certain basic number methods. Again, the notes given here are by no means a definitive theoretical treatise on number theory and representation. The radix of a number is the base in which a number is expressed. Most data processing people are familiar with at least two number systems: binary and decimal. In the decimal notation, each digit in a number is in the range 0 to 9. The position of a digit in a number indicates the value as a power of the base 10. If a digit has a value d (in the range 0 to 9), a decimal number has the form

$$(d \times 10^n) + \ldots (d \times 10^3) + (d \times 10^2) + (d \times 10^1) + (d \times 10^0)$$
$$\leftarrow$$

The decimal number 3567 is thus

$$(3 \times 1000) + (5 \times 100) + (6 \times 10) + (7 \times 1)$$

Similarly, numbers expressed in the binary system use the base 2, with each binary digit (bit) having a value in the range 0 or 1:

$$(b \times 2^n) + \ldots (b \times 2^3) + (b \times 2^2) + (b \times 2^1) + (b \times 2^0)$$
$$\leftarrow$$

The decimal number 12 is thus 1100 in binary:

$$(1 \times 8) + (1 \times 4) + (0 \times 2) + (0 \times 1)$$

Where numbers in different radixes may occur, then a convention is used to show which radix the number is expressed in; this is done by means of a subscript after the number. Using the values shown above: 3657_{10} and 1100_2, any number can be expressed in any radix (with the dubious exception of radix 1!). A radix system of 8 will have the form

$$(e \times 8^n) + \ldots (e \times 8^3) + (e \times 8^2) + (e \times 8^1) + (e \times 8^0)$$
$$\leftarrow$$

where e in this case may have a value of 0 to 7. All the following numbers thus have the same value:

$$35_{10}$$
$$100011_2$$
$$43_8$$

One special mathematical notation is useful here: the Greek "sigma," which means "the sum of." What is to be summed is shown opposite the sigma sign. Thus,

$$\Sigma\ 1, 2, 3, 4, 5$$

is 15. However, the summation sign is used with variables rather than with actual symbols (which, recalling our algebra, are alphabetic characters used to represent a value). Thus,

$$\Sigma\ ab$$

means the sum of a multiplied by b for all values of a and b. This is meaningless in itself unless we specify the sum of a and b for all values of a and b, starting at a given value up to and including another given value. The starting and finishing values are usually given above and below the summation sign. We can thus express a number in a particular radix by the formula

$$\sum_{i=0}^{n-1} d_i p^i$$

where: p = radix
d_i = ith digit in a number
n = number of digits

To show the application of this formula, consider the number 2453_{10}. By straightforward substitution, there are four digits with the radix $(p) = 10$; $(n - 1)$ is thus equal to 3, and i thus takes a value of 3 to 0. Taking each of the digits in turn, this gives us

$$(d_3 \times 10^3) + (d_2 \times 10^2) + (d_1 \times 10^1) + (d_0 \times 10^0)$$

Substituting the values of d, this gives

$$(2 \times 10^3) + (4 \times 10^2) + (5 \times 10^1) + (3 \times 10^0)$$

$$(2000)\ +\ (400)\ +\ (50)\ +\ (3)$$

Radix transformation usually takes place in three stages. The first is carried out to convert a key from character form to a number on which arithmetic can be performed. On most computers the key must be either a number in radix-10 (decimal) or radix-2 (binary). This key is subjected to some processing that converts it from its original radix to another radix. The value so created is then truncated to give a value within the address range used on the storage device. Let us now consider a couple of examples that demonstrate this procedure. First consider a key that is all numeric and is to be processed on a decimal arithmetic unit. The key number in the example is 530476. The radix in the second step is radix-11.

1. Key is 530476_{10}.

2. Interpret the key by employing formula

$$\sum_{i=0}^{n-1} d_i p^i$$

where p is the radix, n is the number of digits in the key, and d_i is the ith digit in the number. This gives

$$(5 \times 11^5) + (3 \times 11^4) + (0 \times 11^3) + (4 \times 11^2)$$
$$+ (7 \times 11^1) + (6 \times 11^{10})$$

Calculation gives

$$
\begin{aligned}
(5 \times 11^5) &= 805255 \\
(3 \times 11^4) &= 43923 \\
(0 \times 11^3) &= 0000 \\
(4 \times 11^2) &= 484 \\
(7 \times 11^1) &= 77 \\
(6 \times 11^0) &= \underline{\quad 6} \\
& 849745_{11}
\end{aligned}
$$

3. Truncate to give four low-order digits:

address is 9745.

For the second example, an alphanumeric key is used: AF719. It is assumed that the key is stored in a typical six-bit character code.

1. Convert the key to a decimal number. The bit patterns of the alpha characters are

$$
\begin{array}{cc}
A & F \\
100001 & 100110
\end{array}
$$

Split each code into 3-bit units. Value of each 3-bit unit is taken as a digit and appended to the original numeric characters of the key (719):

$$
\begin{array}{cccc}
\multicolumn{2}{c}{A} & \multicolumn{2}{c}{F} \\
100 & 001 & 100 & 110 \\
4 & 1 & 4 & 6
\end{array}
$$

Key in numeric form is 4146719_{10}.

2. Perform radix-10 to radix-11 conversion:

$$
\begin{aligned}
(4 \times 11^6) &= 7086244 \\
(1 \times 11^5) &= 161051 \\
(4 \times 11^4) &= 58564 \\
(6 \times 11^3) &= 7986 \\
(7 \times 11^2) &= 847 \\
(1 \times 11^1) &= 11 \\
(9 \times 11^0) &= \underline{\quad 9} \\
& 7314712_{11}
\end{aligned}
$$

3. Truncate to get four low-order digits;

   address is 4712.

For ease of reference powers of 11 are shown in Table 8-3.

Table 8-3. Powers of 11

n	11^n
0	1
1	11
2	121
3	1 331
4	14 641
5	161 051
6	1 771 561
7	19 487 171
8	214 358 881
9	2 357 947 691
10	25 937 424 601
11	285 311 670 611

The radix (p) must be relatively prime to the initial radix of the key—10 in the examples given above. In the examples, radix-11 was used because 11 is prime to 10. Note that the transformation radix (p) is greater than the initial radix; this prevents occurrences of anomalies. Note also, however, that in conversion of radix-10 to radix-11, as demonstrated above, the value 10 can never occur as an 11-ary digit. (The value of a decimal digit is in the range 0 to 9, that of a bit 1 or 0; in other words, one less than the radix 10 and 2, respectively. Thus, it is possible to have an 11-ary with a value 0 to 10.) A transformation radix of 11 is very useful because a multiplication by 11 or power of 11 can be affected in a decimal-arithmetic machine by means of shifting and addition. For example: for (9×11^5),

$$
\begin{array}{rr}
 & 9 \\
+ & 9 \\
\hline
 & 99 \\
+ & 99 \\
\hline
 & 1089 \\
+ & 1089 \\
\hline
 & 11979 \\
+ & 11979 \\
\hline
 & 131769 \\
+ & 131769 \\
\hline
 & 1449459 \\
\end{array}
$$

If the number is processed in binary, then the initial value is in radix-2; a transformation radix of 3 could be used.

The actual mechanics of the conversion process will, of course, depend on the hardware characteristics of the central processor. That is, whether it is a byte, a character, binary word, BCD word machine, etc. Lin (1963) discussed in detail in his paper the distribution of records over storage addresses, including the production of synonyms. Essentially, radix transformation attempts to produce a random distribution of records over the available storage space. Lin demonstrated how a near-random distribution is achieved by using radix transformation on a dozen different types of keys such as names and part numbers. However, his method does have some shortcomings. In some sets of keys, the absence of the 10_{11} value introduces "gaps" in the addresses for a consecutive string of keys. An example is given in the table.

Key	Address Produced by Prime Division (431)	Address Produced by Radix Transformation, Followed by Truncation	
0998	136	1196	196
0999	137	1197	197
1000	138	1331	331
1001	139	1332	332

There is, in fact, a complete series of addresses that cannot be generated by radix-11 transformation. In the preceding case, address 1330 could not be produced without the use of 10_{11} in the key. The number 10 10 10 would generate the address 1330:

$$10 \times 11^0 = 10$$
$$10 \times 11^1 = 110$$
$$10 \times 11^2 = \underline{1210}$$
$$1330$$

but the pattern 10 10 10 cannot, of course, occur in a decimal-format key. Of course a number 101010 could occur in a decimal key, but this would be transformed as $(1 \times 11^5) + (1 \times 11^3) + (1 \times 11^1)$. The result of this may be that addresses are scattered more widely. This could present an appreciable overflow problem for key sets containing many such strings. The results produced by radix transformation are generally so big that truncation or some other method of key reduction is required to produce a number in the appropriate address range.[3]

If we accept that radix transformation as described above produces a near-random distribution over the available addresses, what is the advantage in using this technique rather than, say, prime division? As demonstrated previously, a random distribution must produce synonyms. The *loading factor* (i.e., the num-

---

[3]An interesting warning is found in Buchholz's paper (1963) concerning key reduction by division, following radix transformation. If the divisor is divisible by the radix used in the transformation step, a very bad distribution will result.

ber of records stored in each address) will determine the impact of the synonyms generated. A random distribution will additionally produce underutilized storage space. But, a random distribution is said to be useful in terms of developing an address generation algorithm. (In fact, a number of additional techniques can be used in an address generation algorithm—only the most common "general purpose" approaches have been discussed here.) Lin (1963) summed up the problem quite succinctly. Writing of the problem of developing and implementing an address generation algorithm, he said: ". . . imply perfectly even distribution, which a probabilistic technique on a non-deterministic key set can only approach." Given that it is possible to inspect a key set and determine the hibits no such pattern, the random distribution can be used to good effect. In a recent paper by Lum and his associates (1971) there is this interesting statement: extent to which clusters and gaps occur, and that it can be shown that the clusters and gaps are not very irregular, then an even distribution by such techniques as prime division can be achieved. In those cases where the key set exhibits no such pattern, the random distribution can be used to good effect. In a recent paper by Lum and his associates (1971) there is this interesting statement: "Uniformity in the distribution of the addresses is not synonymous with the mapping of a key into addresses with equal probability. Consequently, as believed by Buchholz and substantiated by the results in this paper, an efficient transformation method should probably preserve whatever uniformity exists in the keys." Thus, there is a place for both techniques—randomizing and other. The method to be used for any one file will depend upon the characteristics of the key set.

In this section we have reviewed the mechanics of the most common methods of key-to-address transformation. Publications describing other techniques are given in References.[4] Later in this chapter, we will consider methods of selecting a particular algorithm for a particular file. Before this, however, we must consider in a little more depth how overflow is dealt with in a randomly organized file.

DEALING WITH OVERFLOW

As discussed earlier, it is inevitable that an address generation scheme will generate synonyms. A synonym has been defined as more than one address being calculated for a number of keys. If the capacity of the storage location cannot hold the synonyms so generated, then synonym overflow will occur.

---

[4]One specific reference that discusses the use of error-correcting codes techniques is G. Schav and N. Raver (1963). This type of technique is sometimes called *algebraic coding*, in which each key digit is considered to be a polynomial coefficient. An example of the application of this technique is described in the paper by Lum, Yen, and Dodd (1971). Similarly, there are many specialized methods for transformation based on hash coding (scatter storage) techniques; see Morris (1968).

This will result in searching when a record is to be retrieved. It follows, however, that the production of synonyms will not in itself generate overflow; the overflow condition will arise only when the capacity of a storage "cell" (track, bucket, block, physical record, etc.) has been exceeded. If the address can hold only one record, then every synonym will result in an overflow record. If the capacity of the addressed locations is two records, then only third and higher synonyms will be overflow.

Overflow is thus a function of the synonyms produced by the address generation algorithm and the capacity of the available storage space. We need two terms to define how a file is stored: the amount of overflow-loading factor and address capacity. The first, the *loading factor*, is the number of records divided by the number of records that could be stored in the file area. If 10,000 records are to be stored in 5000 buckets, each bucket capable of holding three records, then the loading factor (as a rounded percentage) is

$$\frac{10,000}{15,000} \times 100\% = 67\%$$

If the file was stored in 3334 buckets, then the loading factor is

$$\frac{10,000}{3,334 \times 3} \times 100 = 100\%$$

It is obvious, therefore, that if the load factor is greater than 100 percent, overflow records will have to be stored elsewhere because the home file area is too small to hold all records.

The second factor is the capacity of addressed location, measured in number of records. We call this the *address capacity*. If the level of addressing is thus a track, and it is possible to store five records on a track, then the address (track) capacity is 5; if records are being stored in buckets and each bucket can hold ten records, then the address (bucket) capacity is 10. The lower the load factor and the greater the address capacity, the less is the amount of overflow. The greater the loading factor and the lower the address capacity, the more likely is the incidence of synonym overflow.

For ease of reference, let us assume that a file is going to be stored by means of an algorithm that produces a random distribution (Poisson) of records over the available storage space. It is obvious that the loading factor will influence the address range of the file area on the device. A file of 3000 records stored in 3000 buckets gives a loading factor of 100% if each bucket can hold one record. This means that the address generation scheme will be required to produce one address per key and the address range will be, say, 0000 to 2999. If a file is stored in 4000 buckets, then the loading factor is 75 percent and the address range is now, say, 0000 to 3999. Similarly, for the file of 3000 records, storage/loading, etc. would be

> stored in 1000 buckets, bucket capacity 3, loading factor = 100%, address range 00 to 999.

stored in 1500 buckets, bucket capacity 3, loading factor = 66.7%, address range 0000 to 1499.

As stated previously (see the section "A Random Distribution"), given the number of records and the number of addressable locations (e.g., buckets), it is possible to predict the number of synonyms, assuming a random distribution. Figure 8-2 showed the synonyms generated for three file distributions, assuming a random distribution. If we now consider bucket capacity, we can examine the amount of overflow produced. Figure 8-7 shows the original distribution with the bucket capacity superimposed upon it. Note that, as in Fig. 8-2, rounding has been performed to give easily manageable whole numbers. The X axis (left to right) in this figure shows *number of buckets*. This should on no account be confused with *bucket numbers*. Thus, Fig. 8-7(a) shows that 368 buckets have no records assigned. It is a gross error to read this as "the first 368 buckets have no records assigned." The results shown in Fig. 8-7 are summarized in Table 8-4. Each distribution is shown with the appropriate overflow records totaled. Each of the overflow totals is also shown as a percentage of the total number of records to be stored (1000). For example, in part (b) of Table 8-4, it is shown that 90 buckets have 3 records assigned. Thus, 270 records are involved (3 X 90); since the bucket capacity is 2, there are 2 X 90 = 180 records that will be stored in their home buckets and 90 records (270 – 180) will overflow. Another example is given in part (c) of Table 8-4:

21 buckets have 7 records assigned.

Number of records involved = 21 X 7 = 147.

Bucket capacity is 5 records.

Number of records stored in their home buckets = 21 X 5 = 105.

Number of records overflowing = 147 – 105 = 42.

Given a random distribution, it is possible to predict the amount of overflow, provided the load factor and address capacity are known. Table B-2 in Appendix B shows expected overflow for a random distribution. As an example, consider a file of 1000 records assigned to 1000 buckets with a bucket capacity of one record. This gives a loading factor of 100 percent. Consulting Table B-2, address capacity 1, loading factor 100 percent, we see that an expected 36.79 percent of the 1000 records will overflow. (Note that the marginal discrepancies between the overflow percentages shown in Table 8-4 (footnotes) and the appropriate entries in Table B-2 are due to rounding in Fig. 8-5.)

If there is *not* a random distribution in the file, then the figures quoted above will not apply. Nevertheless, they are useful to give very broad estimates of the number of records that overflow. Accepting that synonym generation is bound to occur, how can overflow caused in this way be reduced? As shown in Table B-2, it is possible to reduce overflow by varying the loading factor and/or the address capacity. In the examples shown in Table 8-4, it can be seen that a

Table 8-4. Overflow in Files (Fig. 8-7)

Number of Records, (r)	Number of Buckets Receiving r Records, (B)	Number of Records Involved, $(B \times r)$	Number of Records in Home Buckets, (H); $(B \times c)$	Number of Records that Overflow, (O); $(B \times r) - (B \times c)$
(a) 1000 records over 1000 buckets; loading factor = 100%; bucket capacity (c) = 1				
0	368	0	0	0
1	368	368	368	0
2	184	368	184	184
3	61	183	61	122
4	15	60	15	45
5	3	15	3	12
6	1	6	1	5
Totals	1000	1000	632	368[a]
(b) 1000 records over 500 buckets; loading factor = 100%; bucket capacity (c) = 2				
0	68	0	0	0
1	135	135	135	0
2	135	270	270	0
3	90	270	180	90
4	45	180	90	90
5	18	90	36	54
6	6	36	12	24
7	2	14	4	10
8	1	8	2	6
Totals	500	1003	729	274[b]

(c) 1000 records over 200 buckets; loading factor = 100%; bucket capacity (c) = 5

0	1	0	0	0
1	7	7	7	0
2	17	34	34	0
3	28	84	84	0
4	35	140	140	0
5	35	175	175	0
6	29	174	145	29
7	21	147	105	42
8	14	112	70	42
9	7	63	35	28
10	4	40	20	20
11	1	11	5	6
12	1	12	5	7
Totals	200	999	825	174(c)

(a)Percent overflow:

$$\frac{368 \times 100\%}{1000} = 36.8\%$$

(b)Percent overflow:

$$\frac{274 \times 100\%}{1000} = 27.4\%$$

(c)Percent overflow:

$$\frac{174 \times 100\%}{1000} = 17.4\%$$

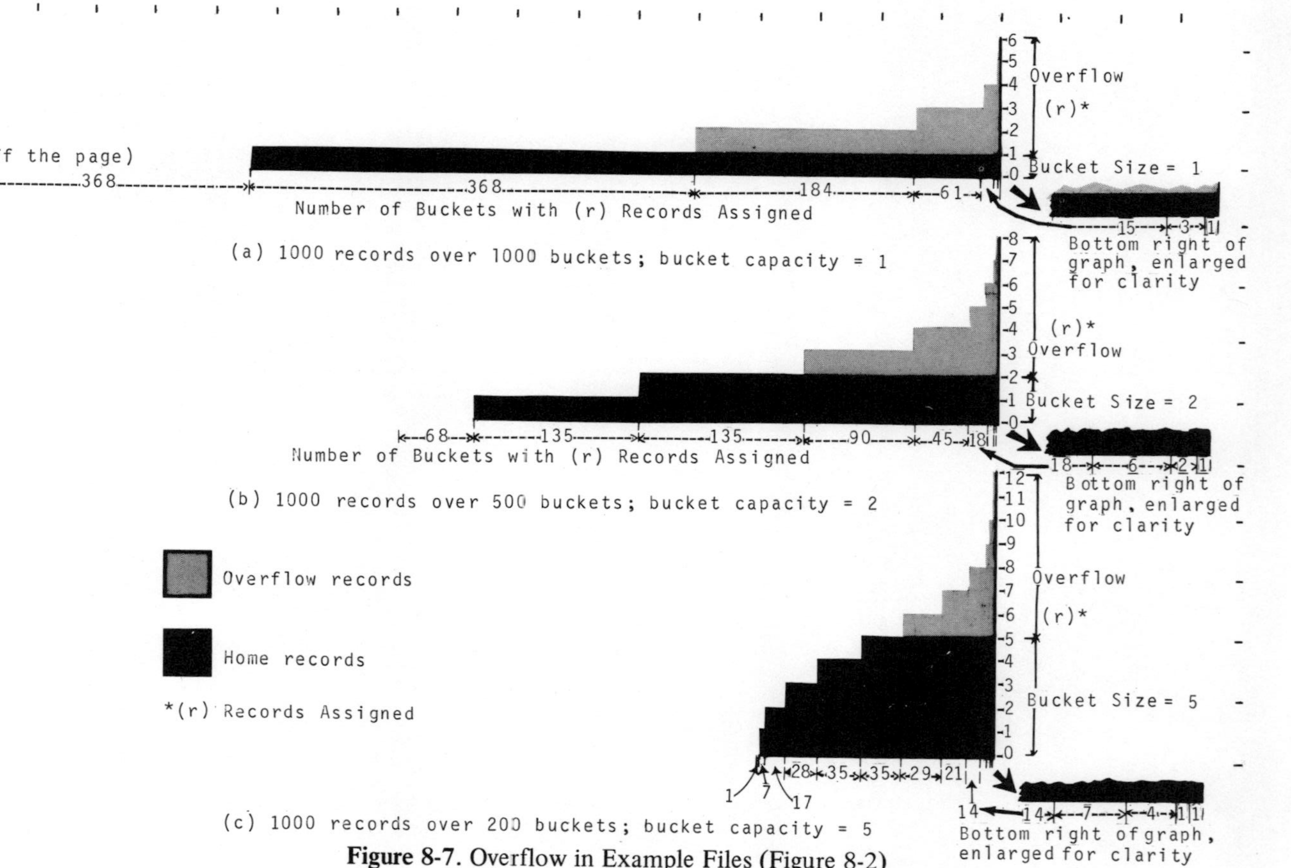

Figure 8-7. Overflow in Example Files (Figure 8-2)

file stored at loading factor 100 percent has overflow (on a random distribution) as follows:

Part (a).   Bucket capacity,   1; overflow = 36.8%
Part (b).   Bucket capacity,   2; overflow = 27.4%
Part (c).   Bucket capacity,   5; overflow = 17.4%

The larger the bucket size, the greater is the read/write time for each individual record access. Assuming that the file in Table 8-4 consists of 1000 records, each 100 characters in length, the bucket sizes are

Part (a):   100 characters
Part (b):   200 characters
Part (c):   500 characters

In this case, therefore, the bucket read/write time will increase for the larger bucket sizes. Because the loading factor is 100 percent in all cases, the file will consist of 100,000 characters:

Part (a):   100 characters X 1000 buckets
Part (b):   200 characters X   500 buckets
Part (c);   500 characters X   200 buckets

Because the loading factor is 100 percent, all additional records will cause a file overflow condition. When the first 1000 records are stored, the file area is filled and additional records cannot be stored in that file area unless an equal number of deletions has taken place.

Let us now consider the case where the loading factor is reduced, keeping the address capacity the same. In this case,

1000 records, each 100 characters in length, are stored in an area with a bucket capacity of 2 records (bucket size = 200 characters); assume a random distribution. Therefore Table B-1 applies.

Table 8-5 shows expected overflow against loading factors of 100 down to 10 percent. Thus, the penalty of minimizing overflow by reducing the loading factor is an increase in file size.

By and large, the penalty of longer bucket read times caused by increased bucket capacity is more acceptable than the drastic increase in file size that results from decreasing loading factor. For example, in one device the difference in bucket read times is

Bucket size =   512 characters; read time =   6.25 ms
Bucket size = 1024 characters; read time = 12.5 ms
Bucket size = 4048 characters; read time = 25 ms

If a system requires a very fast response time and this is critical to the whole operation of the system, then increased file size will have to be tolerated for the minimum access time.

Table 8-5. Impact of Loading Factor on Overflow*

Loading Factor, %	Overflow, %	File Area, Buckets	File Area, Characters
100	27.1	500	100,000
90	23.8	556	111,000
80	20.4	625	125,000
70	17.0	715	143,000
60	13.6	934	186,000
50	10.4	1000	200,000
40	7.3	1250	250,000
30	4.5	1667	323,000
20	2.2	2500	500,000
10	0.6	5000	1,000,000

*Random distribution assumed. File size = 1000 records; record size = 100 characters; bucket capacity = 2 records (200 characters).

How are the overflow records actually processed in the file? This, to a large extent, depends upon the software available, a topic that will be discussed in more detail in Chapter 11. There are two basic ways in which overflow can be handled: by using separate overflow area or by using home (prime) area for overflow. Many minor variations are patterned on these basic themes. Most of the methods use a system of "tags" in the home buckets to reference the location of overflow records.

Separate Overflow Areas

Separate overflow areas may be on the same cylinder or outside the cylinder. In the former case, an overflow record can be retrieved without additional seek time; in the latter, an additional seek will be invariably required. An example of each of the two methods of storage is shown in Fig. 8-8. The use of a separate overflow area on a different cylinder will be very expensive in the use of seek time: Every occasion when an overflow record is to be retrieved will result in a seek. If the percentage of overflow records is large, timing will become excessive. The use of an overflow area within each cylinder may considerably improve access time, but will reduce the home or prime area for generated addresses. (In some software, this approach is prohibited because all addresses within a file area must be consecutive. This means that the overflow area must be defined as a separate file area, which causes processing problems.) If each storage location has a sequential address, such as consecutive bucket numbers within a file area, considerable restrictions are imposed on the address generation algorithm by "gaps" in the address range. This is shown in Fig. 8-9, where the last 20 buckets in each cylinder are allocated to overflow records from that cylinder. This allocation considerably restricts the range of addresses in the prime area; for example,

Home Area	*Overflow Area*
1–80	81–100
101–180	181–200
201–280	281–300
301–380	381–400
.	.
.	.
.	.

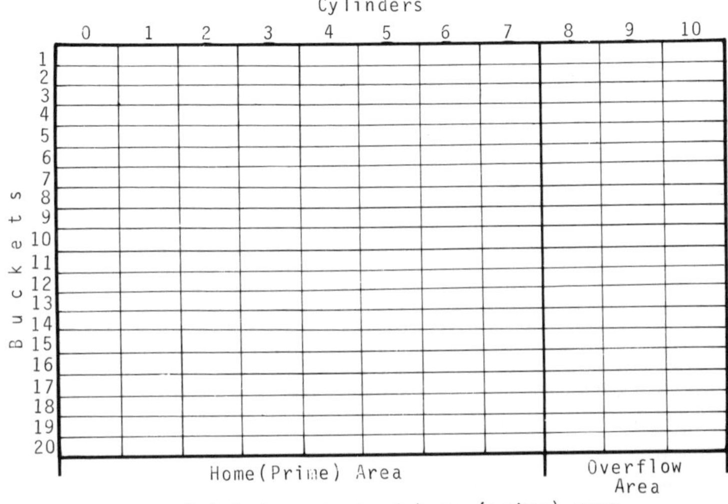

(a) Independent of home (prime) area

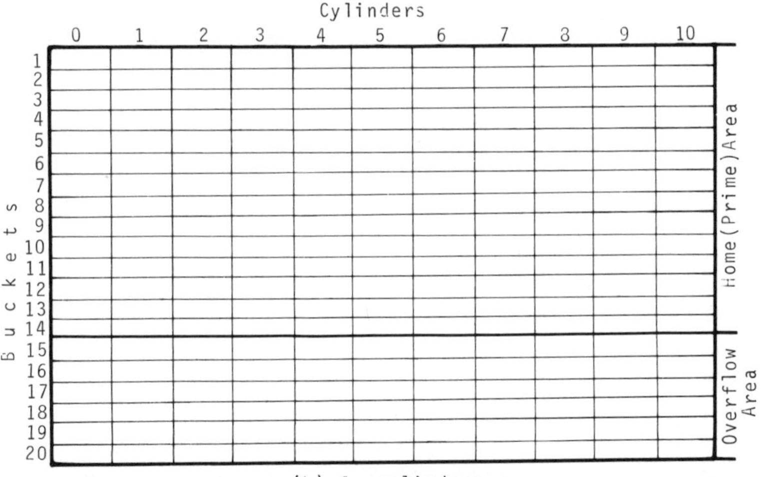

(b) On cylinders

Figure 8-8. Separate Storage Areas for Overflow Cylinders (using cylinders and buckets)

Cylinders

	0	1	2	3	4	5	6	7	
	1	101	201	301	401	501	601	701	Home Area
Buckets	80	180	280	380	480	530	680	780	
	81	181	281	381	481	581	681	781	Overflow Area
	100	200	300	400	500	600	700	800	

Figure 8-9. Restrictions on Generated Addresses

Because the overflow area is dedicated to the storage of overflow records only, it is very difficult to optimize storage space. If overflow occurs sporadically over the file area, it is also difficult to determine the right size of overflow area for all cylinders. A number of tagging systems may be used with a separate overflow area. If an overflow area is located at the end of the file, a technique like that shown in Fig. 8-10(a) can be used. In this method, an overflow bucket is assigned in the area to hold all records overflowing from one bucket in the prime area. To access an overflow record will take three stages:

1. Access home bucket and pick up tag.

2. Seek to overflow area bucket.

3. Access tagged overflow bucket, which contains desired record.

This is very expensive in terms of storage space because each bucket in the prime area which has an overflow record will require a bucket in the overflow area. The marginal advantage is that there is no searching for the required record in the overflow area, as in the following method: The alternative is to use a form of searching, shown in Fig. 8-10(b). Records are assigned to buckets in the overflow area as overflow occurs. Each bucket contains no more than one tag. A chain is thus established between buckets holding records generated from one home bucket. There are many variations of this technique; an overflow record may be tagged by both address *and* key, thereby obviating the need for chaining.

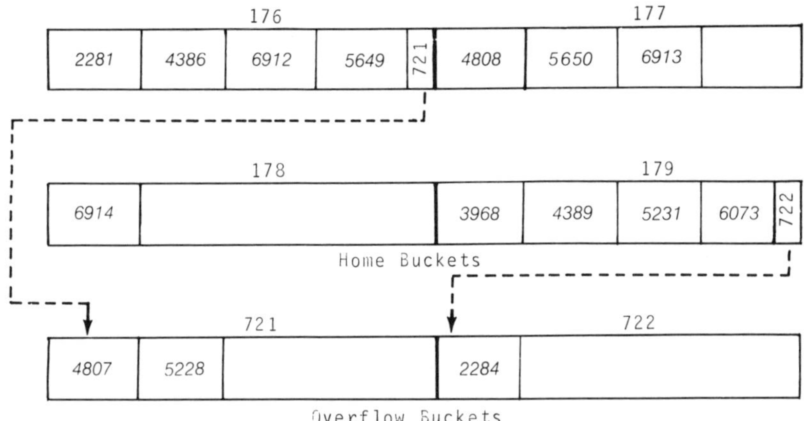

(a)

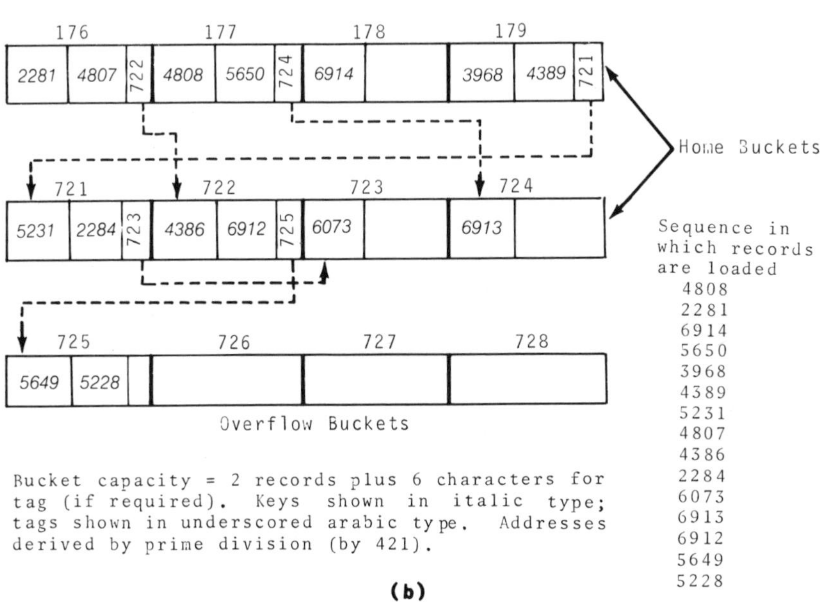

(b)

Figure 8-10. Tagging in Separate Overflow Areas

Use of Prime Area for Storing Overflow

A separate overflow area is wasteful of storage as a whole because it duplicates areas of storage in the main file area. Taking the file examples shown in Fig. 8-7, the following is a list of unused storage space in terms of records:

Part (a):   368 (368 buckets with space for 1 record)

> Part (b):   271 (68 buckets with space for 2 records) plus
>   (135 buckets with space for 1 more record)
> Part (c):   175 (1 bucket with space for 5 records) plus
>   (7 buckets with space for 4 more records) plus
>   (17 buckets with space for 3 more records) plus
>   (28 buckets with space for 2 more records) plus
>   (35 buckets with space for 1 more record)

To set up a separate overflow area in addition to having unused space in the prime area can be very wasteful of storage space. In many instances, therefore, it is better to have overflow stored in the unassigned space in the prime area. This can be done, of course, only if the loading factor is less than 100 percent to allow for overflow after the file has been initially loaded.

As with a separate overflow area, many methods permit overflow records to be stored and retrieved in the home area. Again, however, these methods tend to be variations patterned on two central themes. In this case, the two methods are chaining or closed addressing, and progressive, consecutive spill or open addressing.

Chaining.   This is similar to the technique described for a separate overflow area; the problem is complicated, however, because now there are home and overflow records intermixed in the prime area. Let us consider the simplest case of chaining, one in which the file area is divided into single-record buckets. An example of chaining in such a file is shown in Fig. 8-11(a). As many records as possible are located initially in their home locations. Overflow records are tagged from the home bucket. Should a number of overflow records occur, then a chain of tags is established. The procedure for locating a desired record is as follows:

1. Generate address from record key.

2. Fetch bucket with generated address (i.e., the home bucket).

3. If the home bucket contains the desired record, processing takes place; if the home bucket does not contain the desired record, pick up tag and fetch the tagged bucket.

4. If overflow bucket contains the desired record, process that record; if overflow bucket does not contain desired record, pick up tag and fetch the tagged bucket. Repeat this process until the desired record is located. Or

5. If a bucket is retrieved which does not contain the desired record *and* there is no tag to a further record (i.e., the end of the chain has been reached), record is not on file and appropriate action is taken.

As overflow records occur, they are stored either at the first available storage space *after* the end of the existing chain (located by a search) or by means of a space availability table held at the beginning of the file area. New records are

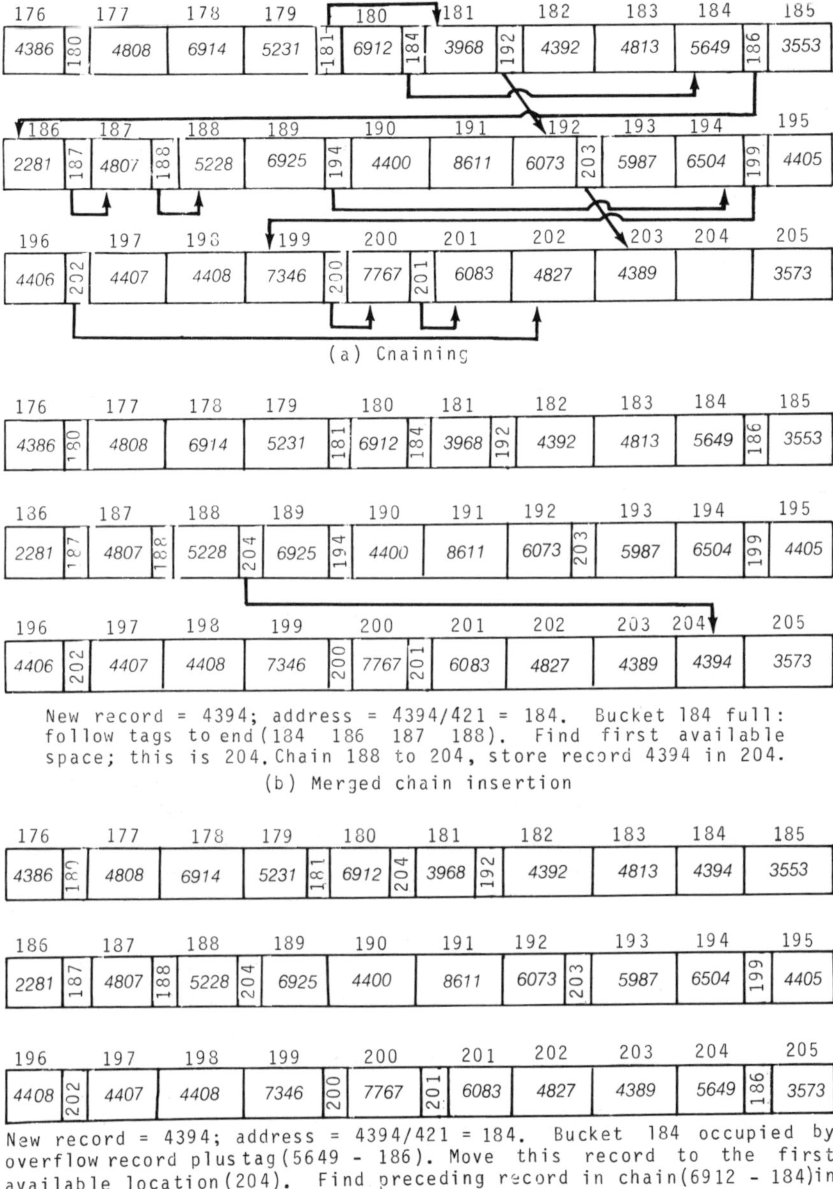

New record = 4394; address = 4394/421 = 184. Bucket 184 full: follow tags to end(184 186 187 188). Find first available space; this is 204. Chain 188 to 204, store record 4394 in 204.

New record = 4394; address = 4394/421 = 184. Bucket 184 occupied by overflow record plus tag(5649 - 186). Move this record to the first available location(204). Find preceding record in chain(6912 - 184)in 280 and alter tag to 204.

Figure 8-11. Chaining in a Single-Record Bucket File. (Records in home bucket are shown in italic type; overflow buckets are normal arabic type.)

thus added by extending the chain. A record deletion, on the other hand, will require changes in the linkages between records in a chain. If records were deleted from the file shown in Fig. 8-11(a), then the tag in bucket would need to be altered to skip the deleted record.

Let us now consider the problem of inserting a new record, the generation of an address for which leads to a bucket containing an overflow record from a previous bucket. Using the address generation technique of prime division by 421, suppose that record 4394 is a new insertion that generates the address 184 but that this address contains an overflow record:

Key	*Tag*
5649	186

There are two ways in which the new insertion can be processed. The first is by the use of *merged chaining*. This is shown in Fig. 8-11(b). The new record is inserted at the end of the existing chain and the tags are altered accordingly. Should yet another insertion come along, then this, too, will be added to the chain, whether it is generated from the 180 bucket overflow chain or from the 184 bucket overflow chain. Each of the overflow-holding buckets in a chain may result in yet another chain sequence.

The alternative method is to preserve independent chains; this is shown in Fig. 8-11(c). This method requires the shifting of the overflow record from a home-addressed bucket to some other location, and the tags in the chain are updated accordingly. In the example shown, the new insertion of record key 4394 generates the address 184, which is already occupied by an overflow record forming part of a chain. This record (5649 – 186) is shifted to a new location, the tags in that chain are updated, and the new insertion is placed in its rightful home bucket. Should a further insertion to a bucket take place, then a new chain is established. This method will require the use of some form of marker associated with each record, designating the record as either overflow or home. To avoid searching, it is necessary to have a *backward* tag as well as a forward tag. Thus, when record 5649 – 186 is moved from bucket 186 to bucket 184, the backward tag to bucket 180 would facilitate an easy alteration of the 180 tag (184) to 204.

Both techniques will require some housekeeping activities (and time) to maintain the tagging system. The method to be used in any one file will depend on the characteristics of that file, i.e., how much overflow will occur, the pattern in the distribution of the overflow records, and the loading factor. Generally, it is wise to keep chains independent; thus the second method would be used. In the first method, merge-chaining (Fig. 8-11(b)), the chains may become quite long, and in a fast-response system this may be intolerable. Also, deletions will more often cause linkage modification in the existing chain. On the other hand, the independent chain system may become unwieldy if insertions are made during main-line processing, since record shifting may occur. But the chains remain shorter, and once a new chain has been formed, processing time is quite low.

If a record is deleted, two options are open. The first is to leave the deleted record where it is but to insert a delete marker. The record can then be deleted when the file is reorganized and the tags are reset. The second is to physically delete the records and to alter the keys accordingly when the delete request is encountered.

Similar techniques may be used for multiple-record buckets. A rarely used method is to store a number of tags in a bucket, each tag associated with one record. For example, the bucket shown below consists of both home and overflow records.

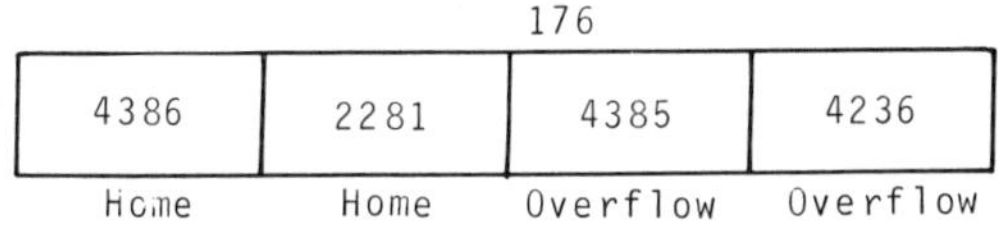

The overflow records form part of different chains:

> overflow record, 4385, from home bucket, 175 chain
> overflow record, 4236, from home bucket, 026 chain

This technique is thus using the multiple-record bucket as though it consisted of a number of separate single-record buckets. A far more common technique, which gets rid of the overhead of storing many tags (as in the system described above), is to use bucket tags rather than record tags. In this method, there is one tag, which references another bucket that contains all the records referenced from the first bucket. Merged chains are therefore a prerequisite for this scheme because a bucket may contain records that are part of the several record chains. An example of multiple-record bucket chaining is shown in Fig. 8-12; each bucket has *one* forward tag.

Ways in which the retrieval time for overflow records can be minimized are discussed at the end of this section ("Loading, Processing, and Reorganization").

Progressive Overflow.   This is also called *consecutive spill*, or *open addressing.* Unlike chaining, it does not require the use of tags. The operating principle requires that records be assigned to their home buckets, with overflow occurring on some buckets. When an overflow record occurs, a forward search is made to find the first available space in which the record can be stored. When space is found, the record is stored. For subsequent retrieval, the home address of the record is generated in the usual manner. When the home bucket is accessed, the

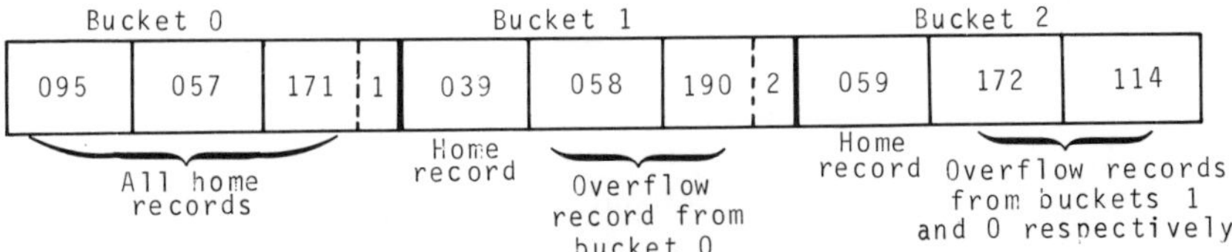

Figure 8-12. Multiple-Record Bucket Chaining

desired record is not found there. A forward search then takes place, bucket by bucket, until the record is found, or a space is found. In the latter case, it may be deduced that the record is not in the file. For the purposes of the forward search (to place the record or to retrieve it), storage is presumed to be circular; for example, buckets . . . 998, 999, 000, 001 are assumed to be in sequence.

An example of processing is shown in Fig. 8-13. In this, single-record buckets are used, but the principle also applies to multiple-record buckets. A file is stored initially as shown in Fig. 8-13(a), with no overflow occurring. A record, key 95, is to be added. Because the home bucket (0) is already occupied, a search is made to find the first available space to take the record. The record is slotted into this space (bucket 3). If a new insert record is generated to an address that already contains an overflow record, there are two options open. Either the overflow record can be moved and the new record inserted into its rightful home bucket, or the new record can be treated as an overflow record and located in the first available space encountered in a forward search.

Deletions are subject to the same options as described previously for chaining —with one important difference. If a record is physically deleted during processing, a gap will be produced and this will cause an erroneous "end-of-search" condition. It is therefore common practice to mark the record with a delete code and to physically delete the record only when the file is reorganized. The only other option is to delete the record physically during processing and at the same time indicate some form of dummy "bucket full" condition to satisfy the search routine. This may be a marker with two meanings:

1. While loading overflow record, meaning is "bucket empty and available for insertion."

2. While searching for an overflow record, meaning is "bucket full and search to continue."

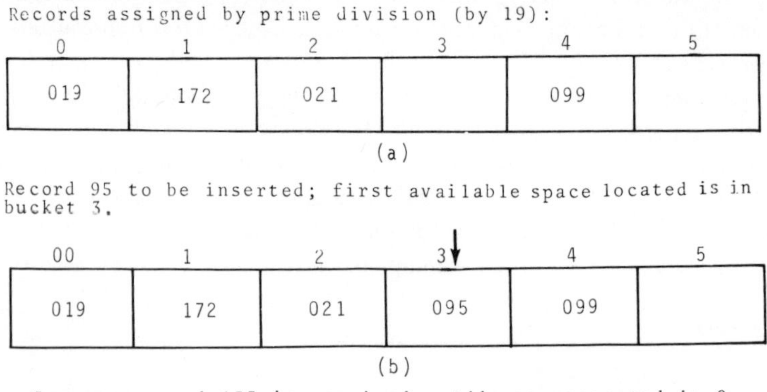

Figure 8-13. Progressive Overflow Method

A detailed discussion on the efficiency of overflow processing is given later. At this point, however, it is possible to make a few very general points on chaining versus progressive overflow.

Chaining requires tags, and there is the overhead of both the storage space required for these and the time required to keep them up to date in load and insertion programs. Chaining, however, gives relatively short search times. Progressive overflow does not require the use of tags (thus saving storage space and tag setting/resetting time), but search times may be considerably longer than chaining. With a low-loading factor, search times will be relatively short, but when the loading factor approaches 100 percent the search times increase significantly. Progressive overflow may also produce localized overflow clusters. This occurs because overflow propagates from one bucket to the next.

A Measure of Efficiency: Length of Search

The *average length of search* is a measure of the number of accesses made before the required record is located. If all records in the file are stored in their home locations, the average access time is 1.0. This means that for one seek/read, the required record is located and accessed. If, on the other hand, there is overflow, then more than one read (and possibly, seek) will be required before the desired record is accessed. The average length of search is defined as

$$\frac{\text{Total number of accesses to fetch all records in file}}{\text{Number of records in the file}}$$

1	2	3	4	5	6	7	8	9	10
001	002	003	004	005	006	007	008	009	010

11	12	13	14	15	16	17	18	19	20
011	013	015	018	012	014	016	017	019	020

Record	Bucket Accessed	Number of Accesses	Record	Bucket Accessed	Number of Accesses
001	1	1	011	11	1
002	2	1	012	11,15	2
003	3	1	013	12	1
004	4	1	014	12,16	2
005	5	1	015	13	1
006	6	1	016	13,17	2
007	7	1	017	13,17,18	3
008	8	1	018	14	1
009	1	1	019	14, 19	2
010	10	1	020	14, 19, 20	3

Total number of accesses: 28

Average LOS = 28/20 = 1.4

Figure 8-14. Length of Search in a Simple File

It is difficult to calculate the length of search a priori. Meaningful length of search figures can be calculated only by simulation. The general principle is described as follows: Suppose there are 20 records in the file and the records generate certain synonyms:

Synonyms	Frequency	Contributing Records
0	10	10
1	2	4
2	2	6

Ten records are thus assigned to their home buckets, four records are assigned to two buckets, and six records are assigned to two buckets. This can be shown by using actual keys and addresses:

Key	Address	Key	Address	Key	Address
1	1	11	11	15	13
2	2	12	11	16	13
3	3			17	13
4	4	13	12		
5	5	14	12	18	14
6	6			19	14
7	7			20	14
8	8				
9	9				
10	10				

Assume that single-record buckets with chaining are used. This means that 14 addresses are generated and 14 records are stored in their home buckets, which in turn means that one access will fetch one of these 14 records. The number of accesses for 14 records is 14. Assuming that records 11 and 13 are stored in their home buckets, then records 12 and 14 will require *two* accesses each. The first access will fetch the home bucket and the second will fetch the record from its overflow bucket. The total access for these records is 4. (Our running total of accesses is thus 14 + 4 = 18.) Now consider records 16 and 17. One overflow record will require two accesses (to home bucket, thence to overflow) and the other overflow record will take three accesses (one to home bucket, one to first chained overflow bucket, and a further access to the second overflow bucket). Since there are two occurrences of two synonyms, the accesses for the six records are

$$2(2 + 3) = 10 \text{ accesses}$$

This is shown diagrammatically in Fig. 8-14. The total number of accesses is thus 28 (i.e., 14 + 4 + 10). The average length of search is thus 28/20 = 1.4.

This is a very simple example. Consider all the assumptions made. Chaining was used. A given overflow record will require $C + 1$ accesses, where C is the record position in the chain. Merged chains will increase the search time. For example, suppose records are inserted in sequence; then record 14 will go into bucket 13 and record 15 will go into a chain. If progressive overflow were used, however, the number of accesses for a given overflow record would be $S + 1$, where S is the number of buckets away from the home bucket of the record.

Length of search (LOS), then is a measure of performance. In a real-file situation, the LOS can be calculated only by simulation of file processing. The object of overflow handling is to minimize LOS. The LOS is an *index* of efficiency. It will, of course, make a great deal of difference if the search involves not only reads but seeks as well.

Loading, Processing, and Reorganizing

In this section we investigate various practical points associated with trying to minimize the LOS for a given algorithm. Overflow has an impact over the whole life of a file. The three major areas considered here are

1. *Loading:* setting up the file on the device and dealing with initial overflow caused by synonym generation against bucket capacity.

2. *Processing:* day-to-day inquiry processing (the *main-line* processing) and dealing with further overflow caused by record additions and insertions, and dealing with record deletes.

3. *Reorganization:* the periodic reloading or tidying-up of the file.

Step 3 is of vital importance. The pattern of overflow and storage used, and LOS *must be constantly monitored.*

Loading.   The way in which a file is loaded is critical when minimizing LOS for initial overflow. There are a number of ways in which the file can be loaded, such as one-pass loading, two-pass loading, and activity loading. In *one-pass loading, all* records are loaded. This means that synonyms generated for a bucket are stored *before* all home records. The suitability of this technique depends upon the method of handling overflow.

When independent chains are used, one-pass loading may be excessively time consuming. The procedure is shown in Fig. 8-15; this example assumes single-record buckets. Every time an overflow record occurs, record shifting and re-tagging is necessary to realign a chain. Contrast this with a *two-pass load* (Fig. 8-16). Records are assigned to their home buckets on the first pass. Overflow records are ignored on this pass. On the second pass, overflow records are inserted in the unused space, and the tags are set up. If overflow goes outside the cylinder that holds the home record, then seek will occur for retrieval. This can be minimized by first sorting the file records into *generated address sequence* before loading.

By and large, LOS for a file with independent chaining is not affected by using a one-load pass as opposed to a two-load pass. If merged chains are used,

The records to be stored and their generated addresses are as follows:

Key	Addresses	Key	Addresses	Key	Addresses	Key	Addresses
001	1	006	6	011	11	016	13
002	2	007	7	012	11	017	13
003	3	008	8	013	12	018	14
004	4	009	9	014	12	019	14
005	5	010	10	015	13	020	14

A. Records 001 to 010 are stored in their home buckets 1 to 10.
B. Record 11 is stored in bucket 11.
C. Record 12 is stored in bucket 12, and tagged from bucket 11.

D. Record 13 is stored in bucket 12 (its home bucket) and record 12 is moved from bucket 12 to bucket 13; the tag in bucket 11 is altered from "12" to "13."

E. Record 14 is stored in bucket 14 and tagged from bucket 12.

F. Record 15 is stored in bucket 13 and record 12 is moved from bucket 13 to bucket 15 and the tag in bucket 11 is altered from "13" to "15".

G. Record 16 is stored in bucket 16 and tagged from bucket 13.

H. Record 17 is stored in bucket 17 and tagged from bucket 16.

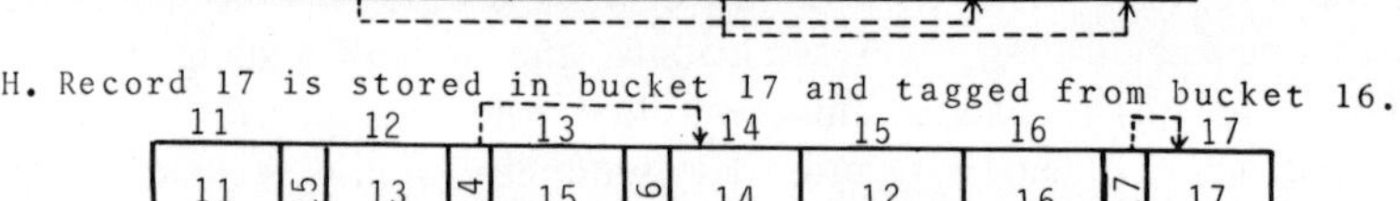

I. Record 18 is stored in bucket 14 and record 14 is moved to bucket 18 and the tag in bucket 12 altered from "14" to "18."

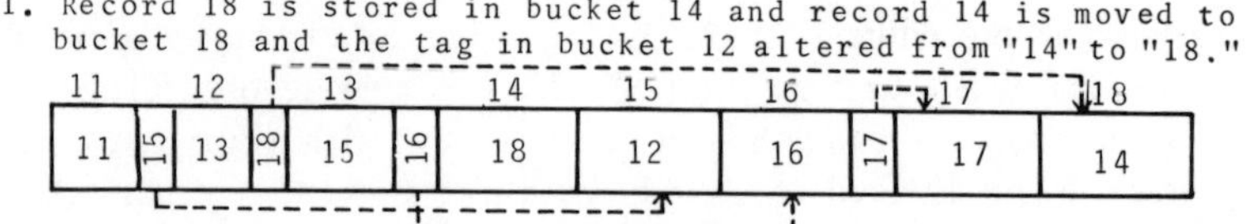

J. Record 19 is stored in bucket 19 and tagged from 14. Record 20 is stored in bucket 20 and tagged from bucket 19. The final form of the file is thus:

Figure 8-15. One-Pass Loading

First Pass

1	2	3	4	5
001	002	003	004	005

6	7	8	9	10
006	007	008	009	010

11	12	13	14	15
011	013	015	018	

16	17	18	19	20

Second Pass

1	2	3	4	5
001	002	003	004	005

6	7	8	9	10
006	007	008	009	010

11	12	13	14	15
011	013	015	018	012

16	17	18	19	20
014	016	017	019	020

Records	Generated Addresses	Loaded on Pass
001	1	1
002	2	1
003	3	1
004	4	1
005	5	1
006	6	1
007	7	1
008	8	1
009	9	1
010	10	1
011	11	1
012	11	2
013	12	1
014	12	2
015	13	1
016	13	2
017	13	2
018	14	1
019	14	2
020	14	2

Figure 8-16. Two-Pass Loading

however, the method of loading will have an important impact on LOS for subsequent retrieval. An example is shown in Fig. 8-17. The average LOS for a one-load pass is 2.4 and for a two-load pass 1.4. In fact, no merged chains are produced in the two-pass load in this example. The same logic applies to multiple-record buckets. If progressive overflow is used, a two-pass load produces the same average LOS as a one-pass load. This is shown in Fig. 8-18.

Activity loading of a file takes into account the likelihood of some records being accessed more frequently than others. The one- and two-pass methods described above assume that all the records stand an equal chance of being accessed: Their descriptions did not, therefore, take into account which record was stored in the home bucket. For example, it was stated in Fig. 8-18 that the

Records to be stored and their generated addresses are as follows:

Key	Address	Key	Address	Key	Address	Key	Address
001	1	006	6	011	11	016	13
002	2	007	7	012	11	017	13
003	3	008	8	013	12	018	14
004	4	009	9	014	12	019	14
005	5	010	10	015	13	020	14

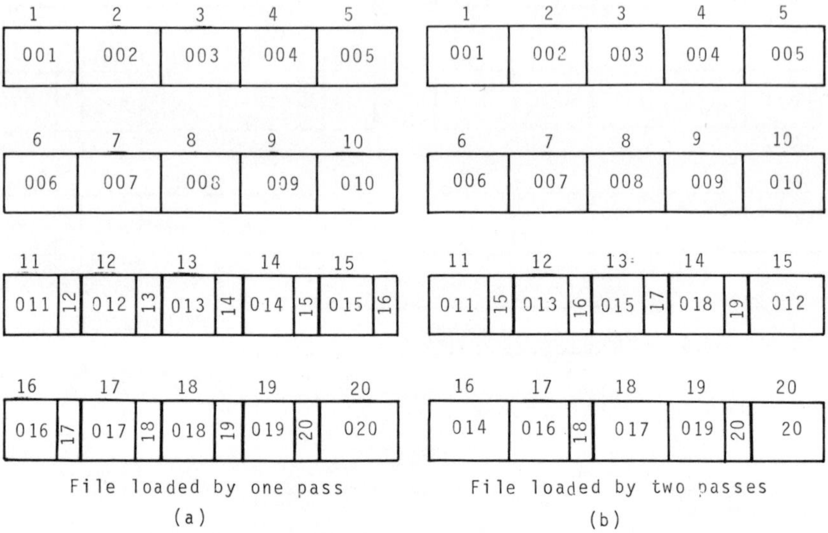

Figure 8-17. Two-Pass Loading: Merged Chains

records 11 and 12 were assigned to bucket 11. Record 11 was assigned to bucket 11 merely because it was the first encountered during loading. The principle of activity loading is that *if* record 11 is requested more often than record 12, then record 11 is assigned to the home bucket. If, on the other hand, record 12 is more active than record 11, then record 12 is stored in the home bucket and 11 is treated as an overflow record. Activity loading not only places the most active records in their home buckets, but also sequences in the records in a chain. The more active a record, the nearer it is positioned to the home bucket; the more infrequently a record is requested, the farther away the record is from the home bucket (i.e., the nearer the end of the chain). Activity loading would thus not affect the average length of search, but would effect processing time because most retrievals (i.e., for the most active records) will be in or near the home bucket. The major problem with this technique is in determining the activity level of each record before loading. Nevertheless, it can be done in some instances.

Two examples that I have come across illustrate how it is possible to "guestimate" activity and to get benefit from an overall reduction in processing time. The first was a type of policy record. It was felt by the users that the older the policy, the less would be the number of inquiries. The more recently that a

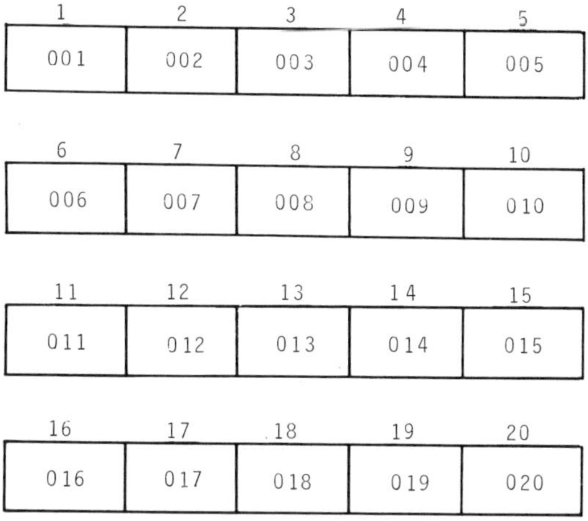

(a) One-pass load

1	2	3	4	5
001	002	003	004	005

6	7	8	9	10
006	007	008	009	010

11	12	13	14	15
011	012	013	014	015

16	17	18	19	20
016	017	018	019	020

Record	Number of accesses
001 to 010	10 (one each)
011	1
012	2
013	2
014	3
015	3
016	4
017	5
018	5
019	6
020	7
	48

Average LOS 48/20 = 2.4

(b) Two-pass load

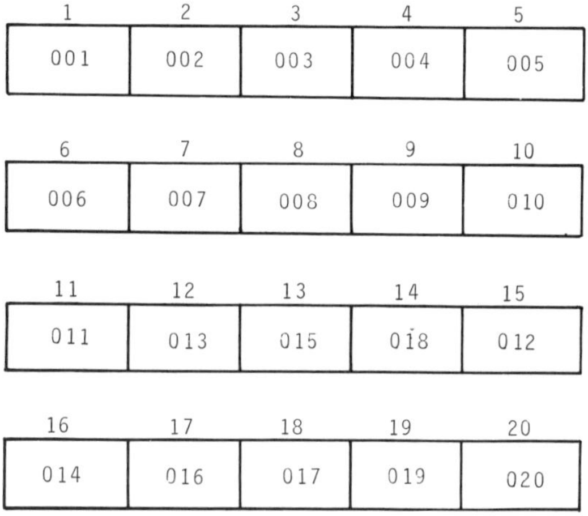 1	2	3	4	5
001	002	003	004	005

6	7	8	9	10
006	007	008	009	010

11	12	13	14	15
011	013	015	018	012

16	17	18	19	20
014	016	017	019	020

Record	Number of accesses
001 to 010	10 (one each)
011	1
012	5
013	1
014	5
015	1
016	5
017	6
018	1
019	6
020	7
	48

Average LOS 48/20 = 2.4

Figure 8-18. File Loading: Progressive Overflow

policy was taken out, the greater would be the number of inquiries. While the policy-aging discussions were going on, the file was loaded by means of an ordinary two-pass technique. Inquiry response times were considerably over-estimated. When the file was reorganized some four months later, it was re-loaded with an activity rate determined by "date since policy raised." The more recent the date, the more active the record, and the closer the record was placed to the head of the chain. Average inquiry-response times decreased by over 30 percent in the next four-month period. The other case where activity loading was used was based on a credit limit of customers. In this instance it was felt that the higher the credit limit, the higher would be the activity. The file was loaded on this basis.

It is more likely, however, that activity *reloading* will be used. As mentioned earlier, files are subject to periodic reorganization (deleted records removed, etc.). During processing, statistics are built up on the activity rate of records. These statistics can then be used to sequence records in chains during reorganization. Activity loading will only make a significant impact on overall retrieval times in files with a very uneven distribution of activity rates, and in which considerable overflow takes place.

Processing

During processing, the address of the required record is computed and the appropriate seek/read takes place to access the home bucket. If the record is not found, the appropriate search routine is activated. As a general policy, for security as much as anything else, deleted records should be identified by a delete marker and the record left where it is until reorganization. If an insert record occurs, the record is stored according to the overflow routine used. If storage space is densely used, it is advantageous to use a "next overflow area available" table. This is a record of the next available space where an overflow record can be stored. This will obviate the need for a search to find a blank area.

It is very difficult to calculate meaningful processing times for *one inquiry*. However, it is possible to estimate an average processing time that will hold true in the long run, i.e., over many accesses. The average length of search may be used as an approximation. The only way that gives a really sound estimate is file simulation during system design. Let us consider a number of general points on procedure timing. Roughly, the timing to access a desired record will involve two steps:

1. The time to access the home bucket after the address has been computed. This will require at most a seek, at least a read.

2. The time to access the overflowed records; this may require more reads and possibly more seeks.

A rough approximation of step 1 is calculated as follows: If the number of cylinders holding the file is equal to C, then the number of seeks of T inquiries may be taken as

$$1 + T\left(1 - \frac{1}{C}\right)$$

If five transactions are to be applied to a file stored on 1000 cylinders, an estimate of the number of seeks would be

$$1 + 5\left(1 - \frac{1}{1000}\right) = 5 \text{ seeks}$$

In effect, T must be large compared with C before we dispense with the general estimate that *each inquiry results in a seek*. We ignore special software constraints, and accept that each inquiry will take one seek, followed by latency and a read to access the home bucket. This will be the best case.

If the record is an overflow, further bucket reads will be necessary. In a small number of cases, when chaining or progressive overflow is used, this overflow may be off the cylinder in a separate area. This will be the worse case, and it should be timed. If the worst case is outside the limits of the response time, then the design will need to be modified.

Reorganization

As the file ages during processing, records are deleted and new ones inserted. It is very important to monitor the response rate of inquiries against file storage utilization. Periodically, the file is dumped onto magnetic tape or some other device and reloaded. Old records are deleted and the file is closed up, with tags being updated if chaining is used. The frequency of reorganization depends upon the insert/delete activity rate. In some files this is so low as to make reorganization necessary only once a year. On other files, reorganization may take place monthly, with a vast improvement in efficiency after reorganization (compared to efficiency just prior to reorganization). Examples of monitoring points are

1. Number of records in home buckets

2. Number of overflow records
   (a) on cylinder
   (b) off cylinder (e.g., in a separate overflow area)

3. If chaining is used, distribution of chain sizes; for example, of 1000 chains,
   > 20 with 2 records
   > 800 with 3 records
   > 150 with 4 records
   > 20 with 5 records
   > 10 with 6 or more records

4. Number of deletes since last reorganization

5. Number of additions since last reorganization

6. Unoccupied space available for overflow

Many of these statistics are compiled during main-line processing by a subroutine tucked in with the processing logic. Certainly, points 1, 2, 4, and 5 may be calculated during processing. Points 3 and 6 may be calculated during processing, starting with the values from the last reorganization.

As discussed in the next section, the evaluation of the address algorithm is not a "one time" process that stops when the system is implemented. The efficiency of the algorithm and the overflow-handling procedures should be continually monitored.

EVALUATING AND CHOOSING AN ALGORITHM

I was once very impressed with an address generation system working in the office of a client whom I visited regularly. The more I saw of the system in operation, the more impressed I became—both storage utilization and processing time were efficient. A number of times I asked about the method being used but never got a satisfactory answer. I finally pinned down the analyst who was responsible for developing the system, and proceeded to pump him as to the method used. He was very vague—and accepted that the system worked—as though by magic; as long as it worked, he wasn't going to worry how. It turned out that the algorithm had been developed by an insurance actuary who was a mathematical genius; the man had since left the company (unfortunately, from my point of view) and nobody had yet unraveled the program coding of the procedure! The analyst who developed the system had been very wise in backing out of the detailed development of the algorithm. (I will be the first to admit that he backed out too much—heaven help the company when they hit a program maintenance problem!) He had been wise because the analyst had no number sense at all, no appreciation of statistics or algebra. The complexity of the key set in this particular system would have soon got him into hot water if he had delved too far by himself. *There is nothing particularly difficult or mystical in implementing an address generation procedure, but it does require hard work and research. If the analyst starts to get bogged down in complex mathematics, he should seek the advice of somebody with a good knowledge of (at least) statistics.* (For those without a reasonable background in mathematics, a number of aside notes have been incorporated in this book to help ease analyst-mathematician communication, if nothing else! Basic textbooks that may be of help are also given in References; examples include Feller, 1950; Holman, 1966; and Vinogradov, 1955.

How does one set about choosing and implementing an address generation algorithm? There is no single, simple, step-by-step guide that, if followed, will give perfect results. However, a number of considerations should be borne in mind. This section reviews these and gives some examples of testing procedures that can be used to evaluate a range of algorithms.

The development of an algorithm is usually an iterative process: design—test—modify, redesign—test—modify, etc. The steps in development are summarized in Fig. 8-19. All the points shown must be considered during design. The constraints, which are preset, are commonly key characteristics (data), and address range and format (device). The latter may be further constrained by the software facilities available; e.g., overflow-handling routines. The key format, range, and distribution must be carefully studied. This is part of the systems designer's axiom: *Know Your Data.* Depending on the size of the file and the resources

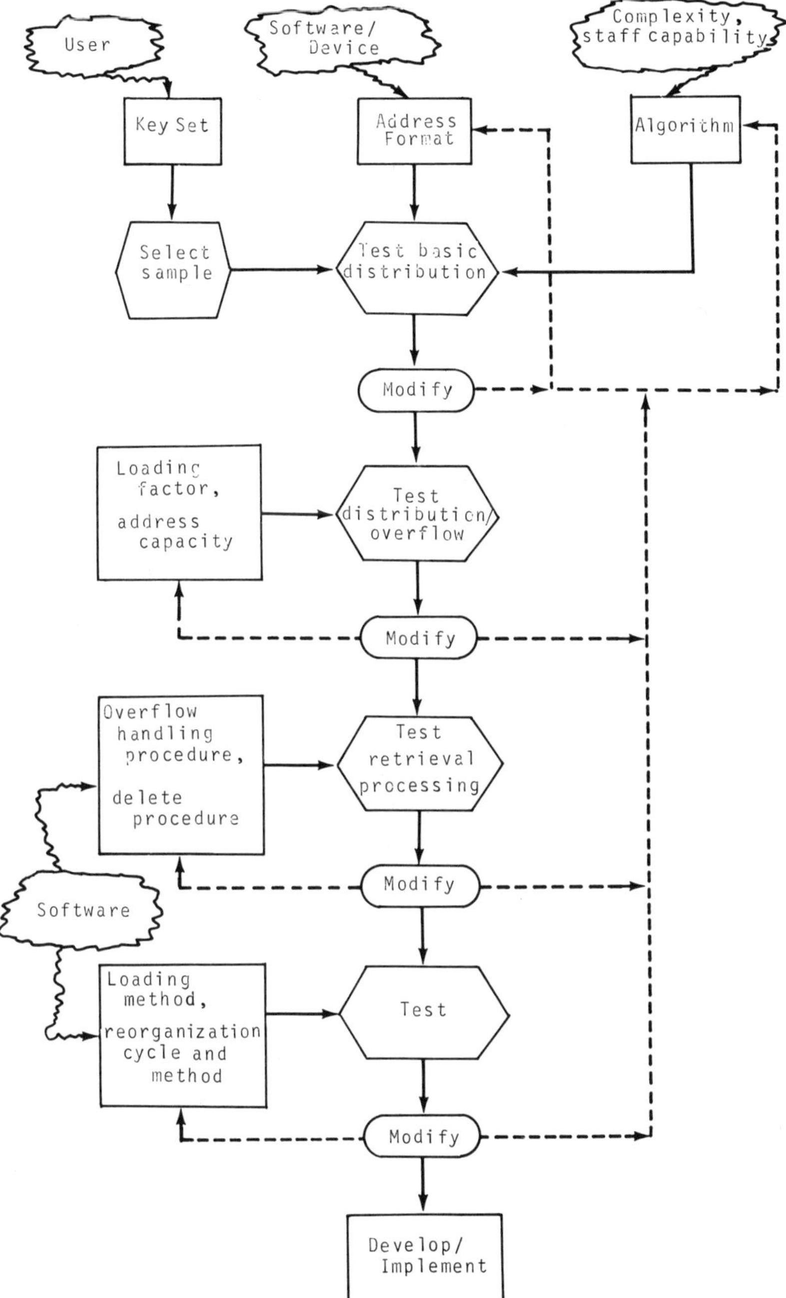

Figure 8-19. Steps in Address Generation Algorithm Development

available, it may be possible to do an in-depth analysis of key pattern. To do this properly, all keys should be input to a digit analysis program. An example output is shown in Fig. 8-20. This shows the distribution of digits in various key positions. If the key contains an alphabetic character, this should be converted to a numeric format. The technique for conversion should be that which will be used in the actual algorithm. The example shown in Fig. 8-20 indicates that key positions 5, 6, 7, and 8 are most evenly distributed, and these can be used in the address calculation process.[5] Thus, analysis of the keys gives a good starting point in algorithm design.

```
Total keys   = 19645
Key length   = 10 characters
Format = all numeric
```

Digit Value	Key Digit Position									
	1	2	3	4	5	6	7	8	9	10
0	19645	10523	7377	3612	2519	1679	1190	2421	215	200
1			3251	5212	2200	1771	2110	2400	348	317
2			4445	3278	2313	1910	2310	2313	577	942
3			4572	2345	1497	2324	1714	1700	712	1677
4		9122		2371	1618	2519	1621	2231	1013	1992
5				3027	1654	2671	1714	1942	4004	2013
6					1963	2421	2645	1773	6241	4451
7					2121	1432	2151	1412	3150	3722
8					1872	1224	2617	1832	1935	2966
9					1888	1422	1973	1621	1350	1365

Figure 8-20. Example Output from a Digit Analysis Program

The address range will depend upon hardware/software facilities available. Still to be determined will be the address capacity and the loading factor. Generally, multiple-record buckets should be used. The loading factor will depend upon the predicted incidence of overflow. These two factors are best set after simulation of the algorithm, using a range of address capacities and loading factors. (If no reasonable loading factor is immediately apparent, a factor of 70 to 80 percent is suggested as a starting point. A synonym overflow rate of about 10 to 15 percent, or higher in some systems, is tolerable.)

Test simulations of the algorithm should be done in careful stages. It is suggested that each method, or trial, should be tested on a sample of keys. Care should be taken in the selection of the sample so as not to distort the distribution by presenting a biased sample. Each trial should apply the sample of keys to the calculation method and to the device addresses generated. An analysis of the results obtained should be made on the computer. The procedure is

---

[5] IBM had a very interesting program 1401 – 01. 4. 034 which performed digit analysis and then set up a conversion method. Results are then evaluated.

1. *Input*
     sample of keys
     address range

2. *Process*
     address generation routine
     analysis routine

3. *Output*
     trial results listing

This is the lowest level of assessment, with the output listing showing

number of synonyms.
number of times that the number of synonyms was produced.
number of contributing records.
cumulative percentage.
totals of records produced.

An example is shown in Table 8-6 of the sample key set over the available storage: the number of synonyms produced and the number of contributing members. A rule-of-thumb address-capacity/loading-factor assessment may be made by manually calculating the amount of overflow. Each of the trials (division by prime, various folding/truncating/extractions, radix transformation, etc.) can thus be initially assessed to see which requires additional work. A complete file simulation incorporating the sample can then be performed to take into account the following components:

Loading factor
Address capacity
Overflow-handling method
Loading method

Table 8-6. Example Output of Synonym Analysis

Number of Synonyms	Frequency	Number of Records	Cumulative Percent
0	36551	36551	56.50
1	8350	16700	82.22
2	2811	8433	95.37
3	501	2004	99.31
4	140	700	99.54
5	32	192	99.84
6	12	84	99.96
7	2	16	99.98
8	1	9	100.00

Total records = 64,689
Total generated addresses = 48,400

The results of this simulation should show results like those in Table 8-6, together with a simulated average length of search. Based on these results, one trial method can be selected and developed further for implementation. On a straight comparison to indexed-sequential processing, using LOS as a yardstick, the length of a search for a trial will need to be better than 2.0 if the address generation method is to prove itself over indexed-sequential. This comparison is made on the basis that record location using indexed-sequential will take at least one access to retrieve the index and one access to retrieve the bucket holding a record.

SUMMARY

Address generation provides a useful alternative to index searching for the random retrieval of records. It can reduce file size by eliminating the need for index storage space, and it can also decrease the access time. It is therefore of use mainly in very fast response systems.

Unlike index methods in which the keys are fitted to the storage with the index as a "buffer," address generation fits the storage to the keys. The penalty for the fast-response rate obtained by address generation is usually a loading factor well below the 100 percent that can be achieved with indexed-sequential processing. If an efficient system is to be implemented, then considerable development work must precede its formulation. In highly volatile systems, the additions and deletions, unless carefully handled, will produce inefficient search times.

Because the file is stored "randomly," sequential record retrieval is difficult. For the production of sequential reports, two options are open: The first is to dump and sort the file to the required sequence; the second is to use some form of chaining system in which tags are used to refer to the next record in logical key sequence. This is discussed in more detail in Chapter 9.

PART THREE

SYSTEMS AND PROGRAMMING

SPECIALIZED FILE STRUCTURES

In Part Two, the basic methods for structuring direct access files were discussed. The three major methods of structuring and processing files were given as sequential, indexed-sequential, and random. These are the bread-and-butter methods of file handling. There are many variations of and extensions to these file structures, as well as to the *record* structures within a file. These enhancements of the basic methods of storing files are described and discussed in this chapter. All the various methods have as a basis the select addressing facility of a direct access device. These methods have been used only since the advent of disk and strip-and-card devices with the ability to access a record directly without serial searching.

RECORD STRUCTURES

In Chapter 5 the segmentation of data into records was discussed. A group of similar records was defined as a file. Most of the examples given previously in this book used a *multiple-record* approach, the most common form of record structure. Each record in a file consists of the same type of information held in an identical format as every other record in a file. An example is a stock file that consists of item or product records. There is one record for each product and all records hold the same type of information. For example, each record holds the following data:

Product number	Unit quantity
Description	Minimum stock
Sales price	Pack size
Cost Price	Stock balance

These fields are present in all records and each has a fixed length. This is the traditional method of structuring records, and has as its basis the early magnetic tape processing concepts. It is but one method of formatting records.

A simple extension to the multiple-record approach is the use of *contiguous records,* which means simply the division of a large file record into a number of smaller records. The reason for such segmentation is commonly some physical limitation such as a restriction in the amount of core storage available, rather than logical limitations such as system-reporting requirements. An example of this record structure is an insurance policy file that has a record for each policy as follows:

1. Policy number
2. Policy value
3. Monthly premium
4. Due date
5. How payable
6. Beneficiary 1
7. Beneficiary 2

This record may have considerable size, mainly because of the name and address entries held in the beneficiary parts of the policy record, items 6 and 7. It is therefore decided to split the record into three contiguous records:

A. Items 1 through 5
B. Item 6
C. Item 7

If the new records are physically contiguous, there is no need to hold the record key (policy number) in records B and C. Thus, the sequence of records will be as follows:

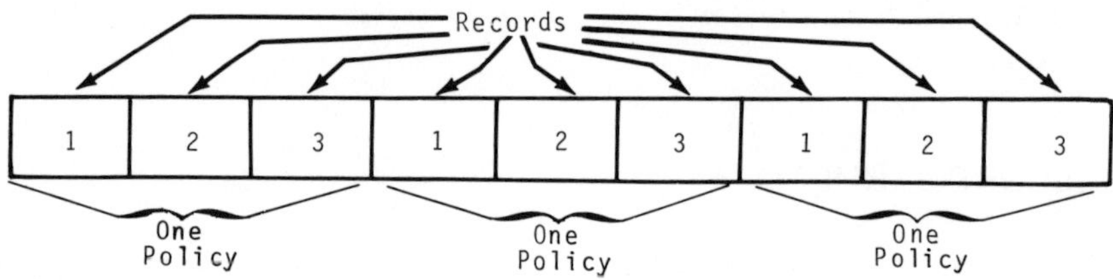

Note that records B and C have no meaning in processing other than when they are read in conjunction with record A; for this reason the records form a dependent series. For all intents and purposes, therefore, multiple and contiguous records use the same approach; i.e., a file consists of a collection of records in which each record of a specific type holds the same type of information in a common format. The group of contiguous records form separate physical records, but contains only one logical record.

A different approach is that of *hierarchical records*. In this approach, a file record is segmented into a number of logical, as well as physical, records. One of the records forms a master record; this is followed by a number of subrecords. Either

(a) the master, *or*
(b) the master and one or more subrecords, *or*
(c) one or more subrecords

is meaningful in itself. The master record may be in multiple or contiguous form. Let us consider as an example an extension to the stock file example presented at the beginning of this section. In this case the master record is a description of the actual stock item: product number, description, prices, pack size, and so on. One subrecord is that of the prime supplier; i.e., the supplier who is usually contacted when more stock is required. Another subrecord is that of a secondary supplier, the one who is contacted whenever the prime supplier cannot satisfy the company's requirements in the time scale. In some instances there may be third, fourth, or even fifth alternative suppliers. Each alternative supplier will have one subrecord, suitably linked to the product master record. In a hierarchical file the number of subrecords and the sizes of the subrecords may be fixed or variable.

It is important at this time to differentiate again between logical and physical records. The hierarchical approach described above relates to *logical records.* The master record and its subrecords need not be physically contiguous. They may be on different files, on different devices, or on different types of devices. The essential problem in practice is one of accessing data and storing data in such a manner that it is readily accessible as required. The storage and access methods described in Part Two applied to simple multiple-record structures. Based on the record structures described here, we now look at more advanced methods that go beyond the multiple-record approach.

DATA STRUCTURES

One view of records in a file structure is that of "owner" and "owned." This is the relationship between records, which depends on how they are cross-referenced. In a straight multiple-record file, no record "owns" any other record. Each record in the file stands alone; there is no cross-referencing between them. Records may be viewed as being related to each other in that they will each have a logical key; if the records are stored sequentially, the relationship is that of a key's being greater than the key in the physically preceding record.

In a hierarchical file, on the other hand, we can say that the subrecords are "owned" by the master. These in turn can "own" further subrecords. This type of file structure is sometimes called a *tree* structure. One record may own a number of records, but each record has only one owner.

Another type of structure is called a *network* structure. This means that a record can own any number of other records, and a record can have any number of owners. The difference between these two approaches is illustrated in Fig. 9-1.

Tree and network structures are thus primarily a means of relating data in one file to another file (or files), or between data in one file only. The method of cross-referencing the data is of prime importance. There are two main methods for cross-referencing data in tree/network structures: chains and chain-modifier ring structures, and lists. The mechanics of these methods are described below, together with examples, and a discussion of the advantages and disadvantages of each method.

Chains

The term *chain* has many definitions and connotations in data processing. *Chaining* is defined here as "a technique of linking logically related records." A

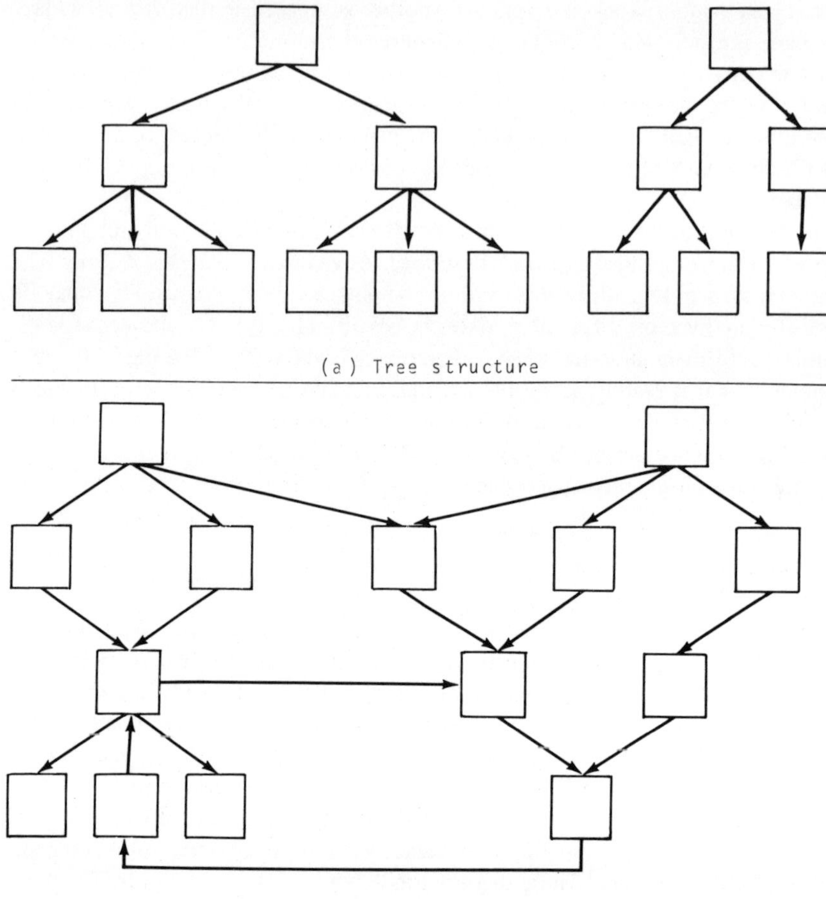

Figure 9-1. Tree and Network Structures

chain is a group of records so linked. A *pointer* is a special reference field incorporated into the structure of a record; a pointer contains a reference to the next related record in logical (not physical) sequence. Records are thus linked together by successive pointers.

An example is shown in Fig. 9-2 where records in a product file are used for stock control purposes. Incorporated in each record is a pointer that references the next record in the file, which is a product supplied by the same supplier. The last record in the chain has a special field in the place of a pointer; this is an end-of-chain marker. The example file is indexed-sequential by product code, and is linked or chained by supplier. This means that records can be accessed by two methods: sequentially, or selectively, by product code; or sequentially by product code within supplier. This is the simplest method of chaining in that there is only one pointer; this is a forward (or downward) pointer. In this case, we can

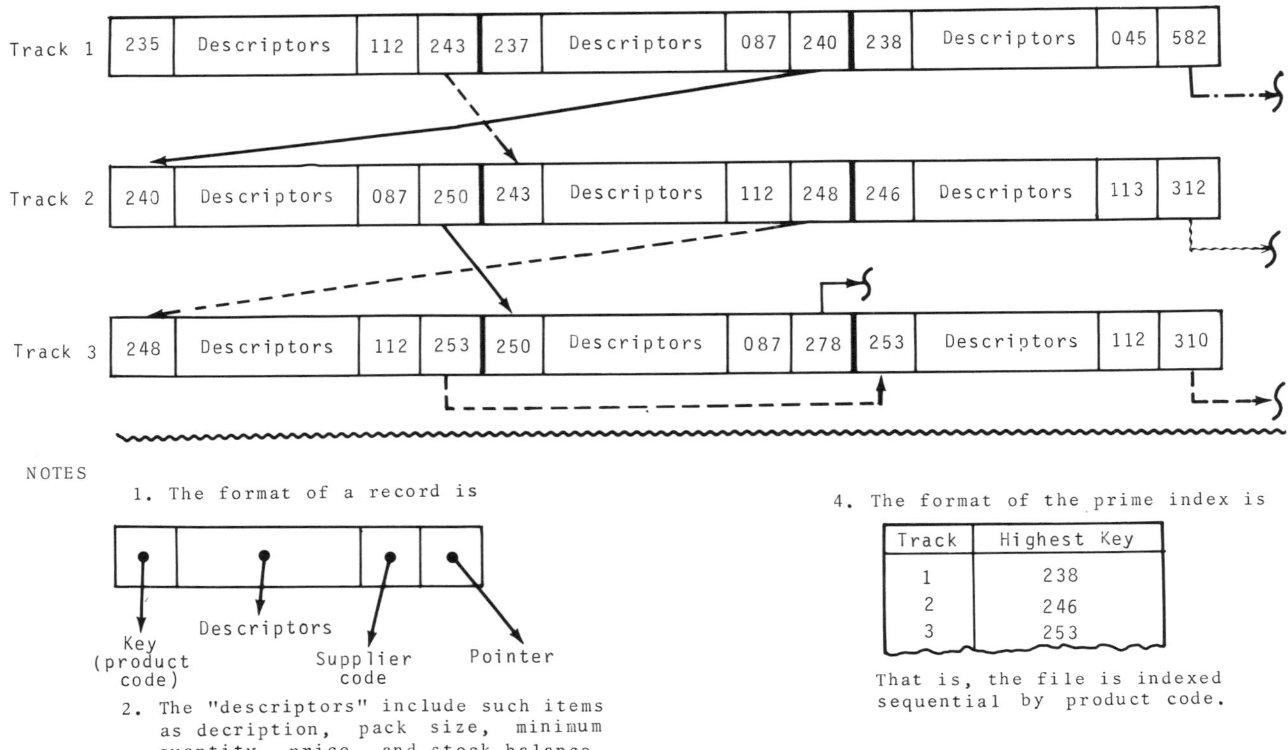

Figure 9-2. A Chained File Using Pointers

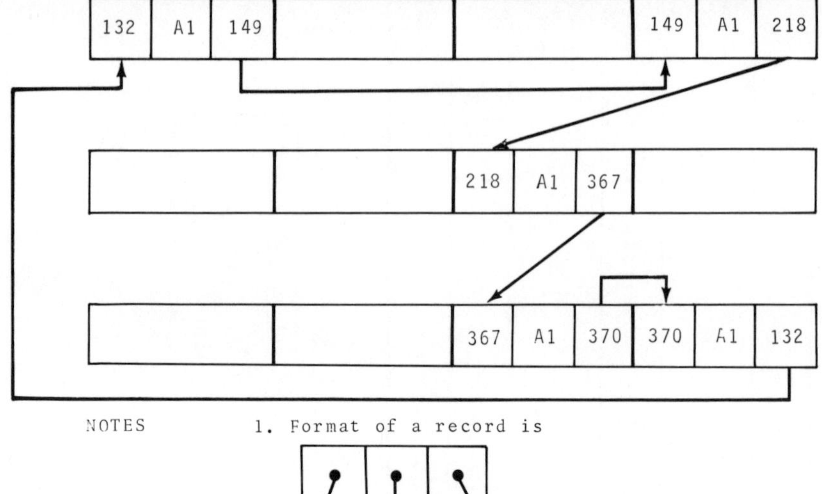

Figure 9-3. A Ring Structure

say that the supplier data field is chained in the file. An additional index may give the location of the first record in a supplier chain. If the file is stored sequentially, the first record in a supplier chain could be accessed by a search of all records, starting at the beginning of the file. The supplier code in each record is inspected until the first record with the desired supplier code is detected. The chain can then be followed to access all product records that apply to that supplier.

An alternative approach is to hold yet another index that gives the address of the first record in any chain. An example of these two approaches is shown in Fig. 9-3. The question presented in this example is: "What is the stock balance on hand for all products supplied by supplier 113?" Without the use of pointers, the entire file would have to be searched and each record examined to see if it had the supplier code 113.

What is the content of the pointer? Depending on the software approach being used, it can be either of the two following methods:

1. *Actual address:* The pointer holds an actual head/track address, or an actual bucket number. This means that all pointers may have to be revised after each file reorganization loading.

2. *Record key:* The pointer holds the logical key of the next record in the chain. To follow the chain, the key is extracted from the pointer and used to access the next record.

The difference between these two methods can be illustrated by a simple example. Suppose that the record key 1421 is stored in location 0200 and is a member of chain A. Record 1732 is the next member in chain A, and is held in location 0271. The file is indexed-sequential. If the pointers hold actual addresses, then the pointer in record key 1421 would hold "0271." If the pointers hold logical keys, then the pointer in record key 1421 would hold "1732." In the latter instance, the chain is followed by extracting the value "1732," which is a key, and matching it against the index.

LOCATING BEGINNING OF CHAIN

This example uses the stock file shown in Fig. 9-2. The problem is to produce a report that lists all products supplied by supplier 113

Method 1

(a) Read the first record in the file (product key 235) and inspect the supplier code. If it is equal to 113, print the stock balance and the product code. Thence follow the chain, printing the product code and stock balance in each record accessed.

(b) If the first record does not have supplier code 113, read the next record. Examine the supplier code. Continue the process until a record with supplier code 113 is found. Thence, print out the product code and stock balance in each record following the chain.

(c) Records (keys 235, 237, 238, 240, 243) will be read and skipped over until record with product code 246 is read. The product code and stock balance in this record is then printed out. The chain is now followed, and record with product code 310 will be the next record accessed. Continue the process until the end of the chain is detected.

Method 2

(a) As the file is created, construct an index that shows the first record in each chain. The start of this index or list will be:

Supplier Code	Product Code
045	238
078	250
087	237
112	235
113	246

> (b) Go to index of supplier chains and locate the first record
> in the chain for supplier 113. Access that record. Follow
> chain via the pointers as described for Method 1.

A modification of the basic pointer system is the circular chain—*a ring structure.* In this technique the chain does not finish with an end-of-chain marker but with a pointer back to the *first* record in the chain. A ring is thus formed, as shown in Fig. 9-3. Processing may start on any record in the chain, and all records can be accessed because of the ring structure.

One of the most important aspects in processing a chained file is the file maintenance—making insertions and deletions. If the logical sequence of records in a chain is of no significance, insertions are simply arranged. If a record is to be inserted in the chain, a pointer is created in the new record to reference the first record in the chain. The address or key of the first record in the chain is generally held in a special control field at the beginning of the file. The pointer in the control field is then altered to reference the newly inserted record. Where the sequence of records within a chain is important, the procedure is as follows: To insert a record, the chain must be followed from the beginning until the insertion point is reached. The pointer in the preceding record is then altered to reference the new record. The original address or key in the preceding record is inserted in the new record, and this then re-establishes the link to the next record in the chain. This is shown in Fig. 9-4(a).

The deletion of records is a slightly more complex matter. Regardless of the logical sequence of the records by the prime key, the record that points to the deleted (dead) record must be located by following the chain. That pointer is then replaced by the contents of the pointer in the dead record. The dead record is thus "skipped" in the chain. (See Fig. 9-4(b).) It may be left physically in its place in the file, with a special delete flag set, or it may be removed from the file. Where the logical sequence of records within a chain is important, the time taken to process a batch of insertions and deletions can be reduced by means of a one-pass loading system. The records in the batch are sorted to logical key sequence *within a chain.* This, of course, presupposes that direct record retrieval is possible by logical keys; e.g., the file is stored indexed-sequential.

In the preceding description, the pointers were *forward pointers.* That is, the contents of the pointers referenced the next record in the chain. In the case of a ring structure, the pointer field of the last record in the chain referenced the first record in a chain. This last pointer field may thus be considered a special kind of *backward* pointer. To facilitate the easy deletion of records (i.e., to adjust the pointers to establish a linkage around a dead record), backward as well as forward pointers can be used in every record. In this case, each record has two pointers. The forward pointer has the same meaning and content as described above.

In a ring structure, the "forward" pointer is used to store the address/key of the first record in the chain. Every other record in a chain has a backward pointer that references the preceding record in the chain. An example is shown in Fig.

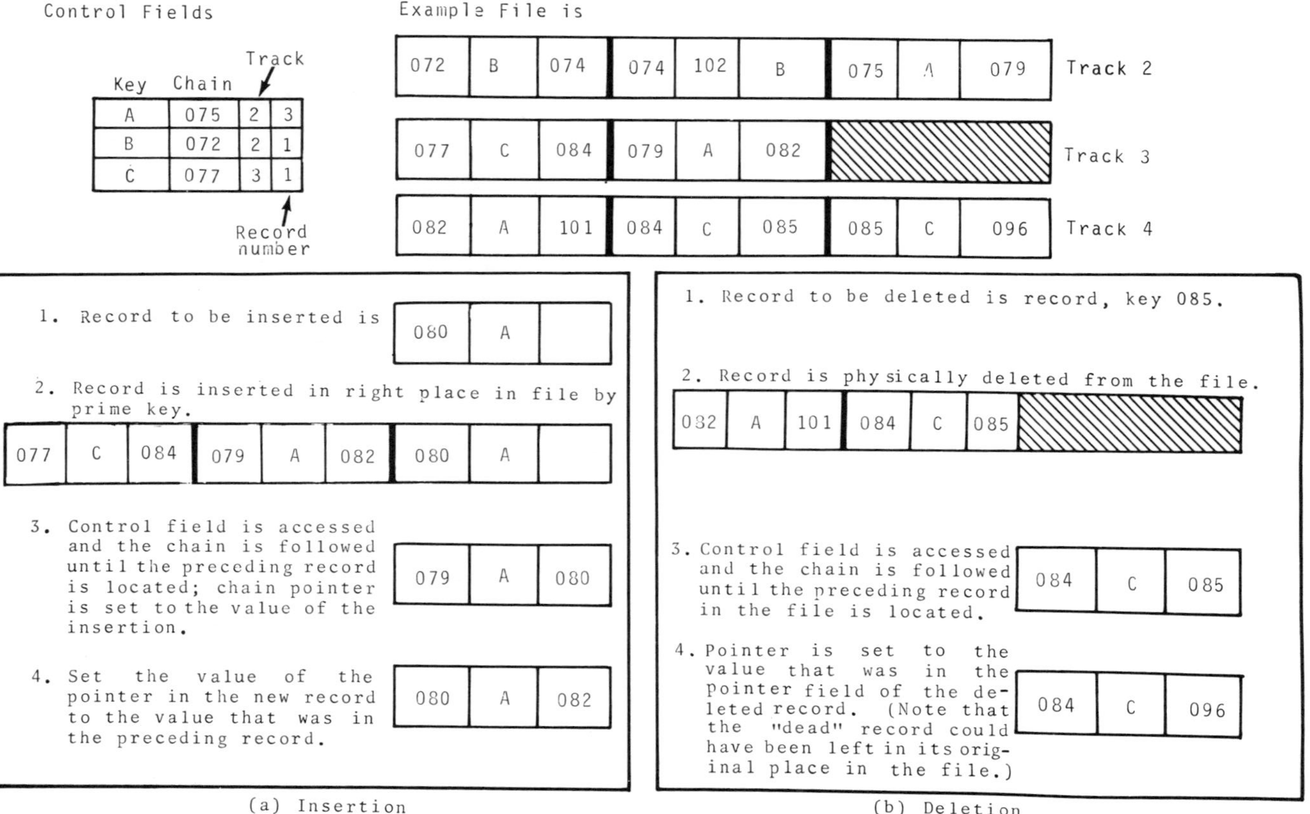

Figure 9-4. Insertions and Deletions in a Chained File

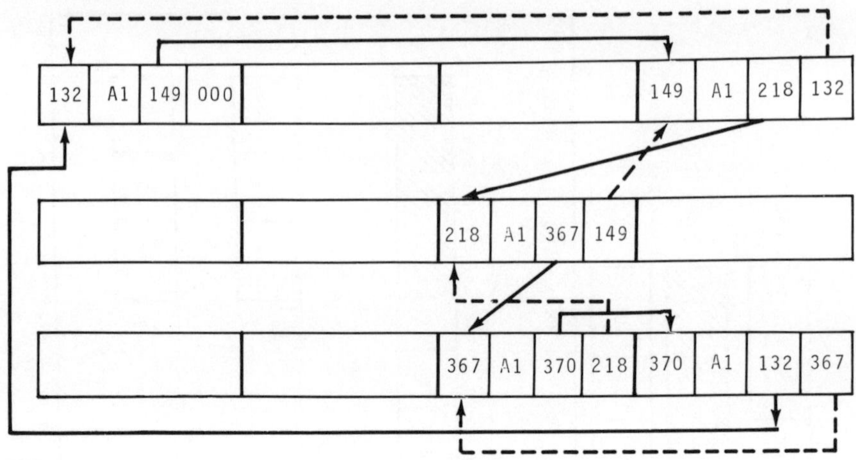

NOTES

1. Format of a record is

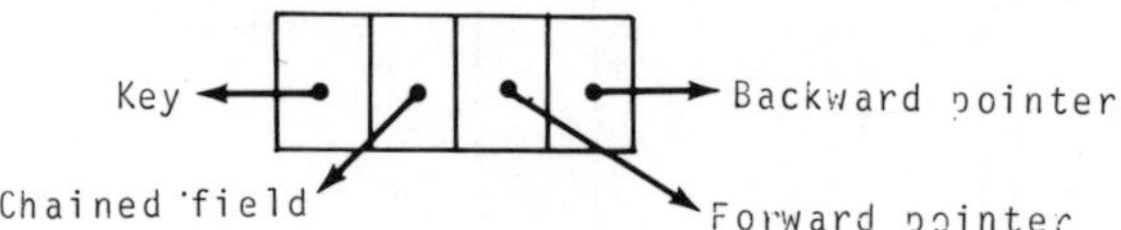

2. Pointer fields hold record keys.

3. The backward pointer in the first record in the chain (key 132) has been set to a special value of 000.

4. For clarity, the contents of a record, other than the key, the chained field, and the pointers are omitted. The contents of records not in the chain are also omitted.

Figure 9-5. Backward Pointers

9-5. These backward pointers can then be used to locate the preceding record in the chain when a record is to be deleted, while the forward pointer is used to locate the next record in the chain. Rather than serial searching, therefore, the deletion of a record is simply achieved by accessing the record to be deleted and then (via the two pointers) accessing the records on either side of the dead record. The linkages in these adjacent records in the chain can then be altered and the records replaced.

Backward pointers thus come into play only during a file maintenance run, although they do have a few uses during actual record processing. The use of two pointers obviously increases record size and the pointer maintenance time during insertions and deletions. For example, adding a record to a file that has both forward *and* backward pointers will require two additional steps:

1. Insert in backward pointer of the new record the address/key of the preceding record in the chain.

2. Change the backward pointer of the next record in the chain to lead (backward) to the new record.

These, then, are the mechanics of handling chained files. In the examples given, we considered a file in which the records were in logical key sequence with the file indexed-sequential. Access to file records could also be by address generation, with the records stored in "random" order. The examples were of a rather simple nature in that they were assumed to have only one chain in a file. Practically, however, it is possible for one file to have a number of chains. This means that we can chain records by any consistent field. For example: The stock file mentioned earlier has

main sequence = stock number; file is indexed-sequential.

chain type 1 = by supplier.

chain type 2 = by product type.

In this example every record would contain a pointer (or pointers) that links it to another record which details a product also supplied by the same supplier. Products are divided into product types. This is a special way of grouping products together and does not show the stock number. Each record in the file will thus have another pointer (or set of pointers) that will reference other records in the same group. An example group of records from the file is shown in Fig. 9-6. In this example, the pointers hold record keys and the actual storage locations have been omitted from the diagram for simplicity.

Similarly, chained ring structures can be used for hierarchical records. Pointers are arranged as shown in Fig. 9-7 and an example is shown in Fig. 9-8. This is an example of a student record file in which data is grouped in three ways: by student, by course, and by semester (term). What are the major advantages of pointer-chained files? They are twofold: They have (1) multiple access and multiple logical relationships, and (2) flexibility of reporting.

It has been demonstrated that it is possible to access data by several keys. One key will be the prime key, that which determines the sequence of the records in the file. This was the product code in the example stock file described earlier. There is, then, the sequence formed by one or more chains; for example, supplier and product type within product code. Data can thus be retrieved in logical sequence regardless of the *physical* sequence of the records. The examples given above had chained fields that grouped the records within a certain category. That is, for example, all products supplied by a specific supplier were chained together, and the products of a type were chained together.

It is also possible to arrange the pointers so that records form a logical sequence totally independent of the physical sequence. An example of this is a policy file used for automobile insurance. The prime sequence of the file is policy number order and the file indexed by this key. However, for some processing, it is necessary to access records by the vehicle registration number. The chained field in the file is thus the registration number, and the first record in the chain is the lowest registration number. This record is chained to the next higher regis-

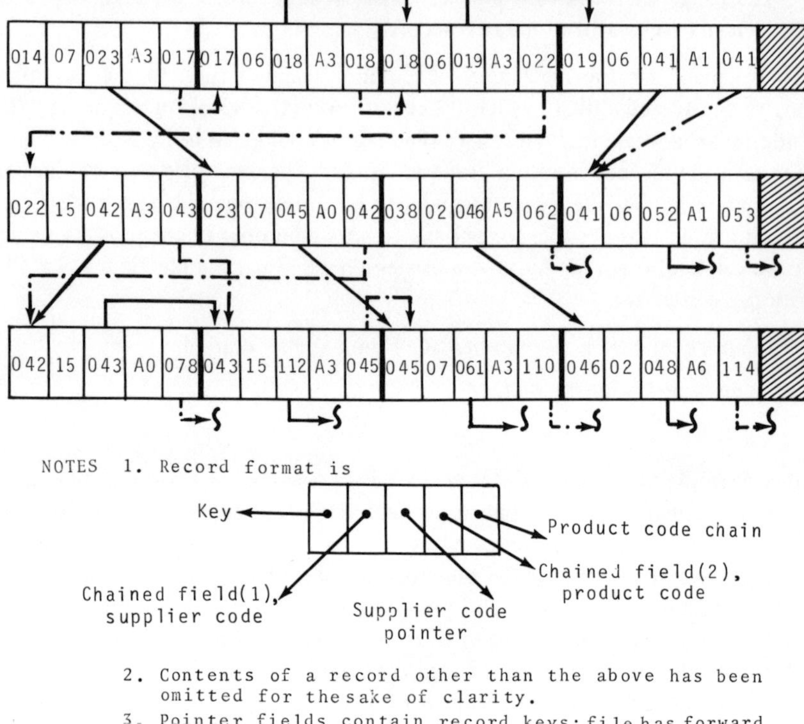

Figure 9-6. Multiple Chains

tration number, which in turn is chained to the record that has the next higher registration number, and so on.

Flexibility for reporting purposes is especially important if additional reports are required after the new system is installed. New reports can be provided without a serial searching of the file and without changing the physical arrangement of the data, as in sorting, collating, merging, etc., with other files. The stock file example given previously could be used to give many different types of reports, as well as serving the function of issue/receipt/balance stock checking. For example, such reports might include the following data:

Report, by supplier, all items that are below minimum reorder quantity (MRQ); MRQ and stock balance are held in the stock record and the supplier chain is followed.

Report all suppliers of product type X; product type chain and supplier code are used.

Report all items of product type X supplied by supplier Z.

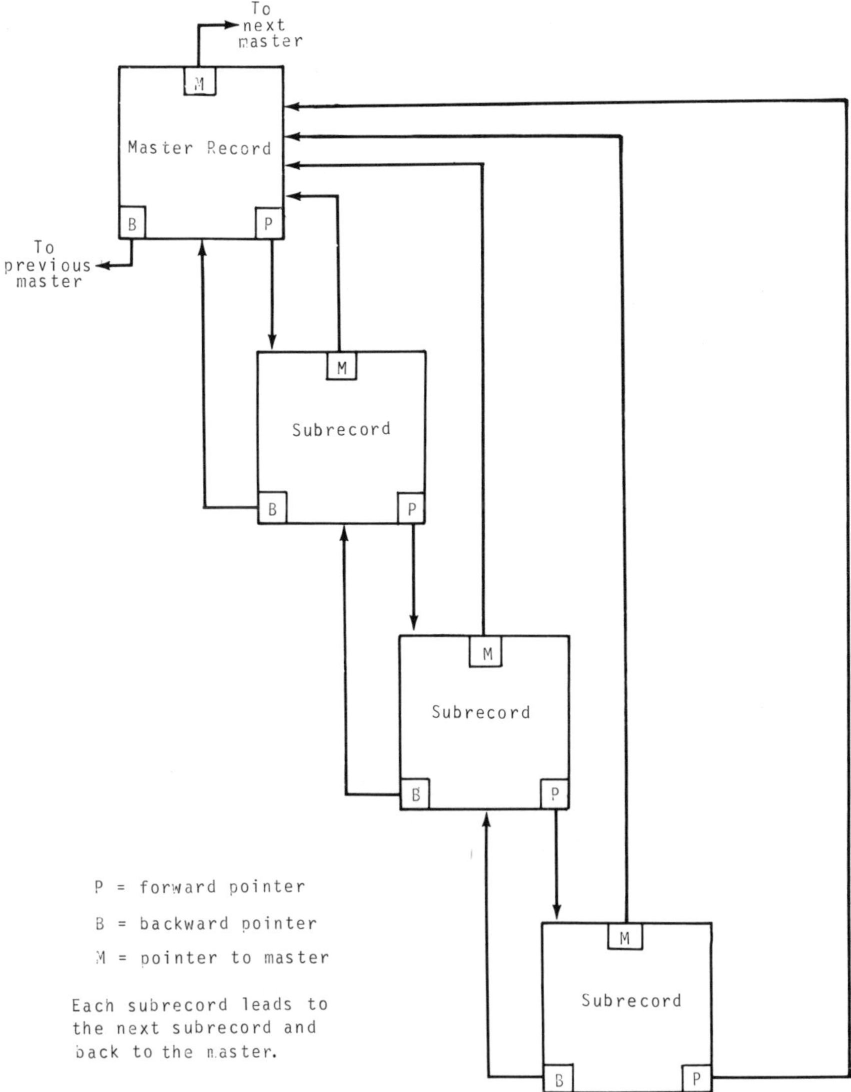

Figure 9-7. Use of Pointers in a Hierarchical File (with forward and backward pointers)

In many systems, new reports can be produced without restructuring the file and will be as efficient to produce as if they had been included in the original design.

There are, however, several disadvantages of the chaining approach. The most serious is the cumbersome updating procedure, which may add significantly to processing time. The seriousness of this depends on the volatility of the data, or the number of deletions and additions in the chain(s). The number of changes to the data within established chains will also be important. In the stock file, the

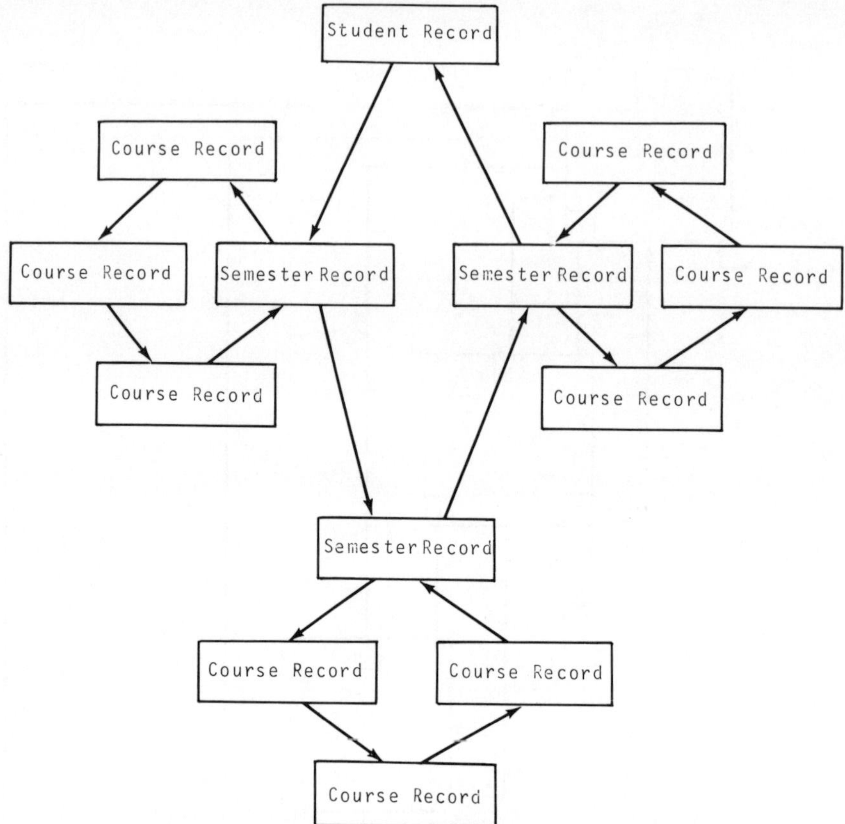

Figure 9-8. Example of a Chained Hierarchical File

number of additions and deletions of stock records will be an important factor, as will the number of times a new supplier is used, the number of times a product is reclassified into a new product type, the number of products obtained from different suppliers, and so on. Each change will require the modification to the forward and backward pointers.

An obvious disadvantage of the chaining approach is in the increased record size caused by the additional space required by the pointers. In the example of the stock file quoted earlier, two fields were chained: supplier code and product-type code. If both forward and backward pointers are used, this means that each record in the file will contain four additional fields for the pointers. If many fields are chained in the file, the basic record size may increase considerably. Similarly, if the chains are long, there is an extended search time to retrieve a selected item. In one file that I examined the record size was increased four- to fivefold by the addition of the required pointers.

The advantages and disadvantages described above need to be weighed very carefully when selecting the file storage and retrieval method. Some of the disadvantages are solved by other methods of cross-referencing data in files. An alternative method—lists—is described below. Although this solves several disadvantages, it does, as we shall see, create some new ones!

Lists

The word "list" is a general term that covers many ways of cross-referencing data in files. The list technique may be used in conjunction with chains in the records. This technique is called the *simple list* approach. We first consider how the simple list technique works and then go on to a method that does not require the use of any pointers in the records; this is the *inverted list* approach.

A *simple list* is defined as an indexing system used when the length of chain through the file is restricted. The chain is fragmented into a number of shorter ones. Each fragment of the chain has its own entry point. The table of entry points forms the list. The fragmentation of the chain depends on the nature of the data in the field being chained. The data being chained may form an independent series, with each entry unique and the chaining being used to give a sequence. An example of this is the automobile insurance file mentioned earlier. In this file there is one record for each insurance policy. The prime key is the policy number—unique to each policy. Each policy record in the file also holds a vehicle registration number, also unique to each policy. Normally, reference is made to the file by the prime key, i.e., the policy number. However, there are instances where the file is accessed by the vehicle registration number.

In this example, we assume that the file is indexed-sequential by the prime key. Each record contains a pointer. The pointer holds the address of the next record in the chain, which is the next higher vehicle registration number. An example of the chained file is given in Fig. 9-9. The control field shown in the figure is held at the beginning of the file. This field holds the track address of the record with the lowest vehicle registration number. To access a desired record, given the vehicle registration number, the first record in the chain is accessed via the control record, and a serial search is made through the file until the required record is located. In a large file the serial length of search may be considerable, but the use of a simple list can cut this LOS to a more viable time.

An example of a simple list is shown in Fig. 9-10. In effect, the list is a table that contains the prime key of every one-hundredth vehicle registration number. To locate a record, the list is searched in much the same way as the prime index. As soon as the search-field (the vehicle registration number) becomes greater than the index entry, the entry point of the chain is located to within 100 records. In this example the entry point is given in the form of the policy number, which is then used to search the prime index and extract the actual address of the record. It is possible, of course, to hold actual addresses in the list itself. This, then, is one type of simple list in which the chain in the file consists of every record and the list holds a number of arbitrarily chosen entry points.

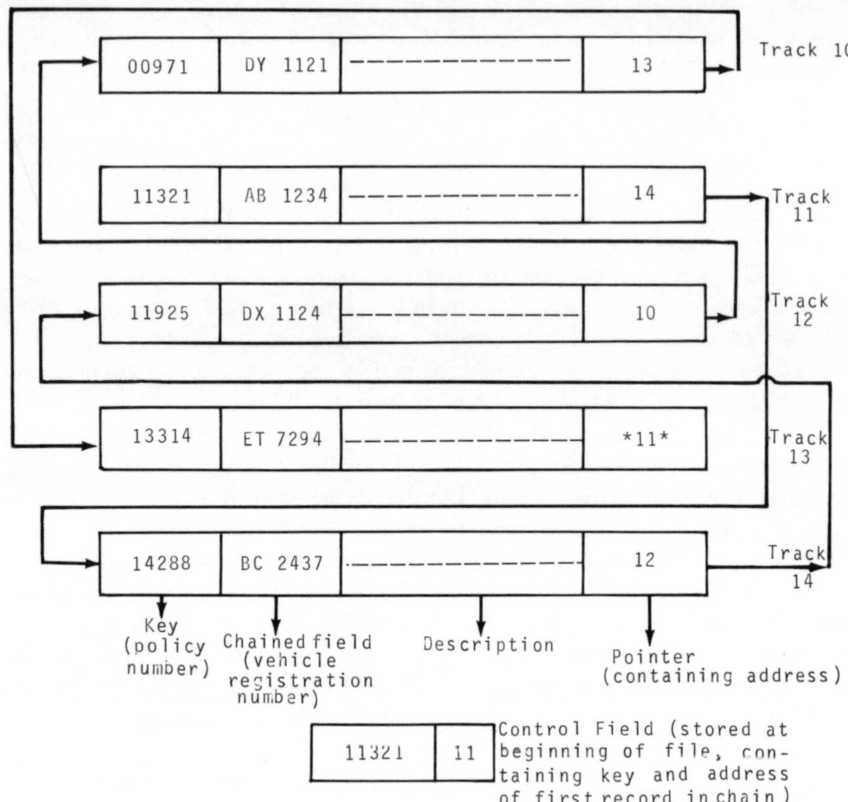

The file is stored in policy number order, with one record per track. A control field stored at the beginning of the file shows where the first record in the vehicle registration number chain is stored. The pointers contain the address of the next record in the chain, which in this case is a track address. Note that the file has a circular chain, with the last record in the chain pointing back to the first record in the chain.

Figure 9-9. Example Automobile Insurance File: Straight Chaining

The alternative method of chaining described previously is one in which records of a particular type are chained together; for instance, where the records of products supplied by a particular supplier are chained together. Let us suppose that the supplier code is a three-digit numeric code. Again it would be possible to have a control record at the beginning of the file to hold details of the lowest product code supplied by the lowest coded supplier. To access records of products supplied by a particular supplier, a serial search would have to be made from the first record of the first chain and on through the file. An alternative would be to use the simple list approach in which the start of each chain is an entry in the list; see Fig. 9-11. The first record in every chain is held in the list and keyed

Vehicle Registration Number	Prime Key (policy number)
AY 1678	90118
BC 2345	01187
BX 0768	34521
DM 0015	87651
DX 4132	21326
EV 9978	00034
FG 0443	13452
JJ 7865	44467
KL 3636	01782

This is an extension to the example shown in Fig. 9-9. Note that in this case the policy number rather than the actual address is being used. Each of the records is stored one per track in policy number order; the file is indexed-sequential. The records are chained in vehicle registration number as before. The simple list as shown at left contains the policy number of every one-hundredth vehicle registration number.

Figure 9-10. A Simple List: Example 1

against the supplier number. Again, to find the records of products supplied by a particular supplier, the supplier code is matched against the supplier codes in the list. In Fig. 9-11 there is one entry for each supplier. When a match is found between the search field and the index entry, the product code of the first record in the required supplier chain is accessed and matched against the prime index. Again the list can be constructed so that the actual address of the record is held in the list.

There are many variations of this theme. If the list contains a great number of supplier codes, but only a few products from each supplier, it may be more economical to hold every tenth supplier code in list. This, of course, presupposes that all records within the file are chained together; i.e., the last record in supplier chain 112 is chained to the first record in supplier chain 113, and so on. Alternatively, it may be that only a limited number of suppliers but a great many products are locatable within each supplier chain. In this case, it would be better to list every tenth product record within a chain; e.g.,

Supplier	Product
112	17894
112	17971
112	18173
113	00768
113	10987
.	.
.	.
.	.

Supplier Code	Prime Key (product code)
001	1346
002	0056
003	8756
004	3452
005	0786
006	2345
007	4545
008	1008
009	9672
010	0787
011	5845

In this example there is one entry for each supplier. Against each supplier code there is in the product number the first record in the chain for that supplier. The records in the file are chained by supplier.

Figure 9-11. A Simple List: Example 2

The approach taken must depend on the reporting requirements and also on the volumes of data, data types, and volatility of the file.

The simple list approach is an extension of the chaining method, the object of which is to reduce the length of search. The *inverted list* approach, on the other hand, does not use pointers in the actual file record. It can be visualized as a series of lists with the pointers held in the lists independent of the data records. This requires one entry for each record in the file. References between records are thus held in the list. An example of an inverted list is presented in Fig. 9-12, which shows the supplier/product code file. The file still has the product code as the prime key; the inverted list has one entry (supplier) for each record and product codes are arranged in sequence within each supplier. If it were required to know which products supplied by supplier 002 were to be reordered (because they had gone below minimum stock level, which is held in each record), the sequence would be as follows:

1. *Access list:* Find the product codes of all those products supplied by supplier 002.

2. *Access the prime index:* Find the address of these records.

3. *Access the records:* Inspect the reorder (minimum) quantity and report.

The lists can be held at the beginning of the file on the same device, or on another device (or type of device). The updating procedures for additions and deletions are the same as those described for chains. The differences are that the records are inserted/deleted in the file area, and all changes to the status and linkages between records are recorded in the independent list area.

Supplier Code	Product Codes
001	1346
	1348
	1447
	1895
	1998
	3076
	3387
	7569
	9981
002	0056
	1056
	1347
	2445
	2678
	3879
	4778
	8799
	9072
003	8756
	8757
	8760
004	3452
	3453
	3454
	3455
	3456
	3457

In this example there is one entry for each stock record. The product codes are in sequence within supplier. No pointers are used in the actual data records. All linkages are via the list.

Figure 9-12. An Inverted List: Stock File

The processing of the lists may be generalized to provide flexible reporting to user requests. With list structures, it is possible to retrieve records from a large file on the basis of variable parameters. These parameters are generally expressed in the form

Report all records that meet condition A and condition B and condition C and condition D, and so on.

A list is maintained for each of the conditions A, B, C, etc. The list for one condition is searched and records with a required condition are identified. The next list is searched and all those records that appear in the second list and the first list are carried over to the next list search. The process is repeated on all lists covering the required conditions. Those records that appear on all the lists searched are the records to be reported. These are then accessed from the main file area and listed, perhaps with some additional processing being performed. Processing time can be considerably reduced if the search begins with the parameter that has the smallest number of records which satisfy that condition. Counters may be used to identify the sequence of searches according to the parameters specified. This technique is often referred to as the *least list principle.*

Let us consider an example of this type of list processing. A series of lists is shown in Fig. 9-13, which refers to a personnel records file. The following conditions are covered:

List 1: Department. Each department has a unique code.

List 2: Seniority. Each employee has been graded according to managerial or supervisory responsibility.

List 3: Sex. Each employee is shown as either male or female.

The file contains one record for each employee, each record holding such information as the following:

Name
Address
Personnel number
Social Security number
Rate of pay
Date of joining company

Note that the illustration in Fig. 9-13 is an extract from the total file. A statistical analysis of the file is shown in Fig. 9-13(a). The personnel manager requests a report as follows:

I require to know the average length of stay of all Grade 3 supervisors in Production, who are also female.

This report can be produced by consulting all three lists. One method of tackling the job is to construct a parameter card that gives the required data:

Grade 3 (supervisors)

Department 67 (Production)

Sex F (female)

Date (today's date)

All records that meet the first three conditions are identified via the lists and then accessed. Each of these records are examined, and by using the date of joining the company and the parameter date, the length of service is calculated. A count of the number of employees is maintained. The length of service is accumulated, and when the last record is processed, the total is divided by the employee count to give the average. This is entered in the output report.

Note that in Fig. 9-13 the lists contain counters of the number of entries. Thus it is known that there are 897 Grade 3 supervisors, 1789 employees in Department 67, and 5653 female employees. There is no way of telling from the lists how many people can be categorized as Grade 3 for department *and* female. In some systems, it is possible to specify exact volumes as parameters, if the user

List 1

Department Code	Personnel Number	Narrative
01	001879	Personnel (23)+
	002345	
	002346	
	002438	
67	000346	Production (1,798)+
	000478	
	000879	
	001003	
	001018	
	001034	
	001035	
	001036	
	001037	
	001045	
	001047	

List 2

Seniority Code	Personnel Number	Narrative
00	002346	Dept. Head (125)+
	002578	
	004765	
	006785	
03	000178	(3) Super. (897)+
	000145	
	000349	
	000455	
	000456	
	000459	
	000467	
	000470	
	000478	
	000480	
	000491	

List 3

Sex Code	Personnel Number	Narrative
F	000047	Female (5,653)+
	000056	
	000060	
	000079	
M	000033	Male (11,217)+
	000036	
	000040	
	000045	
	000049	
	000053	
	000059	
	000062	
	000067	
	000076	
	000078	

*Narrative shown for explanatory purposes only.   +Counter giving number of employees.

(a) Extracts from example lists

```
Number of employees: 16,870          Average number of employees per department: 137
Number of departments: 123           Average number of employees per grade: 703
Number of seniority grades: 24       Number of male employees: 11,217
Number of sex classes: 2             Number of female employees: 5,653

          Maximum number of employees per department: 6,895
          Minimum number of employees per department: 23
          Maximum number of employees per seniority grade: 7,345
          Minimum number of employees per seniority grade: 1
```

(b) Statistical analysis

Figure 9-13. Inverted Lists: Personnel Reporting

has this information available at his fingertips. In this example, we use the values of the counters in the lists on the basis of the least principle, taking the seniority list first, the department list second, and the sex list last. If the lists are in numeric sequence by employee, (i.e., personnel number order), then the list searching time will not be too excessive. The personnel numbers that pass all three levels of the "sieve" are accumulated and the records are accessed.

In the preceding example, there are actually only 34 employees who fulfill all the conditions. Of 16,870 records, only the 34 required records accessed, showing the superiority of the inverted list over the serial search of the whole file. The list-processing time will not be too excessive if the records within the various groups in the lists are in numeric order by personnel number. Assuming that the personnel number is limited to six digits, the lists will not be very long. The example also shows how the lists themselves could be segmented. Master indexes can be held to show the location in the device that contains the part of the list required. From Fig. 9-13, we see that there are 123 departments, 24 seniority grades, and 2 sex classifications. A department index would have 123 entries, giving the location of the list (or start of the list) for each department. Similarly, a 24-entry list would show the location of each part of the list by grade. Finally, there would be a master index showing two entries, the start of the male list and the start of the female list. If these indexes themselves become very large, then further segmentation can be made with even higher levels on index. The hierarchy of lists and indexes for this file is summarized in Fig. 9-14.

Let us now consider the advantages and disadvantages of lists. Essentially, the disadvantages of chaining also apply to simple lists. However, the disadvantage of extended search times is eliminated; this is the *raison d'etre* of simple lists. On the other hand, additional storage space for lists is required, with *no* correspond-

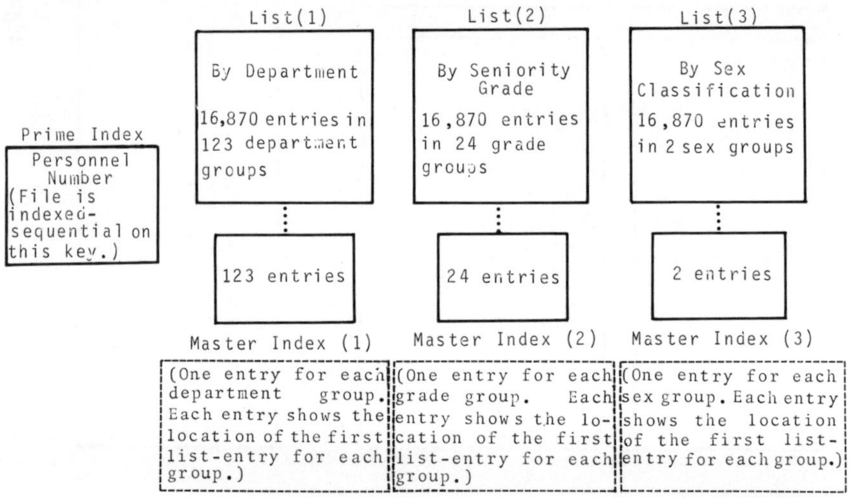

Figure 9-14. Example Hierarchy of Lists and Files for Personnel File

ing reduction in record size to compensate, but the reduced search time in fast-response systems may well be worth it.

The principal advantage of an inverted file is that it allows access to all data with equal ease. This lends itself to a generalized system, allowing the user to describe the search parameters simply without the intervention of computer personnel. More will be said about generalized file processors in Chapter 11. Updating logic is similar to that described for chained files. It will, however, require less time because most of this updating is done in the lists rather than in the main file area. This means that shorter records are being handled, with a consequent reduction in the number of accesses required. Storage space is no more than in a chained file with a similar number of chained keys because the chains are no longer present in the records. In many systems, storage space in the main file area is at a premium, and therefore the separation of the pointers to the independent list areas in an inverted file is very useful.

The logical extension of file inversion using lists is the *involute structure*. An involute structure is one in which the data elements, rather than pointers to records, are organized into lists. Every field belongs to a chain and every item in each chain has an entry in a list. The record, in the sense of a physical group of data fields, ceases to exist. The physical records are replaced by the logical linkages provided in the lists. One or more key fields (search arguments) may be created for each data element. As with inverted lists, it may be desirable to create indexes to the lists. An involute structure therefore permits complete flexibility in file access and reporting, but it is subject to the penalty of an increased overhead in time and space for holding and maintaining the lists.

SUMMARY

In this chapter we have reviewed some of the more advanced methods of structuring files on a direct access device. All the structures rely on the facility for direct record retrieval (i.e., select record addressing) without serial searching. The two methods discussed, chains and lists, are based on the techniques used in the more elementary methods of structuring files. Chains are essentially an extension of the pointer/tag system used for locating overflow records. Lists have their foundation in indexed-sequential files. The methods described in this chapter have two main aims. The first is to permit multikey access, where data is to be retrieved according to various data elements, while the file is stored according to prime key. This is related to the second aim, which is some form of generalized retrieval of information to meet many, often changing, reporting requirements.

This chapter has been largely an introduction to the techniques that can be used. There are many variations of the methods described here, but all use some form of chaining or listing approach. One of the most important aspects of using these methods is the availability of prewritten software to take care of file creation and chain/list maintenance. The great advancement in this field has been an increasing use of generalized file processors and data management languages.

Data Base?

No description of file structures would be complete without reference to "data base." This is perhaps one of the most widely abused terms used in data processing today—abused in the sense of meaning so many different things to so many people. (Indeed, to hear some speakers, it seems that "data base" means all things to all men!) Basic definitions of the term *data base* are:

> A *corporate* data base is all information that exists in the company at any time. An *application* data base is all the information about one part of the company's activities (production, sales, financial accounting, etc.).

Invariably, a data base cuts across departmental boundaries. The modern interpretation of data base is the structuring of generalized files that are system independent and the use of generalized processing/reporting programs. The objective is to create files in such a form that there is complete flexibility in meeting reporting requirements. The traditional approach to systems design is to produce those programs, procedures, and files that meet the user's specific requirements. This means that considerable redevelopment work must take place to modify the system if the user's requirements change at a later date. Using a data-base approach, the time and resources necessary to meet user's new or changing requirements are kept to a minimum.

A data base may exist theoretically with the files stored on media such as hard copy, punched cards, and magnetic tapes. In order to meet the general processing requirements, however, direct access devices are usually required for file storage, and generalized software are used for processing.

The subject of data-base design is deserving of several books devoted to it alone. (Introductory references include Black, 1971; Codasyl, 1969; Kantor, 1967; Smith and Dee, 1971.) What is certain is this: An understanding of data base requires a detailed knowledge of structuring and processing direct access files, since these files are at the very heart of the data-base approach. Equally important is an understanding of the generalized software approaches—principally generalized files processors—as described in Chapter 11.

CHAPTER 10

FILE SECURITY AND CONTROL

BACKGROUND

Protecting the integrity of data in a computer-based system and building in methods of recovery in the event of a failure are vital parts of installation management and systems design. In a commercial sense, we can define a breach of security in an installation as any event caused accidentally or deliberately, which could or does cause the company an increase in costs or a loss in profits or competitive position. This broad definition covers many aspects of the data processing installation: physical damage to plant which delays processing; corruption of data in a file; producing inaccurate reports; theft of master confidential information that is used by competitors; fraudulent manipulation of data; and so on. To see this problem of security in context, we must briefly review the characteristics of a data processing installation which make it so essential to design appropriate safeguards for plant and data.

Centralization and Dependence

The introduction of a computer requires the centralization of information and processing which is unparalleled in modern business. Certainly, a company may centralize many clerical functions assigned to a building or a group of buildings. The centralization implied by a computer-based system takes this even further, to concentration in perhaps three or four rooms. With this centralization has come *dependence* on the computer processing facilities. Consider the two basic levels of system on a computer: record keeping and control systems. At the lowest level there are the record-keeping systems, without which a company cannot survive for long: sales-ledger/invoicing, bought-ledger/payments, payroll, stock recording, etc. Transcending these in importance are the control systems upon which the allocation and monitoring of the company's resources depends so much: inventory control, production planning and scheduling, credit control, etc. Putting these vital systems on the computer means that a degree of dependence exists such that if the computer facilities or accumulated data become unavailable or the data are corrupted or lost, dire consequences can result for the profitability of the company. This degree of dependence and centralization creates real security problems.

Compactness of Data

Allied to the total concentration of data and processing facilities, the magnetic-based storage of data on direct access devices presents unique security problems. In a clerical-based system, for example, the sales ledger occupies reams of paper. To access such data as volume of sales, current trends, cost of sales, etc., would mean going to many decentralized sources of information. In a computer-based system, however, this data may be concentrated on a single disk pack or group of disk packs. The theft and misuse of company confidential information, or the deliberate corruption of data, becomes far easier for the potential troublemaker. Also, magnetic-based information can be damaged by several means.

Lack of Visual Records

In a clerical-based system, the clerks have a day-to-day knowledge of the state of the records. A supervisor could monitor clerks by visual inspection of the records. In a computer-based system, the records are held on magnetic storage media and are updated by an automatic machine process. There would be little point in the day-to-day inspection of each individual record. The accuracy and authenticity of the file information is the joint responsibility of the data processing department and the users. Security problems exist not only in the correction of corrupted data but also in the detection of such occurrences.

Remote Access to Data

The advent of terminal-based systems presents security problems that are now being realized by many companies. These systems permit the interrogation *and alteration* of data from geographically remote resources, with little or no intervening manual checks (and quite often poor computer validation) of authenticity or content. Again, in a manual system, each inquiry, over a telephone, say, would generally be queried by identifying the caller. Alternative methods must be found for protection of computer systems.

Lack of Security Awareness

This is apparent in many computer installations. It can be attributed to two causes. The first is the failure of management to clarify the areas of responsibility for checking the security of plant and systems. Who is responsible for the integrity of the data? Is it the user department who originates the input and who uses the reports? Or is it the responsibility of the computer department who does the day-to-day processing of the data? The failure to allocate the responsibility along clear lines is in itself a security hazard.

Certainly, on the computer side, there has been a distinct lack of security awareness. For example, inspection of the average installation standards manual will generally reveal that the standards have been written with operational expediency in mind, to the detriment of security. Rightly, many installations have been totally committed to getting systems working in the quickest possible time—again to the detriment of security. Inspection of the average program written in the middle 1960s (and of the file protection and recovery procedures) will show stereotyped controls that have not taken into account the special problems presented by a specific system.

It is against this background that we must look at the security and control aspects of using direct access devices. Coping with security affects all functions of the data processing department. In this chapter we are concerned with the problems of security and control of direct access devices and files only. In practice, all facets of security and control are very closely linked.

Security includes three main functions: protection/prevention, detection, and rectification/recovery. The cost of designing, implementing, and running procedures for these three areas must depend on the system and the installation. Each installation, and indeed each system, is subject to differing risks with varying degrees of probability. Similarly, potential losses, in financial terms, will vary from installation to installation: cost of hardware, dependence on processing, confidentiality of information, importance of data availability, and so on.

In this chapter we are primarily concerned with the protection of data, the detection of corruption of or loss of data, and recovery in the event of a failure. Although we are concerned with the security of data on direct access devices, protection/detection/recovery of data is based on many things, such as:

> Hardware: construction and operation
>
> Media: construction, handling, and storage
>
> Operating procedures
>
> System/program controls and recovery

It is these areas that will be considered.

HARDWARE

Modern engineering methods and rigorous product testing have produced direct access devices that are hardy and reliable. In a review of direct access devices about four years ago (Epstein, 1968), it was said that magnetic tape systems achieve an error rate in the region of about one permanent error in 10^8 to 10^9 bits read. For direct access devices, the nominal error rates are 100 to 1000 times better. Recording and reading errors may occur for several reasons, among which are equipment malfunction or damage to the exchangeable recording media. (More will be said about media damage later in this chapter.) The prevention and detection of errors takes place in a number of steps in data transfer: These are summarized in Fig. 10-1.

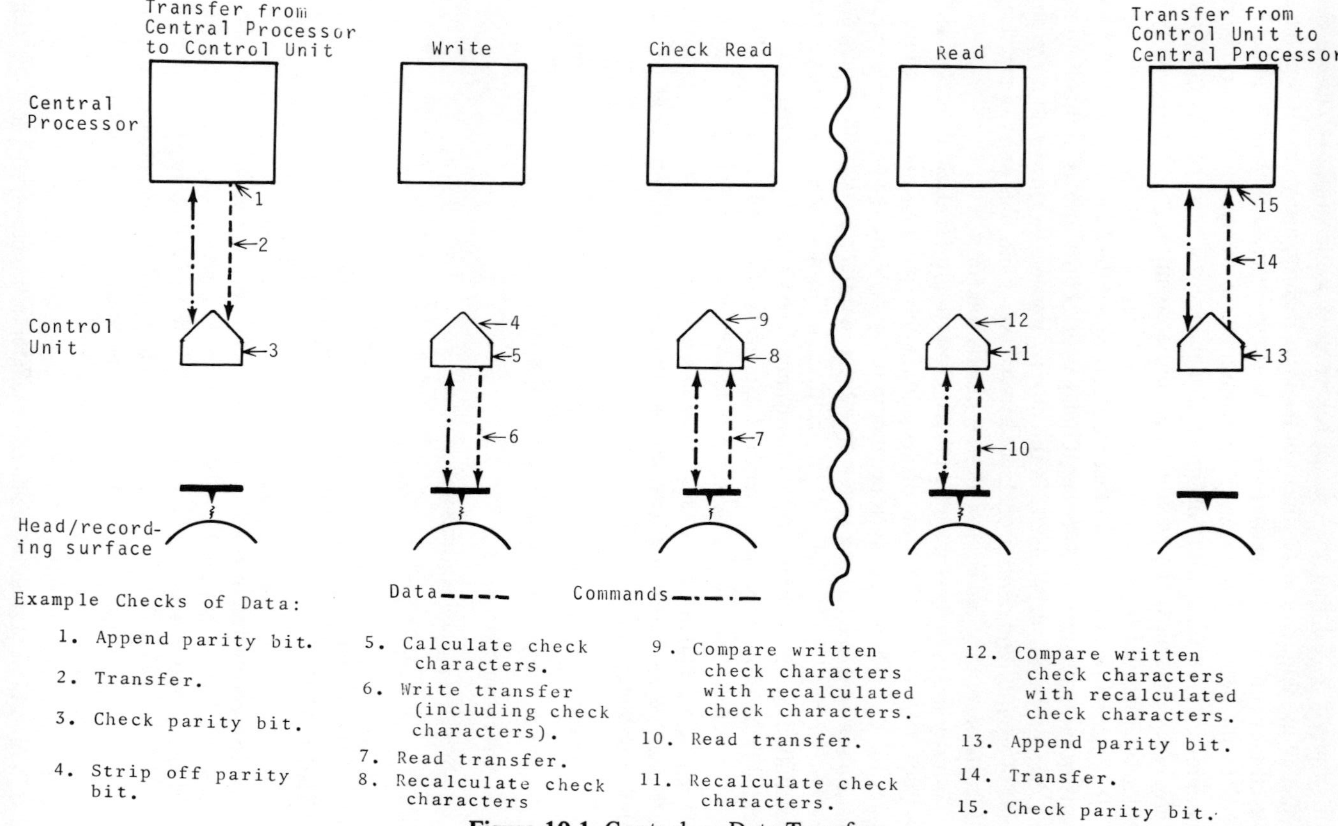

Figure 10-1. Control on Data Transfers

Data transferred from the central processor to the direct access device is monitored by the use of a parity-bit system. Each character, byte, or word is accompanied by a parity bit, as explained in Chapter 1, "Fundamentals of Digital Recording." This will detect dropped or gained bits during the transfer. The next step is the actual recording process. All systems have provision for recording some form of check information together with the data. Some equipment records one parity bit with each word, which is used to check the information on a subsequent read. However, the use of one parity bit per character or byte would be very expensive in terms of storage space. Usually, therefore, the parity bit is stripped off before recording, and one or more special check characters are recorded at the end of a record, block, or track. This means, for example, that there may be two check bytes (16 bits) for 2000 bytes of recorded data, as opposed to 2000 parity bits.

After recording the data and the check bits, there is usually a check read cycle, which reads information into the control unit of the device and recalculates check bits. The recalculated check bits are then compared with the recorded check bits. If the two groups do not agree, the data has been misrecorded and the device signals an error. Either the check read cycle happens automatically on every transfer or it is optional and can be used only if desired. An example of the latter is a WRITE/VERIFY instruction, as opposed to a WRITE instruction, which can be used by the programmer. The check takes place in the control unit and does not take central processor time or space.

Some hardware/software has provision for automatic rewrites if an error is encountered on the check read. A number of attempts are made to write the data; if still unsuccessful, error action is taken. The objective of the check read cycle is to detect immediately any data errors. If the check is left to a subsequent run, possibly a week or so later, it will be much more difficult to re-create the corrupted information. If a recording error is detected immediately, the appropriate action can be taken to record the data somewhere else on the device. There is usually a special control field that specifies the status of, say, a track as "operable" or "defective." If a check read error is repeatedly encountered after a number of attempts to write, this control information is set to "defective," and the track is thereby locked out from further processing. The data is then recorded somewhere else on the device and a substitute track address is used. There are usually a number of spare tracks available for just this occurrence, and by a relatively simple switching operation the local engineer can bring them into use as substitutes for the defective tracks. (Note that manufacturers usually guarantee that a certain number of tracks will be available on the device. The spare tracks enable this obligation to be met.) Additional error interlocks are provided for other conditions such as a timing error, an invalid address, an invalid bit code, or unit disabled.

As described previously, many devices use floating heads. If the heads should accidentally come into contact with the recording surface, serious damage may cause permanent loss of data or damage to the head. To illustrate how this "touch-protection" works, Burroughs disk devices are used as an example. The first line of defense against a crash is the use of a tachometer to measure the speed of the disks. The heads are not allowed to actuate unless the disk is at a safe speed. If, for any reason, the disk speed falls below the safety limit, this slowdown is detected and the heads are prevented from touching the surface. The heads will also retract automatically if there is a failure in power or air pressure. The final protective device is a "touch circuit," which senses electronically the space between the heads and the surface. If the space decreases, the heads have dropped, or there is foreign matter present, the heads are automatically retracted. The touch protection in fixed-disk models is more sophisticated than in exchangeable disk devices.

One of the major security objectives is to prevent the erroneous overwriting of current data. Part of the protection is provided by operating procedures and part by program checks on recorded identification labels on the files themselves. Some devices perform a hardware check through the use of a write-permit key, which is inserted into a lock on the disk drive. Only when the key is positioned correctly can a write order be given to the disk mounted on that unit. Sometimes this key has a more restricted use, namely, the addresses recorded on the device can be altered only when this key is used.

Hardware protection is thus well provided by the design and built-in operating components of the equipment. However, it must be supplemented by good operating procedures and program/system controls. It is a fact of life that failures *do* take place. In designing a system, the question must always be asked: What if . . . happens? The next question is, "how likely is it?" It is good planning to examine the installation and its equipment to identify possible causes of error. Even if there are touch-prevention devices operating with the floating heads, there is always the *possibility* of a crash. If the write/check facility is not used, a subsequent read may reveal data errors that were caused days, weeks, or even months previously. Damage to the media may be caused by an operator (discussed below). It is therefore vital to build into the system some method for recovery if data is lost.

MEDIA CONSTRUCTION, HANDLING, AND STORAGE

Special problems are presented by exchangeable magnetic disk and card packs. With the increasing popularity of exchangeable disk devices and increasing disuse of card/strip devices, this part of the chapter considers the handling of disk packs only. Correct handling and storage of disk packs is a major part of ensuring data integrity. It has been estimated that the great majority of disk faults have been caused by poor handling and storage. To quote from an early IBM manual[1]:

---

[1] *IBM Disk Pack Handling and Operating Procedures,* Form A26-5756-3, International Business Machines.

The disk pack and its cover combine to make a relatively rugged container that can withstand a normal amount of abuse to which it may be subjected while being transported about and placed on tables, shelves, or portable carts and stands. But, because the disk pack is a precision instrument, it should be handled with care.

Media Suppliers

The rise in popularity of exchangeable disk devices has resulted in a dramatic increase in the number of disk pack suppliers. In the early days, disk packs were purchased or rented from the disk unit manufacturer, normally the main-frame manufacturer. With the advent of the independent suppliers, the computer user now has the option to acquire the actual disk packs from a number of different sources rather than from the disk drive manufacturer. This has resulted in intense competition, which in turn has led to a dramatic decrease in price, as much as 50 percent in one year. It also means, however, that the perspective buyer must evaluate many different products, not only for price and terms of business *but also for reliability and servicing.* This is all part of protecting the data in an installation. A faulty disk pack, caused either by substandard manufacture or operator mishandling, may have a serious impact on the running of a system. A few of such failures include the following:

1. A disk containing a master file cannot be subsequently read, and the data held on the disk is therefore locked out of the system.
2. The running of a system is delayed because of a system malfunction caused by a damaged disk.
3. Data stored on a disk is permanently lost.

Confidence in the media construction and in its durability and maintenance servicing is of utmost importance; it is the starting point for ensuring data protection.

The choice of purchasing the media from the main-frame supplier versus an independent source is a matter of no little contention. For example, one point made by a main-frame manufacturer is that because the engineers are frequently on site, the disk packs can be inspected. On the other hand, many independent suppliers offer three monthly specialist checks on the media that they supply. This is often quoted as "free of charge." Regular checks form a vital part of prevention/protection. Another supplier offers, free of charge, a manual disk pack cleaner that is fully automatic. (These can also be rented/purchased independently of the disk pack supplier.) One example is the cleaning device made by Warbash Computer Corporation of America. As has often been pointed out, however, the maintenance cycle depends not so much on frequency of disk usage as on the cleanliness of the installation.

The first rule is to carry out a detailed product evaluation. This follows the basic procedure for assessing any hardware, including such things as checking the servicing resources and talking to existing users of the equipment. Much time and money can be saved by a detailed study of the agreement. All disk-pack suppliers offer guarantees; these should be very carefully inspected. The norm appears to be a two-year "unconditional" guarantee, but there may well be a qualification that this applies only to disk replacement in the case of manufacturing faults. To quote from a magazine article applying to the United Kingdom,

> It is always quite useful to read the small print in a warranty; one smallish company marketing disks guaranteed the disk from the date of original manufacture, not from the date of delivery to the customer site. If the disks are made in America, the time lag between the two dates could be significant. (*Computer Management,* 1971)

OPERATING PROCEDURES

The care and handling of disk packs is normally taught in basic operator-training courses. It is the responsibility of operations management to ensure that all operators receive the appropriate training and that the rules and procedures are followed in day-to-day work. As the IBM manual warns, the packs are robust, but they can be seriously damaged by operator mishandling. There are five golden rules for handling disk packs:

1. Cleanliness is very important; this is part of good housekeeping in the computer room. The environment should be as dust-free as possible, especially important when the disk drives have floating heads. Foreign matter can cause a disruption to the air cushion. Dust in the computer room is normally kept to a minimum by the use of filtration in the air-conditioning system and by dust mats at the doors. The room should be regularly cleaned with a vacuum cleaner or wet mop. Never use any cleaning method that will create or merely move the dust without removing it: brooms, floor buffing with steel wool, etc. The air going into the disk drive is normally filtrated within the drive. Never leave the cover of a disk drive open; the dust will bypass the filter system. This applies whether or not a disk pack is loaded.

2. Never handle a disk pack without a cover. In fact, the construction of a disk pack is designed to prevent removal of the cover except when the pack is being properly mounted on the disk drive.

3. Always lower the pack gently but firmly onto the hub of the drive unit. A sharp impact may cause damage to both drive and disk.

4. Never place a disk pack on a surface not designed to hold it. They should be placed on trolleys or special storage racks.

5. If a disk pack has been dropped, never place the pack on a disk

drive and attempt to use it. It must be first checked by an engineer. Attempting to run a damaged pack can cause further damage to the pack and possibly to the disk drive.

The ideal storage units are those with shelving or cabinets with pull-out, foam-rubber-lined shelves. Some shelving units are mounted on telescopic guide rails that slide easily and are very sturdy. These have the advantage of making the loading and removal of packs relatively easy, as well as making optimum use of the available storage space. Disk packs must always be stored horizontally, the same position in which they are held in the disk drive.

Some installations have to transport disk packs from one location to another. The pack must always be in its two-part plastic cover. The ideal cover is one supplied by the disk manufacturer/supplier. A conditioning period (about 2 hours) is often stipulated. This means that if a pack is removed from the air-conditioned area, it should be acclimatized to the new environment before use. It is also good policy to have the disk inspected by a servicing engineer on its arrival. Any magnetic material may be distorted if placed in a magnetic field of strong intensity. For one manufacturer, this can take place in a field of 50 oersteds. (In one installation known to the author, a major problem was encountered in air transportation of disks during the hijacking scares. All luggage was X-rayed, causing loss of the data held on the disks!)

Labeling and Library Procedures

The last aspect of media handling is the identification and control of the use of disk packs. The major objective is to load the right pack at the right time and to avoid the inadvertent corruption of data by overwriting a valuable master file. Some protection is afforded by hardware checks, such as the write-permit key described previously. Further protection is given by program checks on prerecorded labels at the beginning of a file. All these checks should be seen as complementing and enhancing human checks. Although the multiple-drive units such as the IBM 2314 reduce the amount of disk-pack loading and unloading, the first line of defense in file security is the operator.

The number of disk packs in an installation is very much smaller than the number of magnetic tapes. In many installations, insufficient attention is paid to the correct cataloging of disks. This is just as important with disks as it is with tapes, despite the smaller number of media units. A problem encountered in some installations has been that, in the initial days of disk usage, cataloging of packs was neglected; the number of disks increased, and control over disk usage became difficult. It is always good policy to institute procedures for disk-pack labeling and cataloging as early as possible. The design of a good cataloging system depends on many local factors: the number of packs, the life of information stored on the disks, and how a file is identified to the operating system. It is therefore impossible to define general labeling and library procedures that are ideal for all installations. The discussion here covers the general considerations

(a) Volume serial card

(b) Card holder on drive

Figure 10-2. Visual Labels

Supplier	Type	Serial No.	Volume Serial Number		
Defect Tracks			Released	Withdrawn	
Date Recorded	Due for Release	By	Text	Date Released	By

(c) Example index card

This example presupposes that each pack has only one file on it at a time; it does not allow for multiple-file disk packs.

Figure 10-2. (Continued)

and gives examples of useful forms and cards. The cataloging procedures for disk packs are considerably simpler than for magnetic tapes because the contents are less subject to change.

All disk packs should be identified by a simple, unique code. The format of the code must depend on the operating system that will identify, open, and close files. This is often called the *volume serial number*. In one system described by BASF in Europe, volume serial numbers have the form DA, followed by a three-digit number such as DA 108 (DA standing for "directly addressable"). Some installations also have a library number, which is used for clerical purposes. Most installations, however, rely on the one unique identifying number: volume serial number. It is clearly marked on all disk packs. The system described by BASF uses self-adhesive labels stuck to the trim shield of the disk pack; see Fig. 10-2(a). The number is written twice, at right angles, so that it is visible irrespective of the angle of the cover handle.

A simple card-labeling system is required to identify the contents of a disk pack. Again, BASF have an excellent method for doing this: A plastic pocket on the disk cover can be used to hold the card when the disk is in the cover. Identification of the contents of a disk is also required when the pack is mounted on a disk drive. This is achieved by having a card frame on the drive itself, in which the card is inserted when the pack is loaded; see Fig. 10-2(b). In this example, the identification card shows

library number, usually the same as the volume serial number.

volume serial number.

operator number, the operator responsible for recording the data on the disk.

supervisor's number, the supervisor responsible for issuing the disk.

the date the disk was recorded.

release, the planned release date of the disk from the library.

text, a simple file name identifying contents.

A master index of disk packs, their contents, and status is usually required. An example card is shown in Fig. 10-2(c). The top of the card contains information about the disk and supplier, and the body of the card allows one entry for each use of the disk when it is recorded. It is therefore possible to see the status of a disk at a glance. The index cards may be arranged in two groups: allocated and unallocated, depending on whether the disks currently hold information. In an installation that has many disks for which the user is to be charged for their use, the contents of the cards may be extended to include these details. Punched cards are used if statistics are to be produced by computer. The indexing system may also be used to identify the location and status of backup copies of master files that are stored in remote locations.

By the use of such labeling and cataloging techniques, a measure of protection is afforded: By following the labeling procedure, incorrect disk usage is avoided.

SYSTEM/PROGRAM CONTROLS AND RECOVERY

Basic Controls

It is a normal part of systems design to build in data vet controls. These are the checks made on input data, including range checks, format checks, and check digits. They apply no matter what file storage media is used. The modern concept of the input edit and validate is that only proven "clean" data is in the system when master files are created and updated. All data that is input to the system is passed through the edit/validate program as the first step in the system. Error reports are produced by this program and rejected data is flagged for correction. It is then corrected by the user and/or the data control section, and returned as input on the next run. Tighter checks are required on direct input data via an on-line terminal. To a large extent the checks made on the data on input are independent of the file storage media. However, the quality of the input is especially important when updating is by overlay.

In addition to the accidental corruption of data through error input, on-line terminal systems present a problem of protecting confidential data. In such systems there are several possibilities for protection. Data on the file can be scrambled. A special formula is needed to turn the data into an understandable form; the use of the formula is carefully controlled. Another approach is the use of passwords. These are input by the user through a terminal and checked by a control program. Each user has a unique password that is recognized by the control program. Sometimes users performing different functions or who are at different places on the management hierarchy are entitled to have only certain data. The file data is therefore graded according to the user: One user may have access to certain data but not to other. There are many methods of calculating passwords, depending on the degree of confidentiality. In one system, the password changes every hour—only one user has the appropriate formula to calculate the correct password at any time. (In fact, during the systems testing of this job, there was a program bug in the formula-calculation program, with the result that the program calculated a new password every second rather than every hour. The programmer could not calculate the password faster than the program, and was locked-out of his own program during on-line testing!)

Record counts and control totals can be used in file-updating runs. These controls often compute the number of

input records

new records created

deleted records

changed records

matched records retrieved

and other similar data. If a file is updated by overlay, the file is not copied, as in the case of magnetic tape. The overlay mode is used with selective record retrieval rather than with serial file processing. Therefore, record counts of number of records at beginning of run and of number of records at end of run are meaningless, since only a limited number of file records are accessed. One solution to this is to keep cumulative record counts, checked when the file is read serially/sequentially during, for example, a file copy for maintenance. From a file security point of view, it is generally better to leave the physical deletion of records to a separate file maintenance run than to do it during routine file updating/processing.

Many program controls are concerned with identifying data and its currency and with preventing the erroneous overwriting of data. Most software has provision for creating and checking various identification labels. The content, format, and use of a label depends on the equipment, the software, and the file structure, but is usually similar to that used on magnetic tape files. One example approach is shown in Fig. 10-3, based on an IBM technique. Each unit of media is called a *volume* and is identified by a unique volume serial number. The volume label identifies a particular volume, such as a disk pack, and contains the address of a special control area, called the VTOC (volume table of contents). It shows the arrangement of various file areas on the volume. For example, a disk pack may contain a number of different file areas, as shown in Fig. 2-10. The start and finish addresses of each area may be shown together with the address of the file

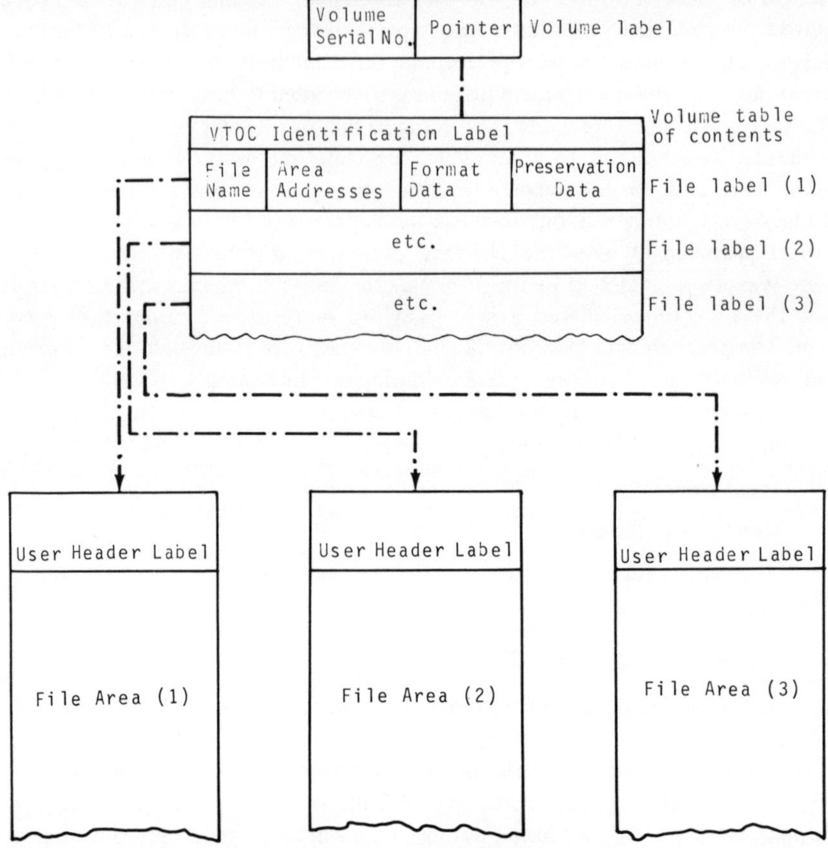

Figure 10-3. Program Labels (after IBM)

identification label for each area. Each file has a label that identifies the contents and the currency of information. (Note that it is also possible to have a file that, for processing reasons, is segmented into a number of areas such as tracks 1 to 25, 50 to 65, and 78 to 100. Each of these areas must be identified and controlled.)

File identification may include a file name, date created, date last-accessed/updated, version, or generation number. There may also be a retention period; this, added to the date created, can be used to form a purge date, which is checked against the current date on subsequent processing runs. If the current date is less than the purge date, no write operation is allowed to take place. If, however, the current date is equal to or greater than the purge date, the data on that area of the device is no longer required and can be overwritten with new data.

Address ranges in control labels are very important, especially when there is more than one file currently on line in one device (e.g., multiple-file disk packs).

They are used to ensure that a program does not inadvertently access another file area and overwrite the wrong data.

Certainly, one of the best protective controls is the use of a careful test plan, with rigorous testing of all disk programs before operational use on live data. Equally important is rigorous program testing after even the smallest amendment to a program, once it is operational. For all the careful testing and operational controls, however, recovery in the event of a failure must always be a consideration in system design.

Recovery

One of the most important aspects of systems design is the formulation of backup and recovery procedures. These are the contingency plans in the event a "what if . . ." condition arises. An old adage in design is always useful to bear in mind: "You can make a system foolproof, but you can't make it damn foolproof." As discussed previously, magnetic tape-based systems have the built-in file copy that affords many opportunities for recovery. The classic method is the use of the grandfather-father-son technique, which permits the reconstruction of corrupted or lost data. In direct access systems where updating is done by overlay, the original data is destroyed by the superimposition of new data. New techniques are thus required to assure recovery in the event of a security failure.

The recovery procedures used depend on many factors, all of which must be carefully studied during design. Among these factors are the following:

What is the probability of a complete loss of data through physical damage to file storage media?

What is the probability of erroneous data being applied to master file records?

How important is the file data? (In some systems, for example, the accuracy and completeness of data is certain files is not critical. In other files, the data may have to be 100 percent complete and 100 percent accurate.)

What is the frequency of processing? (Daily, weekly, monthly, etc.; in batch mode, or on-demand via terminals?)

What is the minimum time delay that can be tolerated between data loss and corruption, and having the data system back in full operation after recovery?

The recovery procedures for a particular file have one major objective: to get an accurate and complete file available to the system within the appropriate time scale so that the required reports and messages are produced at the right time. Within this prime objective, much of the design work is common sense, imagination, and careful planning. Some of the basic techniques for recovery are described below. These are the general methods that must be modified and extended to suit the processing requirements of a specific system. The general guideline in the design and running of recovery procedures is this: The shorter the recovery time, the more time must be spent during normal processing in preparing for a failure—and hence the more expensive the recovery procedures.

All file-recovery procedures have file copying as their basis. The simplest method of recovery is the use of a complete file copy with preserved input. An example is shown in Fig. 10-4(a). The complete contents of a file are dumped at regular intervals, and the input is preserved. The file can be dumped on the same type of device (e.g., exchangeable disk to exchangeable disk) or onto another type of media entirely, such as magnetic tape. The time interval between dumps depends on three conditions:

1. Frequency of processing (daily, weekly, monthly, etc.)

2. Size of file and number of input transactions

3. Tolerable time delay between data loss/corruption and full recovery

All input to the file is retained in a readily accessible form. If the current version of the file is damaged in any way, it is possible to re-create the file by running the previous input against the last dumped copy.

A modification of the complete file copy is the selected, updated record copy. Each time a record on the file is changed, the original file record, possibly together with the input record, is copied out to another device. One method for doing this is shown in Fig. 10-4(b). This technique is very useful in cases where there are a large number of file records and a small number of input transactions. It reduces the frequency at which the master file is completely copied. Consider the start of a day's processing. As a file record is updated, the key/address of the record is written to magnetic tape. At the same time, a special flag is set in the file record. If subsequent transactions are applied to that record, the flag is detected and the key/address copy is inhibited. This means that the key/address of an updated record is written out only once during a day. At the end of the day, the tape is read and the matching master records are read from the file. Each of the records is dated and written to another tape. The tapes produced each day, together with the last full copy of the file, form the basis of backup and reconstruction. If it is required to reconstruct one or more records, the dated tape records are sorted and merged. These records can then be applied to the last complete copy. (Despite the fact that a reduced frequency of complete file copy production may be adopted, the interval between file copying should not be too long; otherwise, the time required to sort/merge the tape records will become excessive in the event of a failure.) The flags in the master records are not set during this process, thus initializing the file for the next processing cycle.

Another variation is the use of two file copies on line at the same time, as shown in Fig. 10-4(c). The claimed advantage of this method is that there is no nonproductive file copying, and an up-to-date version of the file is immediately

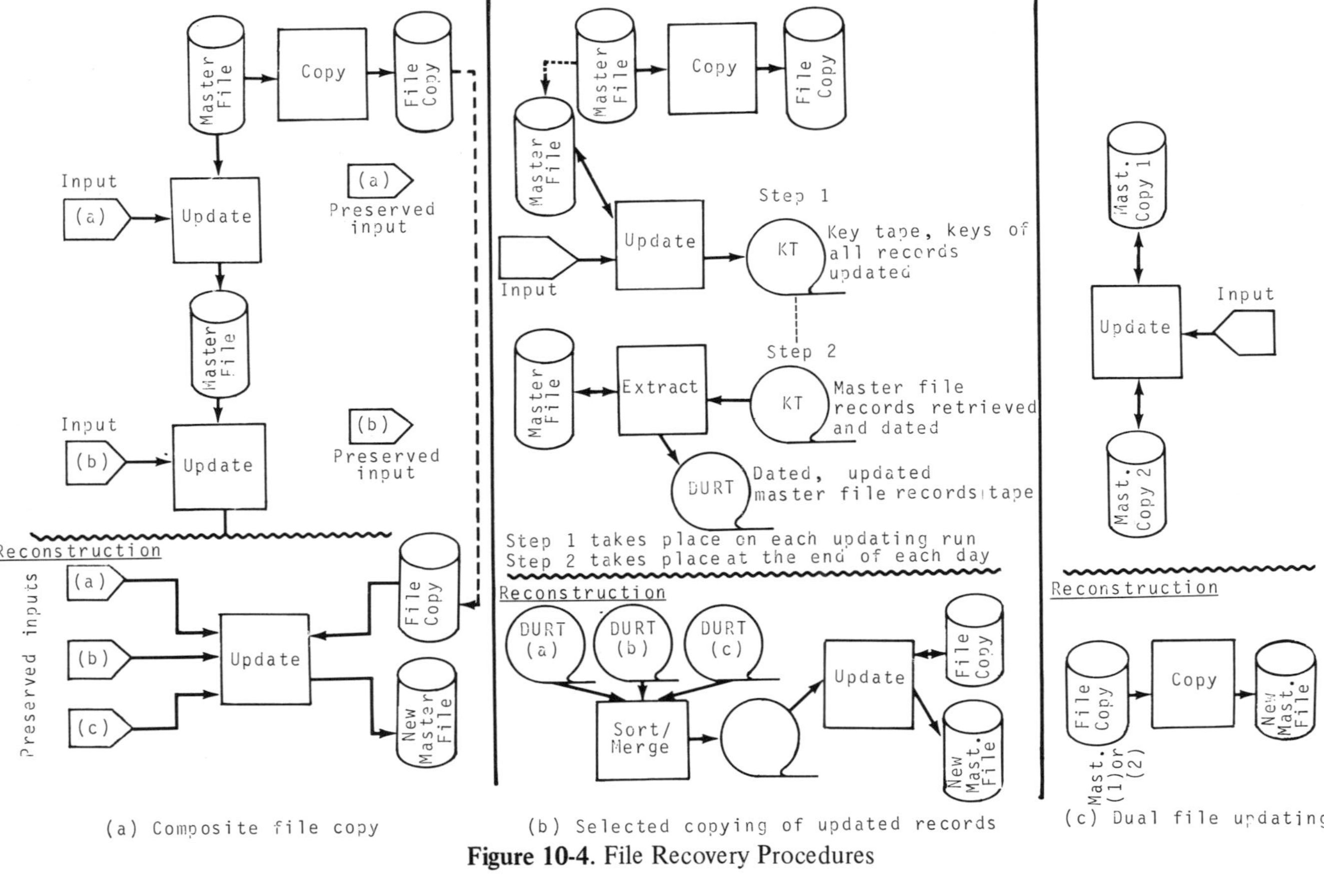

Figure 10-4. File Recovery Procedures

available in the advent of damage to one copy. The time spent on the dual updating is minimal if the two devices are on different channels and the computer has time-sharing/overlap facilities. The two main disadvantages are that the two file copies are together at the same location and at the same time, and that invalid data will be applied to both files simultaneously. The latter problem can be solved only by maintaining yet another, independent, file copy.

The design of the recovery procedures should be done in conjunction with laying audit trails. Audit trails provide perhaps the most comprehensive method for recovery in the advent of an invalid alteration to the file being made. An audit trail is essentially a record of all information that has passed through the system, of the files altered, and sometimes of the programs that were responsible for any alterations. Besides enabling data to be reconstructed, it aids the accountant in making an audit; it may also be necessary to fulfill certain legal requirements. Closely allied to the backup copying procedures are the preservation requirements for audit/user purposes. Depending on the system's requirements, it may be necessary to preserve data for a certain time. The designer must therefore examine the retention requirements, from the point of view of the accountant, user, and legal restrictions. It may be the case that a version of a file can be released immediately when a new file copy is made. In some cases, a file may have to be retained for considerably longer. One solution here is *media cycling,* the principle of which is that, as data ages, reference to it will be made less often and with an increasingly slower response time. The storage media is thus changed as the data ages. For example,

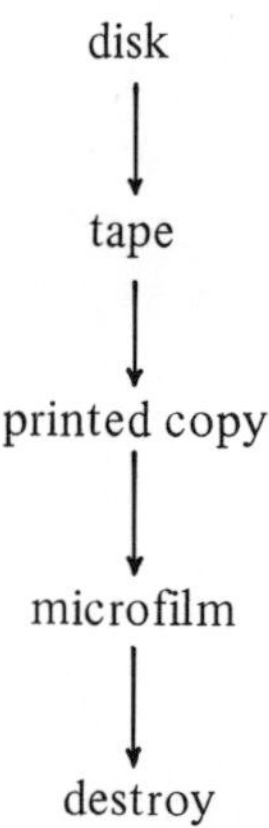

An audit trail can be created by arranging a program to "sign" each record updated. An example is shown in Fig. 10-5. Each file record has two control fields that contain the date and the program reference of the last update. By means of printed reports containing input and file status data, it is possible to trace and correct invalid adjustments. Depending on the characteristics of the system, the reports can be produced daily, weekly, or even monthly.

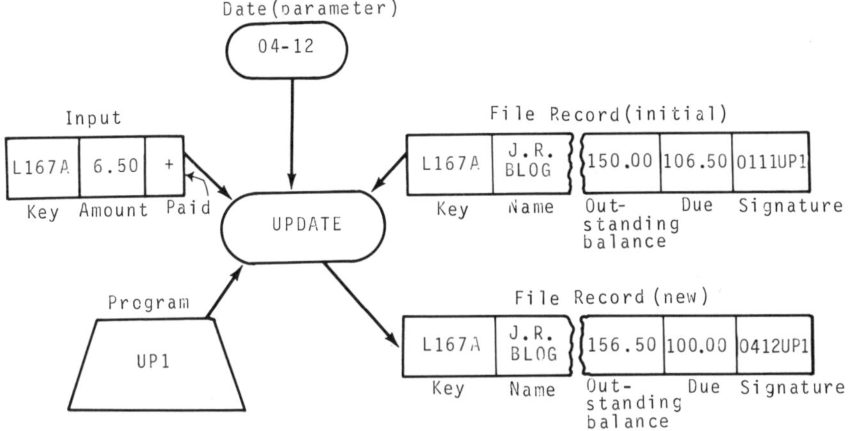

Account Number	Name	Last Reference		Amount Paid	Balance Due	O/S
		Date	Program			
L167A	J.R.BLOG	04-12	UP1	6.50	100.00	156.00

Figure 10-5. Audit Trail: Program Signature

CHAPTER 11

PROGRAMMING AND GENERAL SOFTWARE

THE IMPORTANCE OF SOFTWARE

In previous chapters, direct access hardware and file structures have been discussed. In this chapter, we turn our attention to programming for direct access, give a general review of special problems encountered, and present modern software solutions. In itself, programming for direct access is no more *complex* than programming for any other type of device, such as magnetic tape. It can, however, be far more time consuming; this was certainly the case in the early days of direct access usage, with all the teething problems encountered when new techniques are used. Because there were bugs in both hardware and software for some devices, testing took longer, since files had to be structured and loaded for testing, including the creation of indexes for indexed-sequential test files. With the advent of more flexible *working* software, programming has become far less time consuming. Software in this context means the prewritten and tested programs supplied by a manufacturer, software house, or trade association, or those developed in house. Why is software so important for direct access devices? It is primarily because there are so many "housekeeping" functions and because there are so many options in how files can be structured and processed.

Consider the basic housekeeping functions associated with most direct access files, shown in the following list.

1. File/volume identification, writing

2. File/volume identification, checking

3. Writing/maintenance of all control and address fields

4. File transcriptions

5. File creation: storing overflow records and forming indexes

6. File processing and maintenance: opening new volumes; index searching; detecting, storing, and referencing overflow records; record/block counts; record retrieval; record deletion; index modifications for new records; and closing files.

7. File reorganization: transcription, record additions and deletions, relocation of overflow records to the home (prime) area, resetting of overflow tags, recreation of indexes, and file usage statistics.

These examples of housekeeping functions show that there are many housekeeping operations in processing basic file structures. Even more housekeeping operations will be required if advanced file structures are used: inverted lists, chains, rings, etc. Compared with other devices, there are more housekeeping operations required for direct access usage than for any other form of input, output, or file storage device.

If the user had to produce program coding for all these housekeeping operations, then programming for direct access would require tremendous effort and resources. The rise in direct access usage has therefore been accompanied by an increase in the amount of general software produced not only by manufacturers but also by software houses, trade associations, and the like. Consider, for example, the treatment of overflow records in an indexed-sequential file. There must be program coding to detect the overflow condition, to locate an available area of storage in which to place the overflow record, to move the record to that area and set up the appropriate tag references, and so on. There must also be all the coding required to retrieve overflow records during processing. Complete programs (utilities) are required to do routine file maintenance: deleting records, creating, or re-creating a file; moving overflow records to their rightful place in the prime area; altering the indexes and resetting the tags. All these operations represent a vast amount of coding. The selection and use of the right software is thus of primary importance in programming for direct access.

The software approach depends on the manufacturer and/or the software house. This chapter gives a summary and review of common techniques. There are many minor variations in approach; the rate of development and change in software is far higher than that in hardware. The review here is intended to give the reader a good base for considering technical specifications of various software products.[1]

LEVELS OF SOFTWARE

In discussing direct access software, it is difficult to catalog the vast amount of programs available from many sources. The types of software are summarized as follows:

1. Operating systems (also known as *Executives*)

2. Low-level languages

3. High-level languages

4. Utility programs

5. Data management languages

---

[1]Manufacturers and software houses have been generous in providing information on their products and approaches. However, all software is subject to change. The mention of a package in this chapter does not imply that the package is still available in the form described or, indeed, if it is available at all.

6. Application-oriented file processors

7. Generalized file processors

The first "level" of software is the operating system, or executive program. This is the master control program used in all third-generation computers. It is the "lowest level" in the sense that it is closest to the machine and because the computer cannot be operated without it (sometimes called "firmware" in that it is an extension to the hardware). The operating system is also the most generalized form of software. This means that it is not biased toward any particular application or job. It is used by all programs run on the machine. At the other end of the scale we have complete sets of programs—generalized file processors—which perform most file-handling operations under the control of simple parameters. In some cases, the preparation of the parameters is such a straightforward operation that users can "program" their own reports. In this respect, generalized file processors are closer to the user and farther from the machine. The functions of each type of software are summarized below; they are then discussed in greater detail with examples.

The operating system will carry out the basic tasks of label checking, allocating file areas, setting up control fields, and initiating and monitoring read/write operations. The operating system functions under the control of parameters that come from special input messages (such as job control cards) or via a linkage with a user program.

The next type of software consists of the programming aids: programming languages and subroutines. Most programming languages have been modified to deal with direct access devices. In high-level languages such as COBOL, user programs are written with the aid of powerful macros—source program statements that generate a great deal of machine code. (On a level with this there are the utility subroutines, which are incorporated into the user program.) For example, when an indexed-sequential file is specified, program coding is generated by the compiler, which takes care of index searching, record retrieval, overflow handling, and so on. A recent development in programming languages are the *data management languages*. These are high-level languages (which operate with a compiler) with specialized facilities for structuring many different types of file, maintaining the file, and effecting record retrieval.

Another type of software consists of the "stand-alone" utility programs. These are programs that are completely prewritten and tested; they operate under the control of parameters provided by the user programmer. They include programs for file creation, file reorganization, and numerous sort and transcription operations. The extension to this principle is the *generalized file processor*—a complete set of programs that can be used to create files, update them, and produce reports. A utility program can be used to process any file, irrespective of the type of information it contains. There are also *application file processors*, which handle specific types of files such as files and reports used in production, sales, and finance.

The dividing line between a data management language and a generalized file processor is mainly arbitrary and rather artificial. A data management language is used by writing a source program and converting it to a machine-code object program by a compiler. This is similar to any high-level language. A file processor, on the other hand, has a very simple user-oriented language; data storage uses the directory approach.

File Labels

One feature of file storage is common to all types of software. This is the use of *file labels.* These were introduced in Chapter 10 as a prime aid to security through file identification. The format of a file label differs for different access methods according to the operating system being used. They are the means through which the operating system accesses a file. A file label thus not only identifies a file, but also describes it. As such, it offers the only significant "road map" the user has of finding out how his data is stored on a direct access device.

The content, format, and usage of file labels will depend on the way that the file is structured and the type of software being used. As described previously, the operating system may be considered the "lowest" form of software in that it is through the operating system that the file is actually (physically) accessed. The general schematic is shown here.

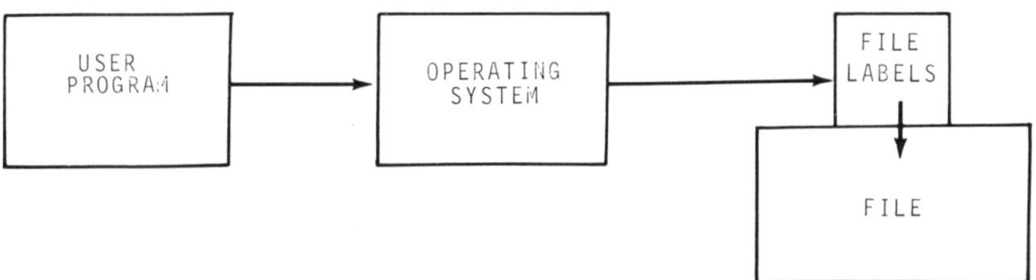

The user program can be any type of program, such as

a user program written in a low- or high-level language.

a supplied utility.

a generalized file processor operating under user supplied parameters.

File labels are thus accessed initially by the operating system. The approach generally taken is to have a common label format for all files accessed by the operating system. In essence, this means that there is some control field stored on the same relative position of all direct access units of storage, such as a disk pack. The control field will be either the label itself or a pointer to the file label. By reference to this field, the file label(s) can be accessed, directly or indirectly, by the operating system.

There may be levels of labels as discussed in Chapter 10 (see section "Labeling and Library Procedures"). In the example shown below, there are three levels of label.

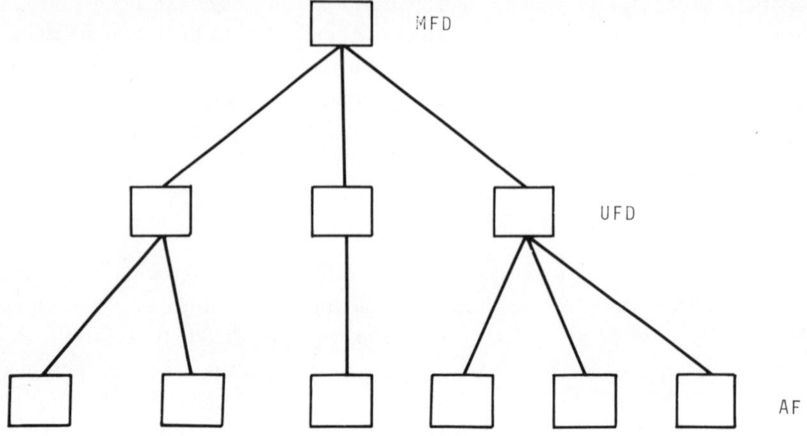

In this case the label is replaced by a series of identification labels forming directories. The MFD (master file directory) contains one entry for each user of the system. This points to a UFD (user file directory), which names the users' files and the appropriate addresses. Each file or file area has its own labels. The number of levels and the content/format of the directory entries/labels will depend on the operating system used. Examples of the possible content of a label area are as follows:

1. File identification

2. Location of the file prime area, overflow area, index area, etc.

3. File structure, including format of track/bucket, including blocking, etc.

4. Next available storage location in file areas

5. File status, such as execute only, read only, additions permitted, general overwriting permitted

6. Control information, such as date and time of creation, date and time of last access, record counts

Thus a label contains a complete description of a file and its structure, in addition to providing security information to restrict access to or usage of any file.

LANGUAGES

The objective of this section is to give a broad review of how programming languages are used to process direct access device files. This provides a state-of-the-art review to give the reader a general background so that he can then study the specification of a particular language. Many languages that were originally designed for processing serial files (punched cards, magnetic tape, etc.) have been modified to permit use with direct access devices. Assembly languages may be used for basic seeking, reading, and writing operations. Because these are low-level languages, they are, by definition, oriented toward the hardware. Each language, therefore, has a different format and a different range of capabilities. It is difficult to generalize about these low-level languages. The discussion here is therefore directed toward high-level languages, which are oriented more toward the user and are more machine-independent.

It is possible to divide high-level languages into two main categories. The first category includes the established languages that have the facilities for handling basic file structures and processing modes: sequential, indexed-sequential, and random processing. The classic example here is COBOL. Most current versions of COBOL have facilities for handling these types of files. Source program statements generate coding (or provide linkages to the operating system or with special subroutines) to deal with sequential record retrieval, overflow handling, and so on.

An extension to the COBOL principle of a powerful high-level language is a *data management language.* This is a language specifically designed to handle the more advanced file structures, such as lists and chains, and tree and network structures. These are not applicable in basic COBOL. One of the main objectives of a data management language is that the files can be defined and constructed independent of any particular processing requirements. This means that a data management language is geared toward the construction and processing of a data base.

Direct Access and Basic COBOL

In the checkered career of COBOL, the language has been consistently modified to accommodate advances in hardware developments. It has been up to individual manufacturers (and software houses) to implement a compiler based on the "universal" COBOL language specification promulgated by the United States of America Standards Institute (USASI). Even the specific standards have been varied to a certain extent by individual implementers of the language. This is hardly surprising when one considers that file-handling techniques must first be based upon *information standards*; i.e., the way in which data is organized on a direct access device and handled by the operating system. Different approaches toward these techniques have been given throughout this book: Hardware-fixed blocks versus variable-track format is a particularly appropriate example. This, in turn, leads to other variations in approach: In a fixed-format track, addressing of overflow records is usually done by tagging within the blocks or buckets. In a variable-format track, overflow records are tagged within an index, and are chained within an overflow area. What is called "serial" processing by one implementer might be called "sequential" by another; what is called "sequential" by one is called "indexed-sequential" by another. With these fundamental differences in approach (defined *before* a standard language was specified), the way in which files are handled in COBOL must vary.

We take as a starting point a brief review of "standard" COBOL: USASI COBOL.[2] In the following discussion, it is assumed that the reader has an understanding of the fundamental structure and operation of COBOL and its use in sequential processing of punched card, printer, and magnetic tape files.

The COBOL mass storage module provides for two techniques for file handling: sequential access with sequential processing and random access with sequential processing. The first is the same as that used for any sequential file: tape, card, printer, etc. This means that records are accessed or written one after another in logical sequence. The other approach allows selected record retrieval. One approach often used is that of an index-register. For sequential processing, this register is loaded with the address of the first record to be read/written. It is then automatically incremented and used to access the following records, without any intervention by the user programmer. When random access is used, the index-register is loaded with a new address each time the file is accessed. For this, the programmer uses an ACTUAL KEY. This is set each time a logical record is to be read/written. The four features of COBOL used in processing direct access files are

> FILE-CONTROL (Environment Division)
> I-O-CONTROL (Environment Division)
> FILE DESCRIPTION (FD) (Data Division)
> VERBS (Procedure Division)
> > CLOSE
> > OPEN
> > READ
> > WRITE
> > SEEK

The format of the FILE-CONTROL paragraph is summarized in Fig. 11-1. Explanations of the features displayed are listed below.

Notes for Figure 11-1

SELECT: Used in the normal manner to name a file, for example,

SELECT DISKFA

ASSIGN: Used in the normal manner to define the medium used; actual content depends on the implementation; for example,

ASSIGN TO DIRECT-ACCESS

FILE-LIMIT: Used to define the limits of the file within which records are to be obtained or placed. The two operands specify the logical beginning and end of the file (or file segment). If the contents

---

[2]Information based on Random Access module, level 2, of USASI COBOL, X3.23-1968.

of ACTUAL KEY are outside these limits, an error action is taken. As will be explained later, there is a READ and WRITE format that contains an INVALID KEY phrase; i.e.,

```
READ file-name RECORD [INTO identifier]
            INVALID KEY imperative-statement
```

The INVALID KEY phrase is executed if the ACTUAL KEY value is outside the specified FILE-LIMIT. (In some implementations, ASSIGN is used to set the file limits.)

ACCESS IS: In the basic version of COBOL, two modes of access are possible: RANDOM and SEQUENTIAL. If RANDOM is specified, then records are retrieved/written according to the value set by the programmer in the ACTUAL KEY field. If SEQUENTIAL is specified, records are accessed in logical sequence by key; the ACTUAL KEY phrase is therefore omitted.

PROCESSING IS SEQUENTIAL: Used to specify that records are to be processed in the order in which they are accessed.

ACTUAL IS: This phrase is required when ACCESS IS RANDOM. The contents of the field with the given data name are used to locate the specified record. The address or a pointer to the address of the record must be placed in the data name before a SEEK, READ, or WRITE statement is executed. For example,

```
SELECT DISKFILA ASSIGN TO DIRECT-ACCESS
ACCESS IS RANDOM ACTUAL KEY IS INDEX-1

. . . . . . . . . . . . . . . . . . . . . . . . . . . .

MOVE 1 TO INDEX-1
L116
    ADD 1 TO INDEX-1
    READ DISKFILA INVALID KEY GO TO L126

. . . . . . . . . . . . . . . . . . . . . . . . . . . .

GO TO L116
```

The definition of the ACTUAL KEY IS field in the data division sometimes requires that a specific picture must be used (depending on the implementation); for example,

```
77 INDEX-1 PICTURE 9 (5) COMPUTATIONAL
```

Whereas the FILE-CONTROL paragraph is mandatory, the I-O CONTROL paragraph is usually optional. It is used to specify the input/output techniques, rerun points, and core areas to be shared by different files.

The FILE DESCRIPTION paragraph (FD) is used to define a given file, the records it contains, and its physical structure (blocking, etc.); see Fig. 11-2. The

```
FILE-CONTROL          { SELECT file-name

ASSIGN TO [integer-1]   implementor-name-1 [,implementor-name-2]...

[ , { FILE LIMIT IS    } { data-name-1 } THRU { data-name-2 }
    { FILE LIMITS ARE  } { literal-1   }      { literal-2   }

  [ , { data-name-3 } THRU { data-name-4 } ] ... ]
      { literal-3   }      { literal-4   }

  , ACCESS MODE IS { RANDOM     }
                   { SEQUENTIAL }

  , PROCESSING MODE IS SEQUENTIAL

  , ACTUAL KEY IS data-name-5 } ...
```

Figure 11-1. Basic COBOL: File Control

```
FD file-name
   [ ; BLOCK CONTAINS [integer-1 TO] integer-2 { RECORDS    } ]
                                               { CHARACTERS }

   [ ; DATA { RECORD IS    } data-name-1 [,data-name-2] ... ]
            { RECORDS ARE  }

     ; LABEL { RECORD IS   } { STANDARD                              }
             {             } { OMITTED                               }
             { RECORDS ARE } { data-name-3  ,[data-name-4] ...       }

   [ ; RECORD ; BLOCK CONTAINS [integer-3 TO] integer-4 CHARACTERS ]

   [ ; VALUE OF     data-name-5 IS { data-name-6
                                   { literal-1

   [ , data-name-7 IS { data-name-8 } ] ... ]
                      { literal-2   }
```

Figure 11-2. Basic COBOL: FD

verbs specific to direct access devices are CLOSE, OPEN, READ, WRITE, and SEEK.

CLOSE: This is used in the normal COBOL manner.

OPEN: The OPEN verb format

$$\text{OPEN}\begin{cases}\text{INPUT file-name} & \text{[,file-name] ...} \\ \text{OUTPUT file-name} & \text{[,file name] ...} \\ \text{I-O file-name} & \text{[,file name] ...}\end{cases} ...$$

is used to initiate processing on the named file: label checking, access to the first record, etc. The I-O option enables files to be updated by overlay (read-process-write back, overwriting the original record). The current label is checked and a new label is written, both in accordance with the compiler's specified conventions.

READ: This has two formats:

(1) READ file-name [INTO identifier] ; AT END
imperative statement

(2) READ file-name [INTO identifier] ; INVALID KEY
imperative-statement

The first format is used in sequential access. The next record available is presented. Basically, the rules for this format are the same as for any sequential file processing (card, tape, etc.). The AT END phrase can be used because the end of file will be eventually encountered. This is not the case with selected record retrieval, and thus format (2) must be used for random access. The INVALID KEY phrase is executed if, at object time, the value of ACTUAL KEY is outside the FILE-LIMITS.

WRITE: This has only one format:

WRITE file-name [FROM identifier] ; INVALID KEY
imperative-statement

This statement is used for both sequential and random access. In the latter case, it operates in conjunction with the ACTUAL KEY clause. The INVALID KEY phrase is executed if end-of-file conditions are detected. It is also executed if the contents of the ACTUAL KEY field are outside the FILE-LIMITS.

SEEK: This is used in random access only, and operates in conjunction with the ACTUAL KEY. The format is

SEEK file-name RECORD

The SEEK statement initiates the access of a storage data record for subsequent READ or WRITE operations. The data name in the ACTUAL KEY clause contains the location of the record being sought. At object time, the contents of the ACTUAL KEY field are tested to see if they are within the file limits. If they are found to be invalid, the INVALID KEY phrase in the following READ or WRITE statement is executed.

Each READ or WRITE statement implies a SEEK; the implied SEEK is not performed if the READ or WRITE is preceded by a separate SEEK statement referencing the same record as the READ or WRITE statement. (One of the advantages in the use of a separate SEEK is in program timing. A SEEK can be given while other processing takes place; a WRITE statement can then be given later when the appropriate location has been accessed or almost accessed.)

These, then, are the basic facilities offered in COBOL. They are restrictive in that overflow handling or indexed-sequential index searching have not been considered. Facilities are therefore required to deal with these conditions.

Extensions to COBOL

In Basic COBOL as described above, there were, in essence, two processing modes:

1. Sequential: Records retrieved in the order they are stored; ACTUAL KEY not used.

2. Non-sequential: The user part of the program specifies the location of the record through the ACTUAL KEY field.

This is a rather restrictive approach to direct access processing; it does not cover overflow handling, index searching, and the like. An example of a more powerful form of COBOL is shown in Fig. 11-3. This is an extract from an actual implementation of COBOL.[3] It shows that the FILE-CONTROL paragraph of the environment division now has an ORGANIZATION clause, an ACCESS clause, and a range of key field clauses. The APPLY clause in the I-O CONTROL paragraph has many different forms; the ones shown here relate to direct access usage:

APPLY RESTRICTED SEARCH
APPLY CORE-INDEX

Each of the clauses is described briefly below, followed by a summary of usage. The file layout assumed is that described under "Variable-Format Track Indexes" in Chapter 7. The three verbs used are READ, WRITE, and RE-WRITE; only the latter is described here because the READ and WRITE verbs operate as described previously.

---

[3] Based on IBM System/360 DOS COBOL: see *COBOL Language Specification* (Program 360N-CB-452), manual form C24-3433-5, updated by Technical Newsletter N28-0245.

```
FILE-CONTROL

      [SELECT file-name ASSIGN clause]

      [RESERVE clause] ...

      [ACCESS IS {SEQUENTIAL}]
                 {RANDOM    }

      [ORGANIZATION IS {INDEXED}]
                       {DIRECT }

      [SYMBOLIC KEY IS data-name]

      [ACTUAL KEY IS data-name]

      [RECORD KEY IS data-name]

      [TRACK-AREA IS integer CHARACTERS]

  I-O-CONTROL
      ....................
      ....................

      [APPLY RESTRICTED SEARCH OF 1 TRACKS ON file-name ...] ...

      [APPLY CORE-INDEX TO data-name ON file-name-1 [file-name-2 ...]].
```

Figure 11-3. Extended COBOL (IBM System/360)

Notes for Figure 11-3

ACCESS: This is similar to before, with the two options of SE-
QUENTIAL or RANDOM. If RANDOM, the file can be indexed
or direct. The latter includes any form of file which uses address
generation. It is up to the user coding to identify the address of the
required record, and to put this in the ACTUAL KEY field.

ORGANIZATION: Three file structures are recognized: sequential
(assumed when no ORGANIZATION clause is recognized), INDEX,
and DIRECT.

An indexed file is one that is stored indexed-sequentially in accordance with the prescribed information standards. In this case it
is a file that has cylinder/track indexes of the form shown in Fig.
7-5. A direct file has a form determined by the user (blocked or
unblocked), with the records stored/retrieved by the user's self-
indexing or address generation procedures.

ACTUAL KEY: This is used, as before, to hold the *address* of a
record. (In this case it is a track address, with the key field defined
as an 8-byte data item in working storage.) ACTUAL KEY is used
only when the ORGANIZATION is DIRECT.

SYMBOLIC KEY: This clause specifies a field that holds the logical key of a required record. It is used to locate the matching file record during reading or rewriting, and to create a key associated with the record during writing. It is required when the file is

ORGANIZATION	*ACCESS*
INDEXED	SEQUENTIAL*
INDEXED	RANDOM
DIRECT	SEQUENTIAL
DIRECT	RANDOM

*Used to specify where sequential processing is to start; the first record to be accessed.

The SYMBOLIC KEY is not used when the processing is sequential on a sequential file because records are retrieved automatically.

RECORD KEY: This is used only when ORGANIZATION is INDEXED; it has several uses: creating an indexed-sequential file, and accessing an indexed file randomly. Simply, the SYMBOLIC KEY is used to access the right track via the indexes, and to match against the key area that precedes the record (unblocked records) or block (blocked records). The RECORD KEY is used for the key-area matching process.

ACTUAL TRACK: This clause allows reading and writing of more than one physical record. It may be used to increase efficiency when adding records to an indexed file randomly. The normal mode of working is the logical record. This permits the transfer of a *physical* record.

APPLY RESTRICTED SEARCH: This clause can be used only when the ORGANIZATION is DIRECT and the ACCESS is RANDOM. When a READ statement is executed, a search takes place for the record, starting at the beginning of the track specified in the ACTUAL KEY. If the record is not found on the specified track, the search is extended to other tracks, and continues until either the record is found or the end of cylinder is reached. The APPLY RESTRICTED SEARCH clause is used to limit the search to the first track only. If the required record is not found on the designated track, the INVALID KEY option in the READ or REWRITE clause is executed.

APPLY CORE INDEX: This clause is used to reserve an area of core to hold the cylinder-level index; it can be used when ORGANIZATION is INDEXED and ACCESS is RANDOM. All or part of the index may be held in core during the processing of the file. If the area is big enough to hold the entire cylinder-level index, then the index will be read once at the beginning of file processing.

REWRITE: This verb is used when files are processed in the overlay mode. The function of the REWRITE verb is to replace a logical record with a specified record (in accordance with the ACTUAL KEY and/or SYMBOLIC KEY). A READ statement for a file must precede a REWRITE statement, and a REWRITE statement can be used only on a file defined as I-O.

The various combinations of direct access device processing are summarized in Table 11-1, which also lists the four main methods of basic file organization and processing. It can be seen that this form of COBOL permits the manipulation of files in the basic form of sequential, index-sequential, or direct. Because there is no standard method for address generation or self-indexing, finding the actual location of a record is the responsibility of the user program. Similarly, there are many ways of dealing with overflow in a file created and processed by address generation. If there are no information standards for this type of file, or if the user does not conform to the standards, then the user must take care of overflow placement and retrieval.

Data Management Languages

Data management languages are specifically designed for file handling, including the advanced file structures such as tree and network structures. The high-level source program is written according to stated conventions and is then translated by a compiler. Many such languages are extensions to COBOL. One of the first that received recognition was produced by General Electric, called IDS (*Integrated Data Store*). The major development today is the work of the CODASYL Data Base Task Group. Both IDS and CODASYL will be used as examples to illustrate the objectives and structure of data management languages.

General Electric's IDS[4] was initially announced in 1964 for use on GE-215 and 225 computers. It was modified and released again in 1965 as an extension to COBOL compiler for the GE-400 and 600 computers. The system uses chaining techniques for linking and retrieving records. It can operate in either a batch or on-line mode. Information is stored as "records," and the logical file organization is determined by the user; the record length is fixed for a particular type of record within a file.

All IDS programs are written in a COBOL-like language (IDS/COBOL) and become part of a COBOL source program after a special IDS translator run. Files are structured using rings, with both forward and backward pointers. The system was designed specifically to handle tree-type structures. (Parts list processing for production was the first application of IDS.)

Programs written in IDS have been used by many large companies besides

---

[4]General Electric Company, Information Systems Division, manuals: *Integrated Data Store Application Manual* (AS-CPB-483A, Rev. 7-67), *IDS Data Base Study* (CPB-491A), *GE-400 Series IDS/COBOL* (CPB-1144).

Table 11-1. File Organization and Access Modes

Method	Organization	Access	Keys	Apply Options
Sequential file accessed sequentially	N/P*	Sequential	N/P	N/P
Indexed file accessed sequentially	Indexed	Sequential	SYMBOLIC used to define the starting record RECORD used to identify the record key	N/P
Indexed file accessed selectively	Indexed	Random	SYMBOLIC and RECORD keys used to locate and identify the desired record.	Core-index
Random file accessed randomly	Direct	Random	ACTUAL used to specify the address of the desired record SYMBOLIC used to identify logical record	Restricted search

*N/P = not present; not applicable.

General Electric's own divisions: U.S. Shell, B. F. Goodrich, Allegheny-Ludlum Steel. Applications have included inventory control, order processing, bill of material processing, and scheduling.

The physical structure of files is based on a *paging/line* technique. The hardware structure is viewed as a number of pages, a page being similar to a block. A block consists of one or more records, called *lines.* Example size is a page (4096 characters maximum) consisting of up to 64 lines (records). The user analyst or programmer defines the size of the page, based on hardware characteristics. Records are chained according to the requirements of the user. This forms a series of master records with associated chains of subrecords. The logical structure and access is by

> randomizing to master record by IDS random number generator.
>
> linking records via chain pointer of master.
>
> linking chain to next record, previous record in chain, master, or all three.

COBOL is extended through modifications to the data division and to the procedure division.

To illustrate the actual form of a data management language, the work of the CODASYL Data Base Task Group will be used. It is stressed that the work of this group is to produce a standard for a language based on COBOL, but no final specification of a common language has yet been produced (CODASYL, 1969, 1971). The name CODASYL represents the Conference on Data Systems Languages, the group principally responsible for the development and promulgation of COBOL. The Data Base Task Group (DBTG) is a subcommittee of the Programming Language Committee of CODASYL. The original report of their findings and proposals was made in October 1968; a later report was made in April 1971. The original report proposed a Data Description Language (DDL) and a Data Manipulation Language (DML). The DDL is a language for describing a data base. The DML is a language that, when associated with the facilities of a "host" language such as COBOL, PL/1, ALGOL, JOVIAL, FORTRAN, etc., allows manipulation of data bases described by the DDL. Its basic principle is that a file can be described independently of the processing procedures. The first report proposed specific semantics and syntax for the two languages. The second report announced the formation of an additional committee, the Data Description Language Committee. Simultaneously, the Programming Language Committee was to develop COBOL extensions for the DML.

The objective of this work is to produce a flexible system that can handle many different file structures (network and tree structures), using many different types of chains and lists, etc., and provide many different methods for processing and maintenance. Three basic definitions are given in the "Major Concepts" section of the April 1971 report:

> A DATA BASE consists of all record occurrences, set occurrences, and areas that are controlled by a specific schema. If an installation

has multiple data bases, there must be a separate schema for each data base. Furthermore, the content of different data bases is assumed to be disjoint.

A SCHEMA consists of DDL entries and is a complete description of a data base. It includes the names and descriptions of all the areas, set occurrences, record occurrences, and associated data items and data aggregates as they exist in the data base.

A SUBSCHEMA also consists of DDL entries. It, however, need not describe the entire data base but only those areas, sets, records, data items and data aggregates that are known to one or more specific programs. Further, it describes them in the form in which they are known to those specific programs and it may also rename them.

The report goes on to define the relationship between the DDL and the DML as the "relationship between declarations and procedure." The relationship between the DDL/DML and the data base management system is neatly summarized in an example; the illustration is reproduced as Fig. 11-4.

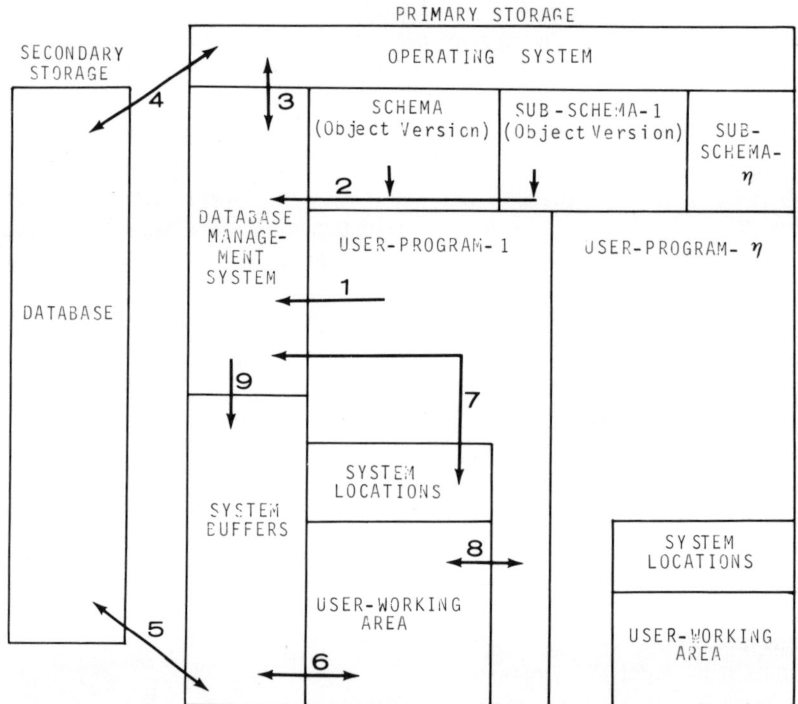

Figure 11-4. Structure of a Data Base Management System. (Courtesy of CODASYL, Data Base Task Group, April 1971 report.)

The DBTG proposals are extensive and introduce many new conceptual approaches, which we cannot go into here. To illustrate some of the ideas in this work, we consider one very small part—the COBOL Data Manipulation Language as described in the April 1971 report of CODASYL, specifically some of the new verbs introduced in the procedure division. The ones briefly explained here are

STORE

INSERT

REMOVE

DELETE

MODIFY

GET

FIND

STORE: This verb is used to add a new record to the data base. The verb STORE allocates space and a unique identifier; it also establishes the relationship between the new information and other information. For example, it may be required to add information about a new product to the data base and this record is to be declared a logical member of a product group set.

INSERT: This verb is used to link an existing record in the data base with one or more sets. The REMOVE verb is the reverse of the INSERT verb: It changes the linkage of a record, but the record remains in the data base.

DELETE: The DELETE verb removes a data record from the data base. It is deleted in the sense that it is no longer available to user programs, but it may still be available to special utility programs and service routines. Not only is a record "removed," but also the linkages between records in a set are realigned.

MODIFY: This verb is used to change data and to make changes in the relationship between data caused by alteration to the data values.

FIND AND GET: These are the verbs used for record retrieval. The verb FIND is used to locate and access a required record. This may result in a search process. It does not make the record available to the user program, but merely locates the desired record and makes it available for a GET command, which provides the record that was previously selected by means of a FIND. For the complex verb FIND, seven alternate formats are proposed. It operates with a *record-selection-expression* (rse). Selection of the record can be by a combination of record-name, set-name, area-name, or position in chain or area (next, prior, first, last).

It can be seen that this approach to using high-level languages opens wide new fields for holding and processing data on direct access devices. It offers many methods for defining relationships between data. How the CODASYL DDL/DML will be accepted and implemented by manufacturers and software houses remains to be seen.

FILE PROCESSORS

Generalized Processor

We must distinguish between the true generalized processor and the application-oriented processor. The former can handle various types of file structures, irrespective of the type of information the file holds. It can handle production data, sales data, or biomedical data; it gives the user complete flexibility to use files and produce reports as he wishes. In some cases, the penalty for this flexibility is inefficient machine usage. Application-oriented processors are, in fact, application packages. They are based on the assumption that there are many things in common between companies with the same commercial application; for example, production systems will generally have the same types of files, and reports can more or less be standardized. The degree of specialization—tailoring the system to the requirements of a particular company—depends very much on the package. The true generalized file processors are discussed here, and application-oriented packages will be dealt with in the next section.

Generalized file processors are the logical extension to general utility programs (such as file loaders) and report-program generators. They can be used with punched card or magnetic tape files, but have been closely associated with direct access files as they have come into prominence. The basic functions of a processor are as follows:

File Creation.   Under the control of user specified parameters, the generalized file processor constructs and stores data records, and sets up the appropriate chains, lists, and indexes. As the file is created, the file processor constructs a dictionary that describes the data in the file. The dictionary is then stored with the file for later use. All programs that will subsequently retrieve and update the file will reference the data via the dictionary.

Updating/Retrieval.   Programs are supplied which, given the parameters that name the data items and processing requirements, will retrieve, insert, change, or delete data records. A program to update a file does not need to contain a description of the file: This is held in the data dictionary formed when the file was created. The file processor uses other portions of the dictionary to control the update; there is very little effort on the part of the user. For record retrieval, the user need specify only that information which he requires; he need not specify how that information is to be obtained. Retrieval requirements are based on contents of data records rather than on the sequence or identification of keys.

Reporting.   The user specifies the content and format of a report in parameter form. The reporting program(s), working in conjunction with the updating/retrieval program(s), will produce the appropriate report. The user programmer need not be concerned with the logical steps needed to perform such steps as editing, formatting, positioning of paper, and performing control breaks.

The constituent parts of a generalized file processor system, and the relationship between them are summarized in Fig. 11-5.

The principal sources of file processors are the computer manufacturers and specialist software houses; many user companies have produced their own processors and some of these models have been sold to other companies. Most computer manufacturers have some form of generalized file processor. Some of these are

Burroughs:	FORGE (*File ORganization GEnerator*)
	FORTE (*File ORganization TEchniques*)
NCR:	BEST (*Business EDP Systems Technique*)
IBM:	GIS (*Generalized Information Systems*)
	IMS (*Information Management System*)

In the July 1971 edition of a catalog of available software, "ICP Quarterly,"[5] no less than 67 generalized file processors are listed; more than three-quarters are the products of software houses and similar companies. Examples of the products of software houses are MARK IV from Informatics and TDMS (*Time-Shared Data Management System*) and ORBIT II from System Development Corporation. The packages consist of from 2 to more than 60 programs, at prices of less

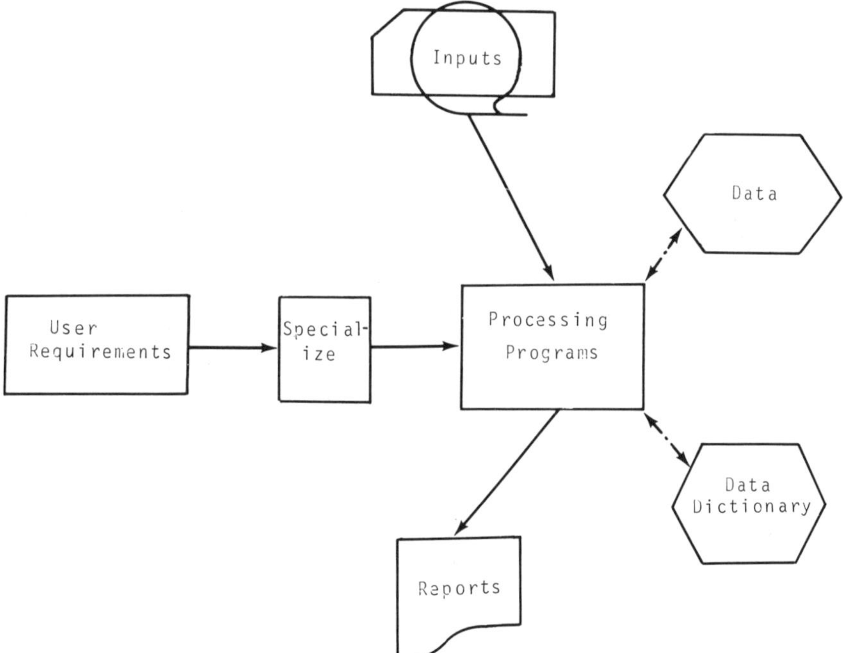

Figure 11-5. Structure of a Generalized File Processor

---

[5]ICP Quarterly, July 1971, International Computer Programs, Inc., 2511 East 46th Street, Indianapolis, Ind. 46205.

than $500 to more than $25,000. They are suitable for running on a complete range of third-generation computers: A generalized file processor is available for practically every make and type of computer. Table 11-2 illustrates a selection of a number of generalized file processors. To show how they are used in practice, some are described below in more detail. These have been chosen because of the techniques used rather than for their current availability.

Table 11-2. Characteristics of Generalized File Processors

Language	Operating Environment	Record Formats	Access Mode	Data Structures
Based on established programming language	Batch On line Free-standing	Fixed Variable Hierarchical	Sequential Indexed-sequential Direct (random)	Random Sequential Indexed *using* Chains Pointers Lists
Free-form language for nonprogramming users				
Conversational				
Tabular				

Data Manager-1 (DM-1) was originally produced by Auerbach Corporation in the middle 1960s. Since it is hardware independent, it could be tailored for a particular configuration. The DM-1 functioned as an extension to the operating system; it is a collection of procedures, executive routines, services, and programs. Data is held in a "data pool" and information about the data is stored in a series of directories. The DM-1 is constructed to work in a time-sharing environment; two central processors are required for time sharing and backup. The data pool is manipulated via a specially constructed high-level language. The original intention was that a user, knowing nothing about the system, could use the free-form language to "program" his own requirements without the intervention of specialized programmers. The data in the pool was stored, using many structuring methods: chaining, lists, indexes, etc. The method used is determined by the system, according to statistical indicators of data usage. The basic organization of the system is shown in Fig. 11-6.

A complete set of languages are available to process data. To create and maintain the data pool, a data definition language is used, naming data, defining structures, and identifying relationships between data elements, etc. Another language is provided for the user to change the data: enter, modify, and change data structure. Finally, there is the query and search language for accessing data: define, retrieve, and display data.

Similar to DM-1 was TDMS, which preceded DM-1 and was introduced by System Development Corporation in 1966. The TDMS has been described as "the big grand-daddy of GFP's". It was designed for use on IBM 360 computers and was operated in batch or on-line mode. The user language was conversational free form; this meant that the user had considerable latitude in specifying processing requirements. This was done by the user on an input terminal as a dialog

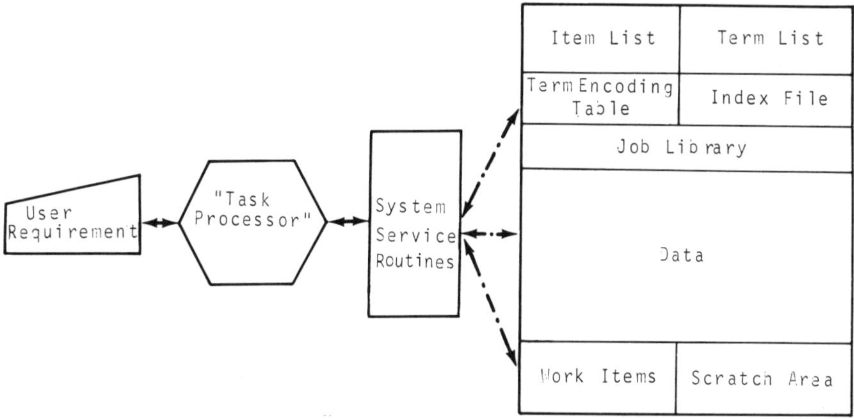

Figure 11-6. Organization of DM-1 (simplified)

with a control program. Its purpose was similar to that for DM-1 in that a non-programmer could use the system. The design of TDMS was based on a very large configuration with high-capacity mass storage devices, high-speed communications equipment, and a large number of remote terminals. Again, the directory-data pool technique was used. Data was held in tree structures. A range of languages was available for use with the system: JOVIAL, TINT (an interactive language with extensive tutorial features for novice programmers), and the TDMS user languages such as the TDMS Operational (User) language. An example set of commands in the latter language is shown in Table 11-3.

The final generalized file processor considered here is Informatics Mark IV. This has the distinction of being perhaps the most successful generalized file processor produced by a software house, successful both in terms of user satisfaction and number of users. Informatics originally produced Mark I for the IBM 1400 series as early as 1962. It was subsequently modified (Mark II and Mark III)

Table 11-3. Example of TDMS User Language Statements

Command	Function
DEFINE	Creates data descriptions in the data dictionary; includes the specification of validity criteria
LOAD	Inputs data with validity checks; creates necessary access tables
QUERY	Access data, for terminal display, from data pool; permits arithmetic operations to be made on data before display
COMPUTE/PRODUCE	Report generation, defining format and content; also ordering and arithmetic operations on data
MAINTAIN	Changing/updating data in the data pool
UPDATE	Define, generate, manipulate, and recall many different display statements

and was finally released by Informatics as Mark IV for the IBM 360. (This package also has the distinction, rightly, of being one of the most closely guarded proprietary packages!) The system operates in batch mode only and can handle fixed- or variable-record formats. Files are assessed sequentially or indexed-sequentially, with nine levels of hierarchical data structure. Again, descriptions of files are independent of the files themselves.

The emphasis on generalized file processors is on getting the nonprogramming *user* to specify his requirements without involving specialist programmers. Because the files are described independently of the processing, changing user reporting requirements can be dealt with speedily. (Informatics, for example, claims that Mark IV normally results in a 10 to 1, or greater reduction, over conventional programming languages in the time required to implement business application systems). The penalty is usually quite time-consuming file maintenance and routine batch updating of record-keeping systems.

Application-Oriented Processor

There are as many application-oriented file processing packages as there are generalized file processors. They are produced by computer manufacturers, trade associations, software houses, and user companies. Examples are

> RACE Certificates of Deposit (covering banking operations); produced by CBM, Inc.
>
> Construction Payroll and Cost Accounting (consisting of 42 programs); produced by Computer Analysis, Inc.
>
> FORESIGHT (financial planning) produced by Computer Co-operatives Ltd., England.
>
> Milk Producers Payroll System (multicompany); produced by Arlington Trust Company.
>
> BOMP Bill of Material Processor; produced by IBM.
>
> MMS Inventory Management System; produced by Manufacturing Management Sciences, Inc.

The division between an "application package" and an application-oriented file processor is a rather fine one. Some application packages, such as scientific processes, have little or no data files. Some packages that do process files require restructuring of the processing programs by actually changing the arrangement of the coding, rather than by the input of parameters.

Compared to generalized file processors, the application-oriented models have files and reports that tend to be more rigidly structured. The latter also tend to have generalized processing procedures for handling data in the system. Although there is less flexibility, the preparation of parameters may be simpler than in some of the generalized file processor languages.

The selection of the appropriate package is a major task, and should be attacked methodically. Not only the product itself but also the supplier and his staff must be evaluated. Special knowledge is also needed for the negotiation of the contract. A package that is eminently suitable for one installation may be completely inadequate for another (Wooldridge, 1973).

DIRECT ACCESS FOR PROGRAM STORAGE

Most of this book has been concerned with the organization and processing of data files. Direct access devices may also be used, of course, for the storage and processing of programs. The impact of direct access on program storage is discussed below.

Faster Compilation/Assembly

A compiler or assembler will be faster in operation than a magnetic tape-based version. This is to be expected because most compilers/assemblers use some form of list-generation technique for cataloging instruction labels, data areas allocated, matching hardware machine codes with mnenomic verbs in the source language. Magnetic tape-based conversion programs use lists in core together with serial search passes of work tapes. The direct addressing of, say, exchangeable disks permits the creation of a number of separate work areas with indexes; this eliminates the need for much of the time-consuming serial searching.

More Efficient Program Overlays

A program that is too big to be held in core, or in that part of core allocated to a particular job, is segmented into a number of smaller units. As a program is run, various parts of the program are held in core, and new segments of the program are brought in as required and overwrite the existing coding. Direct access enables this segmentation to be made more easily with faster processing times. It is possible to construct an index of the location of the various program segments. To load a new segment, it is located on the device via the index and can be read into core without serial searching. Direct access devices also enable dumps to be made of working segments of program. This can be especially important in on-line systems where core storage space is restricted.

Consider a program that is divided into four segments or modules, called modules A, B, C, and D. Module A is the master module; it is read into core at the start of the job and remains there during the whole time that the job is run. Besides holding A, there is sufficient core storage to hold only one other module and its associated data areas. Let us suppose that the program deals with inquiries of many different types. After the job is initiated, module B is called into store, where it operates in one input type. A condition arises such that module D must be called, but module B has not yet finished its processing on the first input. The area occupied by module B, both program and data, is dumped to disk and the coding in module A notes the location of the dump in a small internal index. We will call this B1. Module D is then called in and processed; it is deleted at the end of the run. Another input is received, requiring module B; this input has a higher priority than the initial input (B1), which was being processed when D was called. Module B, in its initial state, is brought in from disk and run against the input. Yet another interrupt occurs and the area currently occupied by B and its data is dumped to disk; we will call this B2. The master module now has disk references to two dumps, the first B1 and the second B2. Module C is called to service the new interrupt; C operates and is then deleted. The second version of B (B2) is called in, executed, and then deleted, and again module D is called. D is run and deleted; the first version of B (B1), whose data was preserved in the dump, is then called in by module A and processing continues. With this number of overlay transfers, direct access systems are vital, especially when the modules are processing on-line input with a fast-response requirement. It is also possible to arrange for selected data areas to be shared between programs.

Library Storage

The principal of program segment handling can be extended to cover complete program libraries. Again, this is very important for on-line (terminal) working. A typical arrangement of computer facilities is shown in Fig. 11-7. This example shows a large computer configuration that is dedicated to terminal working. The jobs are of relatively short duration, with minimal volumes of input and output data. This is typical of computer work in a university bureau environment, where the users are engineers and scientists who run mathematical problems. Note that in this case there are three types of storage linked to the central processor:

1. Fast, small capacity drums, for work-in-progress use

2. Medium speed, very large capacity disks for program library
    storage and long-term file storage

3. Magnetic tape, used for general housekeeping purposes such
    as security dumps

All terminal messages (interrupts) go to the executive control program (operating system). In this example, the executive is very large and is generally held on the fast drums. The small module, which is a permanent core resident, contains an "index" to other parts of the executive, which are called only if required.

Let us consider an example input to demonstrate how the direct access devices are used in the transfers of program and data. A user comes on line and types in a short message. This is received by the executive. At this time the machine is too busy and too heavily loaded to deal with the interrupt immediately. The message is therefore dumped on a fast drum and the executive notes its location. Eventually (in terms of milliseconds or seconds), the message is retrieved. The executive, via various levels of indexes, accesses the required programs from

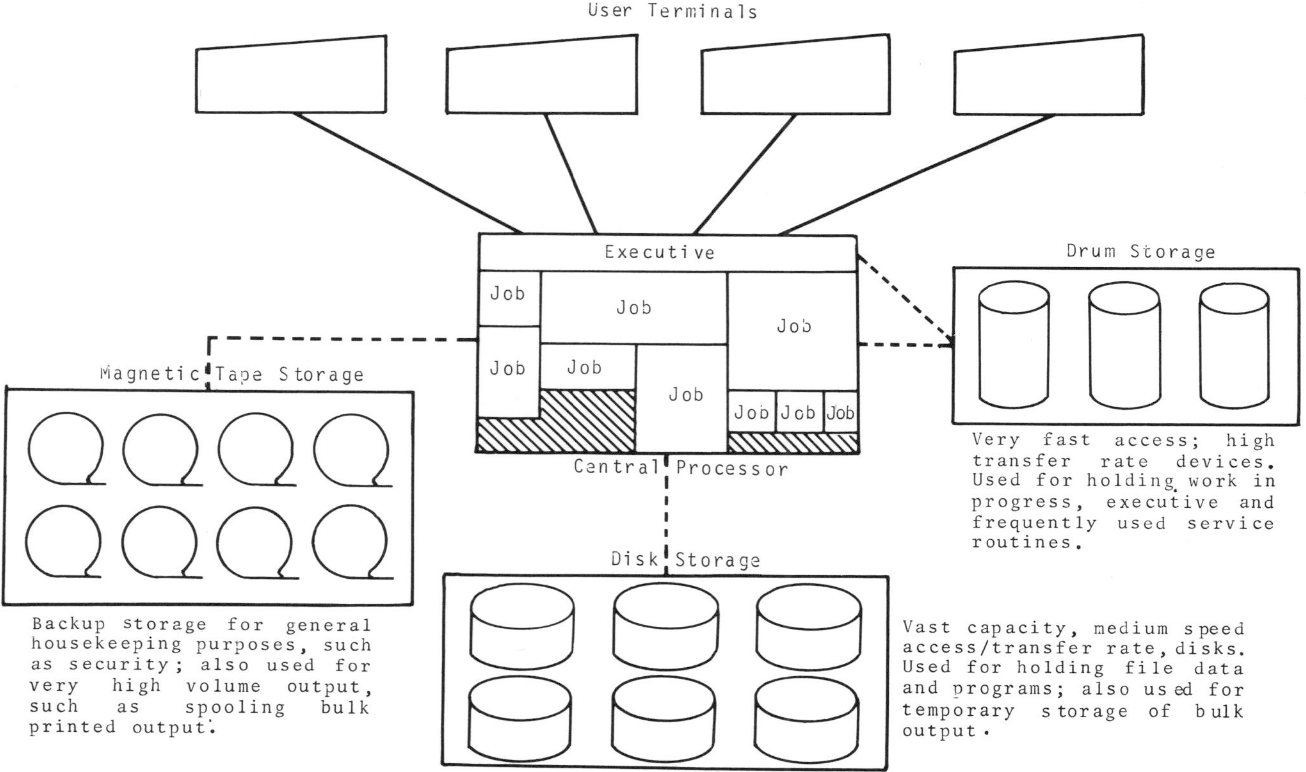

Figure 11-7. Storage Structure in a Large On-Line Terminal System

the library and the data files from the mass storage disks. Processing then takes place; at any time, intermediate results may be written to the fast drum storage if the program has to wait for further information from the user. Final output may be transferred directly from core storage to the terminal; sometimes, however, it is more efficient to transfer the results to magnetic drum storage and leave them there until it is convenient to make the transfer to the terminal.

It can thus be seen that the same methods may be used for program storage as are used in data storage. In the preceding example, indexes were used to locate programs or program segments; some systems use self-indexing or even chaining.

A STATISTICAL APPROACH TO FILE DESIGN

INTRODUCTION

This is a review of basic statistical methods that are relevant to the job of the file designer. It is not intended to be a general introduction to statistics; it concentrates on those methods that are directly applicable to file design. For those readers who wish to extend their study of statistics, a number of excellent books are recommended in the list of References (Feller, 1950; Holman, 1966; Vinogradov, 1955; etc.).

Various tables and charts that are of use to the analyst are given in Appendix B. This review is intended to provide a base of knowledge so that the tables can be applied intelligently, rather than blindly. It is the author's contention that basic statistical methods are a valuable tool in the designer's kit. With intelligent use, charts and tables enable the designer to make certain assumptions about data in a system, thereby giving him an objective starting point in selecting file structures and processing methods. We start by considering two areas in which there is often a degree of uncertainty in the data being handled: timing, and the pattern of file keys and overflow.

Timing

Timing estimates are vitally important in the design of a file structure and the processing methods. Most commercial applications are peripheral-bound (I/O bound). This means that the major timing elements are the input and output operations: The shortest time in which a job is run is determined by the time taken by operations on one or more peripheral devices. If the only peripherals used on a job are direct access devices, it is likely that core operations will be completely overlapped with direct access device operations. Indeed, central processor operations may well be constrained by them. (If slow peripherals are used as well as the direct access devices, the direct access functions may be completely overlapped by slow operations such as card reading or printing.) File design is an iterative process. Each hypothesized design is evaluated, modified, re-evaluated, and so on. Timing is one method of evaluation. Timing estimates are used in several ways:

1. *To see if the results of the file operation will produce reports or messages in the required time scale.* For example, it may be found

that file processing is so slow that the response to an input message from a terminal is unacceptable: the user has to wait too long.

2. *To provide a basis for costing the running of the system.* Where a user is to be charged for the machine time in running his job, he will require costing estimates.

3. *To determine if the job can be run on the existing equipment within the current schedule of operations for all jobs.* Other jobs are being run on the computer. A specific time slot may be allocated to a particular job. On either side of this job, there are other jobs that must be run at a specific time. In this case, computer operations must be certain that a job can be fitted into the schedule. If it cannot be slotted in, then either the run time of the job must be changed (redesign) or new hardware acquired.

One school of thought on timing suggests that, because of the decreasing cost of hardware and the use of multiprogramming, job timing is now of less significance than in the past. It is certainly true that the days when a programmer would spend three man-days saving a few milliseconds are over! However, there are many instances when accurate run-timing estimates are necessary, for the reasons given above. The timing estimates will be based on the volume *and pattern* of input, the size and structure of the file, and the processing method.

The volume of input and the size of a file are relatively easy to assess. This is not to say that either value is fixed, but limits will generally be known. If the volume of input is variable, then a sliding-scale timing estimate may be made, based on various quantities of input. The designer then produces average and maximum run times. The former can be used for estimate (2) listed above, and the latter for estimates (1) and (3), assuming that if the worst case (highest volume) can be accommodated within the response time and operating schedule, then the system is acceptable. However, the pattern of input is just as important as the volume. Consider a simple example: A file is stored on 100 cylinders of a disk. There are 100 input transactions to be applied. The best case will be where all 100 matching file records are sequential on the first two or three cylinders. The worst case will be where there are 100 matching records, each record on a different cylinder and hence 100 seeks.

In some systems, the pattern of input as well as the volume is relatively static. The pattern can be determined empirically by studying selected samples of data. The file can then be designed with this pattern in mind, and accurate timing estimates can be made. *But beware:* The pattern may change as the business changes. In most cases, however, the pattern of input varies, or the amount of time to determine the pattern by observation would be excessive. In this case, various assumptions must be made. It is in this area that the use of simple statistical techniques are helpful.

Key Patterns and Overflow

The problems presented here are similar to the points made above for timing. The pattern of keys will be a major factor in the design of an address generation procedure. How and when records will be added to or deleted from the file will be important in the overflow processing procedures of a highly volatile file. Again, the designer is often faced with uncertainty: He cannot exactly say where records will overflow. There may be a bias in some files; he may know that all new records are added to the end of the file. In other systems, there does not immediately seem to be a pattern.

STATISTICS AND ESTIMATES

It has been shown that the designer is faced with situations in which there is a degree of uncertainty: he cannot determine by observation the exact patterns of data. In any case like this, he produces estimates that must be revised later in the light of experience in running a job. The more reliable the original estimates, however, the better is the product. If the estimates are very inaccurate, the job may need to be redesigned, which means complete reprogramming. (Consider the unhappy user or worried operations manager!)

Some designers use statistics as the basis of all estimates: Statistical methods are applied to the problem and the results are used as the basis for actual estimates. Other designers use statistical estimates to aid their own intuitive judgment. The latter approach uses statistics to give a starting point. The problem is considered, statistical estimates are produced by making certain assumptions, and the results are viewed by the designer. He may "feel" that they just aren't right; he asks himself why, and from this he refines his assumptions. He may drop some of the assumptions or include new ones. The process is repeated until the designer has personal confidence in the result.

We are concerned here, then, with that field of statistics that covers uncertainty and probability, and we are looking at techniques that the designer uses as a guide.

Review of Basic Terms

The probability of any event occurring is given by a numeric value in the range of 0 to 1. Probability 0 means that the event will never happen; probability 1 means certainty—the event will happen. A decimal fraction within the range 0 to 1 indicates various degrees of probability: the closer to 1, the more certain that the event will happen; and the closer to 0, the less likely that it is to happen. The probability of an event's occuring is

$$p = \frac{\text{number of ways event can happen}}{\text{total number of possible outcomes}}$$

The sum of the probabilities for complementary events is always 1.

Let us consider a simple problem, using low, easy-to-handle figures. A file is stored on four cylinders, with five records to a cylinder. Four input transactions are to be applied to the file. What are the chances that

1. all four inputs relate to the records on the first cylinder (or any one cylinder for that matter)?

2. all four inputs relate to different cylinders?

The data for this problem is

    file records = 20
    cylinders = 4
    file records per cylinder = 5
    inputs = 4

We must first make one very important assumption, namely, that each of the records in the file is as likely to have an input applied to it as any other file record. If we were to say that there was some bias in data, then all our work would be incorrect. The next assumption that we will make is that there is no more than one input transaction per record. That is, for four transactions, there will be four master-file records hit. The file is shown diagrammatically in Fig. A-1. For ease of reference, the cylinders have been identified as W, X, Y, and Z, each of the records has been lettered a to t.

1. The chance of the first input relating to a record on cylinder W is

$$\frac{5 \text{ (records on cylinder W)}}{20 \text{ total records in the file}} = \frac{1}{4}$$

2. The chance of the next input relating to a record on cylinder W is

$$\frac{4 \text{ (record on cylinder W as yet unhit)}}{19 \text{ unhit records in the file}} = \frac{4}{19}$$

3. Repeating the procedure, we calculate the probabilities for the next two inputs as being

$$\frac{3}{18} \text{ and } \frac{2}{17}$$

The probability of all four inputs relating to records on one cylinder is thus

$$\frac{1}{4} \times \frac{4}{19} \times \frac{3}{18} \times \frac{2}{17} = \frac{24}{23,256} \quad \text{ or } (0.001)$$

Let us now consider the second problem—the chances of all four inputs relating to master records on different cylinders.

1. The chance of the first input relating to cylinder W (any of the five records a, b, c, d, or e) is 5/20, or one in four as before.

Cylinders

W	X	Y	Z
a	f	k	p
b	g	l	q
c	h	m	r
d	i	n	s
e	j	o	t

Records

Figure A-1

2. The chances of the next input relating to records on the other three cylinders is 15/19. Remember that we have made the assumption that a record can be hit only once. This gives a total of 19 unhit records. We are looking at the possibility of the input's relating to any of the records on the cylinders X, Y, or Z. These three cylinders hold a total of 15 records; hence, 15/19.

3. The probability that the next input relates to cylinders Y or Z is 10/18.

4. The probability that the next input relates to cylinder Z is 5/17.

The probability of all four inputs relating to different cylinders is thus

$$\frac{1}{4} \times \frac{15}{19} \times \frac{10}{18} \times \frac{5}{17} = \frac{750}{23,256} \qquad \text{or } (0.03)$$

Our calculations would be considerably different if we changed our second assumption and said that any number of records could have any number of inputs. For example, it could be the case that all four inputs apply to one file record, or three to one record and one to another. The impact on our calculations would be that the denominator in the probability fractions would remain constant (at 20, the number of records in the file) and the numerator would be altered accordingly.

This example has been worked through in this depth to show the very basic techniques applied and the importance of understanding the assumptions made. In practice, the analysis of a particular file processing situation can lead to some quite complex math calculations. It is for this reason that general reference tables are included in Appendix B. All data in the charts and tables are based on an assumption of a "random distribution," similar to the one made in the assumption that each record stands an equal chance of being hit. Statistical predictions based on probability theory always have the proviso "in the long run." It is completely wrong to assume, for example, that if a chart shows that 50 cylinders are hit in a particular situation, there will always be exactly 50 seeks. Even if the hits are randomly distributed, the table shows that in the long run, over a large number of processing runs, it is reasonable to expect that the number of seeks will average out to about 50.

The material in Appendix B must therefore be used with some caution, and not applied blindly to give a magical figure that will be precise. Data are presented for guidance, to provide a basis for objective comparison with the designer's own estimates. It is suggested that they form the basis for first rough estimates. Examination of the data in a particular job will soon show any bias or skew in the processing.

STORAGE SPACE USAGE IN ADDRESS GENERATION SYSTEMS[1]

This section provides a simple proof for the tables and diagrams used in Chapter 8. Part of the discussion there was concerned with the distribution of records over the available storage space (tracks, blocks, buckets, etc.). The first assumption made was that each of the storage areas (here we call them buckets) was equally likely to receive a record. In other words, a record is equally likely to be assigned to any of the available buckets. Let us use B to indicate the *number of buckets.* The probability of any record's being assigned to any bucket is therefore $1/B$. (If there are 100 buckets, there is a 1 in 100 chance of a record's being assigned to a specific bucket.) The *number of records* to be assigned is labeled N. The assigning of N records to B buckets is thus a series of N independent trials, which, for a given bucket, have a probability $1/B$ of success. From basic probability theory, it is given that the probability of 0, 1, 2 . . . records being assigned to the bucket is successive terms of the binomial expansion:

$$(p + q)^N$$

where $p = 1/B$ and $q = 1 - p$.

We now assume that N and B are large, and it thus follows that p becomes small. The binomial expansion is closely approximated by the Poisson distribu-

---

[1] *Warning—for the mathematically minded only!* The description of this proof in basic terms would require an explanation of too many fundamental terms and concepts.

tion. This is derived from the binomial by letting $p \rightarrow 0$ and $N \rightarrow \infty$ in such a way that Np tends to a finite value m. The probability of exactly r records randomizing to a given bucket is

$$\frac{e^{-m} m^r}{r!}$$

where

$$e = Lt \text{ as } N \rightarrow 0 \text{ of } \left(1 + \frac{1}{N}\right)^N \qquad (= 2.718\ldots)$$

and

$$m = \frac{N}{B}$$

This is given from the Poisson distribution. The "expected" number E_r of buckets in the file containing r records is then equal to

$$B\left(\frac{e^{-m} m^r}{r!}\right)$$

This is the formula upon which the discussion in Chapter 8 is based. By superimposing bucket capacities (the number of records that can be stored in a bucket), the amount of overflow can be calculated quite easily.

APPENDIX B

STATISTICAL TABLES AND CHARTS

These tables and charts are provided for general reference. A description of how to use them and the assumptions that have been made are given with each one. A knowledge of a basic approach to the use of statistics in this field, such as that given in Appendix A, will be useful in consulting these tables and charts:

CYLINDER HITS

Figure B-1 is used to estimate the number of cylinders hit. The required data for use is the number of transactions, cylinders in file, and records per cylinder.

As will be seen in the figure, the latter is really of very little significance unless it is very large or very small. The figure is based on a random distribution of hits over the file.

Procedure for Use

1. Divide the number of transactions by the number of cylinders in the file.

2. If the result of step (1) is 4 or more, assume that *all cylinders in the file will be hit.*

3. If the result of (1) is 0.1 or less, assume that *the number of cylinders hit equals the number of transactions.*

4. If the result of (1) is between 0.1 and 4, then consult Fig. B-1. Apply the result of (1) to the figure and read the number of cylinders hit. This is given as a percentage of the number of cylinders in the file.

Example: A file consisting of 600 cylinders has 600 transactions to be applied to it. Calculation (1) gives 1.0. This is greater than 0.1 and less than 4, so steps (3) and (4) do not apply. Figure B-1 shows that 64% of the cylinders in the file are assumed to be hit, about 380 cylinders.

BUCKET HITS

Figure B-2 is used to estimate the number of buckets hit. A bucket in this case is the smallest level of addressing on a device. It may be a track, a block, or

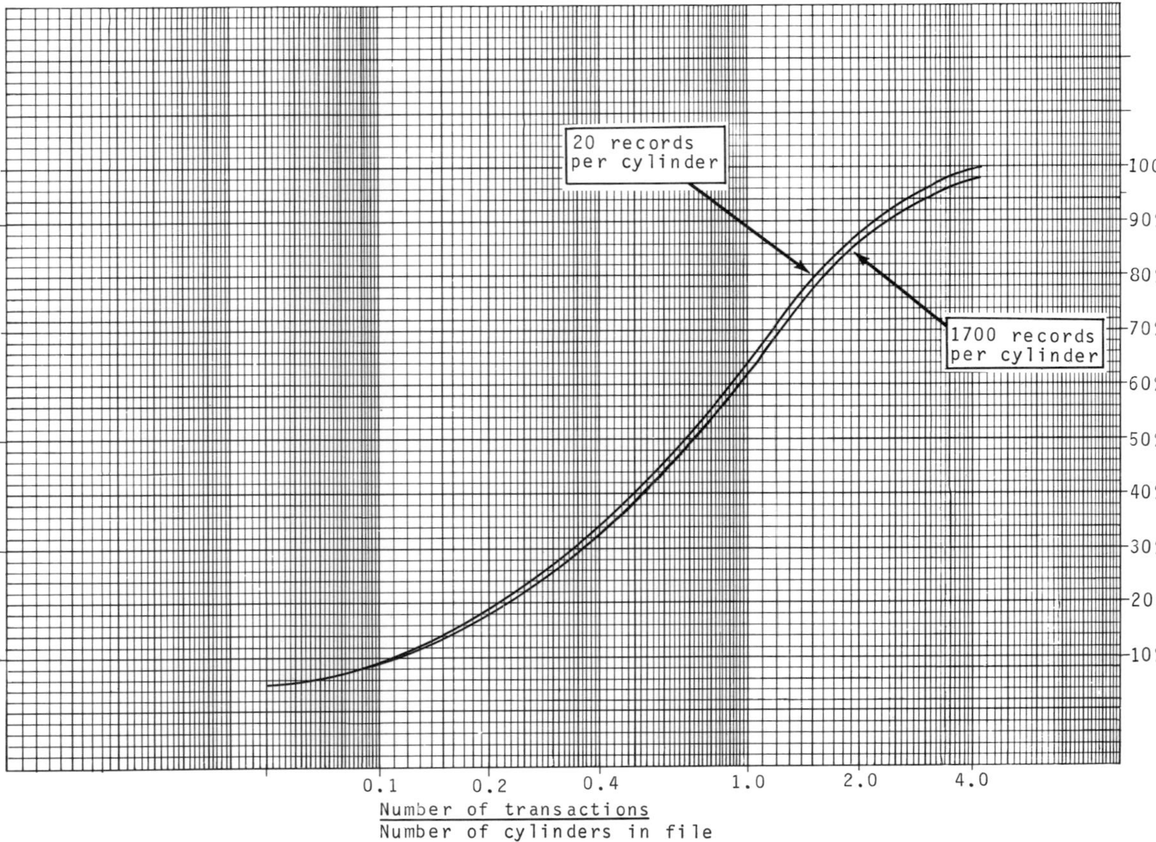

20 records
per cylinder
1700 records
per cylinder
100%
90%
80%
70%
60%
50%
40%
30%
20%
10%
0.1
0.2
0.4
1.0
2.0
4.0
Number of transactions
Number of cylinders in file

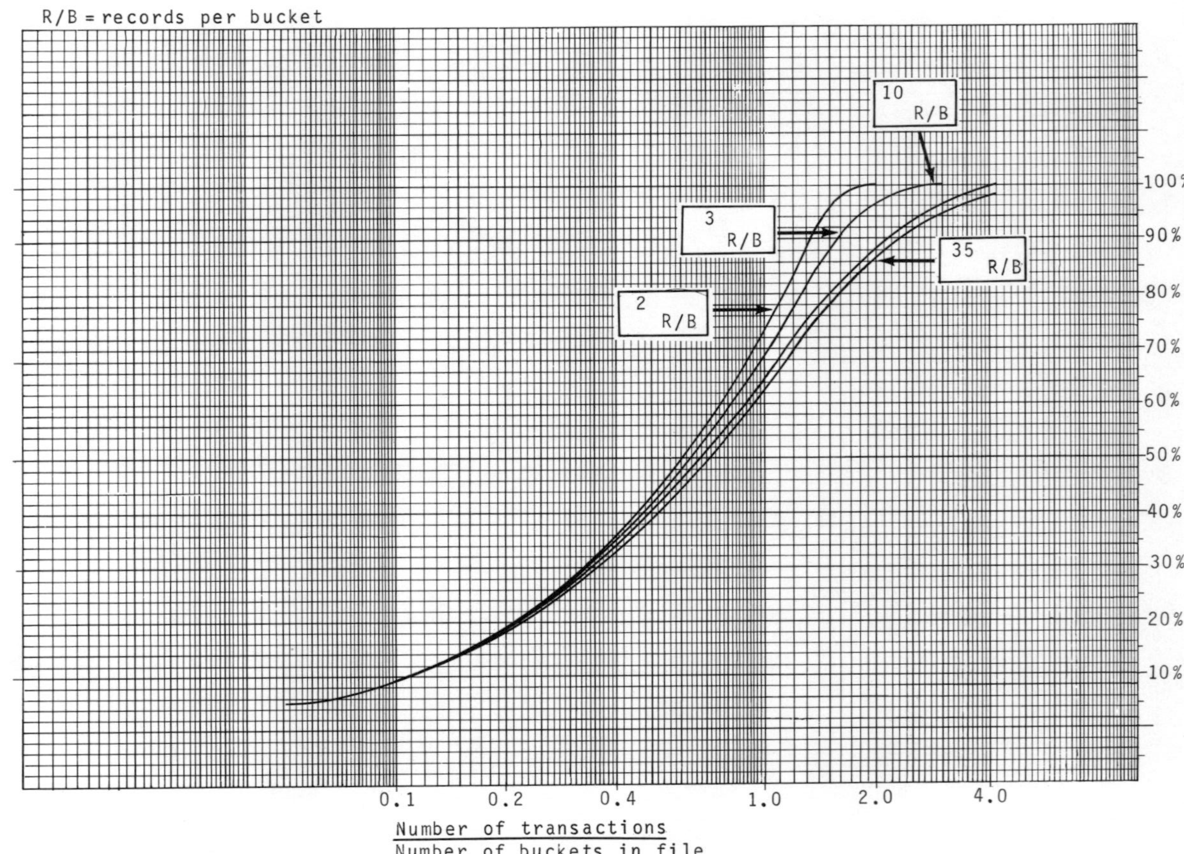

R/B = records per bucket
10 R/B
3 R/B
35 R/B
2 R/B
100%
90%
80%
70%
60%
50%
40%
30%
20%
10%
0.1
0.2
0.4
1.0
2.0
4.0
Number of transactions
Number of buckets in file

a logical bucket. The required data for use is the number of transactions, buckets in file, and records per bucket.

Procedure for Use

1. Divide the number of transactions by the number of buckets in the file.

2. If the result of step (1) is 4 or more, assume that *all buckets in the file will be hit.*

3. If the result of step (1) is 0.1 or less, assume that *the number of buckets hit equals the number of transations.*

4. If the result of step (1) is between 0.1 and 4, then consult the figure. Apply the result of (1) to the figure. Select the curve according to the number of records per bucket. Read off the number of buckets hit; this is expressed as a percentage of the number of buckets in the file.

Example: A file consists of 5000 buckets, and 7500 transactions are to be applied to it. Calculation (1) gives 1.5. Assume that there are 10 records per bucket. Figure B-2 shows that 80% of the buckets in the file are assumed to be hit (i.e., 4000 buckets).

OVERFLOW IN A SEQUENTIAL FILE

Table B-1 can be used to estimate the impact of overflow in a sequential file. This is important in defining the overflow area and in deciding on the record-packing density in a highly volatile file. To use this table, the following must first be estimated:

1. The space in each bucket when the file was loaded or last reorganized, in terms of the number of records that could be held
2. The size of the file as a number of buckets
3. The number of records to be added

Table B-1 allows for record additions only, and is based on a random distribution of records overflowing throughout the file. The table shows the percentage of added records that may be assumed to overflow. In this case a bucket means the lowest level of addressing: a track, a block, or a logical bucket.

Example: A file of 1000 records is loaded into 500 buckets. Each bucket has a capacity of 3 records; the total capacity of the file is thus 1500 records. To allow for expansion, the 1000 initial records are loaded two to a bucket. The space in each bucket for additions is thus 1 record. It is estimated that in the first cycle of operation, some 200 new records will be added throughout the file. Records per bucket is thus 1, and the number of records added (200) divided by the number of buckets for the file (500) is 0.4. This shows that an estimated 17 percent of the 200 input records will overflow.

Table B-1. Percentage of Added Records Located in Overflow Area

RECORDS PER BUCKET*	NUMBER OF RECORDS ADDED DIVIDED BY NUMBER OF BUCKETS IN FILE†														
	0.2	0.4	0.6	0.8	1.0	1.25	1.5	1.75	2.0	2.5	3.0	3.5	4.0	4.5	5.0
1	9.37	17.58	24.80	31.17	36.79	42.92	48.21	52.79	56.77	63.28	68.33	72.29	75.46	78.02	80.13
2	0.60	2.19	4.49	7.72	10.36	14.49	18.73	22.95	27.07	34.77	41.63	47.60	52.75	57.16	60.94
3	0.03	0.21	0.63	1.34	2.33	3.97	5.99	8.32	10.90	16.53	22.40	28.20	33.70	38.80	43.44
4		0.02	0.07	0.20	0.43	0.91	1.61	2.56	3.75	6.83	10.64	14.96	19.54	24.18	28.74
5			0.01	0.03	0.07	0.18	0.37	0.68	1.12	2.48	4.49	7.11	10.26	13.78	17.55
6					0.01	0.03	0.08	0.16	0.30	0.80	1.69	3.05	4.89	7.18	9.87
7							0.01	0.03	0.07	0.23	0.57	1.18	2.12	3.43	5.11
8								0.01	0.01	0.06	0.18	0.42	0.84	1.50	2.44
9										0.01	0.05	0.14	0.31	0.61	1.08
10											0.01	0.04	0.10	0.23	0.44

*Space left in each bucket at last file reorganization, in terms of number of records.

†Since last file reorganization.

BUCKET SIZE	LOAD FACTOR											
	0.1	0.2	0.3	0.4	0.5	0.6	0.7	0.8	0.9	1.0	1.1	1.2
1	4.84	9.37	13.61	17.58	21.32	24.80	28.08	31.17	34.06	36.79	39.35	41.77
2	0.60	2.19	4.49	7.27	10.36	13.65	17.03	20.43	23.79	27.07	30.24	33.30
3	0.09	0.63	1.80	3.61	5.99	8.82	11.99	15.37	18.87	22.40	25.91	29.33
4	0.02	0.20	0.79	1.96	3.76	6.15	9.05	12.32	15.86	19.54	23.25	26.93
5	0.00	0.07	0.37	1.12	2.48	4.49	7.11	10.26	13.78	17.55	21.42	25.30
6		0.02	0.18	0.67	1.69	3.38	5.75	8.75	12.24	16.06	20.06	24.11
7		0.01	0.09	0.41	1.18	2.60	4.74	7.60	11.04	14.90	19.00	23.19
8		0.00	0.05	0.25	0.84	2.03	3.97	6.68	10.07	13.96	18.15	22.46
9			0.02	0.16	0.61	1.61	3.36	5.94	9.27	13.18	17.44	21.86
10			0.01	0.10	0.44	1.29	2.88	5.32	8.59	12.51	16.85	21.36
11			0.01	0.07	0.33	1.04	2.48	4.80	8.01	11.94	16.34	20.94
12			0.00	0.04	0.24	0.85	2.15	4.36	7.51	11.44	15.89	20.58
14				0.02	0.14	0.57	1.65	3.64	6.67	10.60	15.15	19.19
16				0.01	0.08	0.39	1.28	3.09	6.00	9.92	14.56	19.53
18				0.00	0.05	0.28	1.01	2.65	5.45	9.36	14.07	19.16
20					0.03	0.20	0.81	2.30	4.99	8.88	13.66	18.86
25					0.01	0.09	0.48	1.65	4.10	7.95	12.87	18.31
30					0.00	0.04	0.29	1.23	3.47	7.26	12.31	17.93
35						0.02	0.18	0.94	2.98	6.73	11.87	17.66
40						0.01	0.12	0.73	2.60	6.29	11.53	17.47
50						0.00	0.05	0.45	2.04	5.63	11.03	17.20
60							0.02	0.30	1.65	5.14	10.68	17.03
70							0.01	0.20	1.37	4.76	10.41	16.93
80							0.01	0.13	1.14	4.46	10.21	16.86
90							0.00	0.09	0.97	4.20	10.05	16.80
100								0.06	0.83	3.99	9.92	16.77

Source: W. Buchholz, "File Organization and Addressing," *IBM Systems Journal*, June 1963 (Table 4 on p. 99).

OVERFLOW IN A RANDOM FILE

Table B-2 shows the *initial* overflow on file loading caused by synonym generation in a random file. A random (Poisson) distribution has been assumed. The required data for use is

1. Bucket size (in terms of the number of records per bucket, maximum).
2. Load factor: actual number of records to be stored divided by the record capacity of the file area.

These two factors can be applied to the table and the percentage of records which overflow on loading determined. This is a useful guide in determining the bucket size and size of overflow to be allowed. Note, however, that if the distribution of records over the available storage area is biased, then an appropriate adjustment must be made to the results.

"Bucket" in this case means the lowest level of addressing within the device, or that area whose address is computed by the address generation procedure. It may be a track, a block, or a logical bucket.

Example: A file of 6000 records is to be stored in a file area of 1000 buckets. Records are to be stored six to a bucket (this is the maximum). Thus, the bucket size = 6. The load factor = 1.0; the actual number of records (6000) divided by the total capacity of the file = 6 records per bucket X 1000 buckets. Table B-2 shows that, assuming a random distribution, 16 percent of record will overflow initially (960 records).

REFERENCES

Many general papers have been published on direct access devices and file design, in addition to the literature issued by hardware manufacturers and software houses describing specific products and approaches. The references cited here are to those papers that have been used in the preparation of this work, and to which the reader is referred for additional reading. Only those papers that are generally available in a reasonable technical library have been quoted.

Special abbreviations used in the list are:

> Comm. of the ACM, Communications of the Association for Computing Machinery
> Journal of the ACM, Journal of the Association for Computing Machinery
> DPMA Quarterly, Data Processing Management Association (U.S.A.) Quarterly
> IAG Journal, Journal of the Administrative Data Processing Group (IAG) of IFIP
> IFIP, International Federation of Information Processing

Adriaenssens, G. "A General File Organization Method for Real-Time Systems," *IBM Technical Information Exchange,* July 1965.

Anzelmo, F. D. "A Data-Storage Format for Information System Files," *IEEE Transactions on Computers,* vol. C-20, no. 1, January 1971.

Bachman, C. W., and Williams, S. B. "A General Purpose System for Random Access Memories (a description of IDS)," *Proceedings of the Fall Joint Computer Conference,* 1964.

Bell, J. R. "The Quadratic Quotient Method: A Hash Code Eliminating Secondary Clustering," *Comm. of the ACM,* vol. 13, no. 2, February 1970.

Black, N. A. "Optimum Merging from Mass Storage," *Comm. of the ACM,* vol. 13, no. 12, December 1970.

Black, N. A. "Generalized Data Base Management Systems," *IAG Journal,* vol. 4, no. 2, 1971.

Bonn, T. H. "Mass Storage: A Broad Review," *Proceedings of the IEEE,* vol. 54, no. 12, December 1966.

Briandais, R. de la. "File Searching Using Variable Length Keys," *Proceedings of the 1959 Western Joint Computer Conference.*

Broderick, W. J. "An Up-To-Date Review of Mass Storage," *DPMA Quarterly,* July 1966.

Buchholz, W. "File Organization and Addressing," *IBM Systems Journal,* June 1963.

Buegler, R. J. "Random Access File System Design," *Datamation,* December 1963.

Coffman, E. G., and Bruno, J. "On File Structure for Non-Uniform Access Frequencies," *BIT,* vol. 10, no. 4, 1970.

CODASYL. Data Base Task Group, October 1969 Report and the April 1971 Report to the CODASYL Programming Language Committee (available from Association for Computing Machinery).

Computer Bulletin. "Feature Analysis of Generalized Data Base Management Systems," vol. 15, no. 4, April 1971.

Computer Management. "Through the Disk Pack Maze," April 1971.

Cooke, M. J. "The Data Base Revolution," *Systems and Procedures Journal,* March-April 1968.

Corville, A. "The IDS Concept of FILE," *Computer Management,* vol. 6, no. 3, March 1971.

Coyle, F. T. "The Hidden Speed of ISAM," *Datamation,* vol. 17, no. 12, June 1971.

Craver, J. S. "A Review of Electromechanical Mass Storage, *Datamation,* July 1966.

Douglas, W. "File Organization and Search Techniques," *Annual Review of Information Science and Technology,* vol. 1, American Documentation Institute. New York: John Wiley & Sons, 1966.

Dumey, A. I. "Indexing for Rapid Random Access Memory Systems," *Computers and Automation,* vol. 5, no. 12, 1956.

Dumey, A. I. "Considerations on Random and Sequential Arrangements of Large Numbers of Records," *Proceedings of the IFIP Congress,* 1965.

EDP Analyzer. "What New Random Access Memories Mean to You," vol. 2, no. 2, February 1964.

EDP Analyzer. "How to Organize Files," vol. 2, no. 10, October 1964.

EDP Analyzer. "New Approaches to Random Access Files," vol. 2, no. 5, May 1965.

EDP Analyzer. "Data Management: File Organization," vol. 5, no. 12, December 1967.

EDP Industry Report. "Disk Pack Prices," vol. 6, no. 11, April 9, 1970.

Epstein, A. D. "The Technology of Disk Data Storage," *Data Processing Magazine,* September 1968.

Gotlieb, C. C. "Sorting on Computers," *Comm. of the ACM,* vol. 6, no. 5, May 1963.

Gross, H. L. "Card Random Access Memory," *Datamation,* December 1963.

Griffin, H. *Elementary Theory of Numbers.* New York: McGraw-Hill Book Co., Inc., 1954.

Farr, W. W., and Peisel, W. E. "An Optimum Disk Organization for a Virtual Memory System," *Computer Decisions,* June 1971.

Feller, W. *An Introduction to Probability Theory and Its Applicatons,* Vol. 1. New York: John Wiley & Sons, Inc., 1950.

Flores, I. *Computer Sorting.* Englewood Cliffs, N.J.: Prentice-Hall, Inc., 1969.

Flores, I. "Computer Time for Address Calculation Sorting," *Journal of the ACM,* Vol. 7, 1960.

Hanan, M., and Palermo, F. P. "An Application of Coding Theory to a File Addressing Problem," *IBM Journal of Research and Development,* vol. 7, no. 2, April 1963.

Hayes, R. M. "Information Retrieval: An Introduction," *Datamation,* vol. 14, no. 3, March 1968.

Heising, W. P. "Note on Random Addressing Techniques," *IBM Systems Journal,* June 1963.

Hester, C. M., and Harries, G. V. "Interchangeable Random Access Discs (the IBM-1311)," *Datamation,* December 1963.

Hobbs, L. C. "Review and Survey of Mass Memories," *Proceedings of the Fall Joint Computer Conference,* 1963.

Holman, L. J. *Statistics for Business.* London: Pitman and Sons Ltd., 1966.

Johnson, L. R., "An Indirect Chaining Method for Addressing Secondary Keys," *Comm. of the ACM,* vol. 4, no. 5, May 1961.

Kaimann, R. A. "Entry to the File—Randomize or Index, Parts I and II," *Data Processing Magazine,* November 1968.

Kalton, G. *Introduction to Statistical Ideas for Social Scientists.* London: Chapman and Hall, 1966.

Kantor, J. "The Ubiquitous Data Base Concept," *Data Processing Magazine,* May 1967.

Lefkovitz, D. *File Structures for On-Line Systems.* New York: Spartan Books, 1969 (Macmillan in Great Britain).

Lin, A. D. "Key Addressing of Random Access Memories by Radix Transformamation," *AFIPS Conference Proceedings,* vol. 23, 1963 Spring Joint Computer Conference.

Lovell, J. "Concept 315—An Appraisal," *Data and Control* (now *Data Systems*), June 1964.

Lum, V. Y., Yuen, P. S. T., and Dodd, M. "Key-to-Address Transform Techniques: A Fundamental Performance Study on Large Existing Formatted Files," *Comm. of the ACM,* vol. 14, no. 4, April 1971.

Malagodi, A. "The Sequential Compromise," *Data and Control* (now *Data Systems*), May 1964.

Malagodi, A. "Locating the Information," *Data and Control* (now *Data Systems*), June 1964.

Martin, J. *Programming Real-Time Computer Systems.* Englewood Cliffs, N.J.: Prentice-Hall, Inc., 1965.

Minker, J., and Sable, J. "File Organization and Data Management," *Annual Re-

view of Information Science, Vol. 2, American Documentation Institute. New York: John Wiley & Sons, Inc., 1966.

Moroney, M. J. *Facts from Figures.* London: Penguin Books, 1956.

Morris, R. "Scatter Storage Techniques," *Comm. of the ACM,* vol. 11, no. 1, January 1968.

McGee, W. C. "Generalized File Processing," *Annual Review in Automatic Programming,* Vol. 5. New York: Pergamon Press.

McIlroy, M. D. "A Variant Method of File Searching," *Comm. of the ACM,* vol. 6, no. 3, March 1963.

Olson, C. A. "Random Access File Organization for Indirectly Addressed Records," *Proceedings of the ACM 24th National Conference,* 1969.

Patton, P. C. "Data Organization and Access Methods," *Computer,* vol. 3, no. 6, November/December 1970.

Peterson, W. W. "Addressing for Random Access Storage," *IBM Journal of Research and Development,* April 1957.

Poland, C. B. "Advanced Concepts of Utilization of Mass Storage,"*Proceedings of the IFIP Congress,* 1965.

Poole, D. "Indexing for Random Access/Systems for Scanning" (in two parts), *Computer Weekly,* March 2, 1967.

Samet, P. A. "A Note on Radix Conversion for Integers," *Software—Practice and Experience,"* vol. 1, no. 1, January-March, 1971.

Schav, G., and Raver, N. "A Method for Key-to-Address Transformation," *IBM Journal of Research and Development,* April 1963.

Schay, Jr., G. and Spruth, W. G. "Analysis of a File Addressing Method," *Comm. of the ACM,* vol. 5, no. 8, August 1962.

Smith, J. M., and Dee, E. G. "Aspects of Data Base Management—Part 1 and 2," *Data Processing,* vol. 13, no. 2, March/April 1971.

Stevens, W. B. "The Concept of Data Analysis and Control Catalogue for Management Information Systems," *Computers and Automation,* April 1968.

Tainiter, M. "Addressing for Random-Access Storage with Multiple Bucket Capacities," *Journal of the ACM,* vol. 10, no. 3, July 1963.

Taylor, G. "File Structures and Addressable Mass Storage," *Software World,* vol. 2, no. 2, Winter 1970-1971.

Tellier, Harrison. "The Role of the Generalized Program," *Data Processing Digest,* June 1968.

Terdiman, J. F. "Mass Storage Devices and Their Application to a Medical Information System," *Computers and Biomedical Research,* vol. 3, no. 5, October 1970.

Vinogradov, I. M. *An Introduction to the Theory of Numbers.* London and New York: Pergamon Press, 1955.

Walker, B. S. *Introduction to Computer Engineering.* London: University of London Press, 1967.

Wooldridge, S. *Software Selection.* Philadelphia: Auerbach Publishers Inc., forthcoming 1973.

Manufacturers Literature

There are many publications issued by manufacturers which describe their hardware and software products. The reader should contact the appropriate manufacturer for information about a particular device in which he is interested. The references cited here are a representative selection of publications showing a cross-section of hardware/software approaches.

General Electric Information Systems: "GE–615/635–Information Systems Manual," Publication CPD 371F, 1969.

Honeywell: Series 200–Summary Description; Series 200/Model 115–Summary Description.

International Business Machines: Student text, "Introduction to IBM System/360–Direct Access Storage Devices and Organization Methods," 1966 (revised November 1969), Publication C20-1649-4.

International Computers Limited: "Systems Manual." Various volumes describe 1900 series hardware and basic software; "Direct Access," Publication 3383, 1966; "System 4–Information Manual," Publication DP/260, 1966.

National Cash Register Company: "High-Performance CRAM," Publication 4775, 1966.

GLOSSARY

This glossary defines those special direct access terms used in this book. The multiplicity of manufacturers and software houses has generated a large number of synonyms; these are given in the glossary. This is not a general data processing glossary; many good general glossaries will be found in any technical reference library.

access time The time that elapses between an order being given to access a storage location and that location becoming available for use.

activity loading A method of creating a file on a direct access device by *address generation*, in which records that are to be accessed more frequently are loaded first. Records that are required infrequently are loaded last. If *overflow* occurs, frequently requested records are thus in or near the home location. The least-requested records will be farther from the home location.

activity rate (1) Of a file, a synonym for *hit rate*. (2) Of a record, a measure of the frequency of access.

address capacity A measure of the number of records which can be stored in one storage location (e.g., a bucket).

address generation A method of assigning, and subsequently retrieving, records on a direct access device whereby the address of a record is computed from the record key. Also known as *key transformation* and *randomizing*.

algorithm A computational procedure.

band Synonym for *track*.

binary search A method for scanning an index by dividing it successively in half. The maximum *length of search* to locate any specific entry is thus $\log_2 N$, where N is the number of entries in an index.

block (1) *physical:* a hardware segment of a track; also known as a *sector*. (2) *logical:* a user-defined area of storage that is read or written by one read or write instruction; *see also* blocked records.

blocked records A group of records that can be accessed by one read instruction or written by one write instruction.

bucket (1) A logical unit of storage, consisting of one or more hardware blocks. (2) The smallest addressable unit of storage in a direct access device.

byte   A unit of storage consisting of eight bits (usually with a ninth, parity bit). These eight bits may be used to store a character, an eight-bit serial word, or two decimal digits.

chaining   (1) A technique of referencing overflow records from their home locations; also known as tagging. (2) A method of cross-referencing records, one to another, which enables records to be accessed by different keys.

character   The smallest unit of information represented by a symbol 0 to 9, A to Z, or a special symbol (+ * / - (, etc.), represented by a six- to eight-bit code.

consecutive spill   A synonym for *progressive overflow.*

cyclic check   A method for verifying that data has been recorded correctly. A special check value is recorded with the data. On a subsequent read, the check value is recalculated from the data just read and compared with the recorded check value. An error is signaled if the two check values do not agree.

cylinder   A concept of storage: that area of storage which can be read without mechanical movement (i.e., a *seek*).

data point   A synonym for *index point.*

direct addressing   A synonym for *self-indexing.* Sometimes also used to refer to *address generation.*

directory   A synonym for an *index.*

dummy   An artificial record or index entry that contains no meaningful information; commonly used as fillers.

dump   A copy of a file made for control or recovery purposes.

extraction   A computational technique used in *address generation:* taking part of a key for use as an address or for further computation.

field   The smallest unit of meaningful information in a record.

fine indexes   The lowest level of index in an indexed-sequential file.

fixed-track format   Descriptive of a direct access device in which the recording tracks are divided into addressable hardware units; i.e., sectors or blocks.

fixed length   (1) Of a field: all fields of one type containing data in the same format and consisting of the same number of characters. (2) Of a record: all records of a similar type containing the same fields in the same relative position in each record; all records contain the same number of characters. (3) Of a block: all blocks in a file contain the same number of records, each record consisting of the same number of characters.

folding   A computational technique used in *address generation:* dividing a key into parts and performing arithmetic (usually addition) on those parts.

generalized file processor   A software system that creates, updates and processes, and reports from any set of files, using parameter input.

hierarchical records   Data segmented in such a way that some records are logically subordinate to others.

hit rate   A measure of the number of records in a file which are expected to be accessed in a given run. Usually expressed as a percentage:

$$\frac{\text{Number of input transactions} \times 100\%}{\text{Number of records in the file}}$$

home address   (1) A storage location (e.g., a home bucket) into which a data record is logically assigned; as opposed to overflow address. (2) In a software system (IBM), a field that contains the physical address of a track, recorded at the beginning of a track.

index   A list used to determine the location of a record. An index contains a number of entries, each entry normally containing a key and a storage location.

index point   A hardware reference mark on a disk or drum; used for timing purposes.

indexed-sequential storage   A file structure in which records are stored in ascending sequence by key. Indexes showing the highest key on a cylinder/track/ bucket, etc., are used for the selected retrieval of records.

indicative data   Data that identifies or describes; e.g., in a stock file, the product number, description, pack size. Normally, indicative data does not change on a regular, frequent basis during processing (as in, for example, an account balance).

indirect addressing   Any method of specifying or locating a storage location whereby the key (of itself or through calculation) does not represent an address. For example, locating an address through indexes.

inverted file   A file structure in which there is no *chaining* of records. Independent lists are maintained in which record keys are grouped according to the values of specific fields.

involute file   A file in which all data fields appear in lists, and the concept of the physical data record ceases to exist.

key   A field that uniquely identifies a record. For example, an employee number in a personnel record, and customer account numbers in a sales ledger.

key distribution   The arrangement of keys in a given set of records; i.e., the number of keys present from the total range of key values, with the pattern of clusters and gaps.

key transformation   A synonym for *address generation.*

latency   The time taken for a storage location to reach the read/write heads on a rotating recording surface. For general timing purposes, *average latency* is used; this is the time taken by one half-revolution of the surface.

label   A control record used to identify the contents of a file, the date of its creation, and the retention status of the data. A label may also contain data that describes the format of the file.

length of search The number of records or index entries that must be accessed or inspected before a required record or entry is found. The *average length of search* is a general measure of the number of accesses made before a required record is located, calculated by

$$\frac{\text{Number of accesses to find all records in file}}{\text{Total number of records in file}}$$

loading factor A synonym for *address capacity:* the number of records stored in a storage location.

map A pictorial representation of the layout of data in a storage area.

multiple records The simplest arrangement of records in a file in which all records have the same format.

media cycling A method of retaining data in which the storage media is changed as the data ages and reference is made to it less frequently. For example, disk to magnetic tape to printed hard copy to microfilm, etc.

one-pass loading A method of creating a random file, using address generation. All file records are input on one pass, thus causing *synonyms* of some records to be stored before all home records are stored. Contrast to *two-pass loading.*

open addressing A synonym for *progressive overflow.*

overflow The condition when a record cannot be stored in its *home address*; i.e., the storage location to which it is logically assigned on loading.

overlay A method of changing data in a record by overwriting the original record with new data.

parity check A checking system to insure that bits are neither gained nor dropped during a transfer or in recording. A special check bit, a parity bit, is appended to each group of bits transferred: a character, a byte, or a word. In an even parity system, the parity bit is used to make the number of one bits in a group even; if an odd number of one bits is encountered, an error condition is signaled. An odd parity system uses the same logic, but the number of one bits must always be odd.

partial indexing An indexing system in which the indexes contain one entry for each storage location rather than each record. Usually, each index entry shows the highest key in a storage area (cylinder, track, bucket, etc.).

pointer A control field in a record which provides linkage to another record. A pointer may contain the key or the address of the cross-referenced record. Also known as a *tag.*

prime area Part of a file area that is used to store home records; as opposed to part of the file area that is dedicated to the storage of overflow records.

prime division A computational technique used in *address generation;* a numeric value is divided by a suitable prime and the remainder (or part of it) is used as an address.

progressive overflow   A method of handling overflow in a randomly stored file which does not require the use of *pointers*. An overflow record is stored in the first available space and is retrieved by a forward serial search from the *home address*.

purge date   The date on or after which a storage area is available to be overwritten. Used in conjunction with a file label, it is a means of protecting file data until an agreed release date is reached.

quantitative data   A numeric field that records a value; contrast with *indicative data*. It is usually updated in regular processing. An example is any balance figure.

queue   A set of records or messages awaiting processing; usually in a real-time mode; hence queuing.

radix   The base of a number system. For example, decimal is radix-10 and binary is radix-2.

radix transformation   A computational technique used in *address generation*; expressing a numeric key value in another number base.

randomizing   A synonym for *address generation*.

record   A group of fields that are in some way related to themselves and to the key; stored together.

regeneration   Recreating data after all or part of the data has been lost or corrupted.

response time   The elapsed time between input and output being available. Usually applied to on-line systems; the elapsed time between inquiry and answer.

rotational delay   A synonym for *latency*.

rough indexes   The highest levels of indexes in an indexed-sequential file; e.g., indexing device unit or a group of cylinders, as opposed to *fine indexes* that index to a track or bucket level.

search key   The key of a record that is to be located and accessed; e.g., a search key is matched against index entries.

sector   A synonym for a hardware *block*.

seek   Mechanical movement of a read/write head to reposition it from one track to another.

seek time   The time taken for a *seek*.

selective-sequential   Synonym for *indexed-sequential* processing, in which selected records are accessed.

self-indexing   A method for accessing data records by using the key (or part of it) as the address of the record.

sequential processing   Accessing records in ascending sequence by key; the next record accessed will have the next higher key, irrespective of its physical position in the file.

serial processing   Accessing records in their physical sequence. The next record accessed will be the record in the next physical-position/location in the file.

simple list   A method of structuring a file in which records are *chained* and an independent index is kept which gives selected entry points in the chain(s).

string   (1) In sorting, a consecutive group of records in ascending key sequence. (2) Of keys: a group of keys that produce, via an *address generation algorithm*, a consecutive sequence of addresses.

synonym   In *address generation*, the production of the same address from a number of keys.

tag   A synonym for *pointer.*

track   That area of a circular recording surface which is transcribed by a read/ write head.

transaction   An input record applied to an established file. The input record describes some "event" that will either cause a new file record to be generated, an existing record to be changed, or an existing record to be deleted.

transfer rate   A measure of the speed with which data is moved between direct access device and the central processor. Usually expressed as thousands of characters per second (kch/s) or thousands of bytes per second (kb/s).

truncation   A computational technique used in *address generation*; shortening the length of a numeric field by, in effect, dividing the value by the divisor that is a power of the value radix.

two-pass loading   A method of creating a random file, using *address generation.* Records are assigned first to their home addresses wherever possible on the first pass. On a subsequent pass, overflow records are loaded and the tags set up.

variable length   (1) Of a field: fields of the same type which differ in size and may vary in format. (2) Of a record: records of the same type which contain a differing number of fields, which themselves may consist of a differing number of characters. (3) Of a block: blocks that contain a different number of records (which themselves may be variable). Blocks thus differ in size in one file area.

variable-track format   Descriptive of hardware in which the recording tracks are not physically segmented into *blocks*, etc. Storage locations are created by a combination of hardware and software, with the addressing information recorded on the tracks in control fields.

volatility   (1) Of hardware: descriptive of the physical retention properties of a storage device; a volatile store is one in which data is lost on the removal of the power supply. (2) Of a file: the rate at which records are added or deleted from a file.

word   The lowest level of hardware storage in some computers. The size of a word (e.g., 16, 24, or 32 bits) is fixed for a particular machine.

INDEX